The Voice of Fashion

The Voice of Fashion

79 Turn-of-the-Century Patterns With Instructions and Fashion Plates

Edited and with Additional Material by
Frances Grimble

Lavolta Press
20 Meadowbrook Drive
San Francisco, CA 94132

First edition

ISBN: 0-9636517-2-2

Published by
Lavolta Press
20 Meadowbrook Drive
San Francisco, CA 94132

Book design, cover design, scanning, scan editing and coloring,
page layout, and production management by
Frances Grimble and Allan Terry

Printed and bound in the United States of America

Library of Congress Catalog Card Number: 97-7214

Publisher's Cataloging-in-Publication
(Provided by Quality Books, Inc.)

The voice of fashion : 79 turn-of-the-century patterns with
    instructions and fashion plates / edited and with additional
    material by Frances Grimble. -- 1st ed.
        p. cm.
    Includes bibliographical references and index.
    Preassigned LCCN: 97-72141
    ISBN: 0-9636517-2-2

    1. Voice of fashion. 2. Dressmaking--Patterns. 3. Vintage
clothing--United States. 4. Costume--United States--History--
20th century. I. Grimble, Frances.

TT520.G751 1998   646.4'78'04'09041
                              QBI97-41345

Acknowledgments

I'd like to thank my husband, Allan Terry, for providing technical support of every type required. He reconstructed the Diamond Cutting System rulers, drew them for this book, helped edit the halftone scans, and helped design and color the cover. He also kept my hardware and software running, and assisted in innumerable small publishing tasks.

My father, Ralph Grimble, located an April 1906 copy of *The Delineator*. My brother, Bob Grimble, gave legal advice. My parents-in-law, Sam and Aileen Terry, donated funding and industrial warehouse space.

I would also like to thank everyone at our printer, McNaughton & Gunn. Charles Arkebauer of Typemasters provided prepress services and advice.

For my other parents, Sam and Aileen Terry

Contents

Contents

Introduction

Browsing through the stock of vintage clothing or paper goods dealers, one occasionally runs across magazines or books containing scaled-down sewing patterns. These are often marked with numbers that, at first glance, appear to be inch measurements. In some cases they are. However, if the instructions mention "scales," the patterns are designed to be drawn with a patent drafting system that includes apportioning scales. These are special rulers that make it easy for the sewer to accurately draft the patterns designed for that system to fit an individual's body measurements. Each ruler has units of a different size. The rulers for smaller sizes have smaller units, the ones for larger sizes have larger units. Thus the units on the pattern can be used to draft any size. No arithmetic or drafting experience is required; the sewer "drafts by the numbers."

The Diamond Cutting System

The patterns in *The Voice of Fashion* were designed for the Diamond Cutting System, one of many drafting systems used in the 19th and early 20th centuries. Most pattern measurements are projected in proportion to one crucial body measurement—the bust measurement for bodices, the waist for skirts. That is, these patterns have some built-in sizing. However, the system recognizes that height is not necessarily in direct proportion to the bust or waist. The instructions explain how to draft patterns for the larger or smaller person after checking a few crucial measurements with an inch ruler. This combination of proportional and inch measurements makes the Diamond Cutting System a "hybrid" system.

The Diamond Cutting System rulers were reconstructed for this book using a partial set of original rulers, plus information in the magazines. (The visual design has been changed slightly.) The tools supplied with the system also included a folding L-square to hold the rulers while drafting, a "scroll" similar to a modern hip curve, an inch tape measure, and a tracing wheel.

The patterns were drawn from 14 issues of *The Voice of Fashion* dating from 1900 to 1906. My earliest issues were produced by the Voice of Fashion Publishing Company, owned by W. H. Goldsberry up till the November 1900 issue. Goldsberry had published pattern diagram books as early as 1884, and *The Voice of Fashion* as early as 1890 (judging from Library of Congress holdings). Various titles refer to the National Garment Cutter in the 1880s and the Diamond Garment Cutter in the 1890s. The L-square (patent no. 247,339) was patented in 1881. The rulers, and illustrations of them in *The Voice of Fashion*, bear a patent date of 1893.

Despite the differing dates, all Goldsberry's publications may have required the same drafting system. The brief description of Goldsberry's rulers in his L-square patent is consistent with the 1893 rulers. *The Voice of Fashion* offers subscribers who learned the system from either the National Garment Cutter or the Diamond Garment Cutter book of instructions, new instruction books "to replace those worn out or destroyed, as our principles in cutting by using the scales are the same." The same waist lining showing the scroll positions was used in the basic drafting instructions from at least 1889 to 1907 (judging from publications in my possession). And a nightgown pattern published as early as 1889 is repeated in the February 1901 and subsequent issues of *The Voice of Fashion* (with a line added for a V-necked style option).

Drafting the Voice of Fashion Patterns

Using the Diamond Cutting System to draft the patterns in *The Voice of Fashion* is quite easy. First take your measurements over the foundation garments and undergarments you will wear. Choose

1

the right rulers for your measurements and the garment section. The rulers have size labels that correspond to inch measurements. Suppose you wish to draft a two-piece dress with a 34-inch bust and a 27-inch waist. You would choose the size 34 ruler to draw the bodice, and the size 27 ruler to draw the skirt.

Because ruler lengths are limited by the book size, the rulers in appendix A are partial. Directions are given for copying, cutting, and pasting to full length. The rulers may then be glued onto cardboard or inexpensive yardsticks and used for drafting. Or they may be used for measurement only, and lines drawn with a yardstick.

After choosing your rulers, lay out a big piece of pattern paper printed with marks at 1-inch intervals. Pencil a vertical baseline and use your ruler to mark off the measurements shown on the pattern piece. From these, draw horizontal crosslines to the measurements shown. Step-by-step instructions are given in "Using the Diamond Cutting System."

You then draw the curves, for which you need a modern hip/armhole curve and a set of french curves. Choose a curve that fits to the ends of the lines you drew and looks like the pattern shape. You may need parts of two curves. A flexible curve (available from art and quilting suppliers) comes in handy.

From my experience the fitted bodice patterns, such as tight linings, were designed with very little ease. For these I'd recommend using a ruler one to two sizes larger than your bust and leaving large seam allowances. The proportionally determined waist size is small for many modern women, but can be enlarged. Check all back waist, sleeve, and skirt lengths until you become familiar with the system's fitting standards. Note that the "length of skirt" measurements do not allow for the hem or the waistband seam. "Using the Diamond Cutting System" recommends making most corrections for individual measurements during the drafting process. However, the patterns can be drafted as given, then altered by standard flat pattern techniques and/or during fitting.

Projecting the Patterns

These patterns can also be enlarged by projection, although more alterations may be required. Photocopy the pattern piece onto transparency film. Tape a large piece of dotted pattern paper to a wall. Place the transparency on the projector so the pattern's baseline is aligned with a vertical row of dots and the top crossline is aligned with a horizontal row.

Use the Diamond Cutting System rulers to determine what size each piece should be projected to. Use the bust ruler to size bodices and the waist ruler to size skirts. Adjust the projector till the key measurement is correct on the pattern paper. Draw the pattern using a clear plastic yardstick, ruler, and french curves (clear tools don't block projection). Or draw freehand and clean up the lines later. Projected lines look thick; you'll have to decide whether to trace the outsides or the insides. Trace stars, pleat lines, and other internal pattern marks; but note that seam allowances were not drawn to scale.

Most pattern pieces are drawn to some scale. But the original publisher reduced them to fit on the page, and I reduced some further for the same reason. The resulting scales are unusual. More than one may be used in a single pattern, requiring different projector adjustments.

A few wide skirt pieces were drawn to scale at the waist, but narrowed at the bottom. Check the proportions of all wide skirt pieces till you become familiar with these patterns. Measure the waist-to-hem ratio in units, then inches. If the ratios differ, use the system's ruler to determine the correct waist and hem widths. Use an inch yardstick to draw the skirt length along the baseline. Mark where the waist and hem will meet it. Put the pattern piece on the projector and draw the waist curve. Mark the places diagonal seam and pleat lines should start. Then readjust the projector and draw the hem curve, marking where diagonal lines should end. Take the pattern paper off the wall and draw the diagonal lines from waist to hem.

On some pattern pieces, crosslines were spread out vertically to fit the corresponding numbers in, making the drawing longer in that area. This is particularly true at the tops of large pieces

 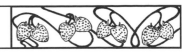

for measurements of 2 and under. A few pieces seem to use different vertical and horizontal scales throughout. I recommend adding large seam allowances to all pieces that look out of scale and taking special care in fitting the muslin.

Finishing a Drafted Or Projected Pattern

Measure edges that will be seamed together. If they're different lengths, check the original measurements and redraw as necessary. Add pattern markings such as pleat lines and stars. Sometimes you must true seam lines where fabric will be folded into darts, pleats, or facings. Fold the pattern like the fabric and redraw nonmatching lines.

The various instructions indicate that some seam allowances are provided and some must be added after drafting. I suggest allowing 1 to 2 inches on side seams, 1 inch on seams of sections that fit tightly or look drawn out of scale, and 1/2 inch on seams of loose-fitting sections. To add a seam allowance, measure out from the pattern edge with a clear plastic ruler. For straight edges measure each end and connect the lines. For curved edges draw short lines at such frequent intervals that they connect. Or use a double tracing wheel to indent the paper, then pencil over the indents.

To finish the pattern piece, draw a grain line following a vertical row of pattern paper dots. Label the piece with the pattern source, garment type, and style date. Indicate how many times each piece will be cut from fashion fabric, lining, underlining, and/or interfacing. Add any marks or notes you find helpful.

Although the Diamond Cutting System produces a good fit, Edwardian patterns assume the sewer adjusts a muslin or lining before cutting garment fabric. I strongly recommend this.

Trim guidelines are given in the fashion plates and descriptions, but pattern pieces and placement markings are often omitted. This is because Edwardian sewers adapted trims to their tastes, substituted trims from other patterns, or copied them from friends' clothes. Of course, you're free to adapt

trims too. Draft and mark them with an inch ruler after completing the rest of the pattern. You can test size and placement on the muslin.

Using This Book

The original sewing instructions are terse, which is typical of Edwardian patterns. However, they are supplemented by the construction, fabric, and trim suggestions in the fashion columns that appear in most issues of *The Voice of Fashion*. The May 1906 issue printed the Diamond Cutting System drafting and sewing instructions instead; these were probably drawn from, or duplicate, a separate manual. I placed them at the beginning of this book. For May, I inserted a column from the April 1906 *Delineator. The Delineator* was a strong competitor, offering more fashion columns and fancy fashion plates in addition to ads for Butterick's precut tissue patterns. Because *The Voice of Fashon* did not offer colored or multiple-figure plates, the cover plate is drawn from the January 1900 *Delineator*.

The Voice of Fashion published patterns for most garments and styles worn by middle-class women, plus some for children and a very few for men. Many designs are similar; a few were reprinted in multiple issues. Since this book lacked sufficient space for all the patterns, I compromised by selecting the widest range of women's fashions available. These include lingerie; home wear (some of which probably doubled as maternity wear); day suits and blouses; afternoon, evening, ball, and wedding gowns; coats; and sports outfits. If a pattern was reprinted, I chose the earliest printing in the issues I own (but I do not own a complete run).

The date assigned to the February 1900 issue is tentative. The cover, which was the only place the date was printed, was missing from my copy. Someone had written "February 1900" on the first page, and this is likely given the styles and pattern-numbering sequence. However, a date late in 1899 is also possible.

A few patterns lacked some relatively complex section, typically a sleeve or vest front; readers were directed to choose from "any other pattern in this issue." In these cases I chose a section

that looked as though it would correspond to the fashion plate when made up and would work with the sewing directions. Sometimes readers were expected to create their own drafts for simple sections such as cuffs; I have not provided these. I arranged the pattern pieces the way they are sewn together, as well as the page size allowed. Both these

and the fashion plates were edited to correct deterioration and printer's errors. The original text has been edited for clarity. I substituted a few modern spellings and terms (such as "peplum" for "peplin"). The fashion columns were condensed to include only information that's useful in recreating the styles. However, I've made every effort to preserve the style and substance of the originals.

I hope you find *The Voice of Fashion* a valuable addition to your library.

——Frances Grimble

Using the Diamond Cutting System

The Diamond Cutting System Tools

The Diamond Cutting System consists of a square, a scroll, a set of scales, a tape measure, and a tracing wheel.

The tracing wheel is used to convey impressions from the pattern to the cloth to be cut.

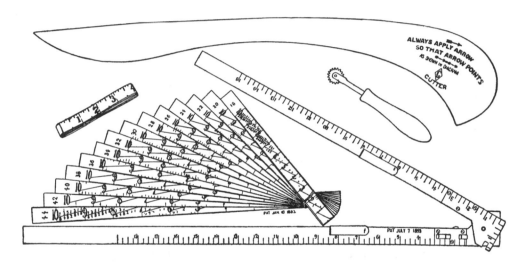

The square is used for all straight lines. Open your square to its fullest extent, and fasten it in position by sliding the small catch at hinge to the left as far as it will go. You will also notice two slides or catches, one on each arm of the square. These slides are for the purpose of holding the scales in position when in use. Fasten or loosen them by moving them either to right or left, as the case may be.

The scroll is used in making all curved lines, as shown below.

The scales are 14 in number. They are used to represent the different bust and waist measurements, and are distinguished by corresponding numbers at one end. They are divided into spaces, and fractions of spaces, instead of inches. The scale is used in connection with the square.

The tape measure is used for taking all necessary measurements before and after drafting patterns, to secure correct proportions.

Taking Measurements

As persons vary in size and form, it is impossible to use the same drafts for all forms. We therefore have a system of measurements which, when carefully taken and applied properly, renders it possible to draft any pattern to fit any person. There are six of these measurements: Bust measure, length of back, waist measure, length of sleeve, width of back, and length of front.

The first measurement to be taken is that of the bust. This measurement always designates which scale is to be used in drafting all patterns above the waistline. To take this measurement place the tape around the largest part of the bust, high up under the arms, taking a close snug measurement, not too tight nor too loose.

Great care must be taken in getting the length of back, which consists of the distance between the large joint at back of neck where neck and body

To get the front measurement, measure the distance from the large joint in the back, where neck and body join, to the waistline in the front. Measure straight over shoulder and straight down front to center of front at waistline. Deduct the width of back at neck, inside the seam lines, and the width of the shoulder seam on front. The remainder will be the length of front from shoulder at side of neck to center of front at waistline.

Forms can be classified into three different classes: Stout, slender, and medium. A stout form is one that has a large bust and short waist. A slender form is one that has a long waist in proportion to the size of the bust. A medium form is one that is between stout and slender. Since there are three classes of forms, so must there be three classes of drafts. A draft must be selected to correspond as nearly as possible with the form for which it is to be used. A draft should be selected that requires little change in the length of back and size of waist.

Drafting the Sample Pattern

The baseline is the basis of all patterns, and is formed by the use of the longest portion of the square. The top or first crossline is a line intersecting the baseline at right angles. The intersecting point is always designated by the letter A, in the upper-right corner of the draft, and is the starting point of all patterns. All lines and measures are from one or the other of these lines, but more often from the baseline. To begin drafting, draw a baseline along the long arm of the square and a top crossline along the short arm. Always begin locating points from the letter A and make a careful copy of the draft just as it is shown in the book.

The arrows shown on the draft are used for two purposes, one to show which way to turn the curve, the other to show how many points to connect. Always turn the curve with the arrow pointing the direction the arrow points in the diagram. If the arrow is between two lines, connect two points; if on a line, connect three points; the point by the arrow being the middle one.

Select a scale corresponding with whatever bust measure you have. If your bust measure is 34 inches, select the scale marked 34. If 36 inches,

join and the exact waistline. The most accurate way of getting this measurement is to place a belt around the waist and then measure the distance from the joint to the lower edge of the belt.

To take the measure around the waist, place tape in position around waist at the lowest point above hip and abdomen and draw the tape as tight as the dress is to be worn. This measure is the tightest one taken.

To take the sleeve measurement, measure from the center of back to wrist joint with arm raised, with elbow level with the shoulder and hand about 6 inches in front of face. Deduct the width of back less 1 inch and the remaining portion will be the correct length of sleeve.

While the lady is in straight position, with arms hanging at her side, get width of back by measuring the greatest distance straight across from armseye to armseye. Since only half of pattern is drafted, divide this measurement by 2. If pattern is to be cut with a seam in the back, add the width of seam as indicated by the draft used.

 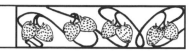
select the scale marked 36, etc. We do not recognize any half inches in this measurement, so should the bust measure be 34 1/2 inches, we advise the use of the scale marked 35. Or if 36 1/2, use the scale marked 37, etc. It is preferable, in such cases, to raise the bust measure 1/2 inch than to decrease it that amount.

To draft the back of this waist form, select the desired scale. Fasten upon the long arm of the square with the end of the scale even with the end of the square. Place the square upon the paper with the angle at the right-hand corner of the paper, with the arms of the square parallel with the edges of the paper and about 1 inch from the same. Draw a line along each arm of the square. Then begin at the letter A and measure each number consecutively on the baseline until all the numbers are taken, making a dot at each number. That is to say, measure 1/2 space with the scale from the corner of the draft and make a dot, then 2 3/8 (from the corner, not from 1/2), then 6. The next number is 10 1/4. This is obtained by making a cross mark or X at the 10 on the scale and moving the square down until its end is even with the X, then measure 1/4 more; this makes 10 1/4. The next number is 15. Make this number by measuring 5 from the X and making a dot. Then again make an X at the end of the scale, moving the corner of the square down to the X measure; 2 and 2 1/2 make 22 and 22 1/2.

This gives all the numbers on the baseline. Now proceed to get the crosslines and numbers. Place the scale on the short arm of the square—be sure to use the bust measure as for baseline. On the top crossline measure 2 3/8 spaces, skip the point representing 1/2, and place the corner of the square at the second point (2 3/8), keeping the long arm exactly on the baseline, and measure 6 spaces on the scale; or at 6 make a dot and from this draw a line to the dot on the baseline.

Move the square down and from this point measure and dot at 5 3/4, drawing line to baseline as before. The next line has two numbers, 1/4 and 3 7/8; dot at each and draw line. The next or fifth

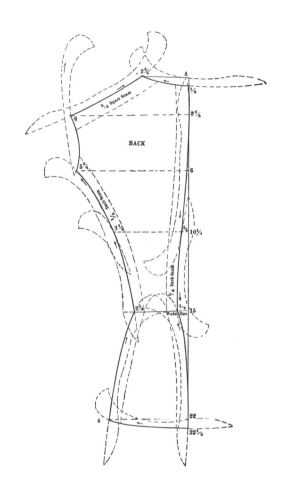

crossline is the waistline and has two numbers, 1/2 and 2 3/4. The last line has one number, 4; dot and draw line.

After getting the lines and measures thus located, take the curve or scroll and draw all the curved lines. Do this by first connecting the points, 2 3/8 top measure line and 1/2 baseline, placing the curve as shown on the draft, and draw a line. This curve is for the back of the neck. Next draw a line from 2 3/8, on the first crossline, to point 6, on the second crossline, then to 5 3/4, on the third crossline, using the small point of the curve. This is the only place where this part of the curve is used. Turn the curve over, move down, and connect points 5 3/4 and 3 7/8, then 3 7/8 and 2 3/4 on the waistline. Turn the curve over and continue the line to the bottom or point 4, then to baseline at 22 1/2, getting the curve for the bottom of the waist. Turn the large part of the curve up and connect 22 1/2,

on the baseline, to point 1/2 on the waistline. Reverse curve and turn over. Then connect from 1/2 on the waistline to 1/4 on the fourth crossline, then 1/4 to 1/2 on baseline.

This gives all the curves and finishes the draft, excepting the seams, which are 1/2 inch with tape measure on each side of the draft. The shoulder is 3/4 space seam with the scale measure. These lines are drawn the same as the outside or cutting lines.

All other drafts are made on the same principle. Do not attempt to make any other draft until the first one is mastered. Read carefully the directions with each draft before making it. Always copy the draft just as shown in the book, except to make the changes necessary for different forms.

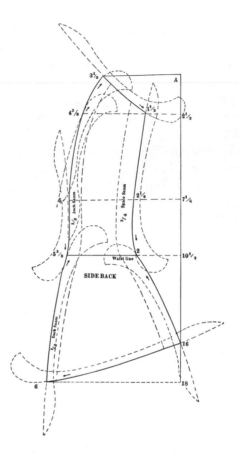

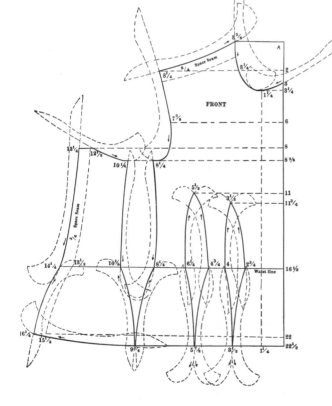

Drafting Patterns For Individual Figures

The proportional measures are: Bust, 32; length of waist, 16; size around waist, 22; sleeve, 29.

Suppose the lady's measurements, for whom you wish to draft a pattern, are: Bust, 34; length of back, 17; and waist, 23. Select a scale corresponding to the bust measure, in this case 34. Always draft your back diagram first (for illustration take the one below). Mark all your points on your baseline corresponding with the numbers on the draft until the number 15, or the point which marks the waistline, is reached. Then take your tape measure and measure from 5/8, the point at neck where center of back begins, down 17 inches, the length of back you wish. This point will fall 3/8 space below point 15. Cancel point 15 by placing a ring around it. Move the square down on the baseline until point 5 on the scale is even with the new waistline point. In this diagram no points fall below the

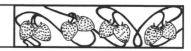
waistline; but whenever there are other points, mark them the same as the numbers call for. Mark off cross and intersecting points in the usual way.

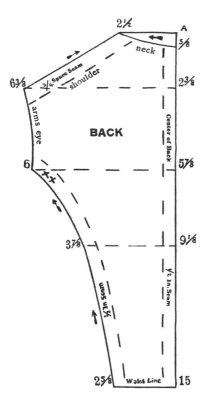

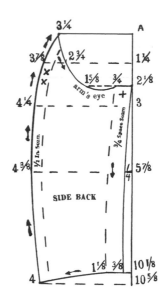

Since you have lengthened the back 1/2 inch, you must also lengthen the side back the same amount. Locate all your points on the baseline till you come to 10 1/8. Lower the point 3/8 space or the same amount as the back was lowered, by canceling the point 10 1/8 and making a new point 3/8 space below. Move your square down the baseline until 1/8 falls at this new point. Make the next point, which is 10 5/8, the same as called for.

Next change the front in the same way and in the same proportion as the other drafts. Change no points above the waistline, except dart points. These are changed only when the amount of change in waistline is 1/2 inch or more; the dart points are changed just half the amount the waistline is changed. Locate all points on the baseline till you come to 10, the line intersecting the first dart point. Since you lowered the waist point 1/2 inch, you

will lower this point 1/4 inch. Cancel your old point 10 and start a new point 1/4 inch below, then move your square down until point 10 on your scale falls at this new point. Lower the second dart line 10 1/2 in the same manner and in the same proportion. The point 15 3/4 indicates the waistline at the underarm seam, so lower this point 1/2 inch, or 3/8 space, to correspond with back and side back.

Get the remainder of your points as they stand. When the pattern is drafted, test the length of front of waist by using your front measurement. Should you desire to lengthen the front 1/2 inch or more, lower the point the desired amount, on baseline which indicates the line intersecting the waistline point of the outside seam of the second dart. In the diagram this point is 16 1/8. This lowers the same amount every point thereafter on the baseline. Now scroll to the new lower dart points made. This will lengthen the front of your waist and yet retain its original shape.

Throughout these diagrams you have lengthened the waistline. But should you desire to shorten it instead, proceed in the same manner, only raise your points the desired amount instead of lowering them. For example, the waist point is 15 and should you wish it 1/2 inch shorter, make a new point 1/2 inch above and move your square up the baseline until 5 on the scale falls at this point. Then

 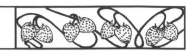
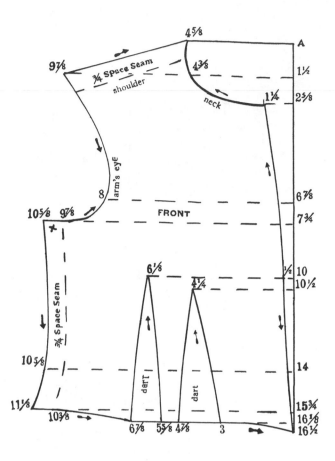

proceed as before. Such drafts should be selected that the raising or lowering of the waistline should not exceed 1 space.

Altering Patterns

After completing the entire draft, with your tape measure the waistline of all your drafts, omitting all space for seams, darts, and hem. If this measurement equals half the waist measure, then your draft is correct. If not, you must make all necessary changes at the underarm seams.

The supposed measure you have is 23 inches, and this draft measures 24, so it is 1 inch too large. Change the pattern at the underarm seam half the amount, or 1/2 inch, taking 1/4 inch off the front and 1/4 inch off the side back where it joins the front. To do this, move point 11 1/8 toward the dart 1/4 inch, or in other words, measure back from the edge of your pattern at waistline 1/4 inch and make a point. Then place your scroll in its original posi-

tion and scroll to the new point. Change only at waistline. Also mark off 1/4 inch on underarm seam of side back at waistline and make a new point. Place your scroll in its original position and scroll pattern to new point. Change your seam lines accordingly and the size of your waist will be reduced the desired amount.

In case the pattern measures too small, enlarge it at waistline by moving your points out and scrolling to the new points made. If the pattern is to be changed 3 or more inches, it is better to change the underarm seams 2/3 the amount and the remaining 1/3 at the seam joining the underarm piece and side back.

To test the length of a sleeve, deduct the width of the back of the pattern being drafted, less 1 inch, from the full sleeve measure. The remainder will be the length of the sleeve. In a plain sleeve begin at the corner marked A and measure down the baseline the full measure (less the width of the back, minus 1 inch). If the tape and the last number (scale measure) are the same, then no change is to be made. But if not the same, raise or lower the scale measure to tape measure, changing point next above the same distance and elbow points half as much. If upper part of sleeve is changed then change lower part the same.

A sleeve with a cuff must also have the width of cuff deducted, less 1 inch for extra seams. For a bell or bishop sleeve, or any sleeve full or pouched at wrist, an extra measurement must be taken to get the inside length of sleeve. Measure the inside of the arm, when stretched its full length, from armseye to thumb joint where wrist and hand join. This measurement, less width of cuff (if one is used), plus 1 inch for seams, will be the length of sleeve sought. For a bell or flowing sleeve with no cuff, take the full arm measurement plus 1 inch for seams.

If you need to change the length of the draft, make your changes the same as in other patterns. However, the point where the draft begins at the baseline should be where you begin to measure for sleeve length, instead of point A. Take your tape and measure from this point down your baseline, the length of your inside sleeve measurement less

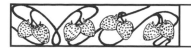 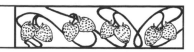

1/2 inch, and make a point. If the number which indicates the lowest point of your inside seam line (and consequently the starting point of lower edge of sleeve), and your tape measurement are the same, no change need be made. But if your tape measurement is greater or less, raise or lower this point to your tape measurement. Raise or lower the starting point of the line intersecting the elbow point just half as much. Get all remaining points just as written.

Patterns for Round-Shouldered Forms. It is sometimes necessary to draft patterns for round- or stoop-shouldered people. Draft back and front as though no changes were to be made. Then on the back at the neckline, at point 5/8, locate a point in from the baseline and up the amount to be changed, which is usually 1/4, 3/8, or 1/2 inches. At the shoulder point 2 1/2 locate point the same distance out and up at neck as was made at back. Now where the curved portion of your pattern should begin, locate a point down your baseline. Scroll in from these new points and locate your new seam lines.

Whatever amount has been added to shoulder seam of back, the same amount must be taken from shoulder seam of front to keep the correct proportion. So make a point in from the shoulder point 4 5/8 and up at neck the same distance as at back at corresponding points. Next locate a point in front, at neck, down just twice the amount of change at shoulder. That is, if you change the shoulder seam 1/2 inch, make a point down front at hemline 1 inch and scroll out neck from these new points. Leave shoulder seam unchanged at armseye. In extreme cases greater changes may have to be made, but if so, proceed in the manner just explained.

Patterns for Stout Forms. Stout people require different drafts in shape and outline than medium and slender people. The same changes are made for stout that are made for slender. If size of waist is to be changed, make changes on the seams joining the two underarm gores, unless a large amount of change is necessary. Then change part on underarm seam that joins front, and on front.

The rule is to change equally all four seams mentioned. If the bust measure exceeds 45 inches, use the following rule to ascertain what scale should be used to get all points on cross and intersecting lines. If the bust measure is an even number, subtract 6, and if an uneven number, subtract 7. Divide this quotient by 2, and the result will be the number of the scale to be used.

For example, if the lady's bust measure is 46 (even), subtract 6. The result will be 40, which divided by 2 will be 20. Therefore select the scale marked bust measure 20. Now when marking off your points on the crosslines do not make a point at the number indicated, but at its double. For example, if the first point should be 3, make a point at 6; should your next point be 10, make it 20, etc. Do this throughout your drafts on all cross and intersecting lines.

For getting all points on the baseline, select a scale which corresponds as nearly as possible with the length of back measurement. For example, if the length of back is 15 inches, make a point 1 inch down baseline from crossline. From this point measure down baseline with tape 15 inches, and make a point. Select a draft whose scale length of back is 12.

To draft this back for a party of 15-inch back measurement, select a scale whose point 12, which number designates the waist point on your draft, will fall on your new point, designating the length of your waist, which in this case will be scale 41. You may not select the correct scale on the first trial, but keep on selecting scales until you get the correct one, always placing the end of your scale even with your crossline. This is termed using the double scale. After selecting your scale get all points on baseline as written.

Drafting Skirts

Use the scale corresponding to your waist measurement to draft your skirt patterns. Regulate the length of your skirt by the use of your tape measure.

Your skirt measurements should be:

Your waist measurement.

Your hip measurement. Measure loosely around the largest portion of the hip.

The length of your skirt in front from the waistline to the floor.

The length of skirt over each hip from waistline to floor.

The length at back at center from waistline to floor.

Draft your front first, and if the last number on draft corresponds with your tape measurement, then no change is necessary. If not, raise or lower the point to the correct measurement, changing points the same as in the waist or other drafts. Change all corresponding drafts in the same proportions. Then take your tape measure and get your correct hip and back measurement if your pattern is not already correct, from the changes already made. Make new points the desired length of your skirt and scroll your pattern from those points. Should you desire a train or sweeping length, allow the desired amount in the back, graduating your sweep from the first gore toward the back.

Special attention should be given to the drafting of skirts for stout people, especially people with high abdomen. Select draft with a narrow front gore and avoid a flare at the bottom of front and at front edge of first gore. To avoid that outstanding effect at front and at bottom of skirt, raise the front edge of the first gore at top 1/2 inch or more, according to the requirements of the party. After raising the points as desired, make a new point, then scroll pattern from this point leaving the other points the same. The same amount that has been added to the top of your gore at front must then be taken from the bottom at front to keep your correct proportions.

When people are decidedly out of proportion, that is when they have a very large waist and short skirt measurement, it becomes necessary to use two scales. One is to be used for crosslines and one for the baseline, the same as when drafting waist patterns for exceedingly large persons.

In selecting a draft, select as short a one as you can and one that flares but little, if any, in front. Now suppose the lady's waist measure is 29 inches and the length of her skirt 39 inches. To use the scale corresponding to her waist measure would make the skirt entirely too short. In extreme cases like this you should make a point on your baseline 1 inch from the crossline, and from this point measure down 39 inches, or the length of skirt desired, and make another point. You would then select a scale that, when measured from the crossline down, whose point which designates the original length of draft falls at your new point 39 inches down. Use it in getting all your points on the baseline. Use the scale corresponding to the waist measure to get all cross and intersecting lines and get your exact points.

Cutting Out

After having drafted all your patterns be very careful in cutting them out, following very closely each and every line of your scrolling. Do not cut out your darts on pattern, but transfer the impression of them to your material with your tracing wheel, as the outline of your darts must be the seam line of same.

It is much more satisfactory to cut all waist lining portions on a crosswise fold of the goods, as they will not then stretch and give so much. To cut the back lining, place your pattern on the cloth so that the center back falls on a crosswise fold of the goods if it is to be cut double. If not, place the line intersecting or following the waist parallel with the lengthwise fold and allow pattern to fall into place on the cloth as it will. To cut the side back place your pattern so that the waistline falls parallel with the selvage or straight weave of the goods, and the position the remaining portion of the draft assumes will be correct. The underarm gore should assume the same position as the side back at waistline. In positioning your front draft, place the line which intersects the waist portion at underarm seam parallel with the selvage.

When the outside portions or forms are to be cut the same as the lining forms, they should occupy the same position relative to the cloth as the lining, only on a lengthwise fold of the goods. Else the lining will stretch in one direction and the outside in another, thereby causing a wrinkle or fold in your waist. Lay pattern for sleeve, both upper

and under portions, upon the cloth so that a line intersecting the elbow points, at both front and back seams, will fall parallel with the thread of the cloth.

Some weaves of cloth have a nap which you will notice always runs in one direction. All portions of your pattern should be placed upon the cloth so that the nap runs downward. Also in figured materials there is often an up and down to the pattern. Care should then be taken to have the figure in all your pieces running in the same direction and right side up.

In all drafts you will notice that only half the garment appears unless otherwise specified. You are then to make a duplicate of each draft in order to produce the full garment. When there is a right and wrong side to the cloth, great care should be taken not to cut the different forms for the same side of the body or both sleeves for one arm. Never cut one form and attempt to cut the second by placing the wrong side of the first on the right side of the cloth. The better way is to lay your pattern on a double fold of your goods with the two right sides together, and cut the two pieces of each form at the same time.

Basting Seams

After having carefully cut your lining and outside portions, place your outside portions on your lining portions with corresponding seams together. Pin the lining at the waistline. Full the lining (from 1/4 to 1/2 inch) on each side from 1 1/2 inch below the waistline to 2 1/2 inches above, the greatest fullness coming at the waistline. Should the waist extend only to the waistline, then full lining above waistline only. This process shortens the lining, but when boned it will be stretched into place. At the front, leave the lining easy each way from top of darts to shoulders, and 1/4 inch full at center of shoulder line.

Great care must be taken in joining the separate parts, smooth, even basting being very necessary. Do not take too long of a stitch, especially on parts that require close fitting. Do not backstitch or draw the thread too tight. Pass your needle through the traced seam on both sides and use great care, as many garments are ruined by injudicious basting.

In joining the back to the side back hold the side back toward you; thus you will baste one side up and the other down. These are the most difficult pieces to join, and it would be well to pin them in position before basting. If the shoulder blades are a little prominent, hold the back a little full where the shoulder blade strikes, to within 1 1/2 inches of the armseye.

The back at the shoulder seam is longer than the corresponding shoulder seam at front. In basting them together, hold the back toward you, baste evenly for 1 inch, then stretch the remaining portion of front shoulder to match the back. Take up all darts on the lines traced for them. If the seam thus formed is greater than desired trim it any desired width.

In joining the sleeve always begin at the wrist. In basting the upper portion of sleeve to under portion at back seam, gather the upper portion to fit the under portion at elbow point when so indicated on the drafts. When no fullness is indicated at this point, hold the upper portion very easy from 1 1/2 inches below to 1 1/2 inches above the elbow point.

In placing sleeve in armseye measure forward on front of waist at armseye, from underarm seam 2 1/2 inches. Place the front seam of sleeve at this point. Baste in armseye to within 4 inches of shoulder seam at front and 2 inches of shoulder seam at back. Gather the surplus fullness at top of sleeve into the remaining 6 inches of armseye. Regulate the fullness as evenly as possible; or if there is a difference in fullness place the greater amount toward the front.

After having basted your garment together very carefully, try it on. If any changes are to be made, make them at the shoulder and underarm seams. In stitching follow very carefully the outline of your basting, straight, even stitching being very necessary.

Finishing Garments

After the stitching and removal of all bastings comes the pressing.

Pressing. Never lay a garment aside as complete until it has been thoroughly pressed. This does not apply to seams alone, but to pleats, tucks, hems, and in fact everything that goes to make up a garment. In pressing lay your goods upon a soft, smooth surface and press them on the wrong side. Avoid all wrinkles or lumps in your ironing sheet. If you press over such irregularities, shiny streaks and spots will appear on the face of your goods. Should you at any time have this misfortune, the shiny parts can be removed by steaming. This again causes the raising of the nap of the cloth. It can be easily accomplished by placing a damp cloth on the parts to be steamed and ironing very gently with a hot iron, removing both the iron and the cloth before thoroughly dry.

In pressing seams, press as flat as possible the seam line, using the point of your iron. Avoid, if possible, making an impression on the right side of your garment of the outer edge of seam. Dampen all parts to be pressed. In pressing skirts and skirt facings, especially portions that have been stitched heavily, it is well to lay a damp cloth on the wrong side and then apply the iron, removing same before dry, and then pressing again without cloth until thoroughly dry.

Seams. All seams should be finished, not only to make a neat appearance inside the garment, but to prevent raveling. There are numerous ways of finishing seams, the most perfect being to bind them with a narrow tape, bought for that purpose. Another way, and a very practical one, is to simply notch the edge of seams by clipping out three-cornered pieces. Again they may be overcast. This does not make as neat a finish but prevents raveling and fraying.

Boning. The seams of a tight waist lining should be boned to preserve the shape of the waist and prevent it from sliding up on the form. There are many kinds of bones, but the most recent and popular is featherboning. It is softer and more pliable than whalebone and can be stitched in place without the use of a casing. If you use the steels prepared for this purpose, they do not conform so readily to the form, besides wear more quickly on the waist.

In featherboning, bone the seam at center of back first, beginning at a point just below the shoulder blade. Place the end of your featherbone in your boner, underneath the foot of your machine and flat on your seam line. Begin at the upper end to stitch bone in place. Stitch in center of bone. Stitch perfectly even with lining for a short distance, and then begin crowding your lining ahead of your bone, not enough to gather your lining but enough to give your bone a rounding effect when stitched in place. This stretches your lining. Cut off your featherbone, back from the end, allowing the casing to extend a short distance over the end of the bone. Overlap this and fasten in place as a finish to the end of the bone.

Next bone the seam that joins back to side back. This seam requires a much shorter bone than the back seam. Begin to fasten your bone at a point where the thread of the cloth in the side back coincides or runs in the same direction with the thread of the cloth in the back. You then place bone in position and stitch it in place as described before. For the next seam, which joins side back to underarm gore, select a bone some longer than the last and proceed in the same manner. The underarm seam requires a bone that extends within 1 1/2 inches of the armseye.

In boning the darts, place end of bone at the extreme point of dart. Stitch evenly for 1 inch. Then begin to crowd your lining until within about 1 1/2 inches of waistline, when you elevate both ends of your bone (taking lining and all) and while in this curved position stitch your bone in place, extending it to extreme lower edge of waist lining. Place a short bone down edge of each lining front and your boning is complete.

Hooks and Eyes. Sew hooks on right front and eyes on left side. If using the plain straight hook (no hump), sew them on both sides, alternating first a hook and then an eye, else they will not stay fas-

tened. Sew the hook on so that the end extends about 1/8 inch back from the front edge of the lining. The loop of the eye should then extend over the edge of the left front a little less than 1/8 inch, sufficient distance for the looping of the hook.

Making Skirts

All woolen goods should be sponged before making up, to remove that shiny appearance and shrink the goods as well. To sponge cloth roll it in a wet sheet wrung out of water, or a strip of muslin for that purpose. Allow it to remain in this damp cloth for several hours. Then remove and press with a very hot iron, always ironing on the wrong side of the goods. It is well to also shrink all canvas before using, in this way.

In joining skirt portions begin at the top and baste downward. Should there be any irregularities in your drafts, they will fall at the bottom where they can be trimmed off without detriment to the skirt. Skirt drafts, as a rule, are so constructed that the bias or most slanting edge of one draft joins the straight, or nearly straight, edge of its corresponding draft. The straight edge of one prevents the stretching of the bias, or partially bias, edge of the other. This is true of all seams excepting the back seam, where you will find two bias, or partially bias, edges coming together. With seams of this sort you should stitch in with your seaming a tape, being very careful not to stretch your seam. This will prevent any further stretching of your seam and an untidy hanging of your skirt.

Skirts are now so constructed that the outside and lining parts are made up as two separate skirts. They may be made on the same or separate bands. The lining is then termed a drop skirt and is very seldom constructed the same as the outside skirt. The most desirable way to construct the drop lining is to use plain drafts for the upper portion of the skirt and finish the bottom with a pleated flounce of about 10 or 12 inches in depth. The flounce can or cannot be set upon the upper portion of the skirt, the most satisfactory way being to sew the flounce to the lower edge.

Such a drop lining can be worn with almost any style of outside skirt. Braid is usually placed on the bottom of the drop skirt for protection. When such a lining is used the outside skirt is faced a short distance from the bottom, and the facing hand sewn or stitched in place, as the case may be.

A facing is a bias strip of cloth of any desired width, stitched to the edge of a garment and then turned back and stitched in place, to strengthen as well as finish the edge and prevent it from raveling. All facings and strapping should be cut on the bias of the cloth to get perfect results. Facings are generally sewed in such a way that when turned over and stitched in place they will fall on the wrong side of the garment. In sewing a facing in position it should be held very loosely, so that when turned and stitched into place, the outside portions will fall easy and not be drawn in wrinkles.

This is especially true in walking skirts or in any facing where many rows of stitching occur. In cases of this sort it is well to stitch your facing on without basting. Place your facing under the foot of the machine, with your facing first and your skirt next. Allow your facing to run under the machine foot easy. At the same time pull your skirt the least bit to prevent it from feeding quite so fast. This causes your facing to go on much fuller than your outside, and when turned over appears in folds almost like a ruffle. Do not let this annoy you, but fold over your facing and baste it down in place as best you can, allowing the fullness to fall straight, as it should. The turn your skirt over, stitching on the right side as many times as desired. When through you will find that all that fullness, that was so annoying to you, has been taken up with the continued stitching. You will have a smooth surface, both on wrong and right side of skirt.

There are many different kinds of bindings for skirts, but the most favored at the present time, especially for drop skirts, is skirt braid. When the bottom of the skirt is faced prior to putting on the braid, the braid is put on by hand and faced down at the upper edge only. The lower edge is left loose and extends a short distance below the skirt to protect it. Braids put on in this way never draw the skirt. When a braid occupies the position of braid and facing combined, then it must be sewed at both edges.

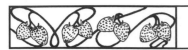 

Making Jackets

There is no branch of the work that requires more thought, care, and attention than ladies' tailoring. A large amount of the success in making jackets must be acquired from actual practice. Your drafting, basting, sewing, and pressing principles are the same for all.

In jackets you have no boning but a lining and an interlining to consider. Your jacket fronts, collar, and cuffs should be interlined with tailor's canvas, or better still, linen crinoline; this is to give stiffness and form to these parts. For warmth as well as to give your jacket that soft, finished outside appearance, you should interline the entire garment with what is termed felt lining.

Cut your lining and outside portions the same except the back, which should be cut wider than the outside back, the surplus fullness being arranged in a pleat down center of back. Place your felt lining next your goods and your canvas next your felt. Stitch the lining and the outside portions separately. Then place them wrong sides together, thereby avoiding all seams on the inside of your jacket when finished.

Cut your collar on the bias and so that the nap or twill of the cloth will extend from the seam in the back, where collar joins, toward the front. The under and outer portions of the collar should be lined separately. The under portion should be stitched back and forth to the canvas very closely, so that when the collar is rolled over in place there will be no loose, baggy effect on the underside. In stitching collar to neck join all portions in the seam and then face your jacket lining over it.

A great amount of the general appearance of a jacket lies in the pressing. The heavy materials used for these garments make heavy and thorough pressing very necessary.

The same principles apply to the making of long coats.

February 1900

Anything plain is a rare exception, and some of the new productions in trimmings, materials, and also ready-made articles are simply marvels of beauty.

Just which, if any, of the many pretty ideas in neckwear has the most favor would be hard to say. All are very high and fit the neck very closely, and everyone seems to have some new and original idea in the way of trimming or arranging the fluffy lace, the plain bow, or the long sash ends that are sometimes formed in a bow at the throat, cross on the bust, and have another bow in the back, from where the ends fall loose. Some very stylish collars are of black velvet, stitched in white, with a little bow of black velvet lined with white silk.

Pleats and tucks are seen on all manner of dresses and wraps. Some of the newest skirts are tucked either entirely or in clusters, some lengthwise and some on the bias. Bias tucking is beautiful in the thin materials for evening wear. In these tucked skirts the tucks usually end within a few inches of the bottom of the skirt, from where they have a pretty flare and usually have insertions set in below the tucks. Box-pleated backs are one of the greatest successes. Some of the skirts have single and some double pleats. In some skirts the pleats hang free from the waist, while in others the pleats are stitched at their edge to a distance of 6 or 8 inches below the belt, or waistline. Tucked backs are also very pretty, and the tucks usually run 10 or 12 inches below the waist. Waists are usually tucked to match the skirt. The new waists made entirely of tucking are very pretty.

One special feature is bolero effects, which are seen in every kind and shape. A very pretty notion is the velvet muff, which is usually profusely decorated with bows of ribbon, lace, flowers, etc. With handsome calling and visiting gowns small shoulder capes, made very gay in bright velvets, pretty laces, ribbons, and even ostrich tips, will be worn.

Some new capes are very beautiful, fur lined and elaborately stitched and strapped. Some are set onto a yoke and may be ever so fancy about the collar. Some turned-up collars are lined with shirred chiffon and have a bow of ribbon at the throat, with long ends, and many have a drapery about the shoulders. Some of the most handsome capes slope backward from the bust line and are quite long in back.

Jackets are very short, the eton being a popular cut. The ones in persian lamb and astrakhan are especial favorites, and usually have collar and revers of a contrasting fur. Even an edging of a different fur gives a pretty effect.

Among the novelties of the season are fur-covered hats. Some have brims lined with fur, others have crowns of fur, while others have their rims and crowns bordered with fur. The effect is usually more becoming where fur is associated with velvet, than where the hat is made entirely of fur. Panne velvet is one of the most popular materials. The association of fur with all manner of lighter fabrics and flowers is quite a departure from the ordinary, yet the effect gained is very beautiful and altogether desirable.

One of the most fashionable materials for dressy wear is panne velvet, as it comes in such a variety of beautiful shades. Some new alpacas are quite pretty. It is almost impossible to tell some of the best qualities from silk. They are employed extensively for accordion-pleated ruffles. Foulards will again be very fashionable for spring and summer wear. Some of the most beautiful new taffetas are outlined in flower or scroll designs. The edges of these designs are finished with a fine cord, the inside portion of the design is cut away, and some have lace or net inserted, while some of the smaller patterns have not. Garments made of these materials require a silk or satin lining.

Silk-finished henrietta is a very pretty and comparatively inexpensive material. For making entire costumes it is not as suitable for ladies as for misses and children, though it makes pretty shirt-waists, yokes, sleeves, vests, panels of skirts, etc. Also there are brocades in the most exquisite patterns. Spangled robes are seen in great variety. In some of the more expensive silks are patterns with encrusted medallions of rare lace; others are embroidered in gilt and silver tinsel. One favorite way of trimming all manner of costumes is with narrow bands of fur.

Ladies' Promenade Costume

Use the scale corresponding to the bust measure to draft the waist, which consists of lining back, side back, and front; half of back; upper front; upper and under revers; vest; collar; and two sleeve portions. Use the scale corresponding to the waist measure to draft the skirt. Regulate all lengths by the tape measure.

Join the back and side back and adjust the upper back to them by basting around the edges. Interline the revers with good canvas and line them. Sew the smaller one to the front edge of upper left front and the large one to the front edge of upper right front. Line the upper fronts with the same material of which you line the revers. Take up the darts in the lining fronts. Lay on the upper fronts and join all together in the underarm and shoulder seams. Line the vest and finish its edges. Tack it to the lining front at the right side and underneath the upper front. Secure it to the left lining front by hooks and eyes. Make foundation for collar of two or three layers of good canvas well machine stitched and see that it fits nicely before covering. Cover in any way the fancy may dictate. Baste sleeve up and fit it to the arm before stitching, as the size of the arm varies considerably in persons of the same bust measure. Also see if it sets properly before stitching in the armseye.

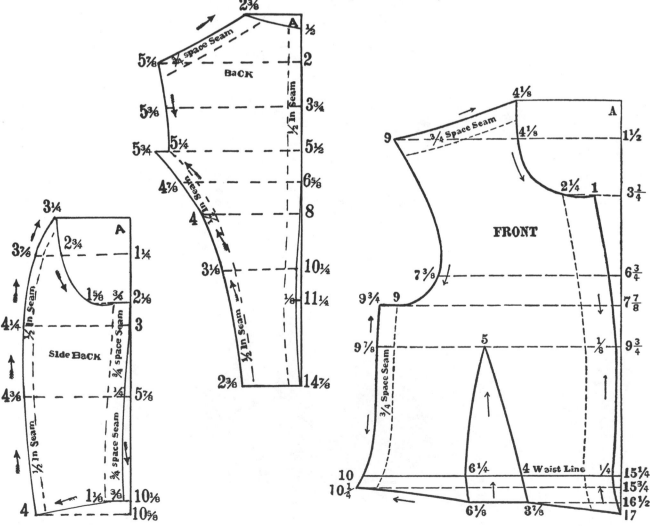

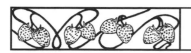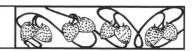
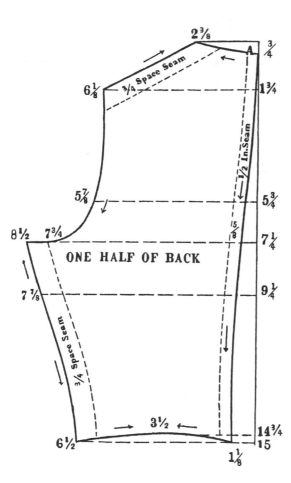

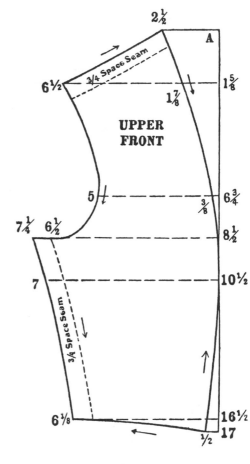

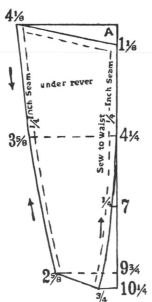

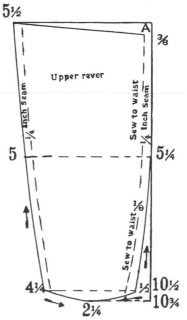

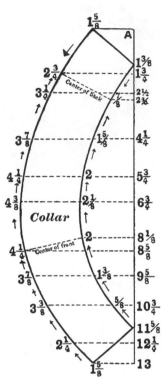

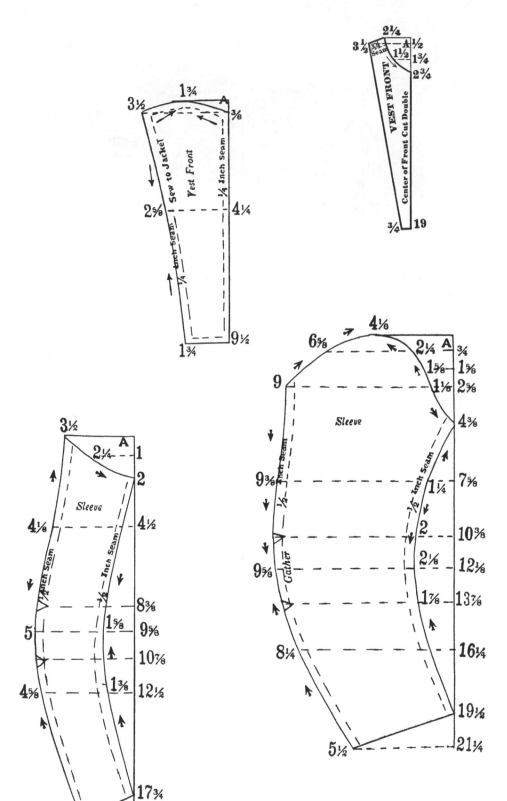

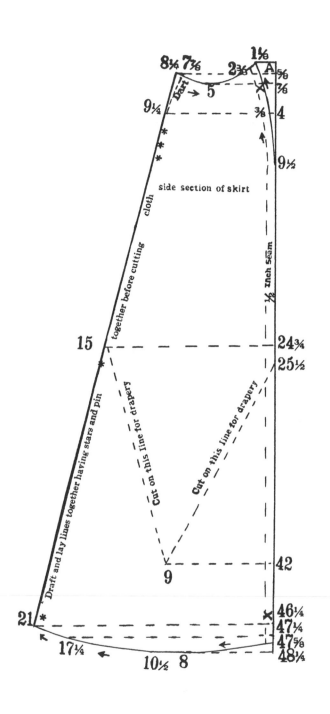

side section of skirt

together before cutting cloth

Dart

Draft and lay lines together having stars and pin

Cut on this line for drapery

Cut on this line for drapery

½ inch seam

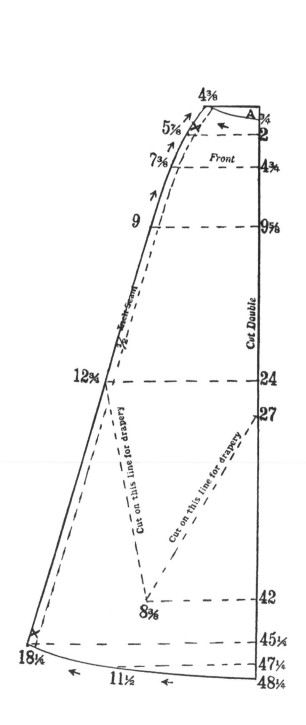

Front

Cut Double

Cut on this line for drapery

Cut on this line for drapery

½ inch seam

23

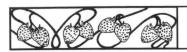

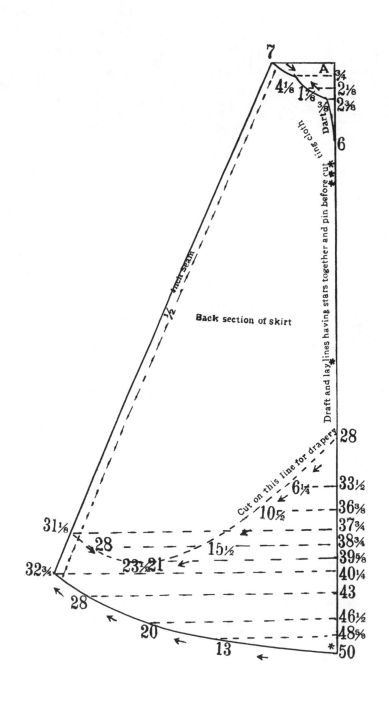

Back section of skirt

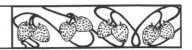
Ladies' Evening Costume

Use the scale corresponding to the bust measure to draft the waist, which consists of lining back, side back, underarm, and front; full back; full front; back yoke; front yoke; and drapery for front. Use the scale corresponding to the waist measure to draft the skirt. Regulate all lengths by the tape measure.

To make with low neck as illustrated, cut the back and front lining away on the dotted lines. Gather the full waist parts and sew to the yokes. Join the lining back and side back and adjust the upper full back and yoke. Cut an upper and lining section, both from the same underarm gore. Take up the darts in the lining fronts. Join the upper part together with the lining in the underarm seam at the right side. Face the lining front at the left side at shoulder, armseye, and underarm seam, and on the upper side, with a facing about 2 inches wide. Gather the full front to fit the lining front at its lower edge. Face it to hold gathers in position, and close it at the left shoulder and underarm seam with hooks, and loops made of buttonhole twist. Close

the lining down the front with hooks and eyes. Hem the drapery at its lower edge, and join it in underarm and armseye at the right side. Gather it at the left side as illustrated. Or lay in small pleats and cover the end with a bow, rosette, buckle, or in any manner suitable. Sew it in with the yoke at the top. The armseye at the top is finished with a straight piece of the silk draped across the top of the arm, its upper edge sewed in the armseye. Its lower edge is hemmed and finished in the same manner as the front drapery, and both the back and front end are caught up in the same manner as the left end of the front drapery.

The lace is made over a foundation skirt of silk, and is embroidered in steel and silver spangles. A full satin ruffle finishes the bottom. The same satin is used to drape the front and armseye, also forms the yoke and is embroidered.

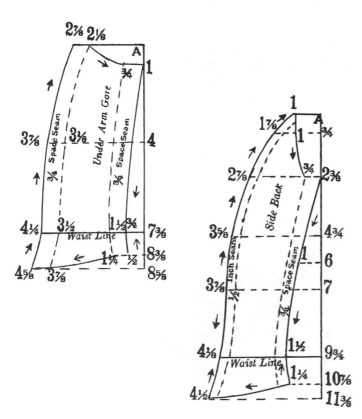

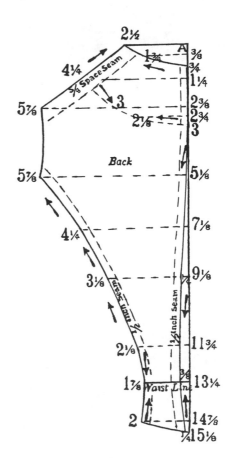

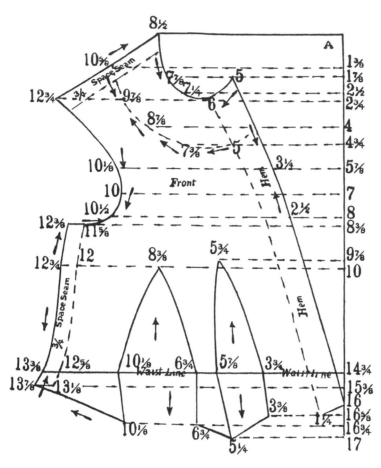
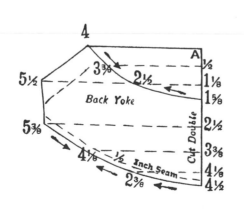
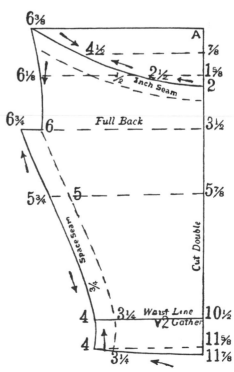

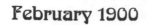

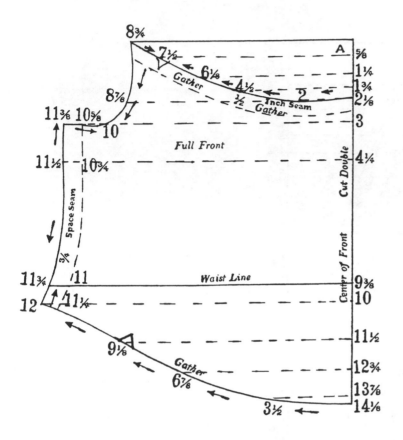

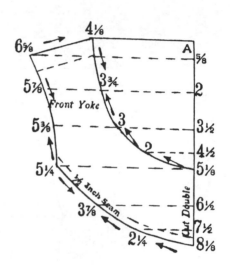

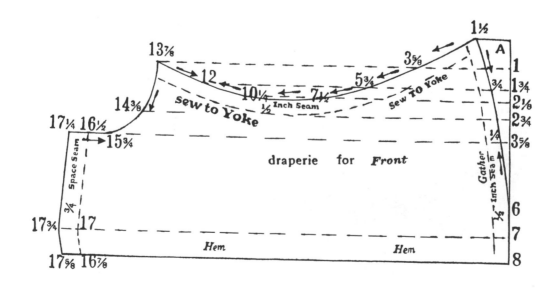

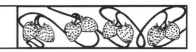

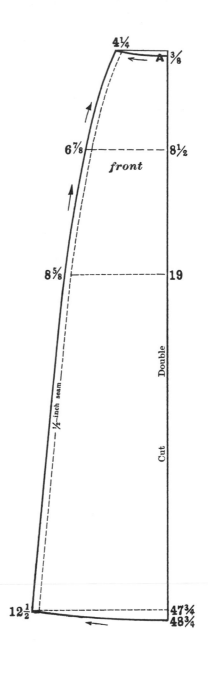

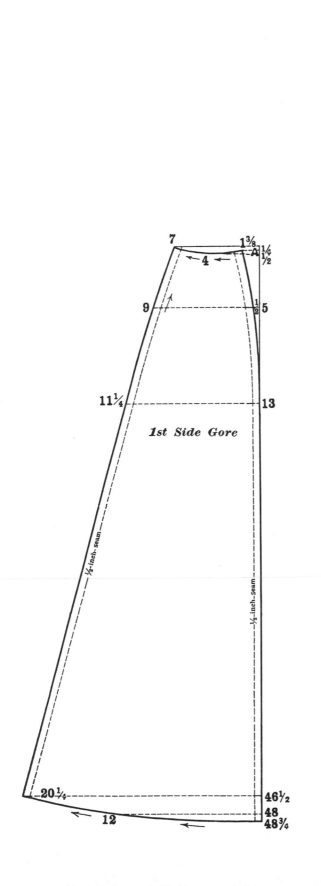

1st Side Gore

front

29

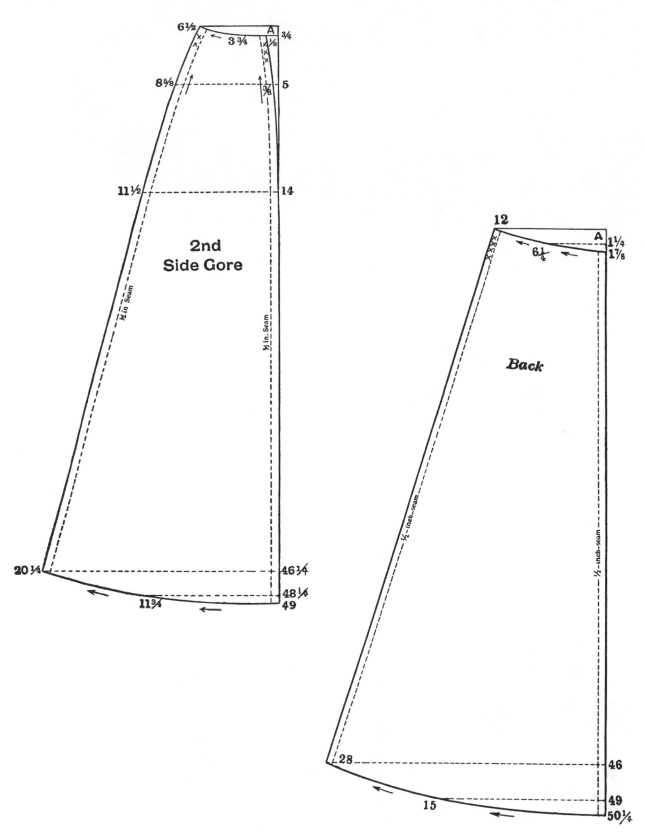

2nd
Side Gore

Back

Ladies' House Toilet

Use the scale corresponding to the bust measure to draft the entire dressing sacque, which consists of back, right and left fronts, three pieces of standing collar, fichu, and two sleeve portions. Use the scale corresponding to the waist measure to draft the skirt. Regulate all lengths by the tape measure.

Join the sacque parts as illustrated. Gather them at the neck to fit the collar. The seams of the collar are left open about 2 inches from the top and faced inside with satin. Pleat the fichu according to stars and notches, and drape around the shoulders, or secure the pleats by placing straps underneath. In this way it may be worn or not, as desired. Make and adjust the sleeves in the usual way.

Join the small front and side sections of the skirt according to the Xs. Gather the ruffle and sew to them and join all to the back width. The back may be either gathered or laid in a box pleat.

This dressing sacque is of china silk, in pale green with a pink and white figure, trimmed in ecru lace, silk, and ribbon. For a lady of medium size, it requires 3 1/2 yards of china silk 36 inches wide, with 2/3 yard of white or ecru silk for the fichu. Skirt of gray cashmere; 4 yards of 42-inch cashmere required.

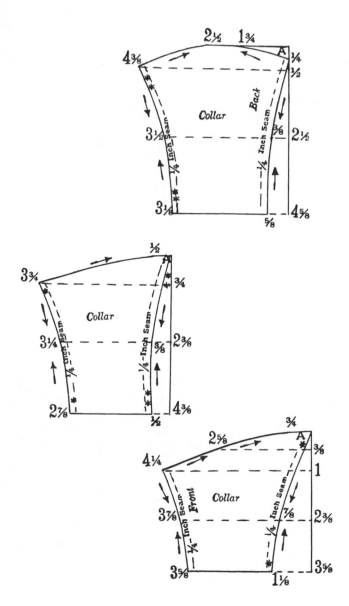

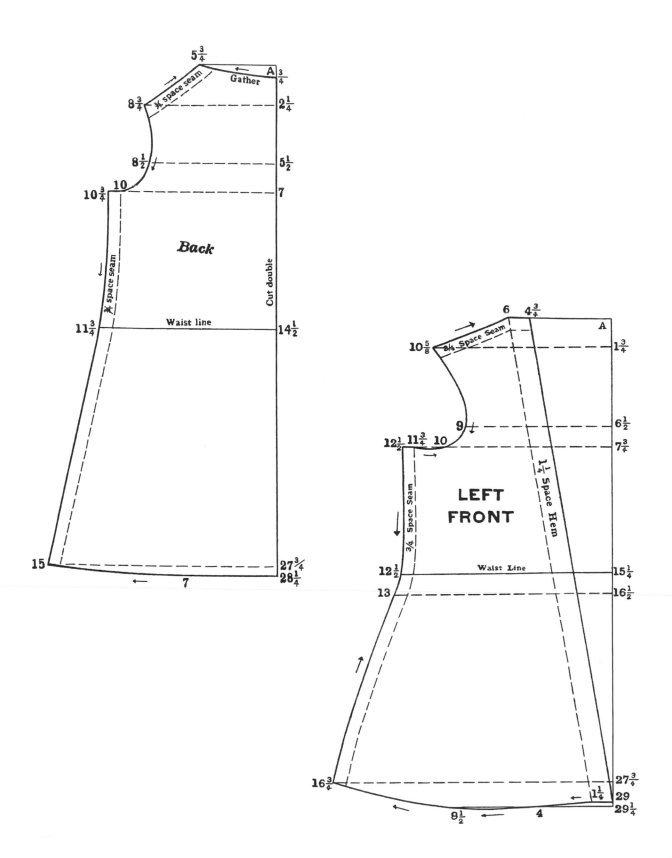

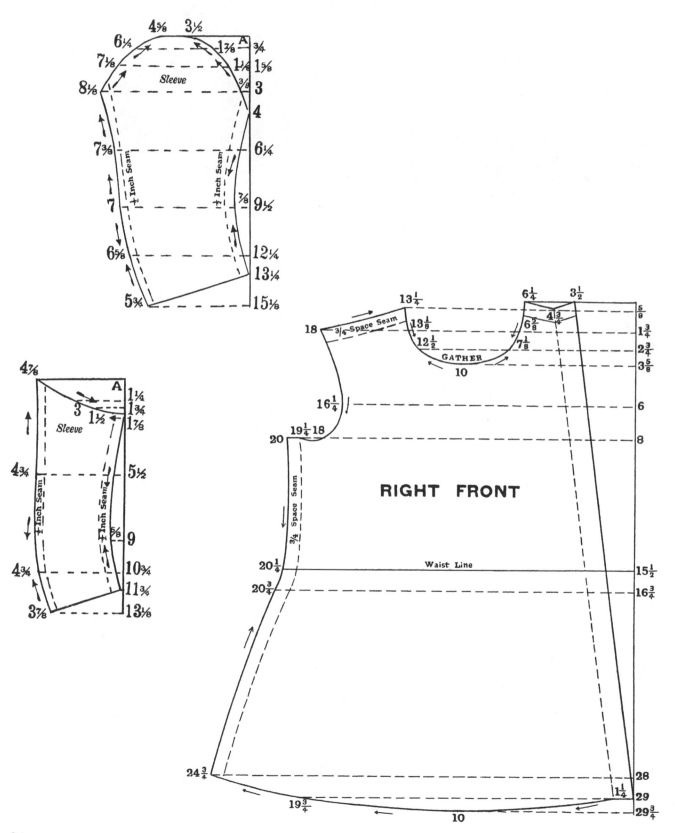

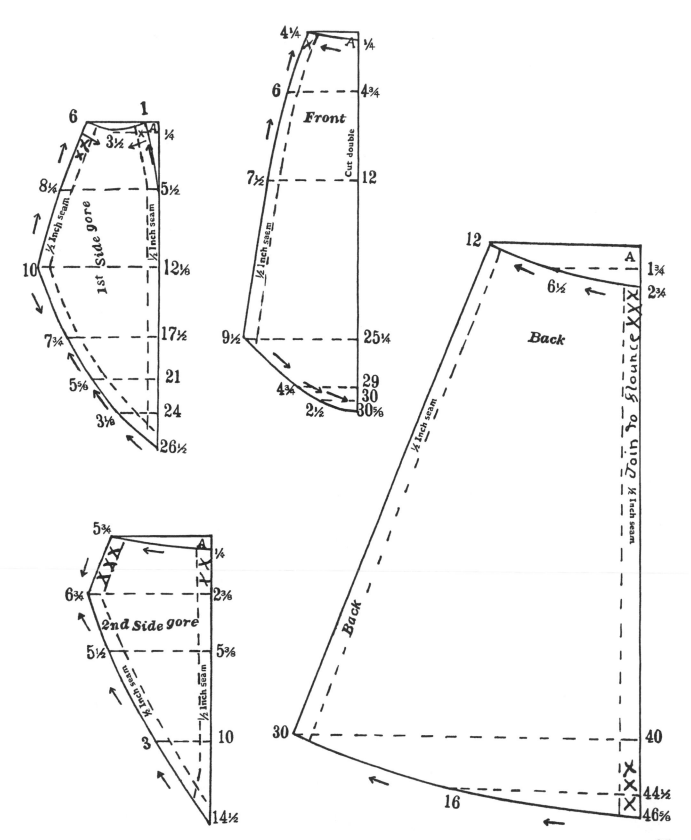

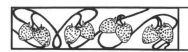

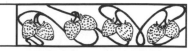

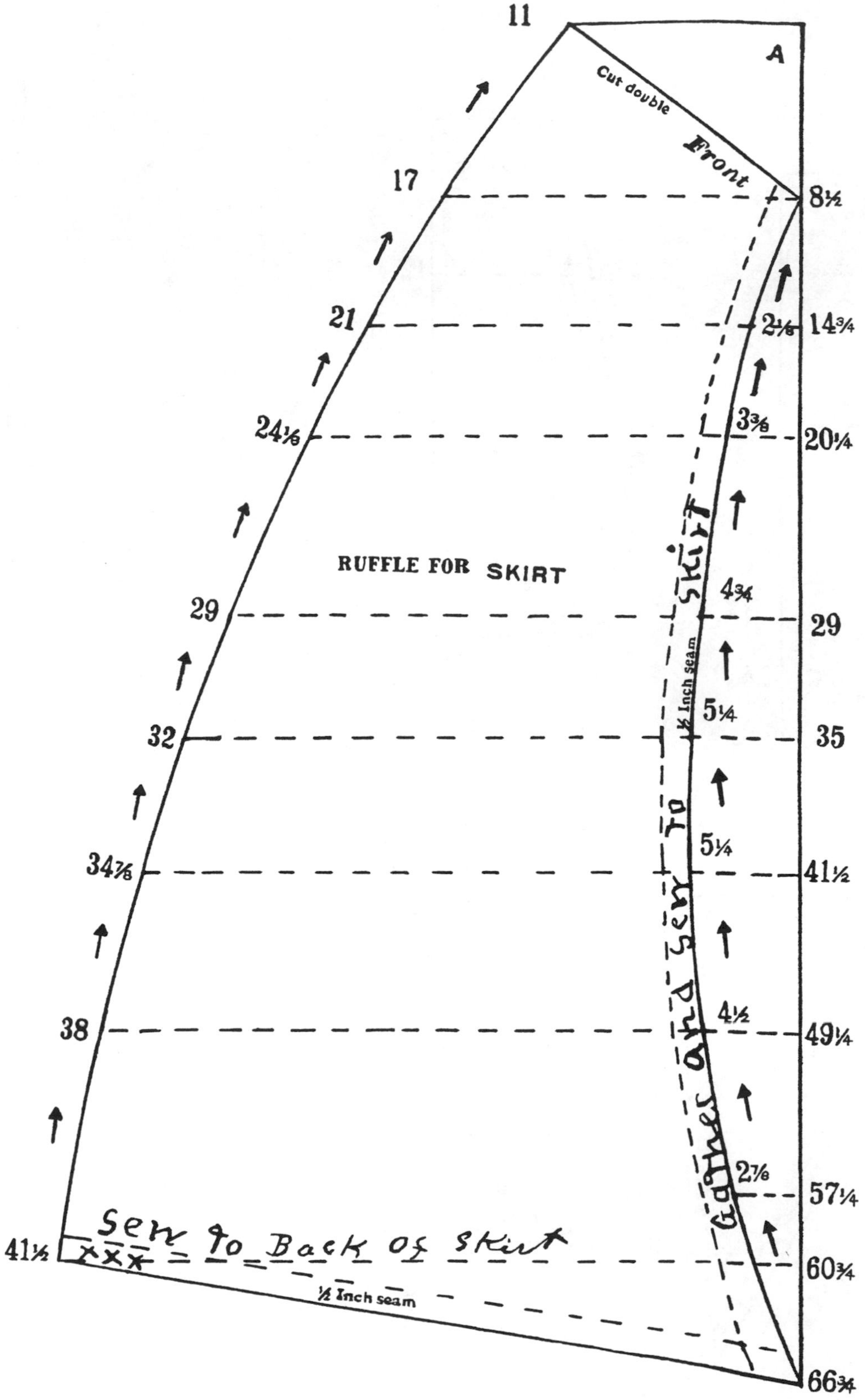
11
A
Cut double
Front
17
8½
21
2⅛
14¾
24⅛
3⅜
20¼
RUFFLE FOR SKIRT
29
4¾
29
½ Inch seam
32
5¼
35
34⅞
5¼
41½
38
4½
49¼
2⅞
57¼
41½
Sew to Back of skirt
xxx
60¾
½ Inch seam
66¾
Gather and sew to skirt

May 1900

Some of the most beautiful spring costumes are of crepe and gauze, and are simply a mass of tucks, shirring, ruffles, and flounces. Light dresses have the preference for dressy wear. Draped bodices are very popular, which is one reason for soft tissues being used so extensively.

In colors, faded tints seem to be given the preference. In the new materials some favorite shades are gray, prune, marine, purple, violet, old rose, pink, pale green, and many others. It is said that one of the leading costumes this summer will be a skirt of white broadcloth worn with a black waist or jacket. If a jacket, there should be a white blouse or vest. Red jackets will often be seen with these white skirts, and also with skirts of black.

A new feature is an undersleeve, known as the lingerie sleeve, which extends from the short sleeve to the wrist, and in many instances well down over the hand. It simulates an undergarment, therefore should be made of thin materials. A waist with a blouse or vest front and in the bolero or empire effect, may have the blouse or vest of the same material, which makes the effect of an undergarment more emphatic.

The popularity of the bolero cannot be disputed. There are all kinds and shapes—sometimes a mere suggestion of a jacket formed of a bit of lace, a contrasting material, or a real eton. Some come to the waistline, some an inch or two above, showing a fancy belt or girdle, and some come barely below the bust line. Some beautiful ones are made entirely of lace and are very pretty worn over a waist of a contrasting color.

A novelty in waists is the ones made of ribbon united with alternate rows of lace insertion or a contrasting shade of ribbon. Entire costumes made in this way will be seen. A foundation may be cut from tissue paper. The ribbon and insertion is sewn on this in alternate rows until the paper is entirely covered, then the paper is torn away.

Another novelty is the handkerchief waist. All manner of the bright colored squares are used, the borders principally for the trimming and the solid colors for the body. Some shirtwaists have a bolero effect. The waist is usually made of some plain color and the bolero of tucking, insertion, etc.

Lace has reached such a degree of popularity that it is one of the most important articles in the manufacture of garments. The allovers, especially, are used in making entire garments of every description, even light wraps for evening wear. The ones in ecru or gray (which is a term used for the natural color of the thread) are exceptionally pretty. Some of the favorite kinds are renaissance, plauen cluny, etc., for the better trade. Some laces for making entire costumes come so planned and cut to pattern that the seams are almost invisible when made up. They should have a colored lining, and may have a chiffon skirt immediately beneath the lace and matching the lining in color. Scalloped and waved laces are also very beautiful and are used as bands and appliqués, on both dresses and wraps.

Foulards have many and varied designs. The ones having a fine interlaced design as with branches of coral are extremely beautiful. Others have designs of fruit attached to stems, others have serpentine patterns, while some have a Japanese effect. Crepe de chine, crepe de paris, and all manner of these clinging effects are in vogue. One very late novelty has an embroidered floral design border; below some borders falls a fringe which can be employed very effectively for trimming. Gauziness seems to be the most desirable effect in woolens, and the silk and wool mixtures for spring and summer. They are most satisfactory when a taffeta or silk lining is employed. Among these soft materials are transparent poplins. Some of the prettiest grenadines have a ribbon effect in some color, joining strips of the sheer material in black, upon which is embroidered a floral design. Some cotton

grenadines have lace insertions, while others have allover lace effects. Then there are the countless sheer and plainer effects, such as cobweb veilings which are admirably adapted for all the pleated, shirred, and tucked modes. Where the stylish clinging effect is desired, corded and tucked silks will remain popular. Some corded taffetas show the cord in some contrasting color. Another new material is lace canvas; in this we see beauty united with durability. Some have a floral colored design on a white ground. Another popular material is khaki. It is very heavy and will be used a great deal for outing suits. Piqué, linen, duck, etc., will remain fashionable in making these outdoor garments.

There will also be seen quite handsome afternoon gowns constructed from plainer materials, but of course they will be more elaborately decorated than the ones for the street and outing occasions. Wash silks are handsomer than ever, though, like most other materials, they seem softer.

The new neck scarf with its tasseled, fringed, or lace ends is very pretty and is seen in all the pastel shades, also black and white. It is usually wide and is either passed twice around the neck and tied into a bow in front, or formed in a large bow and held in place by a fancy pin. The made butterfly bow is very popular, yet the effect is rather stiff. Even on shirtwaists fancy stock or standing collars are used quite extensively.

The bow, rosette, or knot, having long ends and placed on the dress in odd places, is quite a fad. Some are made from the dress material and trimmed at the ends, while others are of ribbon, lace, etc.

The more elaborate hats are simply masses of lace, tulle, chiffon, fancy braids, foliage, flowers, and fruits. Some have the crown and brim lining of flowers or foliage, with here and there a cluster of berries, and the rim covered with lace or chiffon layered in folds and massed around the lower part of the crown. Others are made entirely of leaves and flowers, or foliage combined with fruit or berries. Some very softening and beautiful effects are produced in tucked or shirred chiffon, crepe tulle, etc., with little or no trimming but the extravagant massing of these materials. The newest shapes in sailors will be those with very narrow rims and high, wide crowns, and those having the rims narrower in back, which have more possibilities in the way of trimming.

Ladies' Tailor Made

Use the scale corresponding to the bust measure to draft the entire jacket, which consists of back, underarm, front, revers, rolling collar, and sleeve. It will be seen that the back and side back pieces are attached together, and the three front pieces are drafted in the same manner. See instructions on the diagrams for opening on the different lines, and join pieces just as they are placed on the diagram. Use the scale corresponding to the waist measure to draft the skirt. Regulate all lengths by the tape measure. Be sure to raise or lower the pleat the same amount as the skirt portions.

Sew seams of jacket and lining separately. A lightweight interlining should be joined with the jacket seams, as it will ensure a better finish to the seams. Make the sleeves in the same manner. The revers have no interlining, as the peculiar cut makes a soft finish necessary. The back collar is made, lined, and interlined in the usual way.

The interlining in the skirt usually extends to the top of the pleat. The pleat is interlined the same as the skirt. Use special care in getting all the different parts in their proper places, joining them according to the Xs.

This pattern will develop nicely in any of the materials for summer outing costumes, as well as wool suitings. It may be worn with any shirtwaist. For a medium-sized lady it will require 6 yards of 42-inch material, or 9 yards of 36-inch goods.

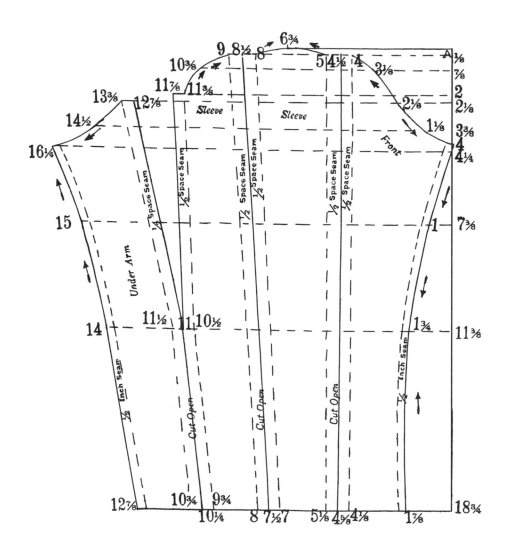

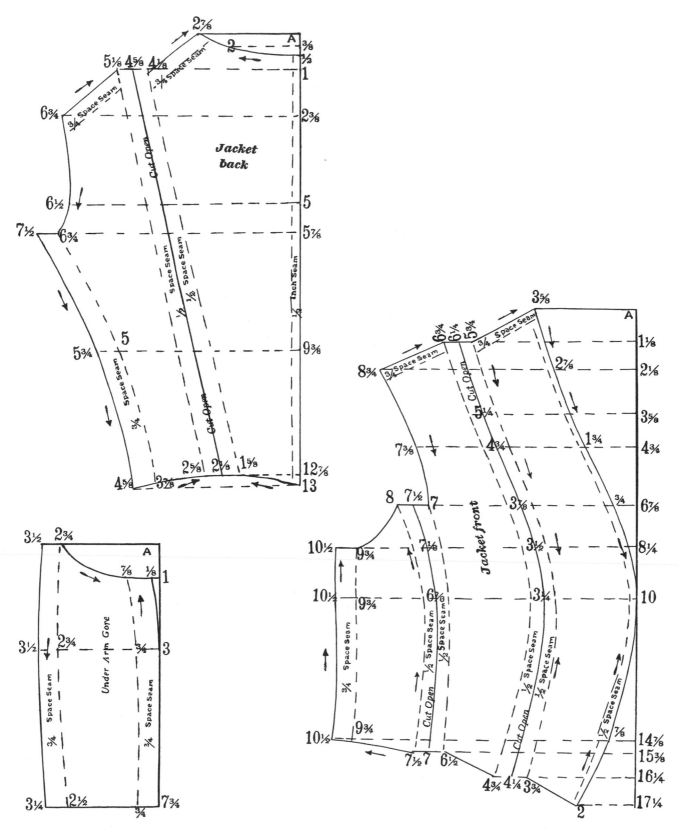

Jacket back

Under Arm Gore

Jacket front

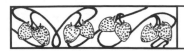
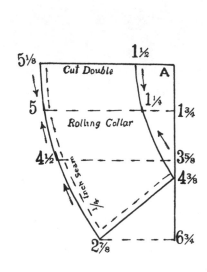

Cut Double

5⅛   1½
   A
5   1¼   1¾
Rolling Collar
4½   3⅝
   4⅜
   ¼
2⅞   6¾

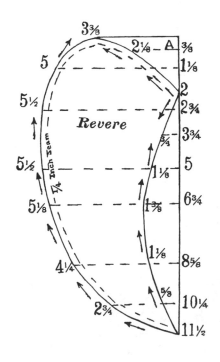

3⅜
5   2⅛   A   3⅛
   1⅛
   2
5½   2¾
Revere   ¾   3¾
5½   1⅛   5
   1⅜   6¾
5⅛
   1⅛   8⅝
4¼
   ⅝   10¼
2¾   11½

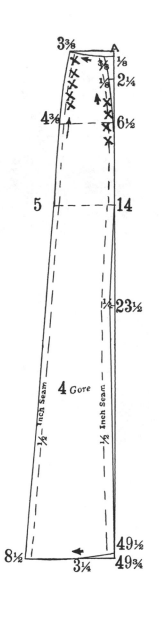

3⅜   A
   ⅜   ⅛
   ⅛   2¼
4⅜   6½
5   14

¼ 23½

4 Gore

½ Inch Seam   ½ Inch Seam

8½   49½
   3¼   49¾

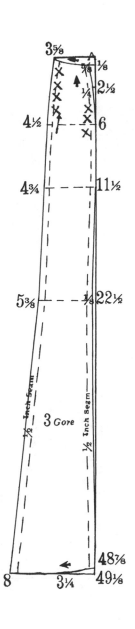

3⅝   A
   ⅝   ⅛
   ¼   2½
4½   6
4¾   11½

5⅜   ¼ 22½

3 Gore

½ Inch Seam   ½ Inch Seam

   48⅞
8   3¼   49⅛

42

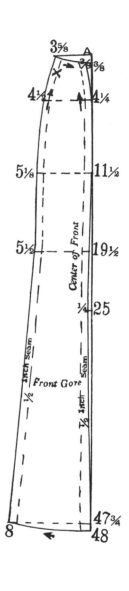

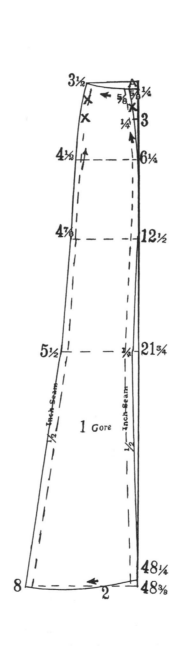

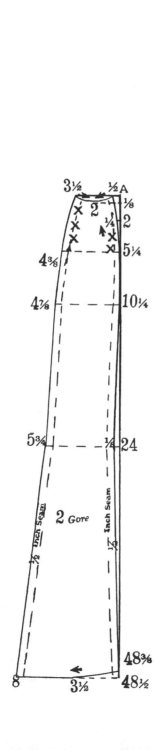

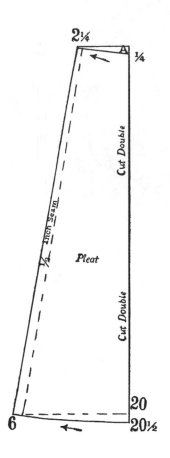

2¼

¼ A

½ Inch Seam

Cut Double

Pleat

Cut Double

20
20½

6

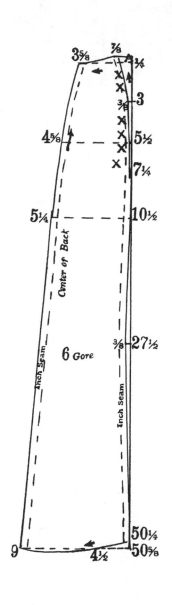

⅞

3⅝ A ¼

X
X
⅜ 3
X
4⅝ X 5½
X
X 7¼

Center of Back

5¼ 10½

Inch Seam

6 Gore ⅜ 27½

Inch Seam

50¼
50⅝

9 4½

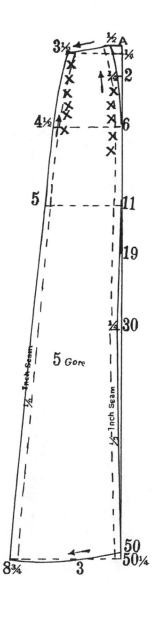

½ A
3½ ¼
¼ 2
X X
X X
X X
4½ X X 6
X X
X

5 11

19

¼ 30

5 Gore

½ Inch Seam

½ Inch Seam

50
50¼

8¾ 3

Bridal Costume

Use the scale corresponding to the bust measure to draft the waist, which consists of lining back, side back, and front; upper back and front; two vest fronts; collar; and two sleeve portions. Use the scale corresponding to the waist measure to draft the skirt. Omit the lines and figures for scallops when drafting a plain skirt. Regulate all lengths by the tape measure.

Join the lining back and side back. Overlay lining back at its upper part with the satin to a depth of about 4 inches. Cut away the upper back on the circular line and finish the upper edge with a facing of the same material. Adjust upper back to the lining. It has no fullness at the waistline. Overlay the lining fronts, with the satin to come below lower vest and back under the side fronts. Round the lining fronts at their upper and front edges, as illustrated, and finish with narrow piping, continuing it around the back. Tuck the goods for lower vest before cutting. Sew it to and underneath the front

edge of the right upper front. Fasten it at the left side underneath the front edge of the upper front. Make the foundation for the collar to fasten in back, and tack it to the lining for the small upper vest. Try them on to see if they set properly. Cover with bias folds stitched to represent tucks, commencing at the bottom of the vest and continuing to the top of the collar. Cut the upper portion of sleeve away at the top as illustrated, or in any shape the fancy dictates. Fill the space with tucks of satin. The waist is finished at the bottom with a narrow roll of the goods, or may be worn underneath the skirt band and a belt of crushed ribbon.

This costume is of pearl gray and white satin, and trimmed with cream lace and flowers. The white is used for the front of the waist, collar, and upper parts of sleeves. Material required for a medium-sized lady, 11 yards of 24-inch gray satin, with 2 yards of the white.

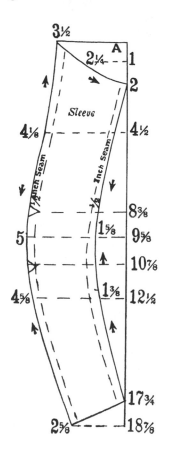

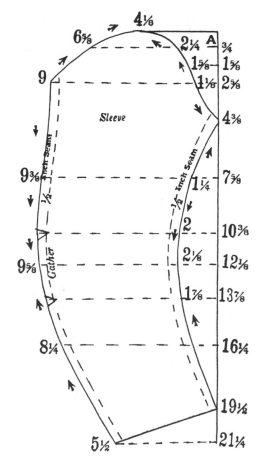

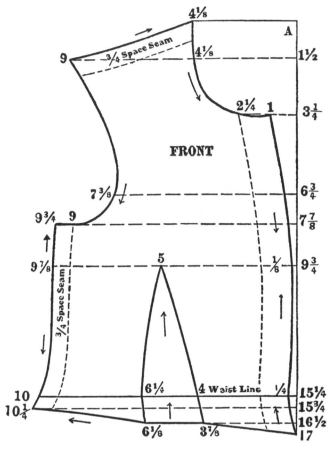

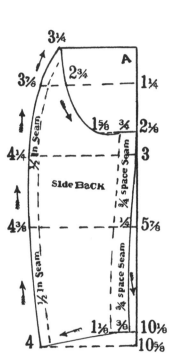

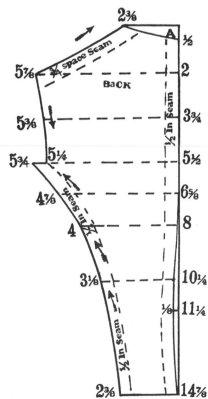

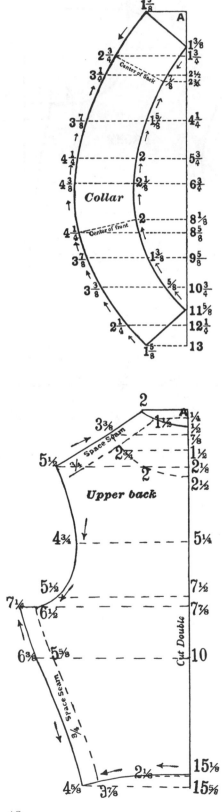

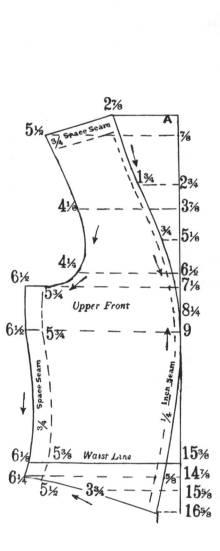

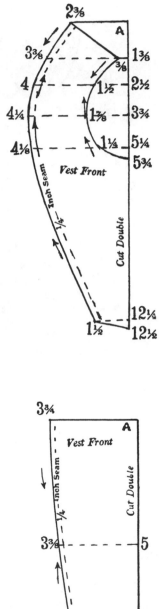

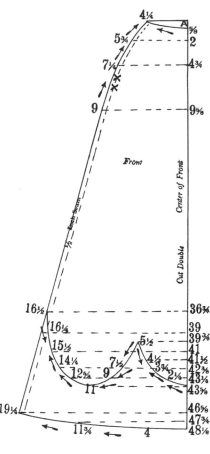

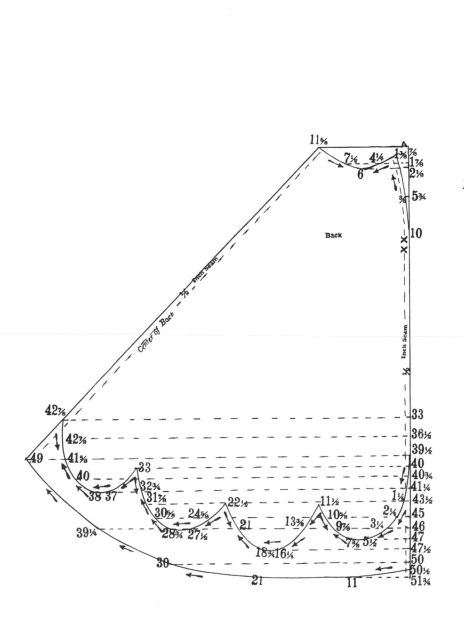

Ladies' Tailor-Made Suit

Use the scale corresponding to the bust measure to draft the waist, which consists of back, side back, side front, small front, large or lining front, vest front, revers, rolling collar, small collar, and sleeve. Use the scale corresponding to the waist measure to draft the skirt. Regulate all lengths by the tape measure.

Cut a facing for the side front, by the front edge and to come about 1 inch back beyond the line that is to join the small front. Place right side of facing to that of the side front. Sew from the upper edge and entirely around the scallops and to the bottom of the waist. Slash all the squares at inside corners of the scallops to 1/4 inch deep and on the bias to ensure a smooth edge all around when turned. Baste and press the edges, stitch, and lay it onto the small front. Place them onto the lining front, and finish as any other waist. Line and interline the collar and revers. Join them to the waist as illustrated, with the upper end of revers coming up over the collar. The foundation of the small collar is covered in front with folds, and an upper collar is set over this and cut out in front in a fancy shape. A strap that is lined and stitched is set in, in both the front and back of the armseye, the front one overlapping the one in back and held in place by a button.

Cut the left side of the front skirt gore 4 inches wider than the right to allow for the scallops. They are cut the same as those on the waist and finished in the same manner. Line and interline the skirt in the usual way.

This dress was developed in very light tan and cream cloth, with white satin vest and white pearl buttons. For a lady of medium size it will require 5 yards of 42-inch goods, or 7 1/2 yards of 36-inch material.

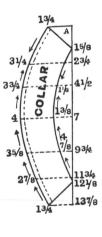

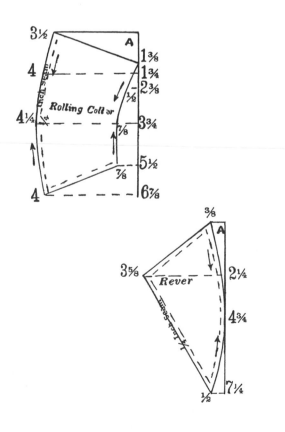

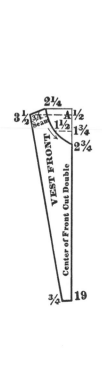

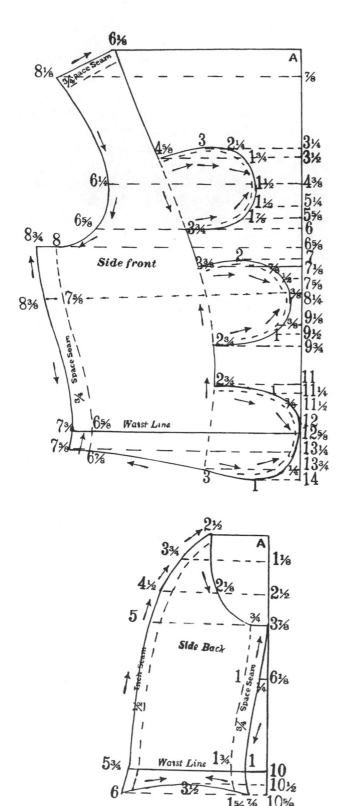

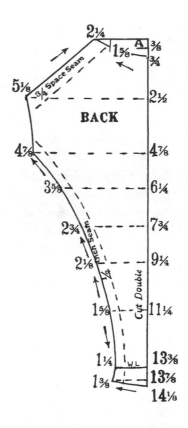

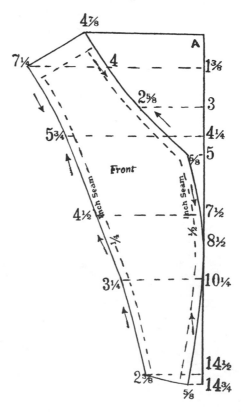

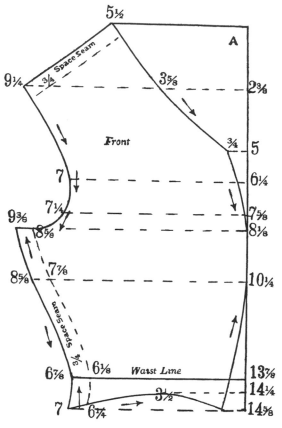

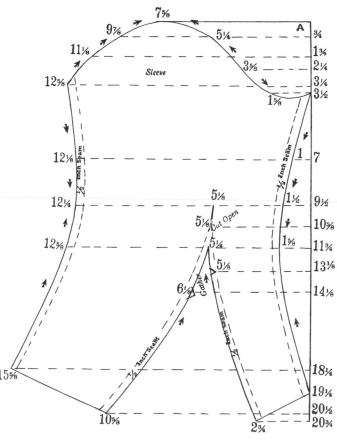

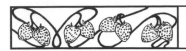

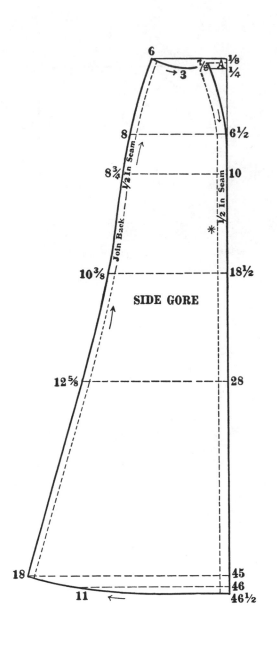

6   ⅛→A ⅛

3   ⅛   ¼

8   6½

8¾   10

½ In Seam

Join Back

½ In Seam

*

10⅜   18½

SIDE GORE

12⅝   28

18   45

46

11 ←   46½

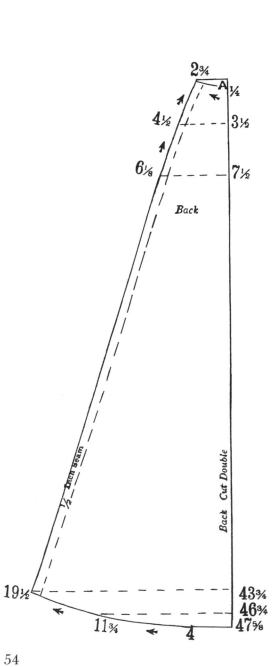

2¾

A ¼

4½   3½

6⅛   7½

Back

½ Inch Seam

Back Cut Double

19½   43¾

46¾

11¾   4   47⅝

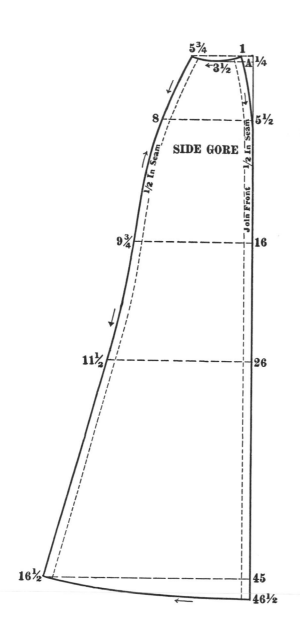

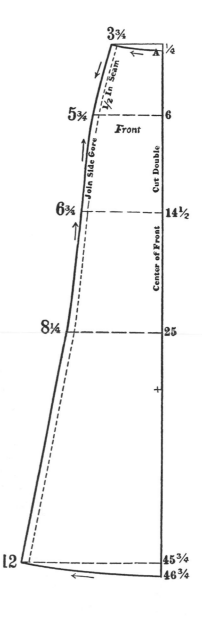

55

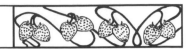

Ladies' Promenade or Calling Costume

Use the scale corresponding to the bust measure to draft the waist, which consists of lining back, side back, underarm, and front; back and front tucked shirtwaist parts; yoke; collar; and sleeves. Use the scale corresponding to the waist measure to draft the skirt. Regulate all lengths by the tape measure.

The lining may be omitted if desired. If used, it is joined with upper waist into the armseye and neck. Tuck waist as shown on the diagrams. Gather on the curved dotted line in the front. The goods is tucked for the upper sleeve portion, is basted to sleeves, and the undersleeve cut away beneath the tucks. The band is laid on the skirt and the skirt cut away beneath in the same manner.

This dress is pink cambric with a white polka dot, trimmed in white insertion and yoke of embroidery. For a medium-sized lady it will require 10 yards of 36-inch goods.

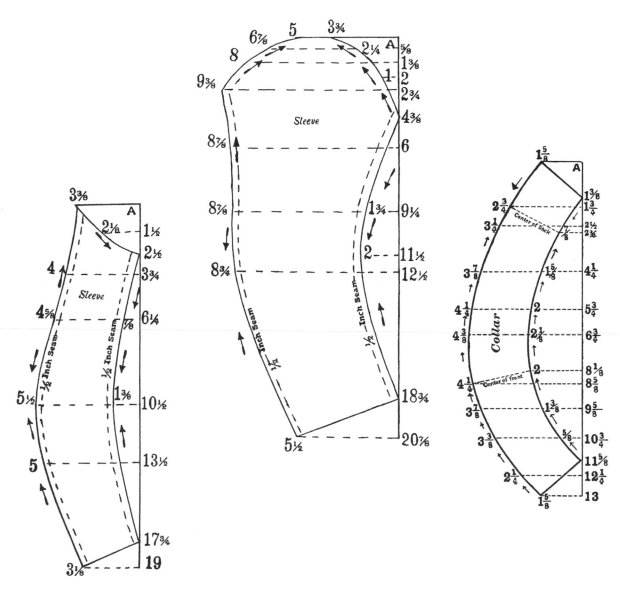

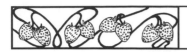
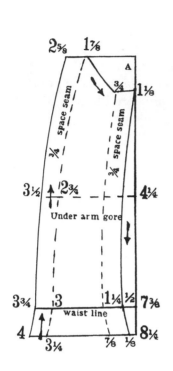

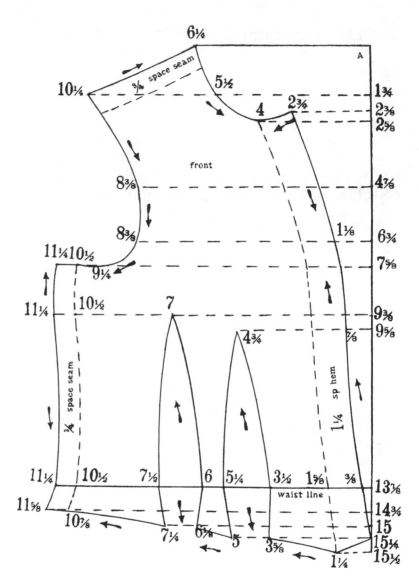

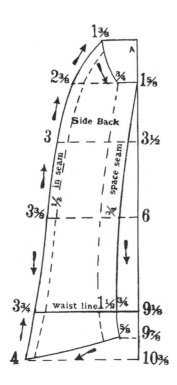

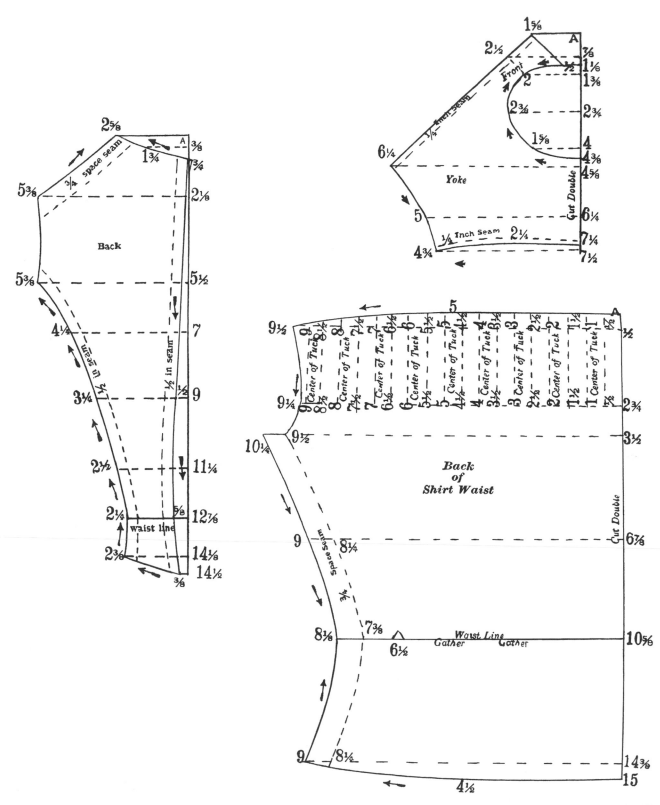

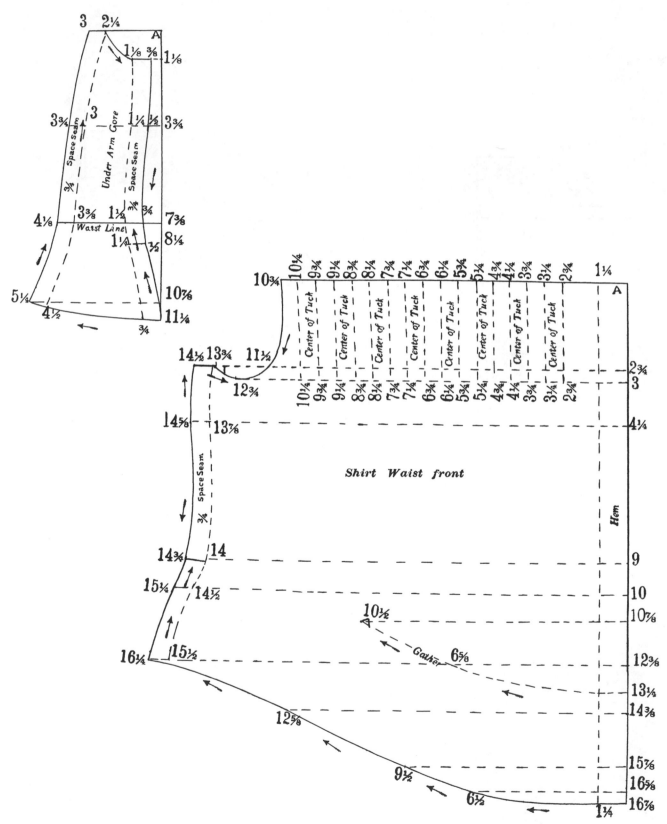

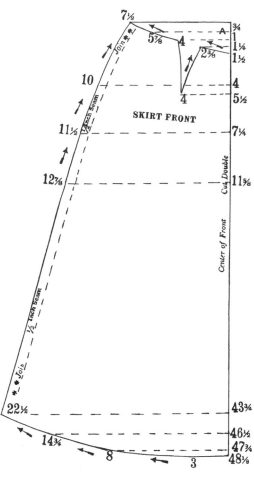

SKIRT FRONT

Center of Front

Cut Double

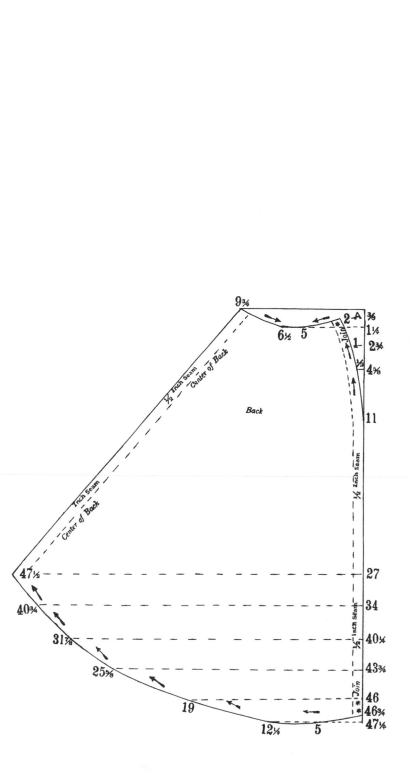

Back

Center of Back

½ Inch Seam

61

 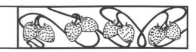

Ladies' Ball or Reception Toilet

Use the scale corresponding to the bust measure to draft the waist, which consists of back and front yoke, full back, full front, and three sleeve portions. Use the scale corresponding to the waist measure to draft the skirt and overskirt. Regulate all lengths by the tape measure.

Gather the full waist parts from the notches in the tops and sew them to the yokes. Gather them at the bottom from the notches to fit a band the size of waist and about 1 1/2 inches wide when finished. Or a tight waist lining may be used and the neck cut out the same as the low neck of the yoke,

or left high and finished with a stock collar and fancy guimpe effect. The lining in the sleeves may be omitted and a casing formed of the seam, through which a tape is run and the sleeve gathered up as short as desired.

This dress is of silk poplin, insertion, and lace. For a lady of medium size it will require 11 yards of 36-inch material, or 7 1/2 yards of 42-inch goods, with 2/3 yard for yoke.

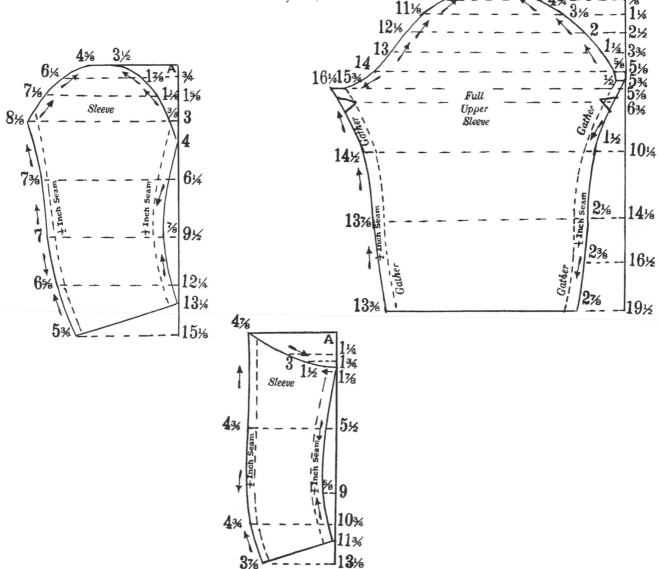

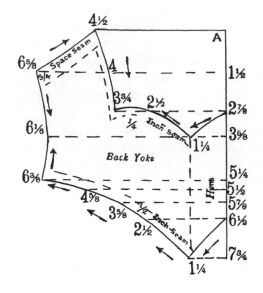

Back Yoke

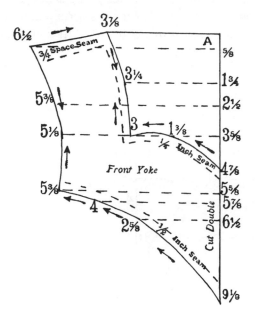

Front Yoke

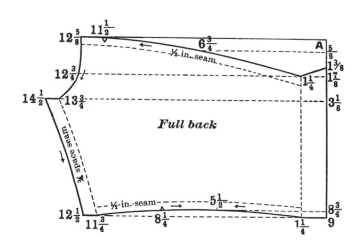

Full back

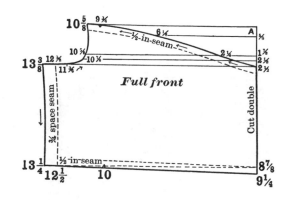

Full front

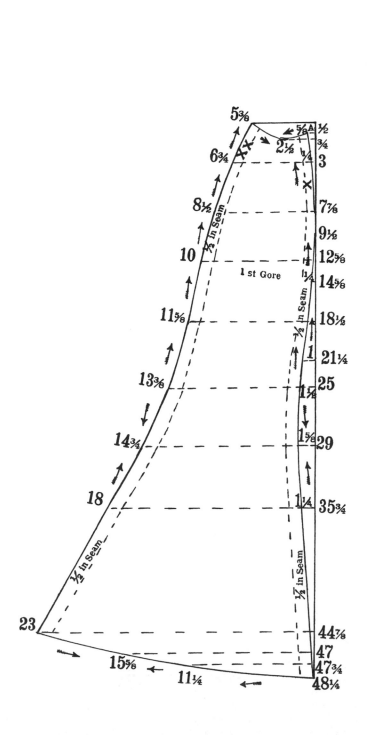

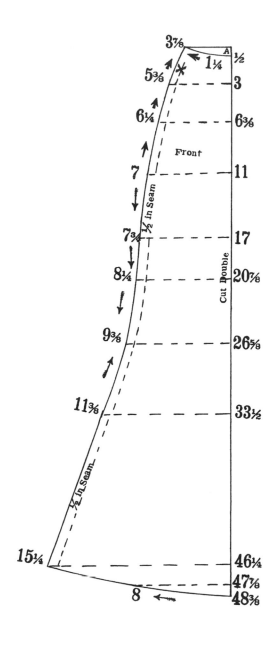

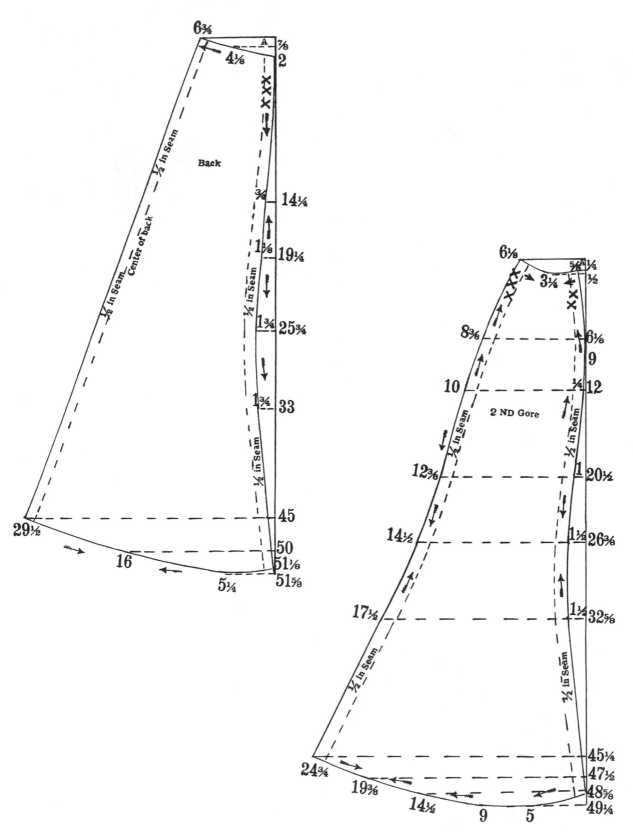

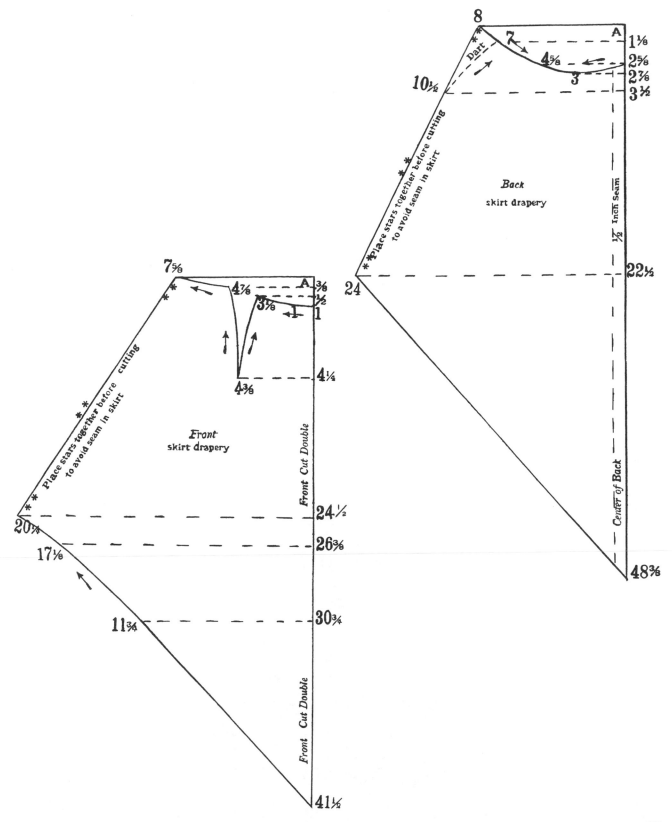

 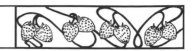
Ladies' Reception or Evening Costume

Use the scale corresponding to the bust measure to draft the waist, which consists of lining back, side back, underarm, and front; upper back; two upper fronts; collar; three jacket parts; and two sleeve portions. Use the scale corresponding to the waist measure to draft the skirt and overskirt, or skirt drapery. Regulate all lengths by the tape measure.

Join the back, side back, and underarm. Adjust the upper back and gather the extra fullness at the bottom. Adjust the upper fronts and gather at bottom to fit waist. Gather two extra rows at the sides, over which ribbon velvet is tacked. The small jacket may be made entirely separate if desired. Small pieces of velvet that are lined with silk and curved at their outer edge are set in at the neck and armseye. Finish the neck of the dress with a nar-

row band. Make the collar in the usual way, and tack over this band to fasten in the back. A rosette of ribbon is placed at the left side of jacket over the fastening, from where to the bottom of jacket is carried a cascade of lace.

Cut skirt drapery for the different sides as instructed on the diagram. There is only one piece of the two U pleats used for the back of the underskirt and it is gathered onto the band.

This dress is made of very pale green satin, with a pink polka dot, embroidered in marshal neil roses and buds. Black ribbon velvet trims the waist sleeves and collar, and is used to hold the drapery together at the sides. Jacket of ecru lace. Black velvet revers on jacket at the neck and armseye.

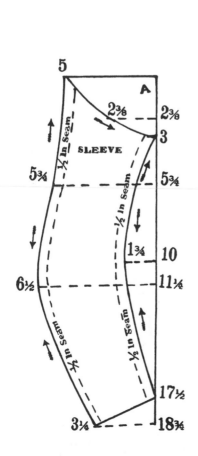

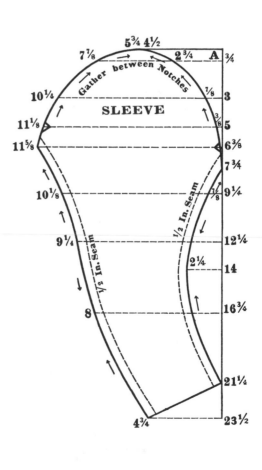

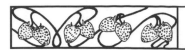 
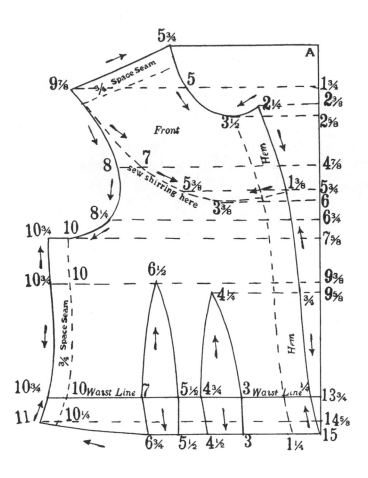

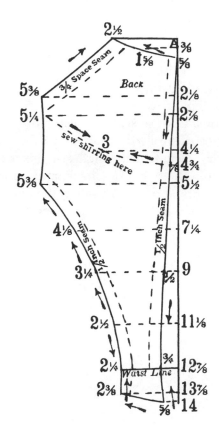

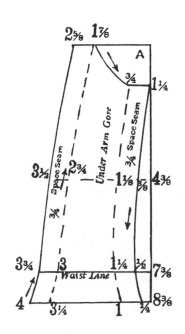

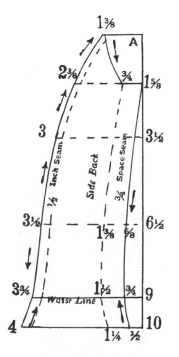

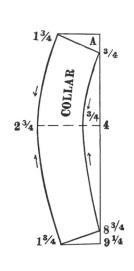

COLLAR

1¾   A   ¾

2¾   4   ¾

1¾   8¾   9¼

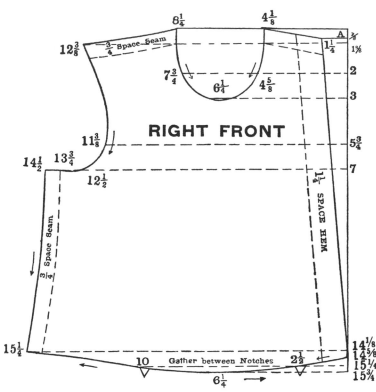

RIGHT FRONT

8¼   4⅛   A   ⅜

12⅜   ¾ Space Seam   1¼   1⅜

7¾   6¼   4⅝   2   3

5¾

11⅜   7

14½   13¾   12½   1¼ SPACE HEM

¾ Space Seam

15½   10   Gather between Notches   2½   14⅛   14⅝   15¼   15¾

6¼

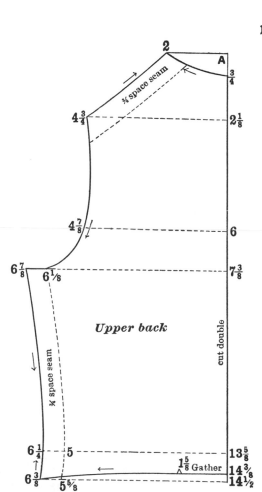

2   A   ¾

¾ space seam

4¾   2⅛

4⅞   6

6⅞   6⅛   7⅜

Upper back

cut double

¾ space seam

6¼   5   13⅝

6⅜   5⅝   1⅝ Gather   14⅜   14½

2¼   A

5¾   ¾ space seam   1

4⅝   3

4⅛   ⅝   5

4⅛   6¼

6⅞   6⅛   7

Left upper front

6½   5¾   9½

¾ space seam

5¾   5   14   14⅝   14¾

1¼   ⅜

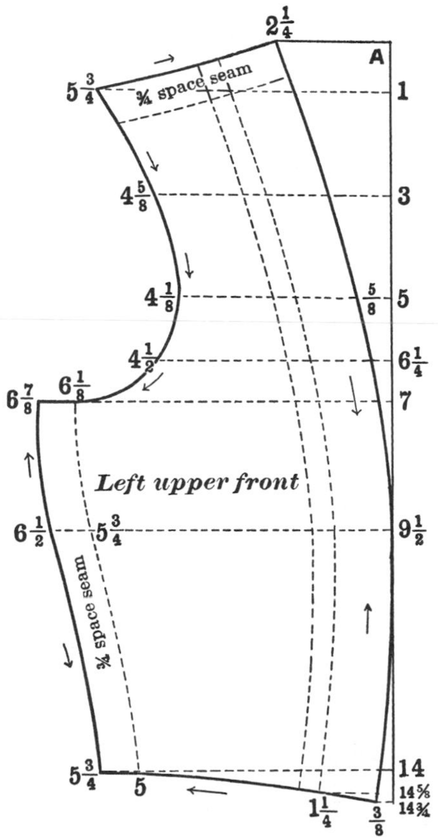

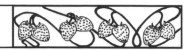

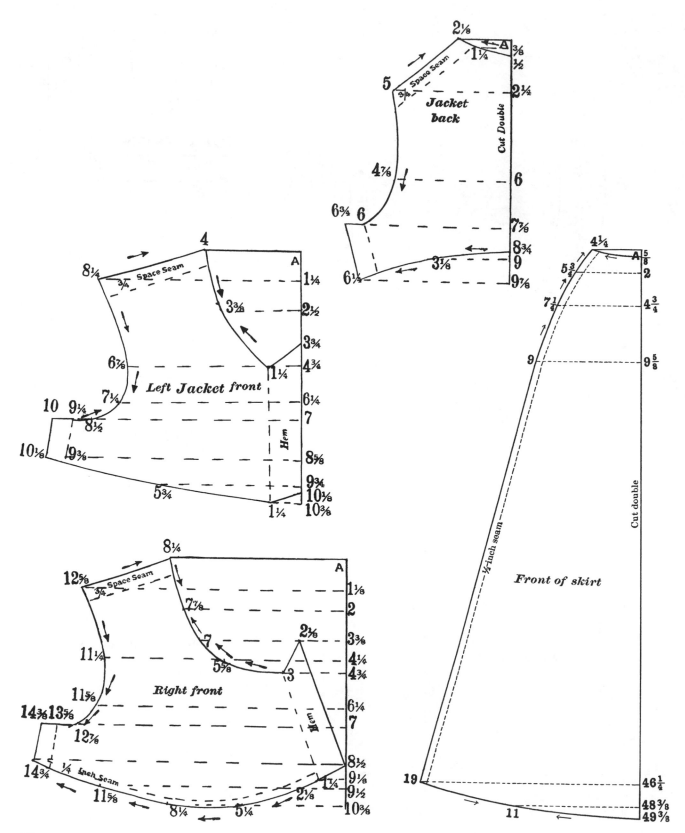

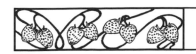

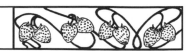

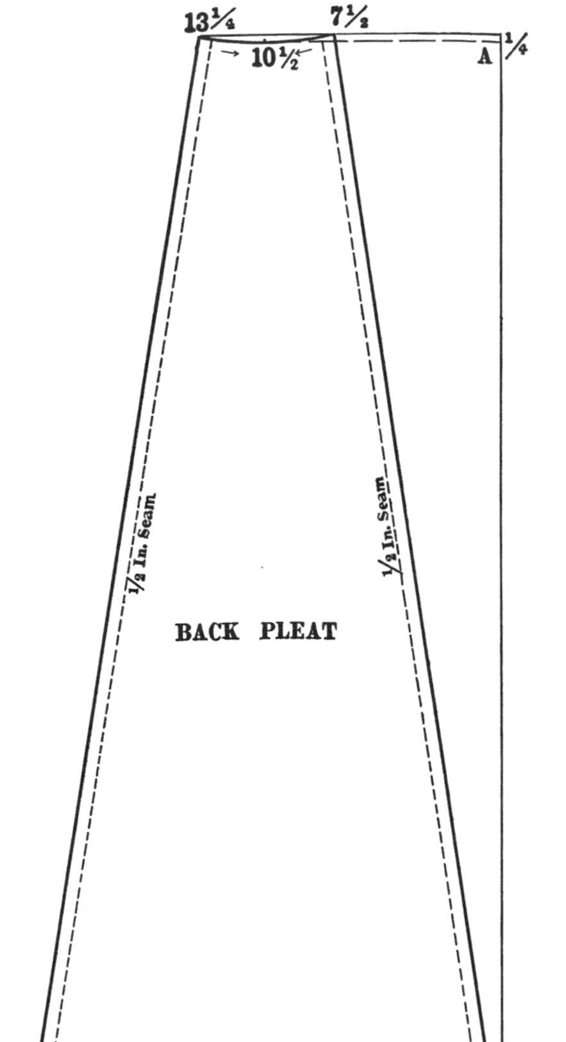
13¼
7½
10½
A
¼
½ In. Seam
½ In. Seam
BACK PLEAT
21
48½
49¼
12¾
8½

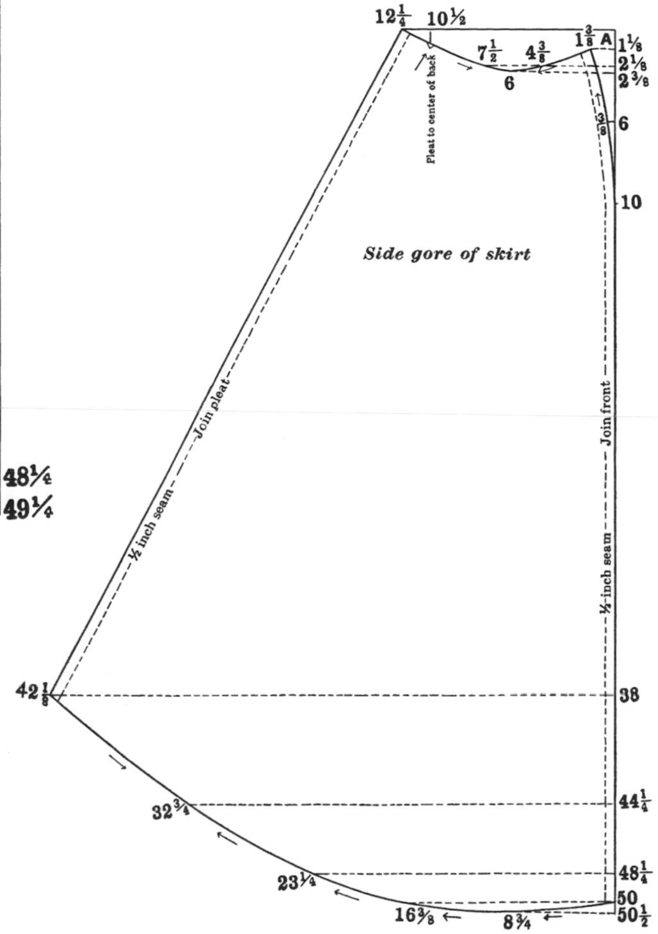
12¼
10½
7½
4⅜
1⅜
A
1⅛
2⅛
2⅜
6
Pleat to center of back
⅜
6
10
Side gore of skirt
Join pleat
½ inch seam
Join front
½ inch seam
42⅛
38
32¾
44¼
23¼
48¼
50
16⅜
8¾
50½

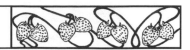
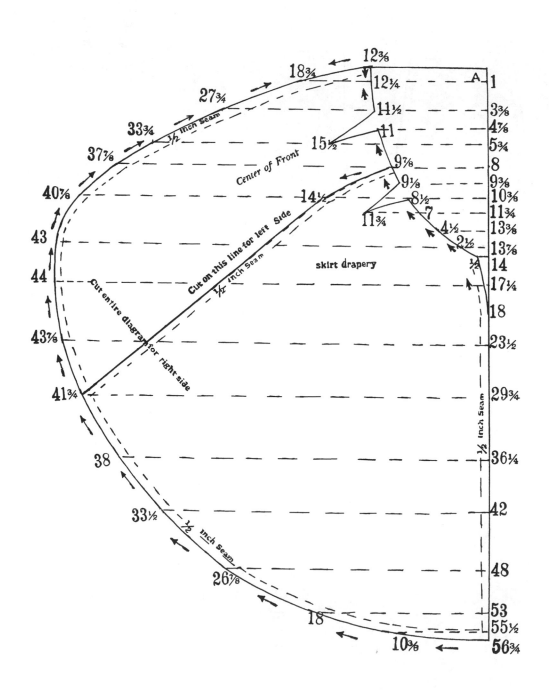

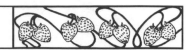
Ladies' Carriage or Calling Costume

Use the scale corresponding to the bust measure to draft the waist, which consists of lining back, side back, underarm, and front; upper back; gathered front; shoulder drapery; seamless yoke; collar; and two sleeve portions. Use the scale corresponding to the waist measure to draft the skirt. After drafting flounce, ascertain by tape measure if it is the proper width and add to or take from accordingly. Regulate all lengths by the tape measure.

Join the back, side back, and underarm, and adjust the upper back. Gather the extra fullness at the bottom. The upper back is cut away from beneath the yoke, when the yoke is made fast to dress, as is also sometimes the lining, letting neck and shoulders show through the lace. Sew the seam in the gathered portions and gather as instructed on the diagram. Join the upper edges to the lower edge of the yoke in front. Face the left lining at the left underarm and armseye on its upper side. Close the lining fronts with hooks and eyes. Finish the gathered portion to position at the left underarm and armseye, with hooks and loops. Hem the shoulder drapery and sew around the lower edge of the yoke, from the left shoulder seam across the back and to the center of front. From the left shoulder seam to the center of front it is faced at the top, and fastened in front after the yoke and full front have been fastened at the left side. Make the sleeve in the usual way and take care in its adjustment, to get the seams set properly.

This dress is of tan silk with a dark brown and black figure, and has a border of lace set at the foot and trimming the waist.

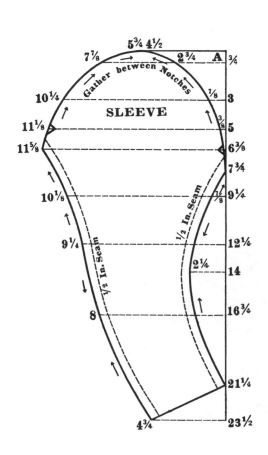

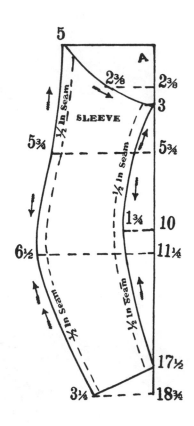

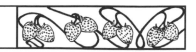

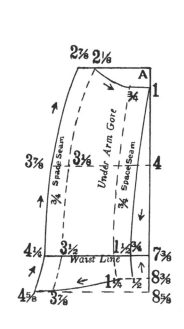

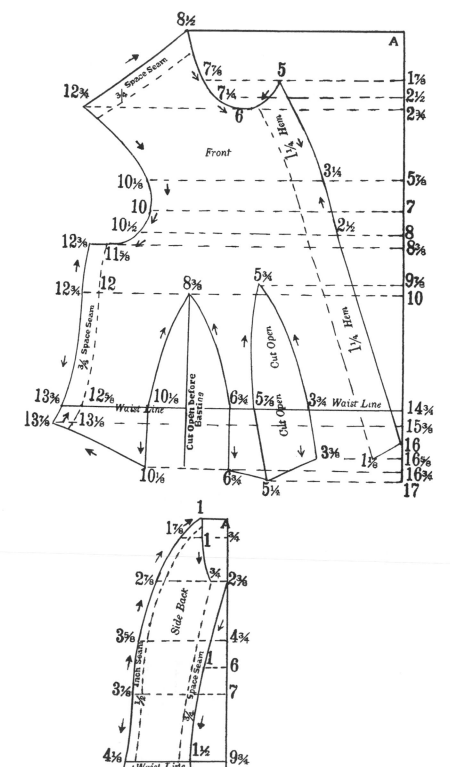

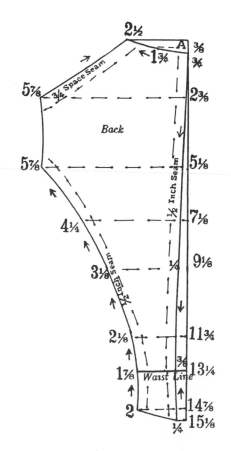

Under Arm Gore

Front

Back

Side Back

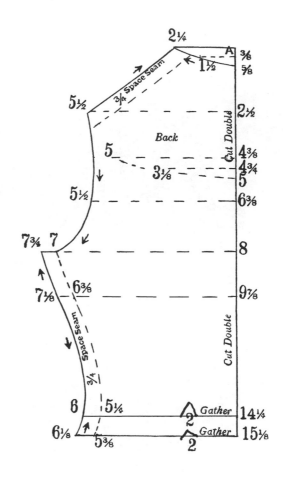

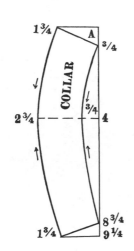

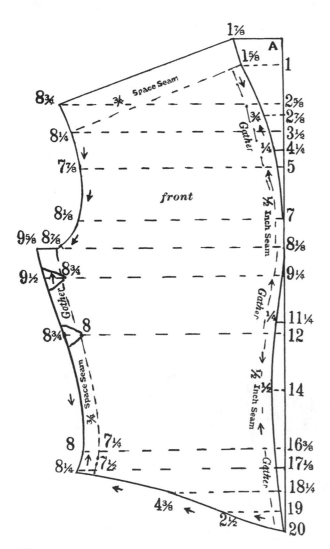

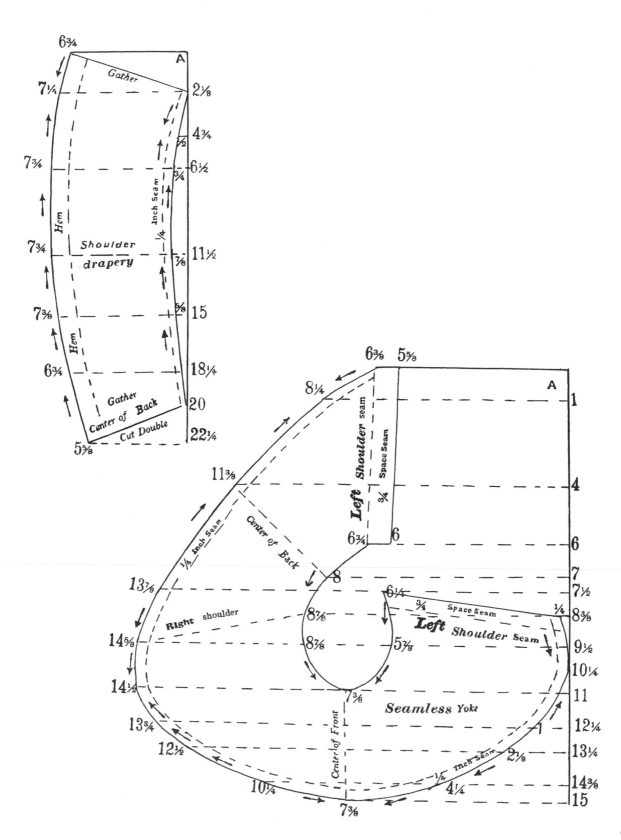

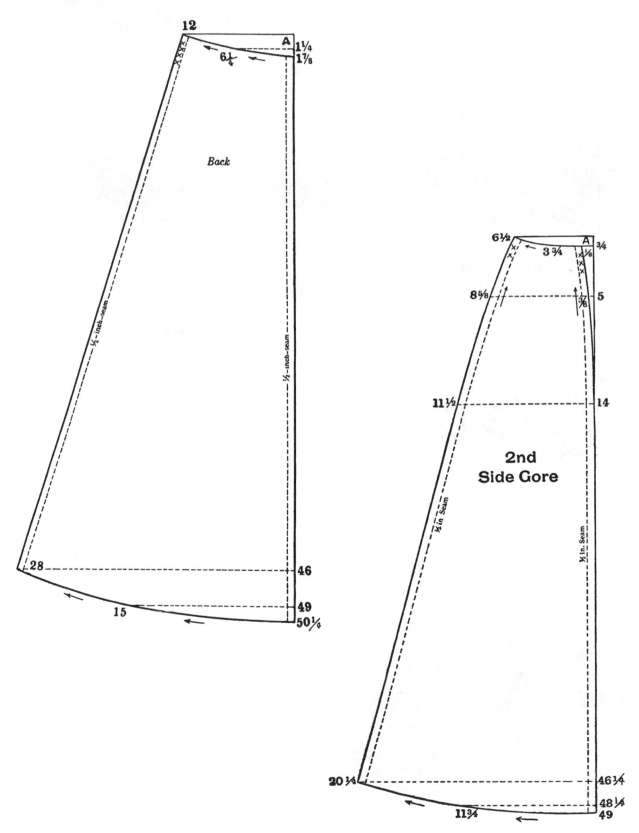

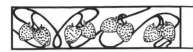

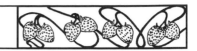

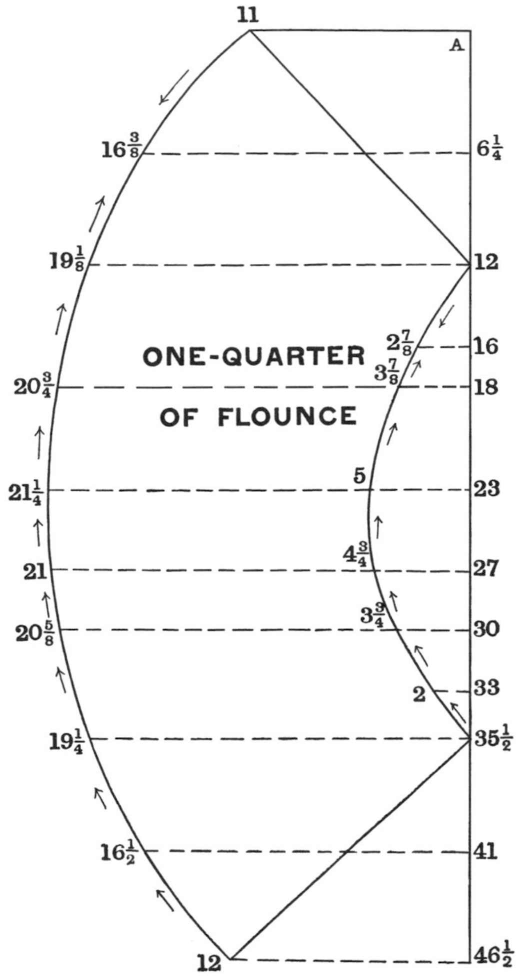
ONE-QUARTER
OF FLOUNCE
11
A
16 3/8
6 1/4
19 1/8
12
2 7/8
16
3 7/8
18
20 3/4
5
21 1/4
23
4 3/4
21
27
3 3/4
20 5/8
30
2
33
19 1/4
35 1/2
16 1/2
41
12
46 1/2

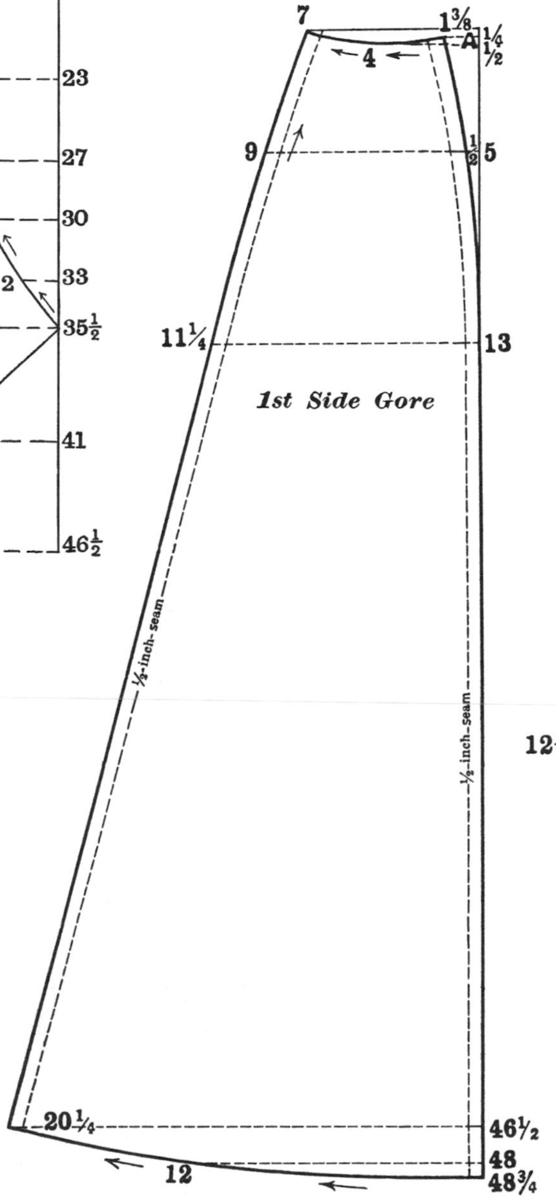
1st Side Gore
7
1 3/8
1/4
A
1/2
4
9
1/2
5
11 1/4
13
1/2-inch-seam
1/2-inch-seam
20 1/4
46 1/2
12
48
48 3/4

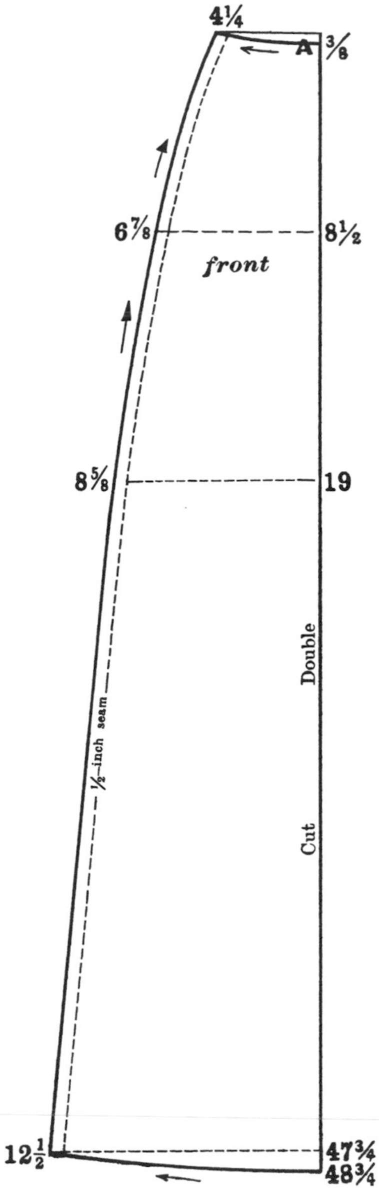
front
4 1/4
A
3/8
6 7/8
8 1/2
8 5/8
19
1/2-inch seam
Cut Double
12 1/2
47 3/4
48 3/4

 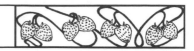

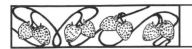 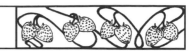
Ladies' Tailor-Made Suit

Use the scale corresponding to the bust measure to draft the entire jacket, which consists of back, side back, underarm, front, collar, and two sleeve portions. Use the scale corresponding to the waist measure to draft the skirt. Regulate all lengths by the tape measure.

Join the different parts of jacket in the usual way. Join the seams of the upper and lining portions separately. Face the front back with the upper material, almost to the dart. Interline the collar and revers with canvas. Join the under portion of collar with the canvas to the neck of jacket. Bring the upper part over and secure with an overcast stitch. The darts are covered with braid, which is carried on a curve into the armseye to represent the side front seams. The jacket fronts are cut off more square than the diagram; that, however, is a matter of taste. Make and adjust the sleeves in the usual way, being sure to set them properly to prevent their twisting. Make, line, and interline skirt in the usual way.

The dress is gray cloth, trimmed with black braid. For a lady of medium size it will require 5 1/2 yards of 42-inch material, or 4 1/2 yards of 54-inch goods.

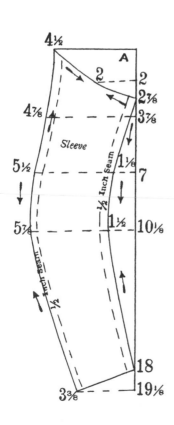

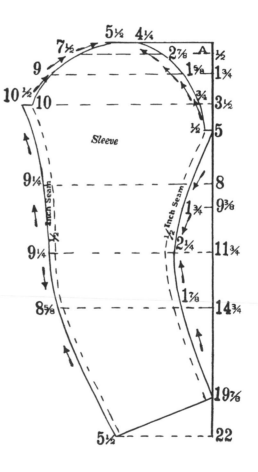

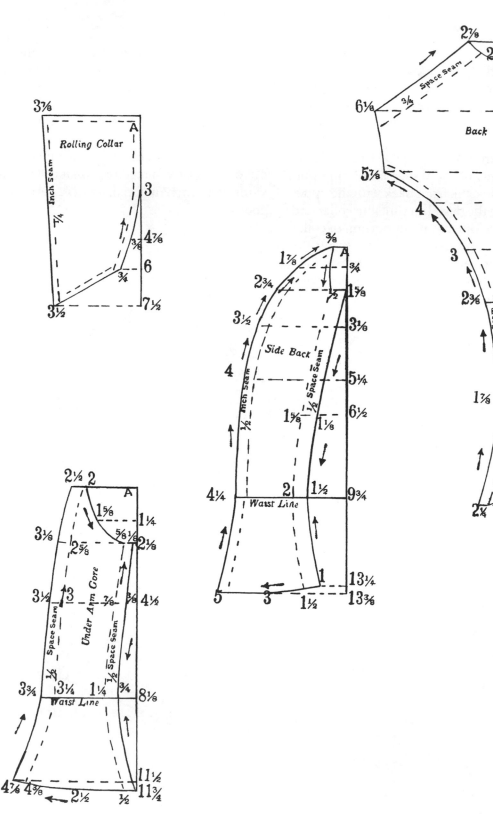

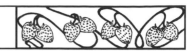
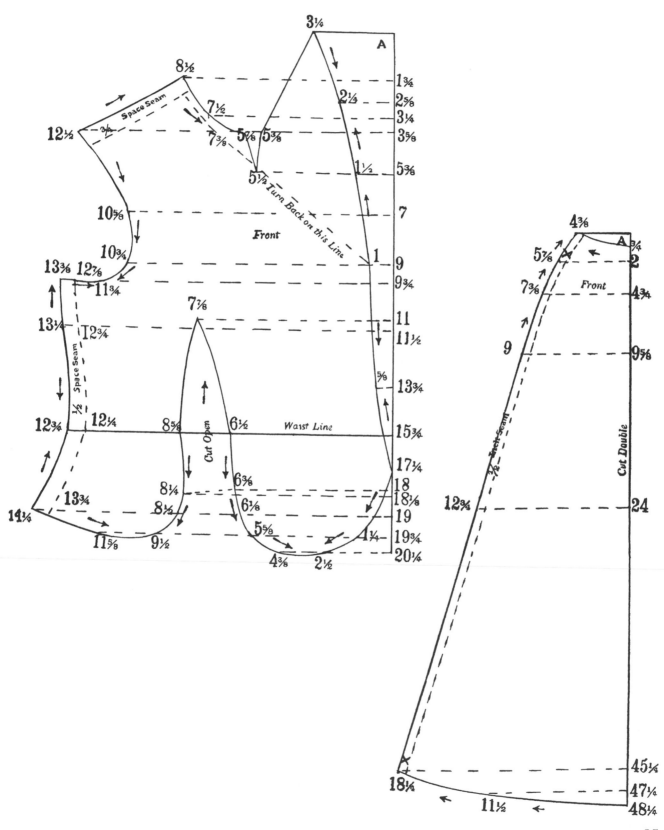

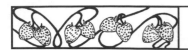

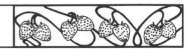

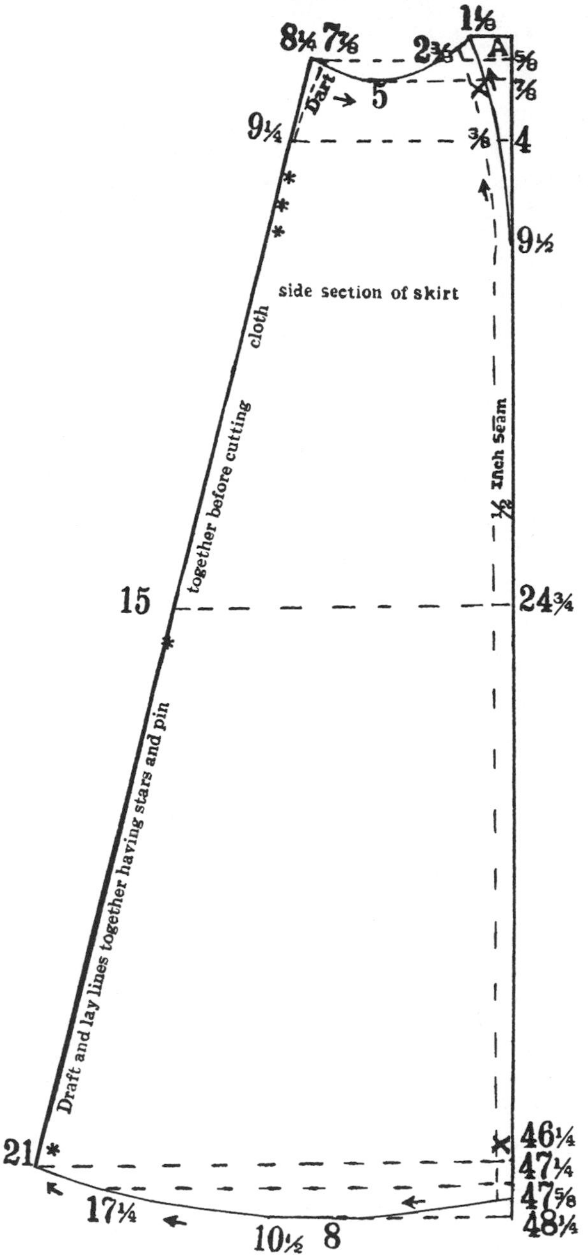
8¼
7⅞
2⅜
1⅛
A
⅝
⅞
Dart
5
9¼
⅜
4
9½
side section of skirt
Draft and lay lines together having stars and pin together before cutting cloth
½ Inch Seam
15
24¾
21
46¼
47¼
47⅝
48¼
17¼
10½
8

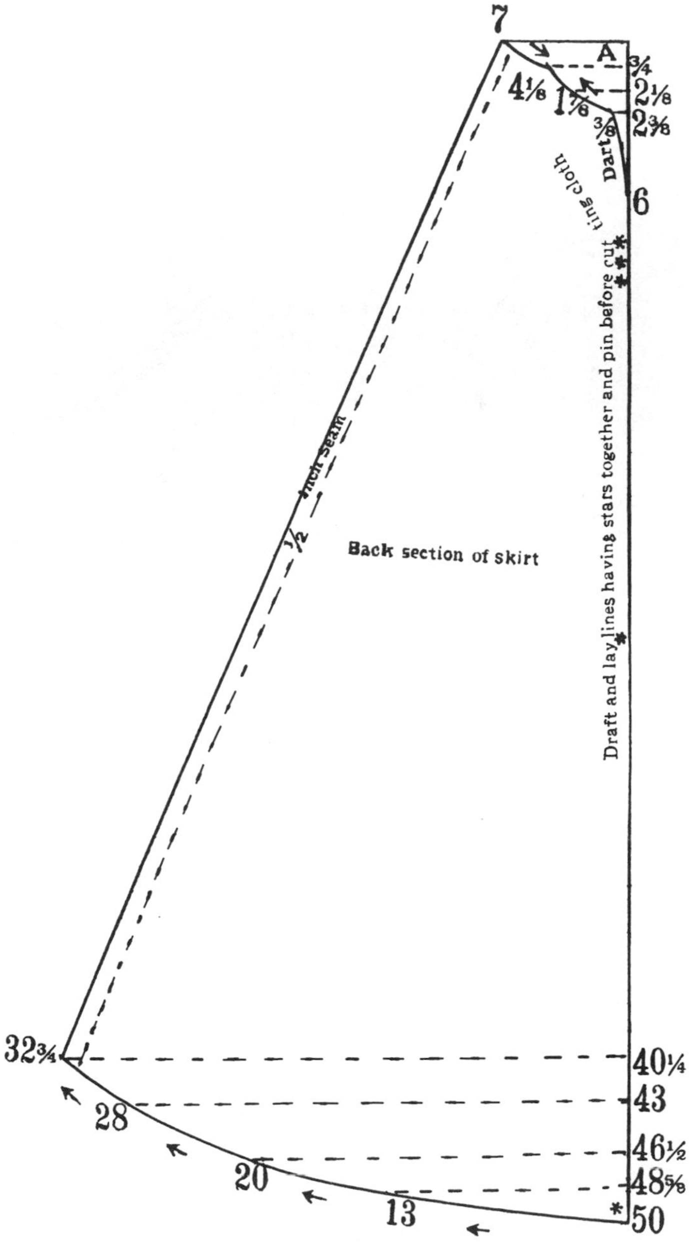
7
A
¾
4⅛
1⅞
2⅛
2⅜
⅜
Dart
6
Draft and lay lines having stars together and pin before cutting cloth
½ Inch Seam
Back section of skirt
32¾
40¼
28
43
20
46½
48⅝
13
50

August 1900

Some skirts are made with long yokes, with the lower part gathered, pleated, or tucked to fit the yoke. Only very thin materials are gathered, as heavier materials have a clumsy effect if gathered about the hips. Many beautiful skirts are seen in brocades, opening over plain petticoats, either in taffeta, or in many instances for summer wear of white materials.

In some blouse waists sleeves are considerably fuller. Some have the full bishop sleeve gathered in a band to fit the wrist; some have a puff set on above the elbow or at the top. Some shirtwaists have fronts forming revers over an attached chemisette; the back may be plain or laid in tucks or pleats. Waists have more of the blouse effect, though not quite so pronounced as for some time past; some have it both in front and in back.

Some dressing sacques have loose fronts and fitted sides and back. One very pretty one was cut off about 3 inches below the waist across the back, and the length completed by a ruffle gathered on with a heading about 1 inch wide.

Quite a note of distinction is obtained by applying a touch of black, in ribbon, velvet, chiffon, tulle, etc., to an otherwise plain gown.

Boleros are seen in many fancy shapes. Some are high at the neck, others are cut in a V or round neck, while others are cut in scallops and fancy shapes. Some useful ones that may be worn open or closed have a coat collar and pointed revers, and usually dip slightly in front. Very pretty boleros are made of pleated taffetas, and may be worn with most any style of garment.

Some of the prettiest jackets have no collars or revers whatever. This feature also distinguishes many gowns, and the pretty and cool low round, square, or V-shaped necks surely will be much approved.

One very pretty style of tie is tucked lengthwise through the center far enough to form the stock, and the ends left untucked, either tied in the front or fastened with fancy pins. There is a fad for wearing narrow black ribbon velvet over white collars. One or more bands are worn, sometimes tied in a small bow in the front or secured with a fancy pin. Black velvet girdles with long ends are very pretty and stylish. Broad girdles of silk or satin are worn with summer frocks; they are boned in the back and at the sides, but a stiff effect is avoided. They are secured beneath a fancy bow, rosette, or buckle, or may have pulley ties.

In dress materials there is none more popular than the foulards, both silk and satin. The cotton ones are made into exceedingly pretty costumes, but the satin ones will be preferred to the Japanese foulards. They are a trifle heavier, and more suitable for evening and promenade costumes as the evenings grow chillier. Linen bands are seen on foulards having white grounds with a colored design. Piqués and linens are too useful to be discarded. Some are elaborately trimmed in stitched bands of a contrasting color in scroll or other fancy designs. Even gold braids are used to some extent on piqué and linen suits.

A style that will be very popular will be the long coats made entirely of heavy lace. They are very rich in effect and are (of course) intended to be worn only for dress occasions. Separate skirts of glacé mohair are very serviceable. Also short skirts made of double-faced cloths of light weight, worn with a shirtwaist of some substantial material such as piqué, linen, madras, or lightweight flannel. This makes a very suitable costume for long walks, outdoor sports, etc., and one can venture out without the necessity of a jacket. Old-fashioned mohairs and alpacas in browns and grays are again revived, and are especially recommended for serviceable wear.

Challises and organdies have an established popularity. Beautiful dresses for yachting and other outing purposes are made of khaki, trimmed in red silk and brass buttons. A tie of red silk worn with such a dress adds to its beauty.

In millinery the association of black and yellow, and black and white, is a noticeable feature. Fancy yellow and butter-colored straws are often trimmed in black roses and velvet. Some have high narrow crowns and straight rims, and a wide band of velvet to cover the crown. Very coarse straws are bent in all sorts of shapes. Poke shapes are still fashionable, and especially becoming to youthful faces. Short-backed sailors are still a favorite. The extravagant use of all manner of fruit, flowers and foliage has by no means diminished.

In outing hats the styles are many. Some have their brims faced in straw. The prettiest are draped around their crowns in various ways, and with different materials. A pretty novelty is the full gathered veil. Narrow black velvet ribbon is usually employed to draw up the veil at the top and about the neck. When the veil is once adjusted it is a great protection to the hat as well as the fluffy arrangement of the hair, both against dampness and wind.

Some of the more substantial parasols for coaching, etc. are of satin, either in black or colored with contrasting bands of satin stitched on with many rows of stitching. Others are decorated in ruchings of satin, ribbon, chiffon, or net. Some beautiful ones are made in corded and tucked silks. As a rule the handles and handle decorations are very large and quite elaborate. Many are hand painted or stained to represent fruits, foliage, etc. Some very popular handles represent golf sticks.

In parasols as well as millinery and everything pertaining to a woman's toilet, pastel colors are losing popularity.

Ladies' Tailor-Made Costume

Use the scale corresponding to the bust measure to draft the entire jacket, which consists of back, side back, underarm, front, vest, collar, and two sleeve portions. Use the scale corresponding to the waist measure to draft the skirt. Regulate all lengths by the tape measure.

Join all the jacket parts in the usual way. If lined join the linings and upper sections separately. Turn the jacket up at the lower edge and toward the upper side. Cover the edge with a bias band stitched on; the one that covers the front edge continues up over the dart seam. Bands are stitched around the armseye to simulate a bolero. Bands also decorate the sleeves and form the fastenings in front. Line the vest to make it firm. Finish it at the top with a band the size of neck and to fasten in the back. Buttonholes may be worked in this band the same as for a shirtwaist, and a linen collar worn

instead of the fancy stock. Place the back seam in sleeve at the second seam below the shoulder seam. Place the front seam about 1 1/4 inches in front of the underarm seam for a lady of 35 bust; vary this distance according to the scale used.

Make the skirt in the usual way. In this instance it has no lining or canvas facings; it is simply hemmed and trimmed with bias bands of the contrasting color of linen.

This dress is of tan linen trimmed with blue, with vest and collar of white. The collar has several rows of narrow ribbon velvet laid on at regular intervals and a rosette of white taffeta at the side. White pearl buttons complete the decorations. For a lady of medium size it will take 8 yards of the tan linen, and 3 of the blue.

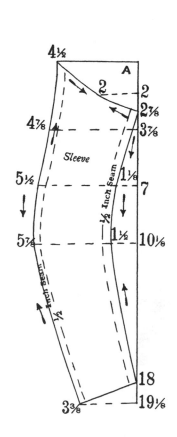

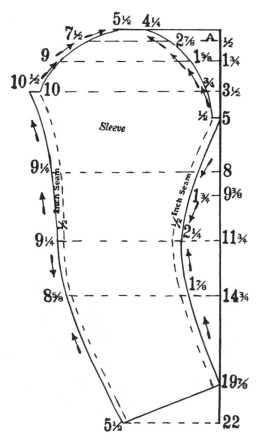

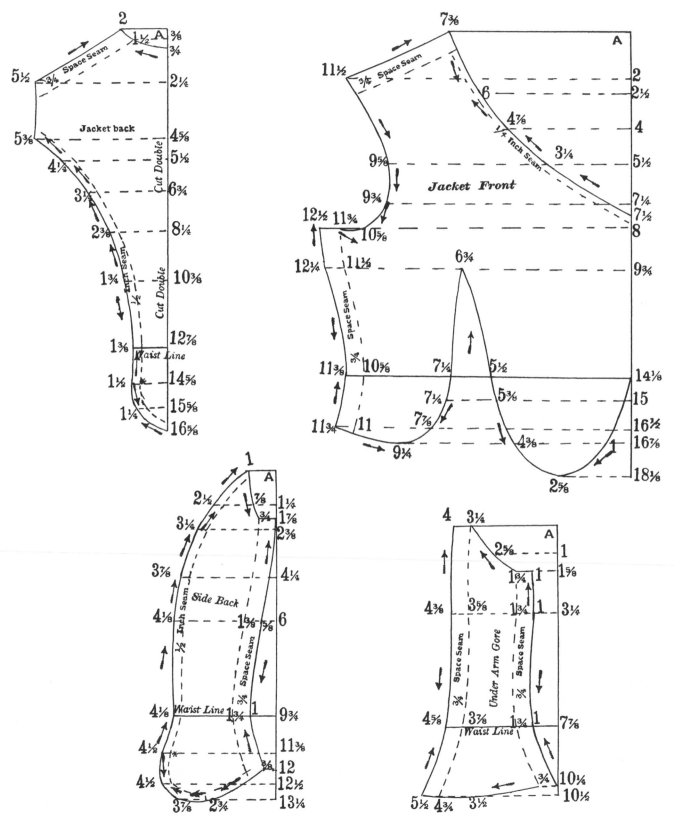

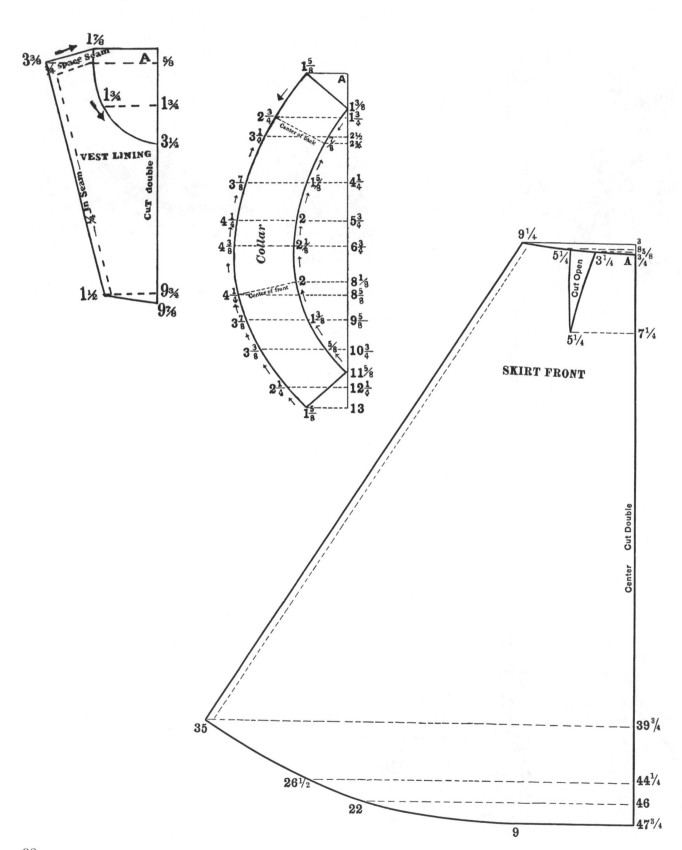

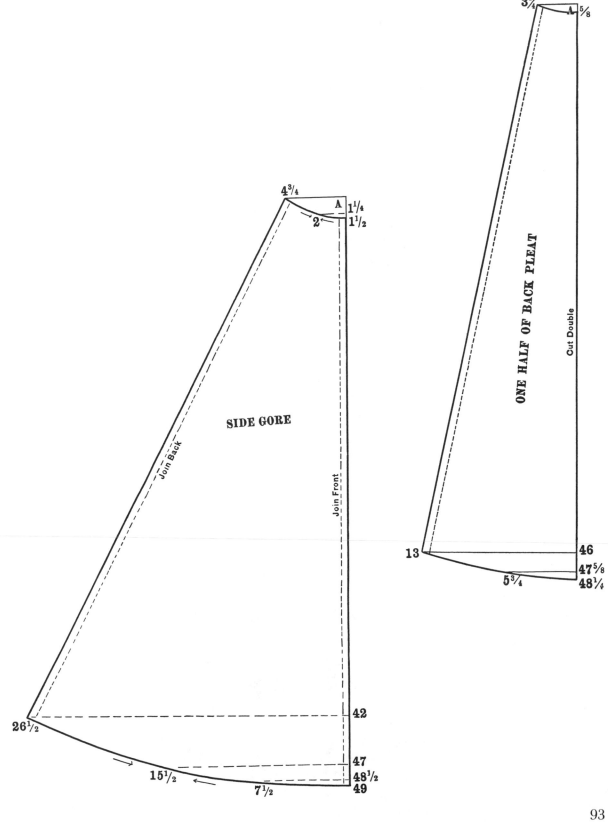

Ladies' Evening Dress

Use the scale corresponding to the bust measure to draft the waist, which consists of back, side back, underarm, front, full front, full back, zouave jacket front and back, and two sleeve parts. Use the scale corresponding to the waist measure to draft the skirt. Regulate all lengths by the tape measure.

Join the back and side portions and adjust the full back, gathering the extra fullness at the top and bottom. Cut both an upper and a lining section from the underarm gore. Take up the darts in the front, adjust the full front, and gather the extra fullness at the top and bottom. To make the sleeves as illustrated, cut a plain sleeve from the dress material, baste on the bands of insertion as far apart as desired, and cut away the material underneath, leaving 1/4 inch for a seam at either edge of the em-broidery. Turn it either way and stitch the insertion fast. Make the jacket parts in the same manner. Join them to the waist before finishing, and finish all together at the neck.

Make the skirt in the usual way. It is finished at the top with a narrow band, and the waist worn underneath this band.

This dress is of pale blue foulard silk, with a red polka dot. It is trimmed in ecru insertion and narrow silk braid. For a lady of medium size it will require 14 yards of silk 24 inches wide, or 10 yards of 36-inch material.

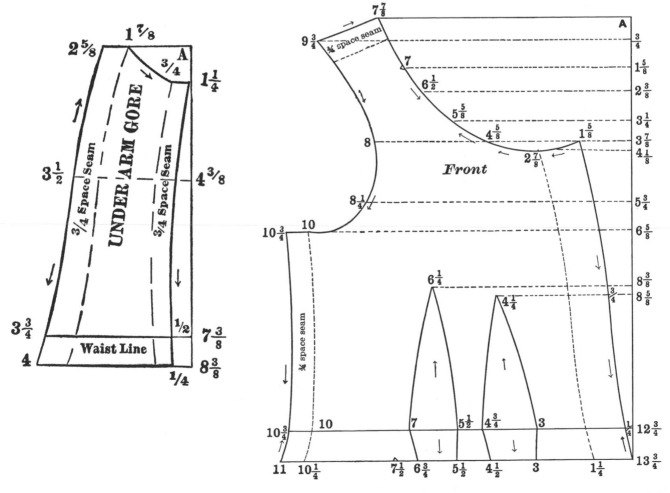

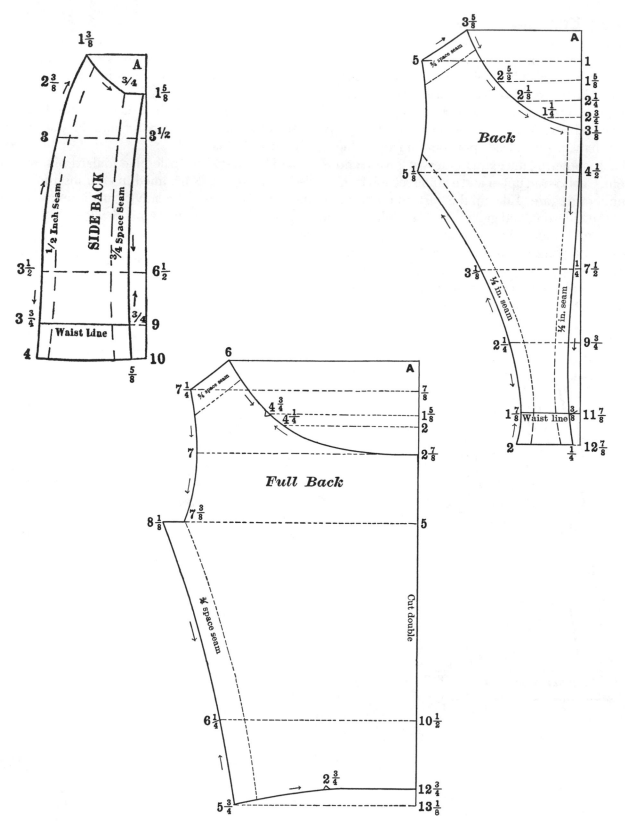

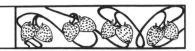
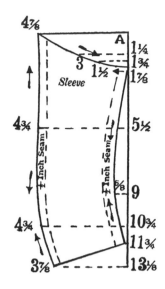

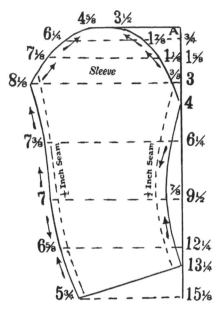

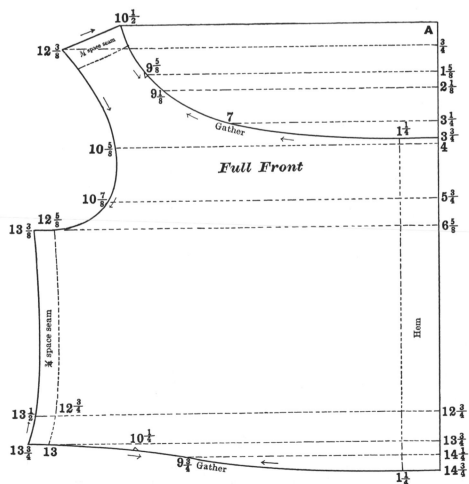

Full Front

97

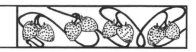

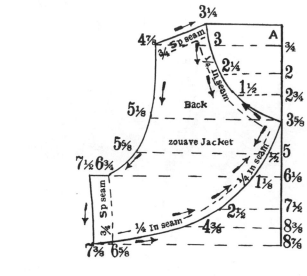

Back

zouave Jacket

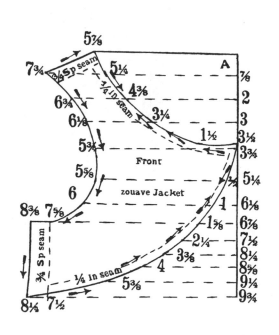

Front

zouave Jacket

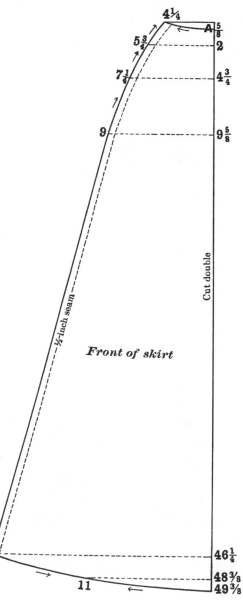

Front of skirt

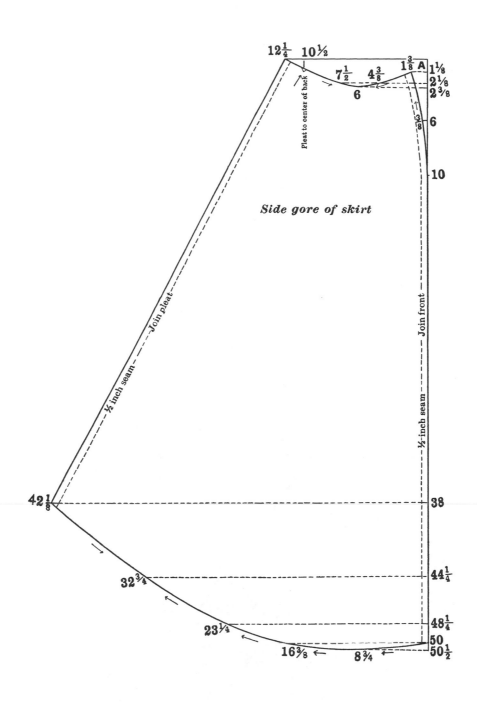

Side gore of skirt

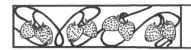 

Ladies' Calling Costume

Use the scale corresponding to the bust measure to draft the waist. For the lining this consists of back, side back, underarm, and front. For the tucked waist it consists of back, underarm gore, right tucked front, left tucked front, yoke, vest, collar, and sleeve. The lining may be omitted if desired. Use the scale corresponding to the waist measure to draft the skirt. Regulate all lengths by the tape measure.

Gather the upper back along the upper edge from figure 3 to the center of the back. Sew to the yoke around the back lower edge that is formed by the baseline from 4 1/2 to 2 and from 2 to 2 3/8 at the top line. The curve at the top is the armseye part of the yoke. The front notch is formed from 5 3/8 at the top to 7 3/4 and to 6 1/2. Gather the extra fullness at the bottom of the upper back, and stitch to narrow band to hold in position. Tuck the fronts between the sloping lines. Cut off on the upper sloping line and sew to the yoke. Leave the last slope of the right tucked portion free to finish with a narrow band. Finish the front slope at the left side with a facing. Finish the front edge of the left side tucked portion with a facing. Hem the left edge of the right tucked portion, lap it over the left

side, and bring the left yoke to the front over the tucked portion. The fastening will be concealed. After hemming the right front, stitch the edge of hem to represent a tuck. To make this collar to fasten in back, cut double on the line marked center of front and cut off on the line marked center of back. Make foundation for collar of two or three layers of canvas and stitch them securely together. Tack it over the vest front and cover with folds to represent tucks, stitching each one fast. Set back seam of sleeve at back seam of underarm gore, and front seam about 1 1/4 inches in front of underarm seam.

Tuck the parts belonging to the skirt, and cut off on the sloping lines at top. If tucked as represented, the tucked portion cut double will fit the points. The points may be carried to the back, if so desired, by laying the front and back together, cutting the points in the back by those in the front, and omitting the circular flounce. After sewing up the seams in the tucked portion, stitch along each seam to represent a tuck, which conceals the seam.

This dress is of white figured muslin.

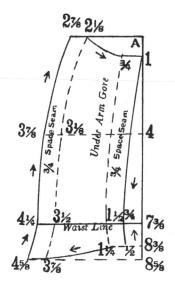

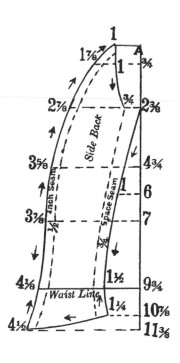

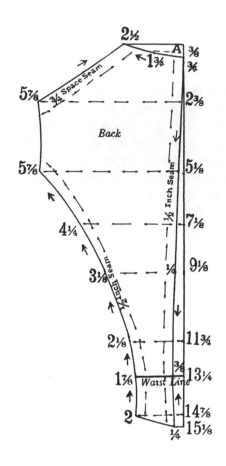

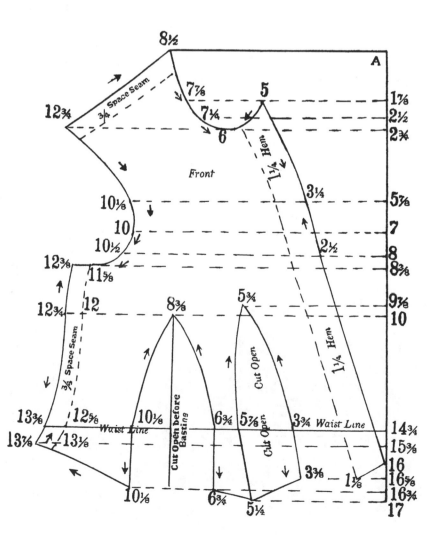

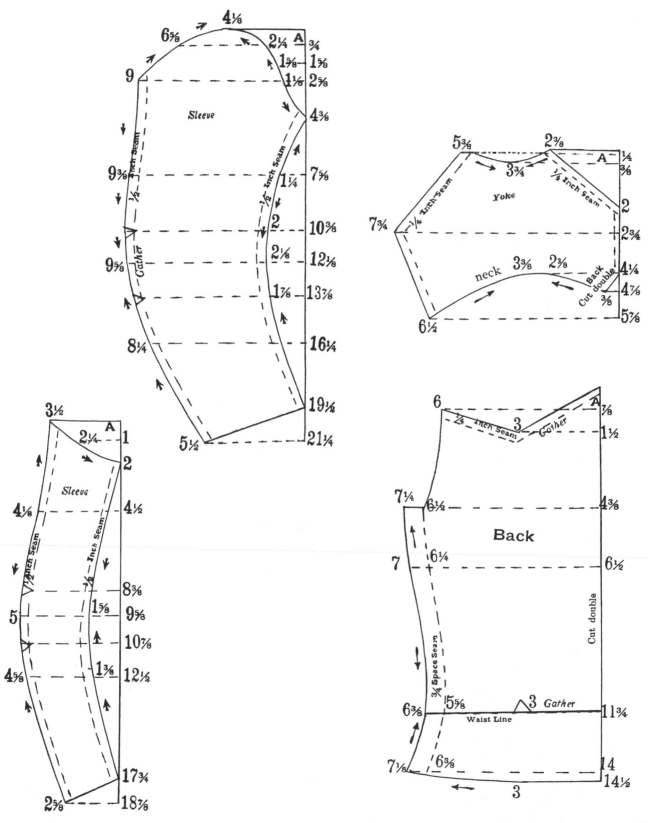

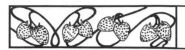

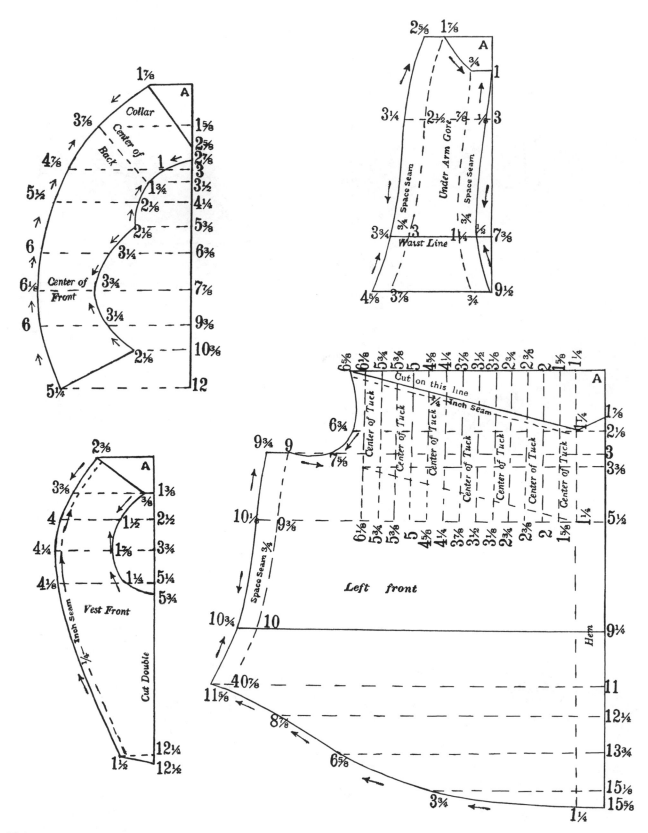

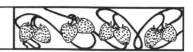

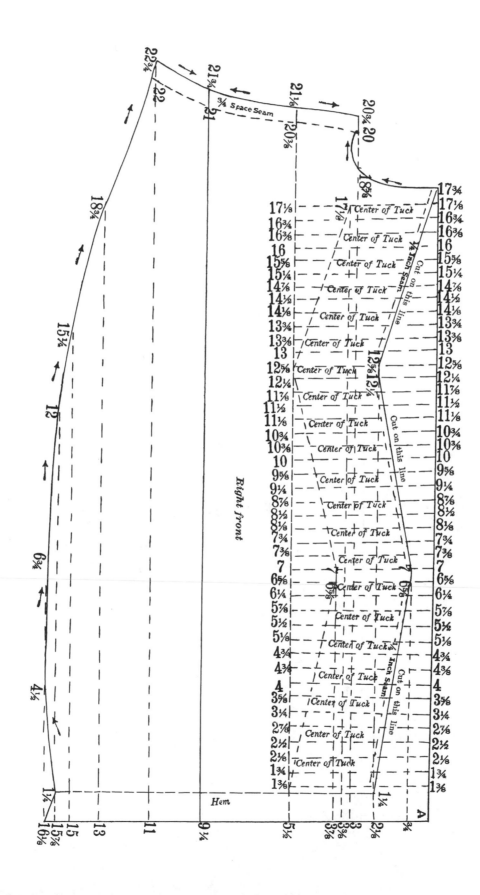

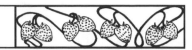

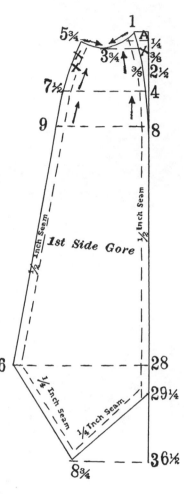

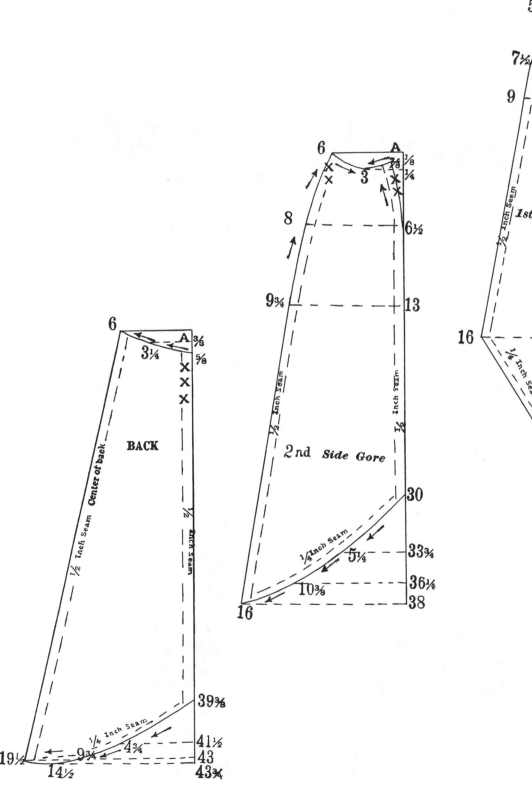

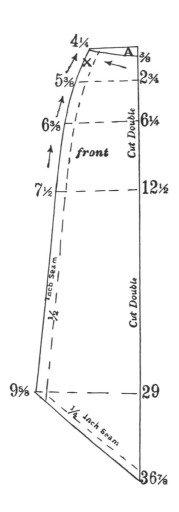

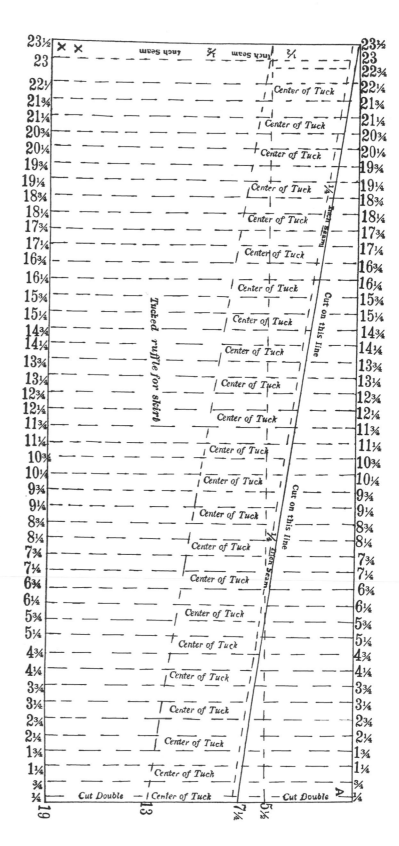

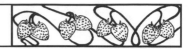

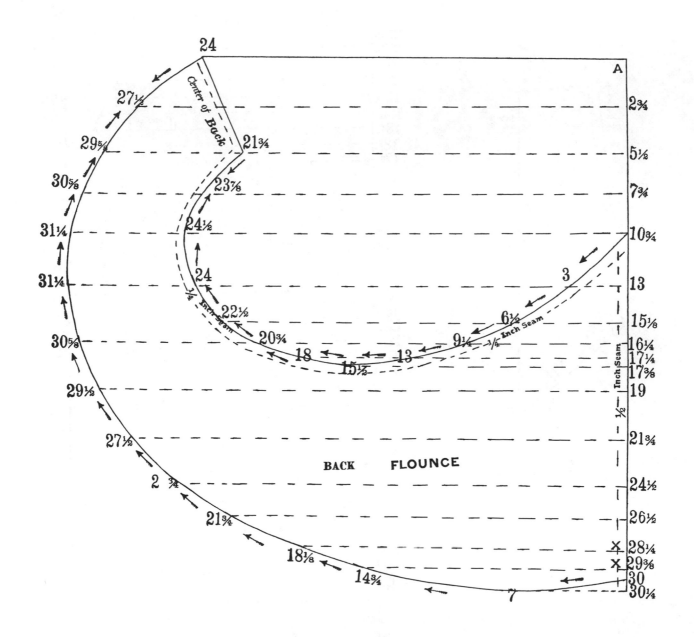

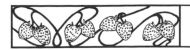 

Ladies' Costume

Use the scale corresponding to the bust measure to draft the waist, which consists of back, side back, underarm, front, upper back, upper front, jacket front, jacket ruffle, collar, sleeve, and scalloped sleeve cuff. Use the scale corresponding to the waist measure to draft the skirt. Regulate all lengths by the tape measure.

Join the back and side back and adjust the upper back. Take up the darts in the front and adjust the upper front. Cover the upper part of the front lining with the material to be used for the yoke to meet the upper edge of upper front. Gather the jacket ruffle at its upper edge to fit the lower edge of jacket from the front to figure 3 1/4. Sew the upper circular part of ruffle to lower circular edge of jacket plain. Make, line, and interline collar in the usual way. Finish neck of dress with a band to fit neck, and tack collar over this band. Make the sleeves in the usual way. Set the point at 3 5/8 in

top of sleeve at the second seam below the shoulder seam, and the front seam about 1 1/4 inches in front of the underarm seam. Place the right sides of the lining and upper portions of the cuff together, seam all around, and turn. Sew it to the lower edge with the ends of cuff at the inside seam of sleeve and finish with a facing. Make skirt in the usual way.

This dress is of grenadine and allover lace, with yoke of insertion and ribbon. Dress is made over taffeta. For a lady of medium size and height it will require 7 yards of 36-inch material, or 9 to 11 yards of silk.

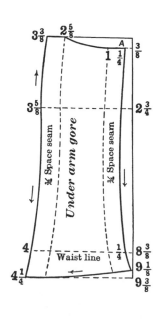

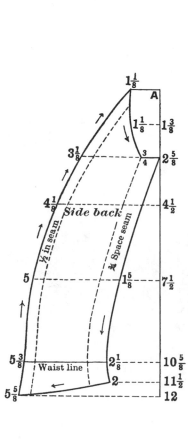

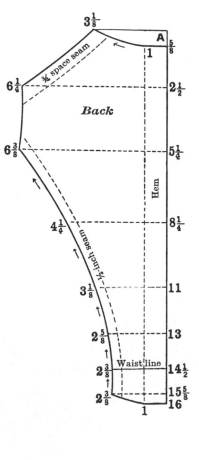

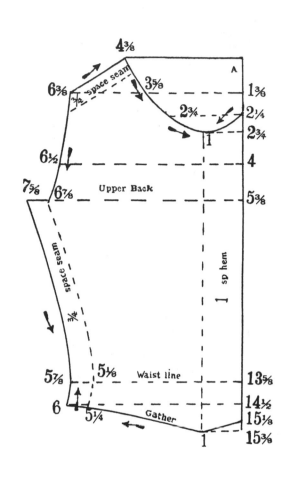

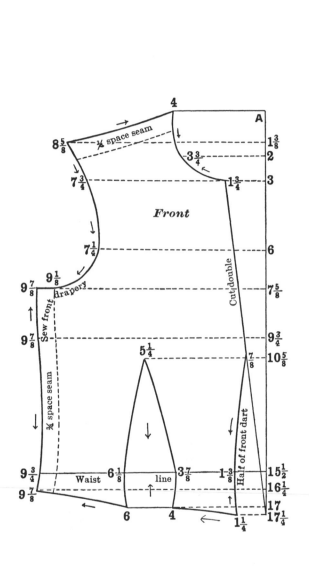

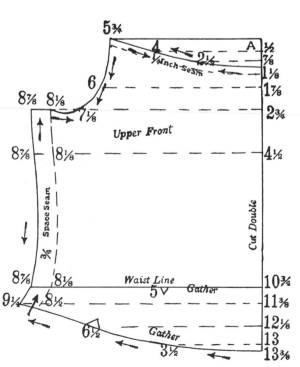

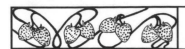

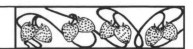

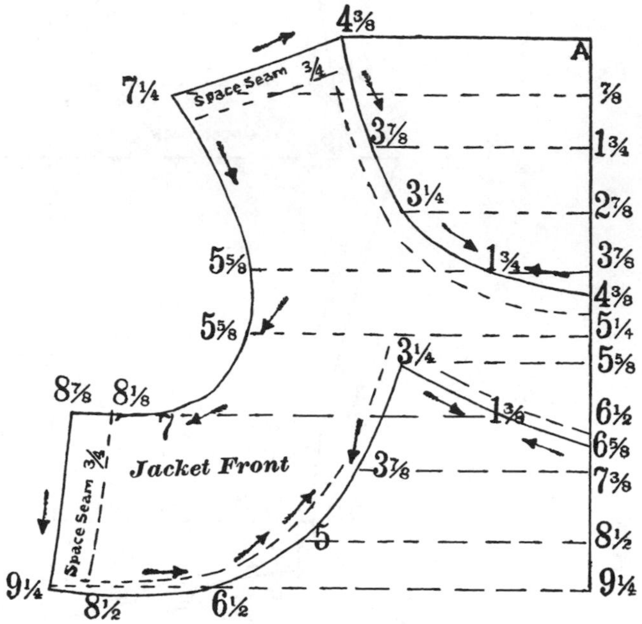
Jacket Front
Space Seam 3/4
Space Seam 3/4
A
4⅜
7¼
⅞
3⅞
1¾
3¼
2⅞
5⅝
1¾
3⅞
4⅜
5⅝
5¼
3¼
5⅝
8⅞
8⅛
7
1⅜
6½
6⅝
3⅞
7⅜
5
8½
9¼
8½
6½
9¼

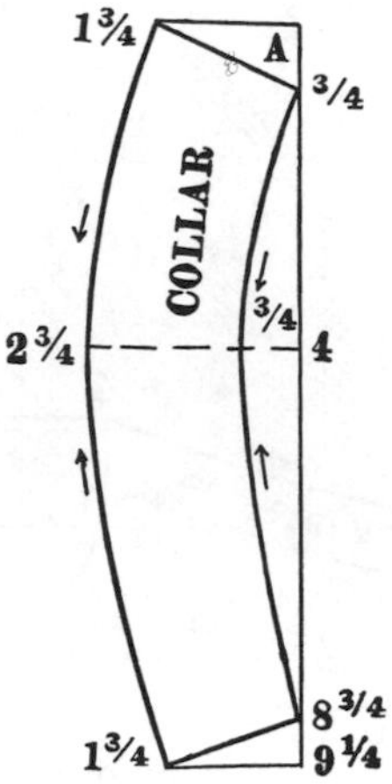
COLLAR
A
1¾
3/4
3/4
2¾
4
8 3/4
1¾
9 1/4

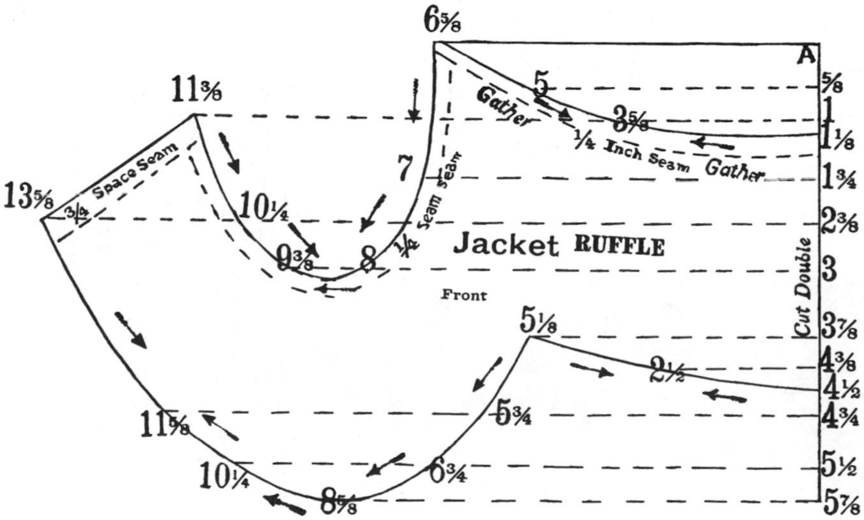
Jacket RUFFLE
Front
Cut Double
Space Seam
3/4
Gather
¼ Inch Seam
Gather
¼ Seam
A
6⅝
5
⅝
11⅜
1
3⅝
1⅛
7
1¾
13⅝
10¼
2⅜
9⅜
8
3
5⅛
3⅞
4⅜
2½
4½
11⅝
5¾
4¾
6¾
5½
10¼
8⅝
5⅞

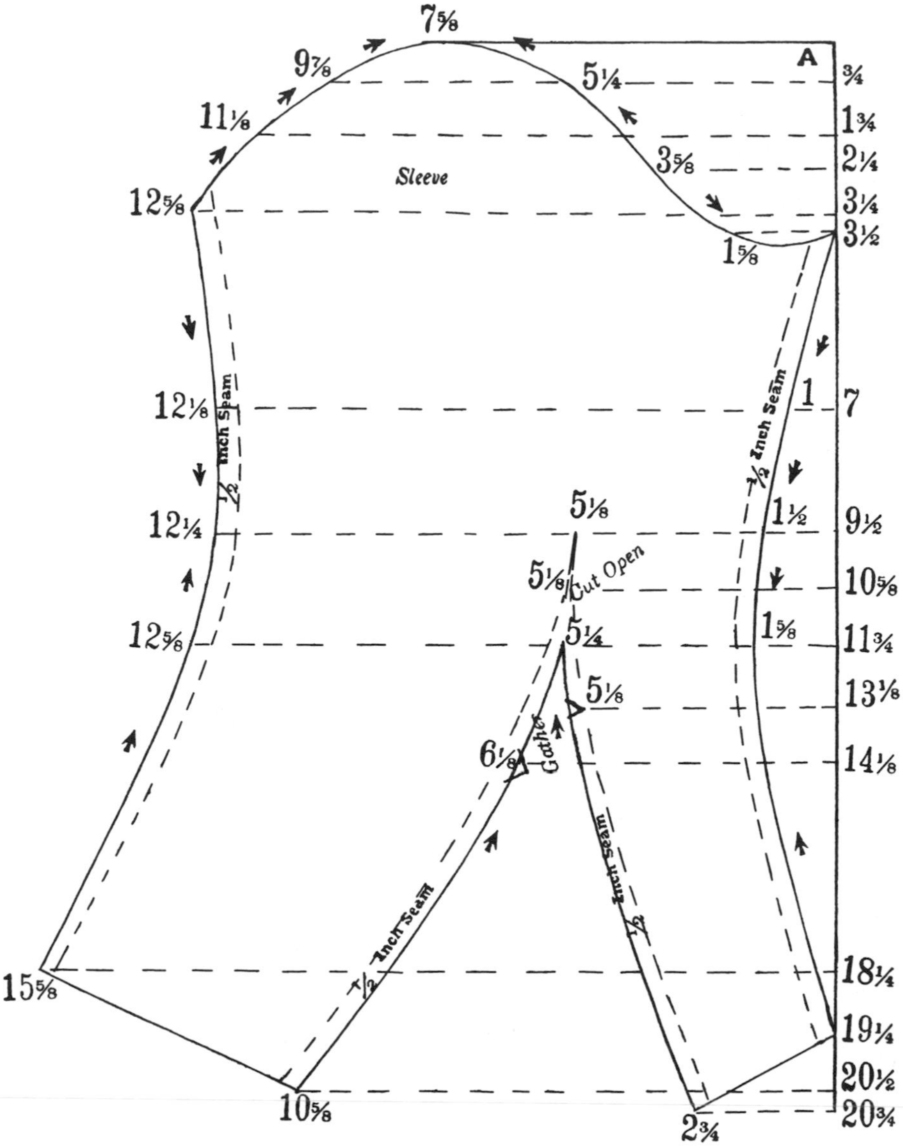
Sleeve
A
7⅝
9⅞
11⅛
12⅝
5¼
3⅝
1⅝
¾
1¾
2¼
3¼
3½
1
7
12⅛
½ Inch Seam
12¼
12⅝
5⅛
5⅛
Cut Open
5¼
5⅛
6⅛
Gather
1½
9½
10⅝
1⅝
11¾
13⅛
14⅛
½ Inch Seam
½ Inch Seam
½ Inch Seam
15⅝
18¼
19¼
20½
10⅝
2¾
20¾

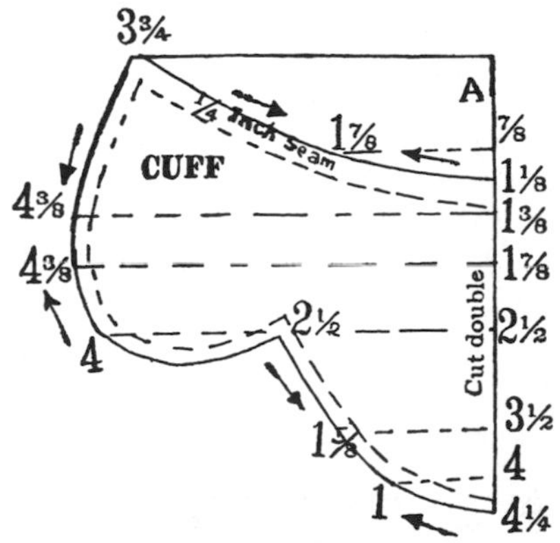
3¾
A
⅞
¼ Inch Seam
1⅞
CUFF
1⅛
4⅜
1⅜
4⅜
1⅞
2½
2½
4
Cut double
3½
1⅝
4
1
4¼

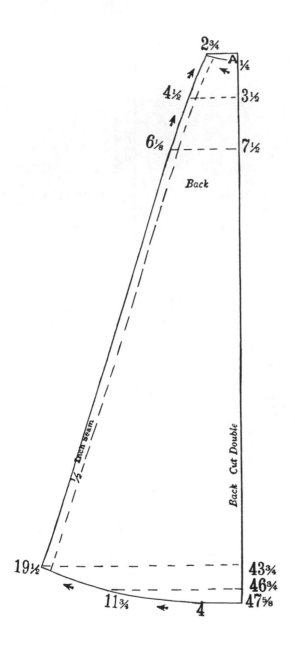

2¾
A ¼
4½   3½
6⅛   7½

Back

½ Inch Seam

Back Cut Double

19½   43¾
            46¾
11¾   4   47⅝

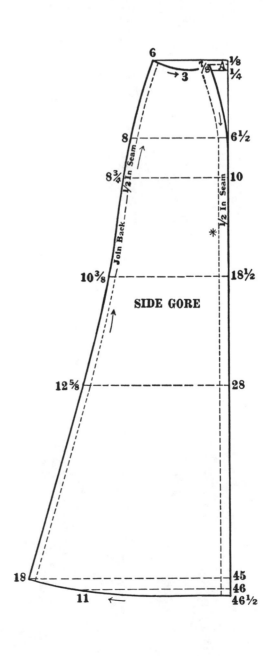

6
⅛ A ⅛
3   ¼
8   6½
8¾   10
½ In Seam
Join Back
½ In Seam
½ In Seam

10⅜   18½

SIDE GORE

12⅝   28

18   45
          46
11   46½

114

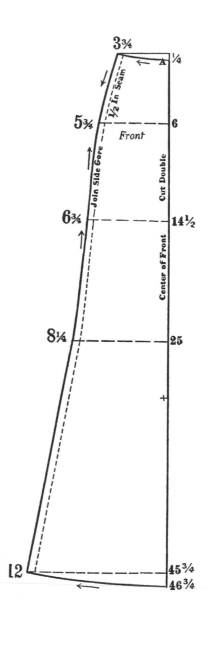

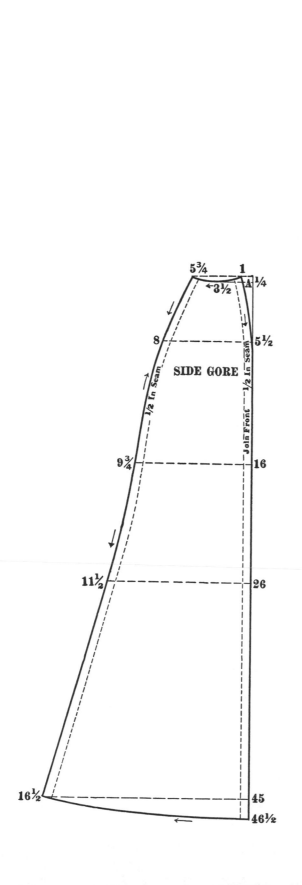

SIDE GORE

 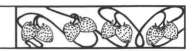

Ladies' Sailor Suit

Use the scale corresponding to the bust measure to draft the waist, which consists of back, front, back yoke, vest, small collar, large collar, and two sleeve portions. Use the scale corresponding to the waist measure to draft the skirt. Regulate all lengths by the tape measure.

Gather the back at its upper edge, from the center of back to figure 4 1/4, and sew to the yoke. Join the back and front portions. Line the sailor collar. Sew it to the neck and roll back as illustrated. Finish the neck of vest front with a band to fit the neck. Make collar and tack it over this band. Make

the sleeves in the usual way. See that the seams are not set high enough to cause the sleeves to draw, or the seams to twist. Sew sleeve into the armseye with a binding. Join the different parts of skirt as instructed on the diagrams.

This dress is of tan linen, trimmed with gold braid. Amount of material required for a lady of medium size will be 8 yards of 36-inch goods.

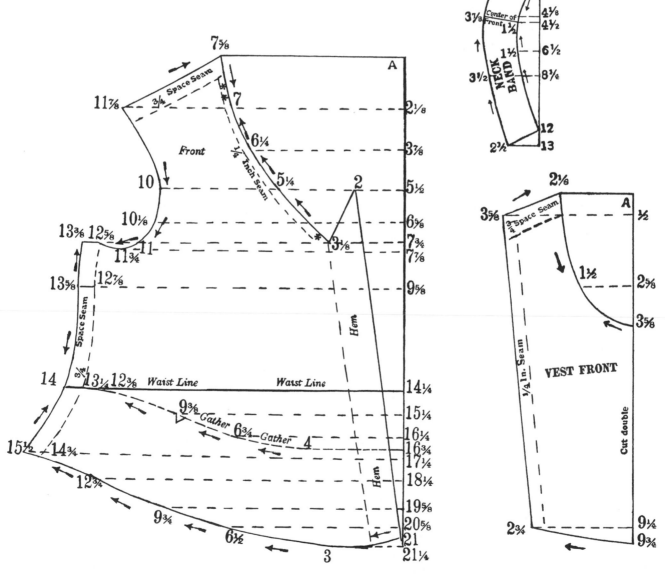

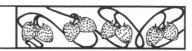

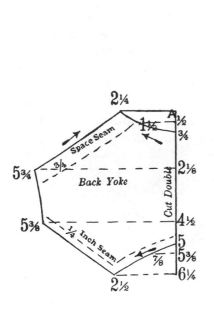

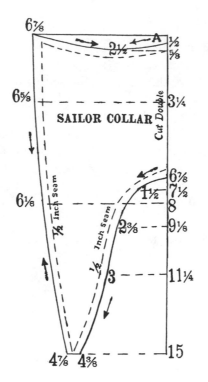

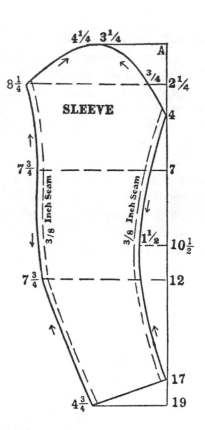

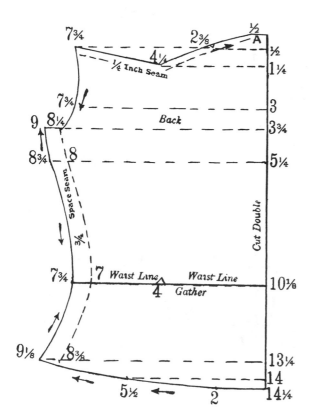

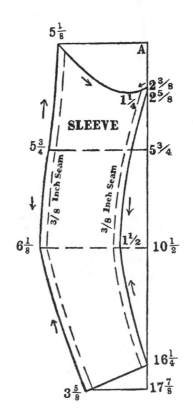

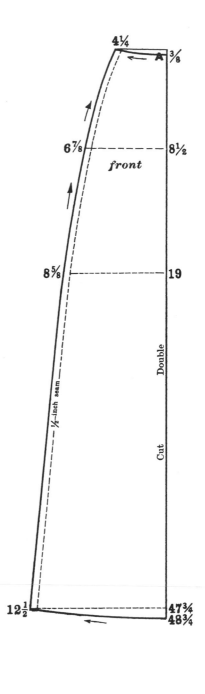

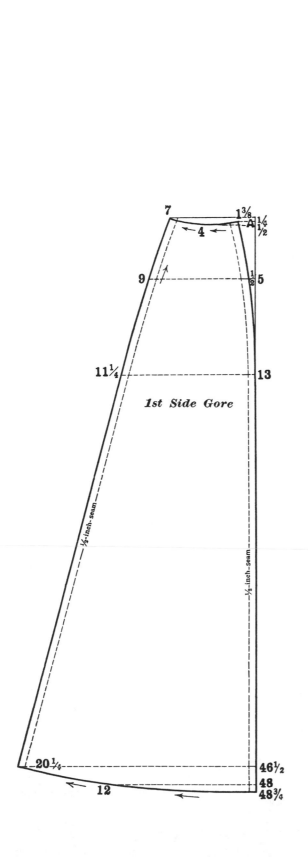

1st Side Gore

front

119

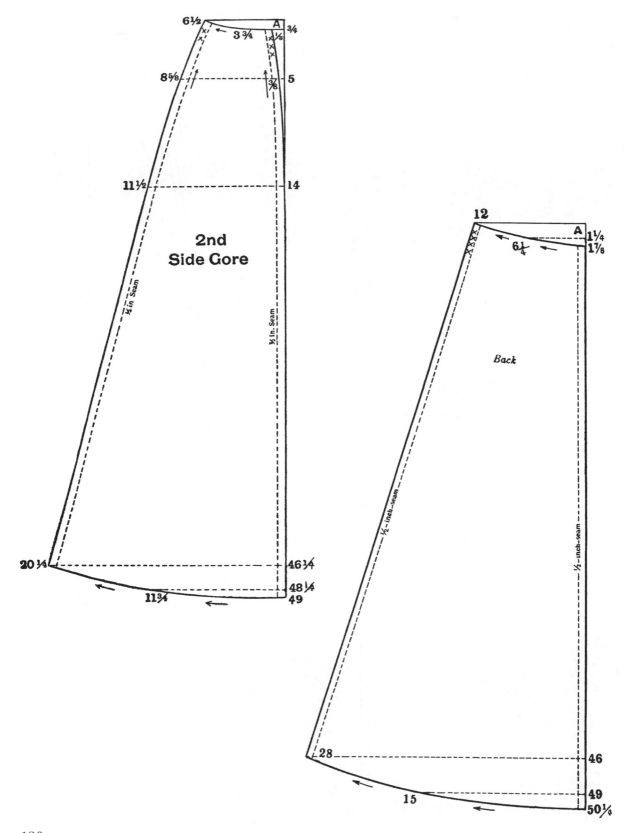

2nd
Side Gore

Back

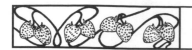 

Ladies' Calling or Evening Dress

Use the scale corresponding to the bust measure to draft the waist, which consists of back, side back, underarm, front, upper front, vest front, collar, two sleeve portions, and cuff. Use the scale corresponding to the waist measure to draft the skirt. Regulate all lengths by the tape measure.

Join the backs in the usual way. Face the upper fronts on their undersides back beyond the line to turn back on, with the material to be used for the revers. Finish the edges and roll them back. Make the vest front of the material to be used for the vest. Fasten it in the right shoulder and armseye and under the front edge of the right upper front. Fasten it at the left shoulder seam and under the left upper front with hooks and eyes. Line flaring cuff and sew it to the lower edge of the sleeve. Bring the upper fronts together to form a V shape at the waist. Place the back seam of the sleeve at the second below the shoulder seam, and the front seam about 1 1/4 inches in front of the underarm seam. Finish neck of waist with a band. Make the collar in the usual way and tack it over this band.

When making the skirt, the insertion and tucks are first put on to form the squares. Then the goods are cut away and the edges finished with a narrow ruffle of the embroidery.

This dress is made of pale lavender organdy, with a figure of black. Amount required for a lady of medium size is 9 yards of 36-inch material, or 13 yards of 24-inch goods. The embroidery for the flounce should be the length of 1 3/4 times around the skirt, at the point where the ruffle is to be sewed on.

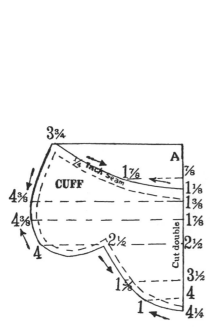

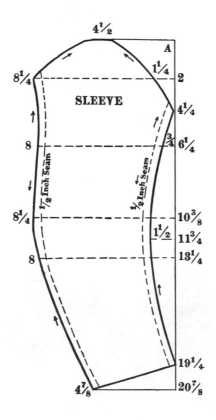

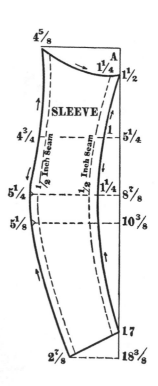

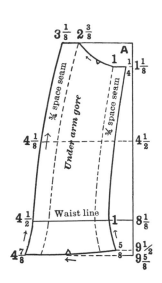

Under arm gore

¾ space seam

¾ space seam

3⅛ 2⅜
1
1⅛
1¼
4⅛ 4½
4½ Waist line 1 8⅛
1
4⅞ 5 9½
8 9⅝

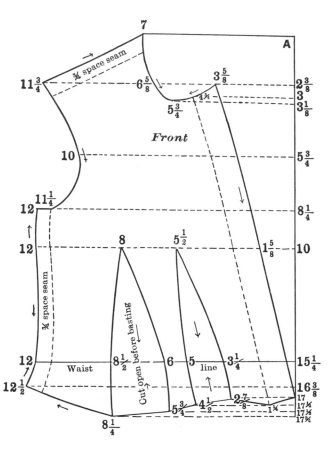

7
A
11¾ ¾ space seam
6⅝ 3⅝
2⅜
3⅜
3⅛
5¾
Front
10
5¾
11¼
12 8¼
12 8 5½
1⅝ 10
¾ space seam
12 Waist 8½ 6 5 line 3¼ 15¼
12½ 16⅜
17
Cut open before basting
5¾ 4½ 2⅞ 1¼ 17¼
17¼
8¼ 17¾

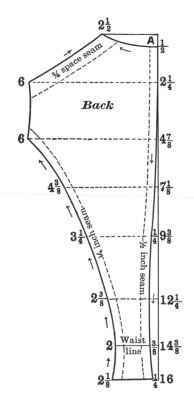

2½
A ½
6 2¼
Back
6
4⅞
4⅜
7⅛
¾ inch seam
3¼ ½ inch seam 9⅜
2⅜ 12¼
2 Waist line 3⅜ 14⅜
2⅛ 1¼ 16

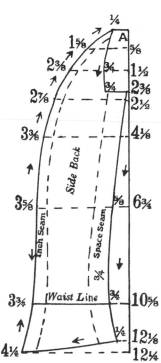

¼
A
1⅝ ⅝
2⅜ ¾ 1½
¾ 2⅜
2⅞ 2½
3⅜ 4⅛
Side Back
3⅝ ⅝ 6¾
Inch Seam Space Seam ¾
3¾ Waist Line ¾ 10⅝
1½ 12⅛
4¼ 12¼

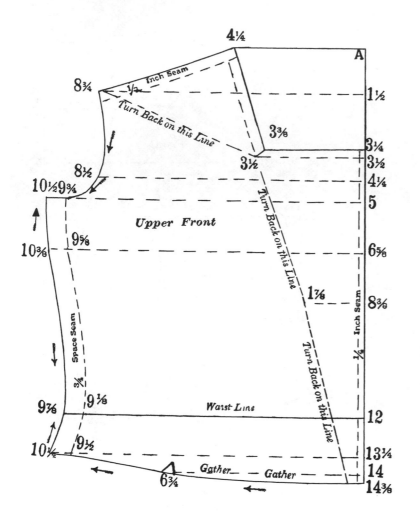

Upper Front

Turn Back on this Line

Inch Seam

Turn Back on this Line

Space Seam

Waist Line

Gather — Gather

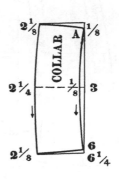

COLLAR

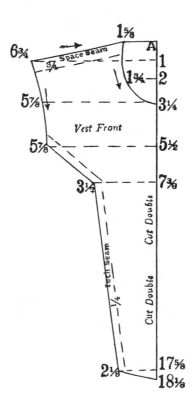

Vest Front

Space Seam

Cut Double

Cut Double

Inch Seam

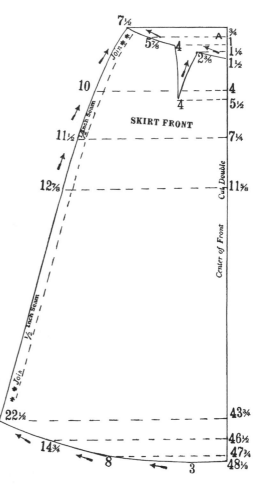

SKIRT FRONT

Center of Front

Cut Double

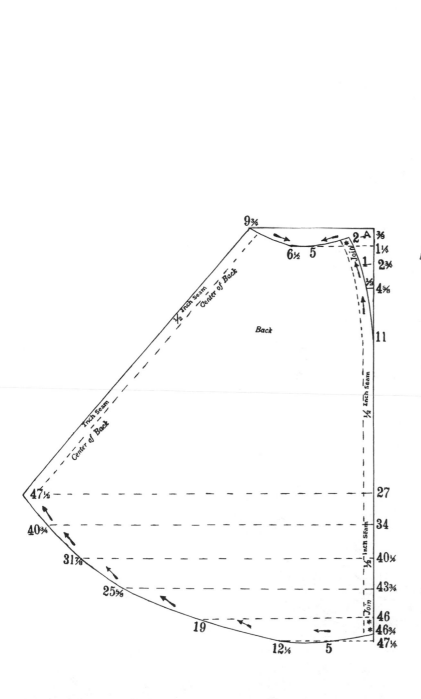

Back

Center of Back

Ladies' Afternoon or Evening Dress

Use the scale corresponding to the bust measure to draft the waist, which consists of back, side back, front, upper back, upper front, vest front, revers, sleeve, and sleeve puff. Use the scale corresponding to the waist measure to draft the skirt. Regulate all lengths by the tape measure.

Join the back and side back and adjust the upper back. Take up the darts in front and adjust the upper front. Sew the side of rever next to the baseline underneath the upper front at the right side. Line the rever like any other rever. Fasten at the left side, as illustrated, with buttons. The vest front is made entirely separate from the waist and fastened in back with a band the size of the neck. Tuck the goods for vest before cutting. Make and adjust the sleeve in the usual way, being careful to set it in properly. The sleeve is finished at the bottom with a ruffle that falls over the puff. Gather the puff at its

edges. Sew upper edge to the lower edge of the sleeve and finish the lower edge with a band to fit the arm.

The skirt diagrams are for the foundation skirt. The upper tucked skirt is shaped from straight material, and as much fullness allowed in the back as desired. The hip curves necessary are secured by holding the skirt full in the tucks.

This dress is of white taffeta, trimmed in black velvet, black ribbon velvet, and cream lace. Amount of taffeta required for a lady of medium size, 14 yards of 24-inch material or 9 yards of 36-inch material.

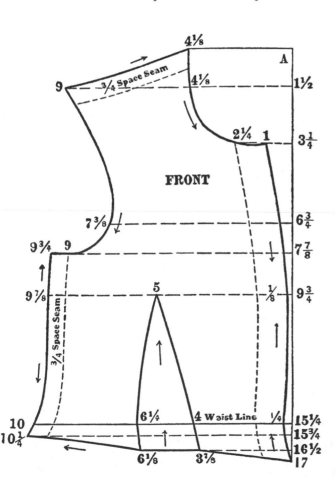

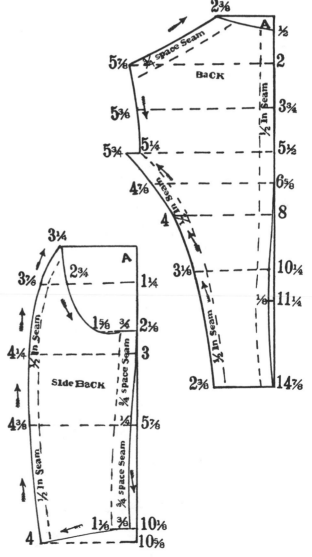

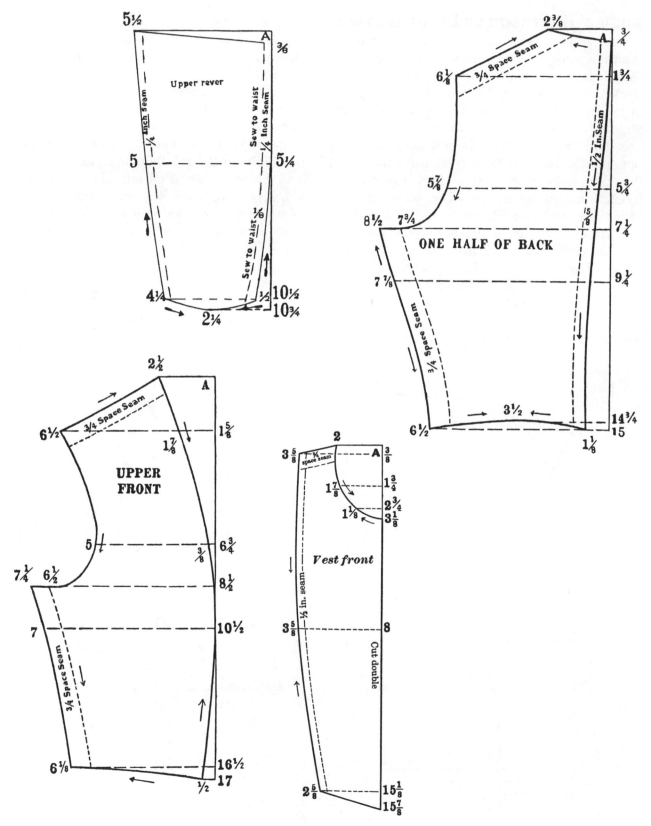

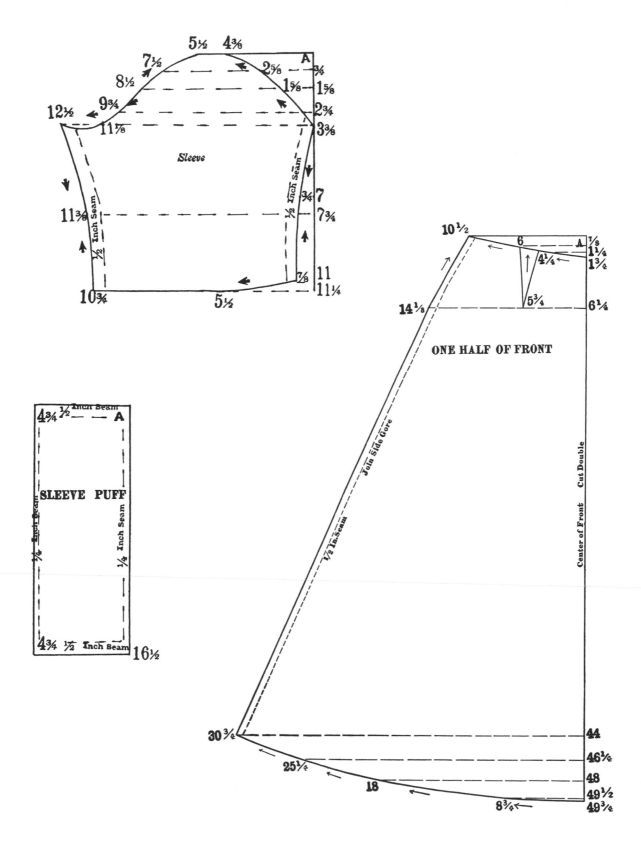

Sleeve

SLEEVE PUFF

ONE HALF OF FRONT

Join Side Gore

1/2 In. Seam

Center of Front   Cut Double

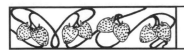

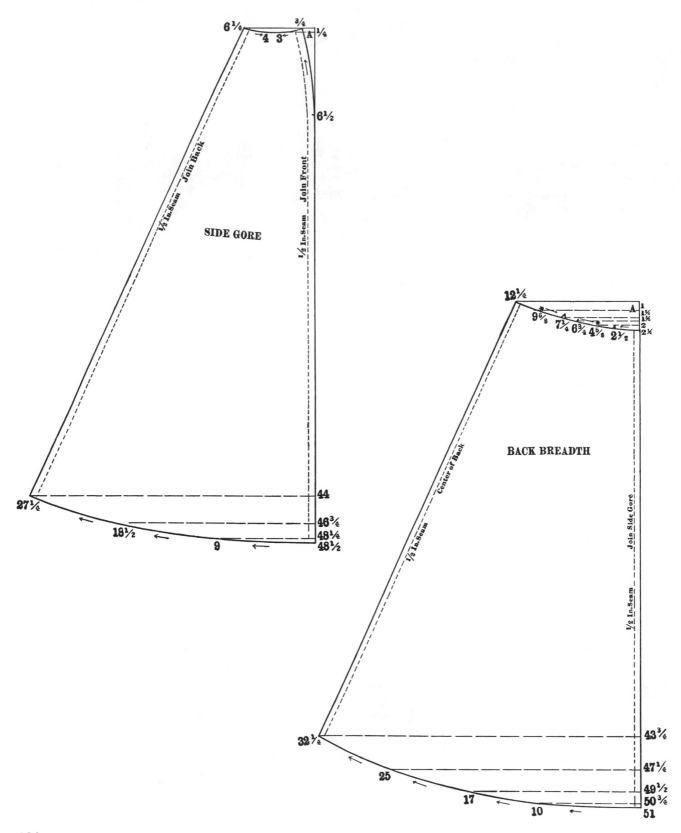

Ladies' Tea Gown

Ladies' Tea Gown

Use the scale corresponding to the bust measure to draft the entire costume, which consists of back, side back, underarm, lining front, upper front, full front, jacket front, sleeve, and sleeve puff. Regulate length by the tape measure.

Take up the darts in the lining front. Gather the full front at its upper edge to the width across the front. Lay on upper front and the jacket front. Cut away the lining front to fit the square neck. Cut the upper and lining section of the back portions from the same pattern. Join the sleeve and puff together in the armseye, and finish each one at the lower edge with a band. Tack the crushed band across the front with the end at right side under the upper and jacket front. Fasten it at the left side with hooks and eyes. Finish wrapper at the foot with a facing, which may be interlined or not as desired.

A yoke in the back of the same lace as the jacket fronts is very pretty. It may be laid on over and finished separately at the bottom from the wrapper, and shaped in a scallop to match the jacket fronts.

For a lady of medium size, this garment requires 7 yards of 36-inch figured goods, and 4 1/2 yards of plain silk for the front and sleeves. Lace for the jacket fronts, 1/2 yard.

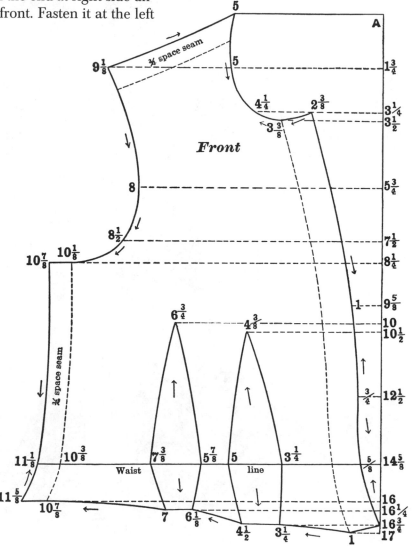

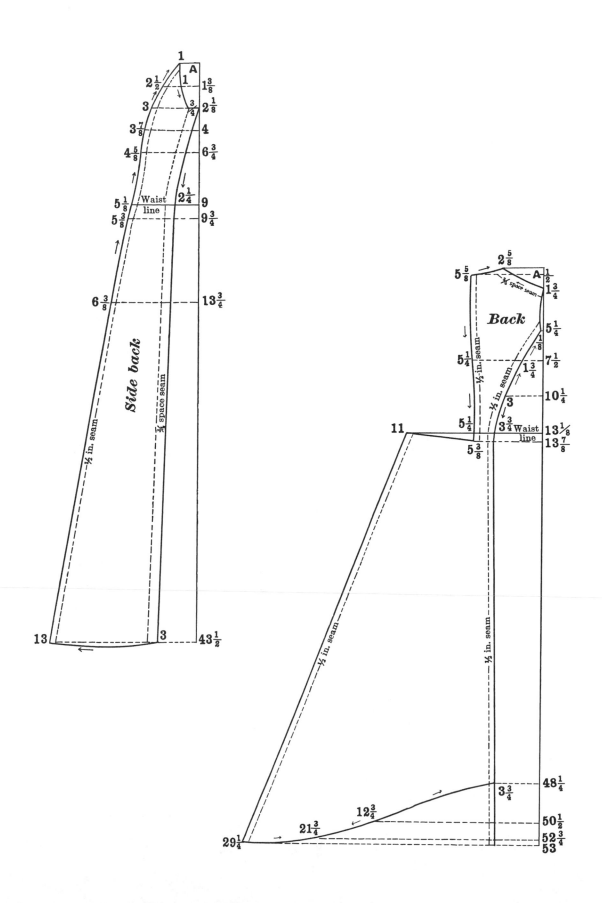

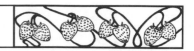

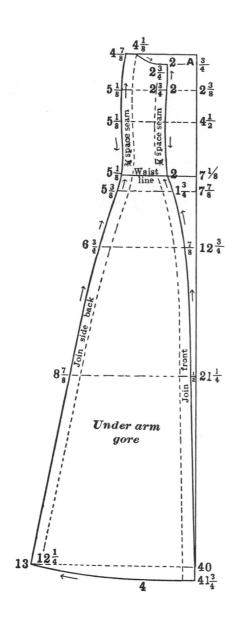

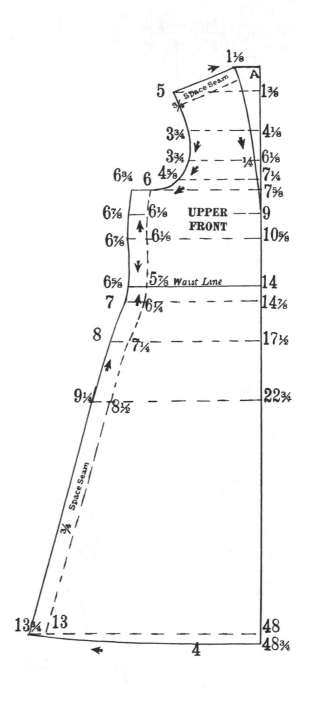

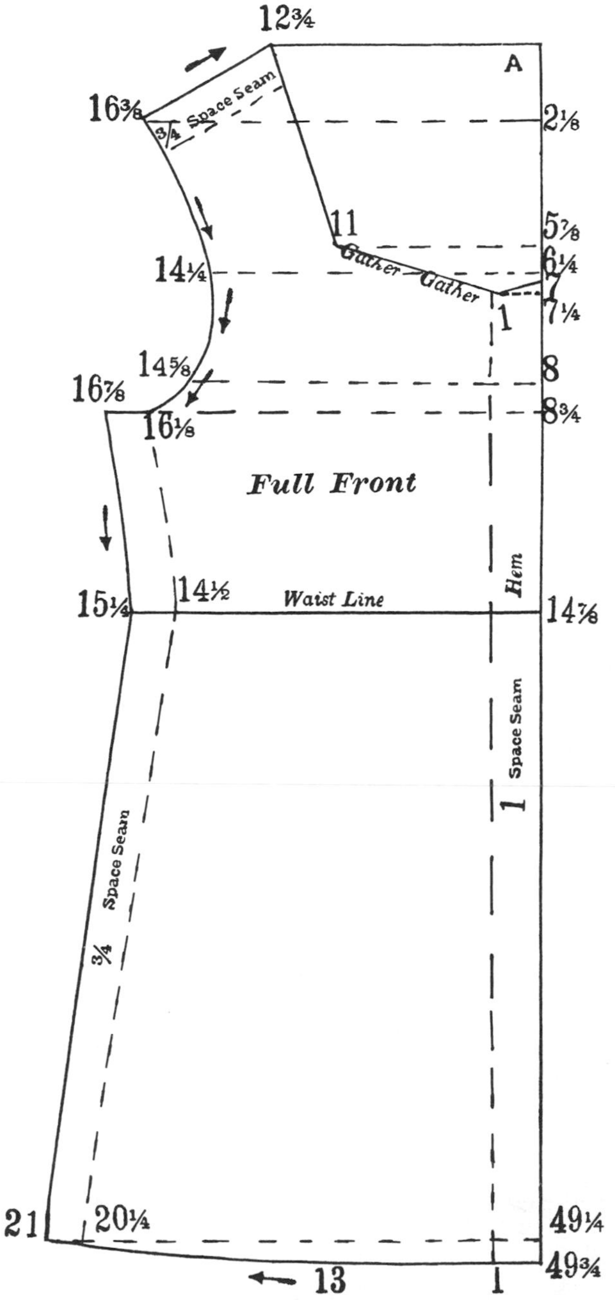

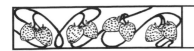

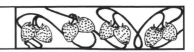

12¾
A
16⅜
¾ Space Seam
2⅛
11
5⅞
Gather Gather
6¼
14¼
1
7¼
14⅝
8
16⅞
16⅛
8¾
Full Front
Hem
15¼
14½
Waist Line
14⅞
Space Seam
1
Space Seam
¾
21
20¼
49¼
49¾
13
1

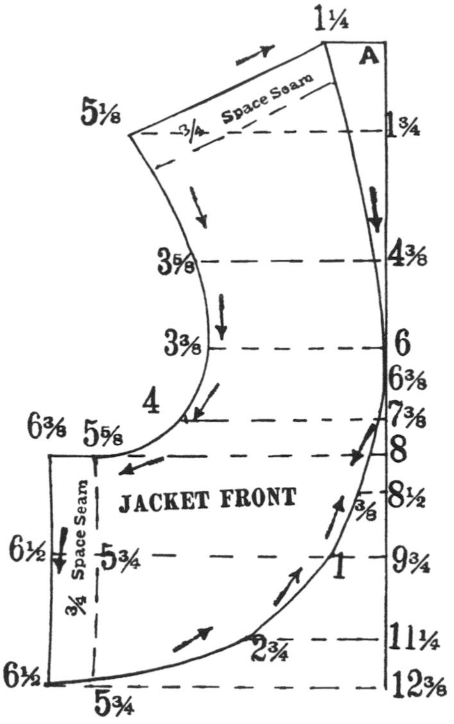

1¼
A
5⅛
¾ Space Seam
1¾
4⅜
3⅝
3⅜
6
6⅜
4
7⅜
6⅜
5⅝
8
JACKET FRONT
8½
⅜
6½
Space Seam
¾
5¾
1
9¾
2¾
11¼
6½
5¾
12⅜

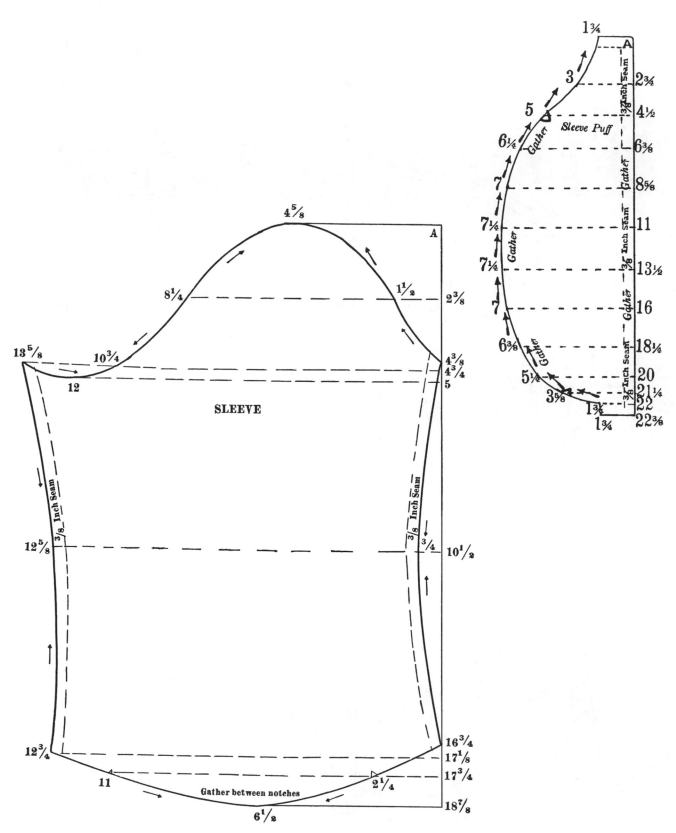

November 1900

There seems to be more attention given to the sleeve than to any other part of the costume. In trimming there seems no limit and but one general rule, and that is that the trimming of the sleeve be in harmony with that of the corsage. One is sometimes puzzled to think what to do to avoid the appearance of narrow and slanting shoulders, which the majority of these sleeves give, as the upper part remains tight fitting in most cases. Sometimes a short square yoke with straps dropping slightly over the shoulders, or a drapery deftly arranged over that part of the shoulders where they appear narrowest and most drooping, or small epaulettes standing slightly out on the shoulders, to some extent overcomes this one objectionable feature.

Another very important change is the mode known as the Juno bust, and the decided dip at the waistline in front known as the Marie Antoinette dip. To secure this effect one must wear and have the costume fitted over one of the new low-bust corsets. These corsets vary in form. Some are extremely low, while others are medium in form, and some are shorter or longer over the hips. These different styles are made more for different forms than to secure different results. The long-waisted effect makes the waist appear more tapering and reduces the size of the shoulders. To secure a perfect result the skirt must be shaped and adjusted to fit the outline of the waist at the bottom. This is done by curving the skirt as low in front as the waistline is to be dropped. Instead of finishing with a band (in the usual way) at the top, finish with a narrow facing or piping. Great care should be given when cutting skirts, to shape them in accordance to the attitude habitual to the wearer.

There are quite a few arrangements giving the effect of a double skirt. Some skirts are composed of two materials, usually the lower half of one material and the upper half of the other. These different materials are usually not joined on a straight line, but may be curved, pointed, horizontal, or have the effect of a graduated flounce.

The old-fashioned scarf that was almost indispensable to the well-dressed woman several seasons ago is again striving for notice. It is sometimes suggested in the scheme of the trimming, and again is seen wound around the shoulders and the loose ends hanging down the front, in some cases almost reaching the bottom of the dress.

The most popular winter coats reach to the knees or lower. Very long coats, entirely covering the dress, are more for warmth and comfort. They are for the streets on wet or cold days, traveling, the automobile, etc. Some of these coats are in the box style, while others have fitted backs and sides and are loose in front. Some sleeves are very fancy in cut. Some cloths have mixed colors and small patterns. It is predicted that this will be a season of velvets.

For costumes for general wear there are many new, beautiful, and useful materials in woolens, and silk and wool. Poplins and mohairs have a large share of favor, particularly covert coatings in many rich, deep, and medium colors. Fancy velvets will be much used in parts of costumes. A great many of even the heavy materials for street and tailor-made dresses come in extremely light shades. Even white will be seen in tailor-made gowns and jackets.

Many of the most beautiful fall wedding and evening dresses may be obtained without the great expense usually attendant upon these occasions, by use of the beautiful imitation silk linings. These are so skillfully designed that they cannot be detected from the genuine article when they form the foundation for the lace overdress. Lace overdresses often come already cut and sewed together, so that one only has to do the fitting and finishing to complete a beautiful costume.

 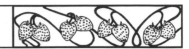

Buttons will be used extensively as a means of decoration, both on dresses and on wraps.

In millinery we see some very daring and original designs. Soft felts are favored for both walking and dress hats. Some beautiful hats are of white panne, usually having pretty high crowns. Some of these are almost entirely covered with black jets in scroll and floral designs. Some have their rims lifted at one side and lined with tucked chiffon. Chenille will be woven into small toque and hat shapes. Some toques are made entirely of plumage. Flowers will not play any great part in millinery except those made of satin, velvet, etc. Hats as a rule will not be trimmed high. Ribbed velvet will be a favorite for trimming. The "mercury" silks are beautiful for draperies, but too expensive to be used extensively. Polk bonnets of felt are so changed to suit the desired arrangement that they will be quite useful.

Scarlet will be a favorite color in millinery. Silk and velvet ribbon bows are used extensively for decorating the hair. One beautiful ribbon has a satin ground with raised velvet figures of a contrasting color. Brilliant green will be used extensively on hats, dresses, and wraps. Brilliant green belts are quite a novelty.

Fashionable furs will combine the plain boa and collarettes with full neck ruffles. These ruffles are made in most all kinds of fur, except those having extremely long hair. They are finished with a cluster of tails, etc., as the collarettes are usually finished, or may have a bow of tulle, chiffon, or ribbon that has long ends. The ruffles sometimes have an inside ruffle of the same material that forms the bow and ends.

Ladies' Calling Costume

Use the scale corresponding to the bust measure to draft the waist, which consists of back, side back, front, upper back, upper front, vest front, small vest, revers, rolling collar, small collar, and sleeve. Use the scale corresponding to the waist measure to draft the skirt. Be very careful in drafting the flounce, so that the pleats will be of a uniform size. Regulate all lengths by the tape measure.

This skirt has the new gathered back. Where flounce is not used the skirt may be cut wider and gathered more in back.

Join the back and side back and adjust the upper back. Take up the darts in front. Cut the left upper front on the line given for that purpose. Cut the entire diagram for the right front. Line the revers, rolling collar, and small vest. Join the small rolling collar to the back of neck, and the front of the upper fronts. Join the revers and small vest to waist as illustrated. Face the upper fronts with silk to a depth of at least 2 inches. Cut the center front vest of either the waist lining or silk. Cover it with folds. The folds are cut on the bias; each one is stitched on very close to the edge, and the next one overlapping it far enough to conceal the stitching.

The tops of the sleeves and the collar are trimmed in the same manner. The slight fullness at the top of the sleeve is gathered to fit the armseye. The bottom is gathered to a band that is made without an opening and just large enough to slip over the hand easily.

The waist may be made the desired length and gathered or sewed to a band the size of waist, or the bottom simply finished with a facing. This figure has the new Juno bust and Marie Antoinette dip. The skirt was curved to a depth of 1 inch from the center of the front, the curve terminating on the hips, and the belt given the same curve to ensure the desired effect. The skirt is finished with a narrow facing instead of being bound. The dress is worn over one of the new low-bust corsets.

If the different sections of the skirt flounce are cut separately, join according to the small Xs. If desired the flounce may be cut crosswise; the sections are pinned together before cutting. Be sure to omit the seams, by laying the dotted lines marked for them directly over each other. Pleat, joining stars to stars and notches to notches.

To make this costume as represented requires 12 yards of 42-inch goods or 15 of 36-inch material. The revers, rolling collar, cuffs, and skirt are trimmed in linen appliqué.

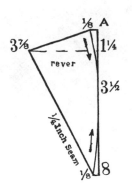

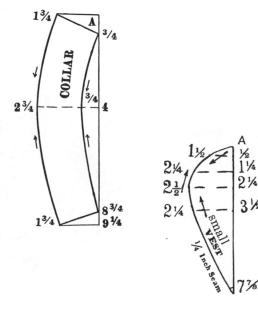

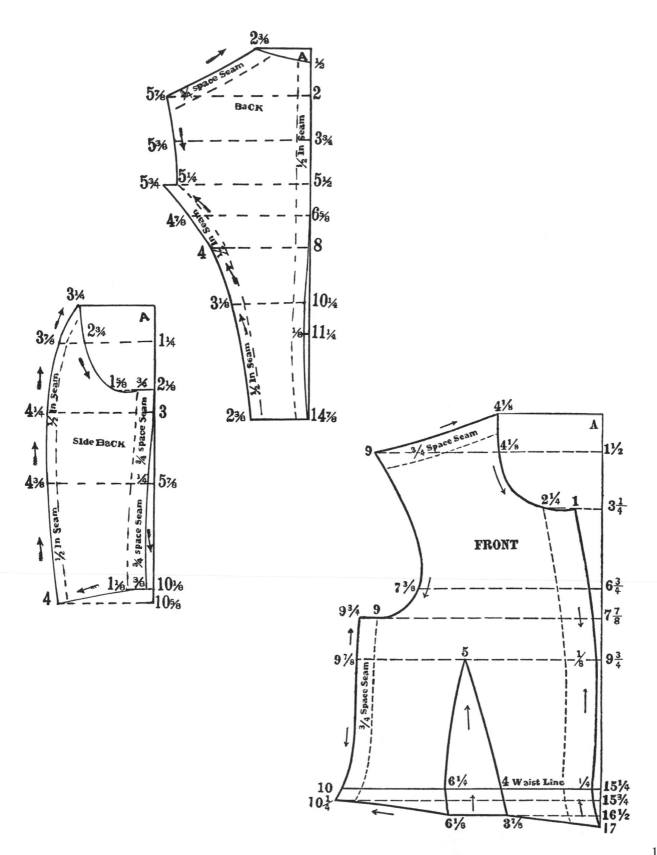

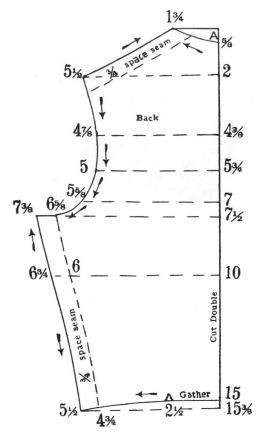

Back

1¾

A ⅝

5½ ¾ space seam 2

4⅞ 4⅜

5 5¾

5⅝ 7

7⅜ 6⅝ 7½

6¾ 6 10

¾ space seam

5½ Gather 15

4¾ 2½ 15⅜

Cut Double

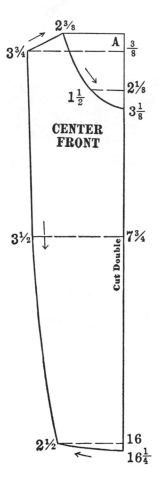

CENTER FRONT

2⅜

3¾ A ⅜

1½ 2⅛

3⅛

3½ 7¾

Cut Double

2½ 16

16¼

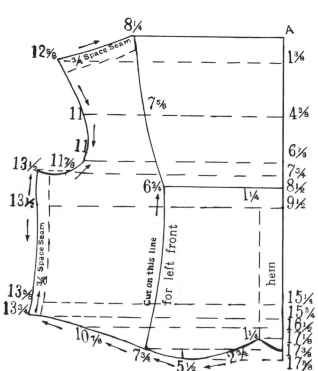

8¼ A

12⅝ ¾ Space Seam 1⅜

7⅝

11 4⅜

11 6⅛

13½ 11⅞ 7¾

6¾ 8½

13½ 1¼ 9½

Cut on this line for left front

¾ Space Seam

hem

13⅝ 15¼

13¾ 15¾

16¼

10⅞ 1¼ 17⅛

7¾ 5½ 2½ 17⅜

17⅝

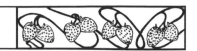

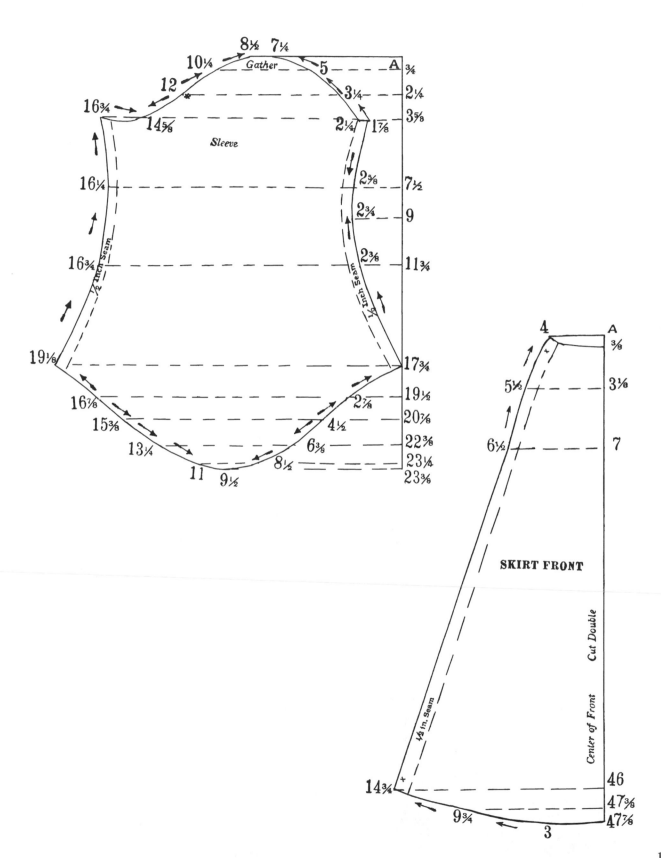

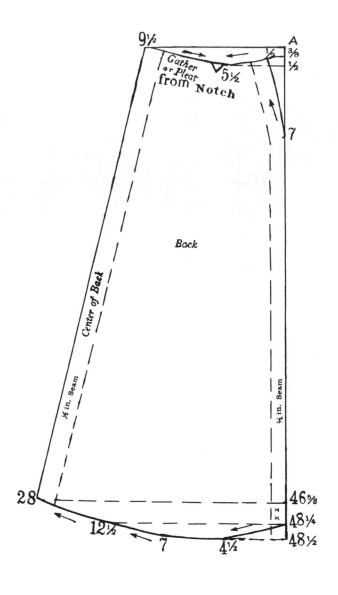

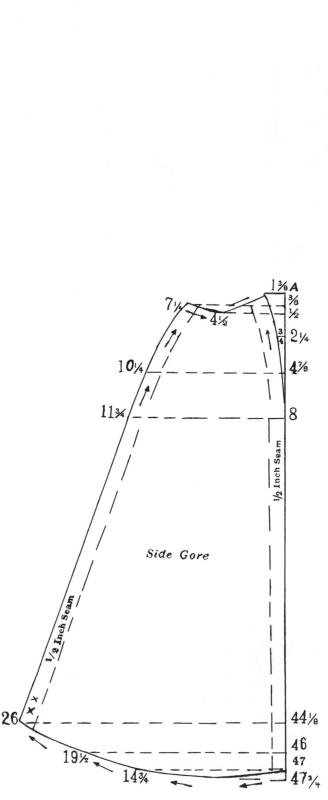

144

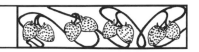
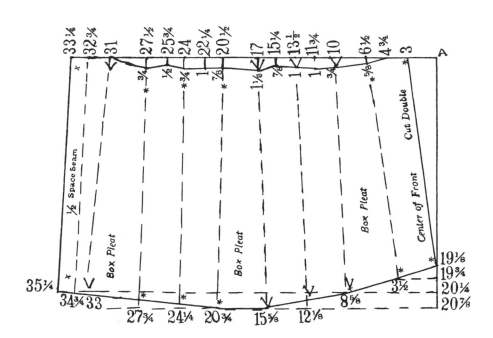

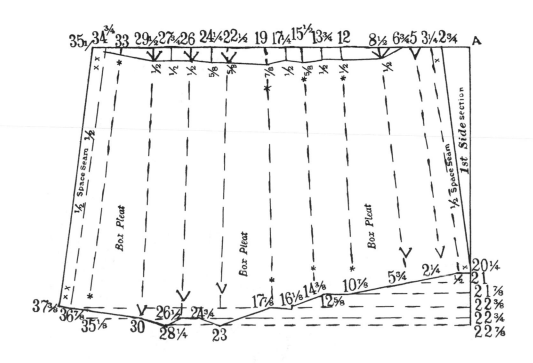

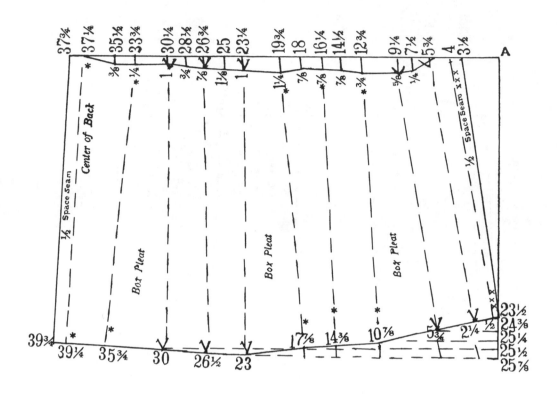

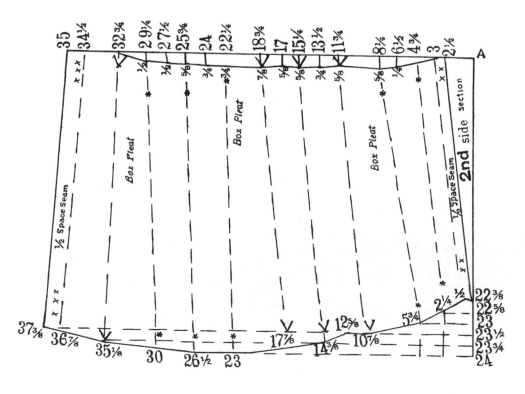

146

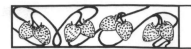
Ladies' Dinner Dress

Use the scale corresponding to the bust measure to draft the waist, which consists of back, side back, underarm, front, upper back, right and left upper fronts, double rever, collar, and two sleeve parts. Use the scale corresponding to the waist measure to draft the skirt. Regulate all lengths by the tape measure.

This is one of the new figures with the low bust and dropped waistline in front. The waist is dropped from the underarm seam on a slant to the desired depth in the front. The skirt is curved down in the same manner. This dress is worn over the new low-bust corset, and the belt adjusted to suit.

Join the back portions. Adjust the upper back and gather the extra fullness at the bottom. Cut the tucked vest by the front lining part by laying the dotted line for hem on a fold. Cut only wide enough at left side to come under the edge of the left upper front, and cut long enough to come at least 2 or 3 inches below the upper edge of the right upper front. The vest, if too loose at the lower edge, may have two small and very short darts taken. Cut the lower rever by the entire diagram, and the small one on the inside line as instructed. The rever may have a very light interlining, and should be lined with silk. The lace at the side of the vest is tacked under the front edge of the left upper front. The end at the top is all caught together under the ribbon rosette.

The lower end should be finished with a narrow hem or binding. It is spread out to form a fan shape and fastened under the upper edge of the right upper front. Cut the lining for sleeve the full size of the pattern and make the lower part of the tucked goods the same as the vest front. The upper part is covered with the dress material to come over the edge of the lower part, and where the two materials join, is finished with the lace flounce that has a narrow heading of chiffon. Finish the neck of the dress with a narrow band. Make the collar and tack over this band. Or buttonholes may be worked in the band and a linen collar worn same as with a shirtwaist, over which is tied a soft ribbon.

This dress is of old rose taffeta, with black net overdress with flounces of deep ecru lace headed with ruchings of chiffon. Vest and lower part of sleeves are cream silk. Stock and ribbon on left side of waist are pale lavender. The amount of material required for a medium-sized lady is 10 yards of 24-inch silk, or 11 yards of 22-inch silk, with 1 1/2 yards of silk for lower sleeves and vest. The lace for the overdress can usually be bought ready cut for sewing.

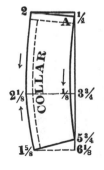

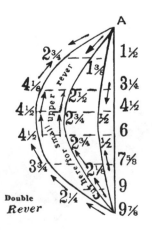

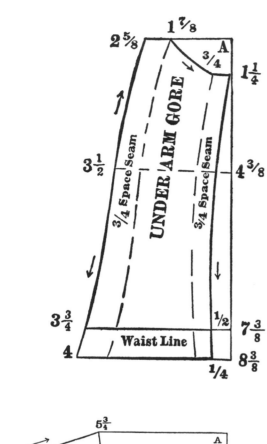

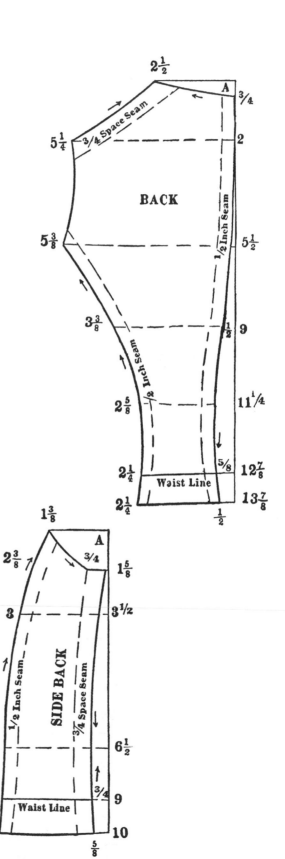

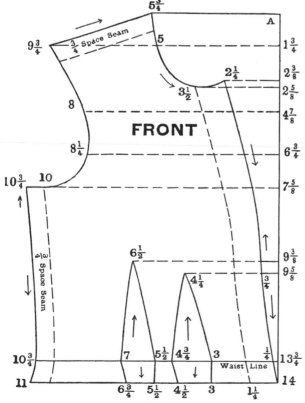

149

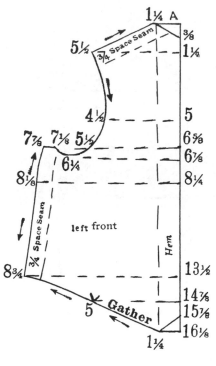

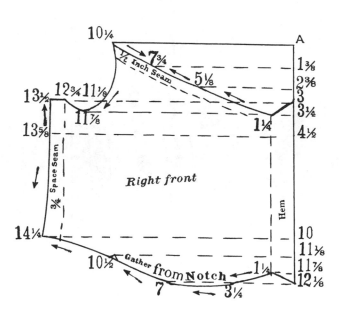

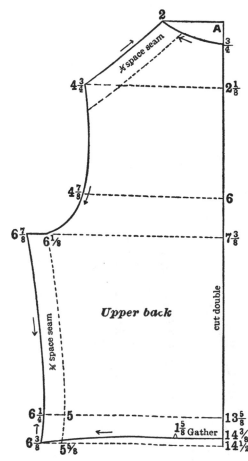

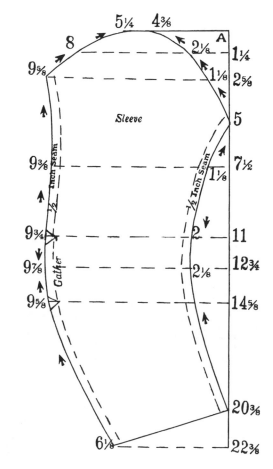

150

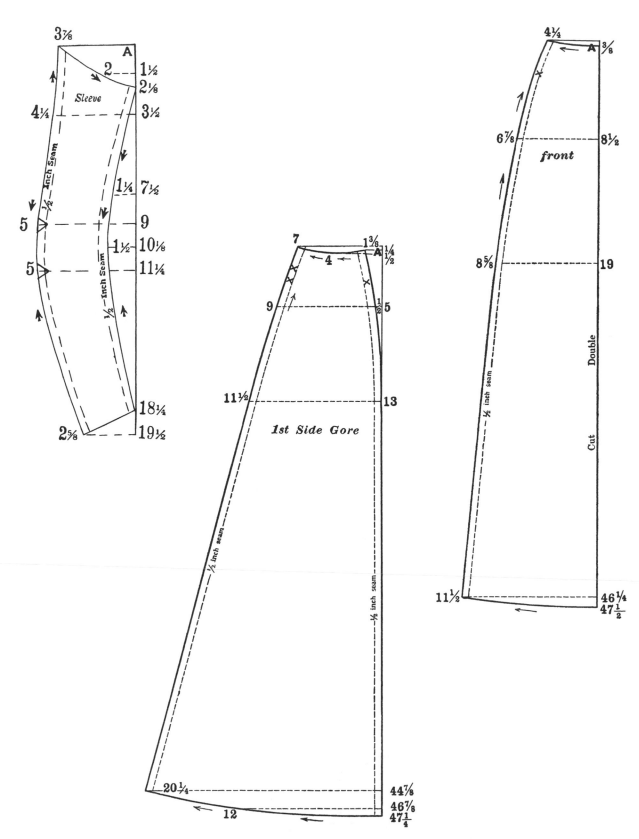

Sleeve

1st Side Gore

front

151

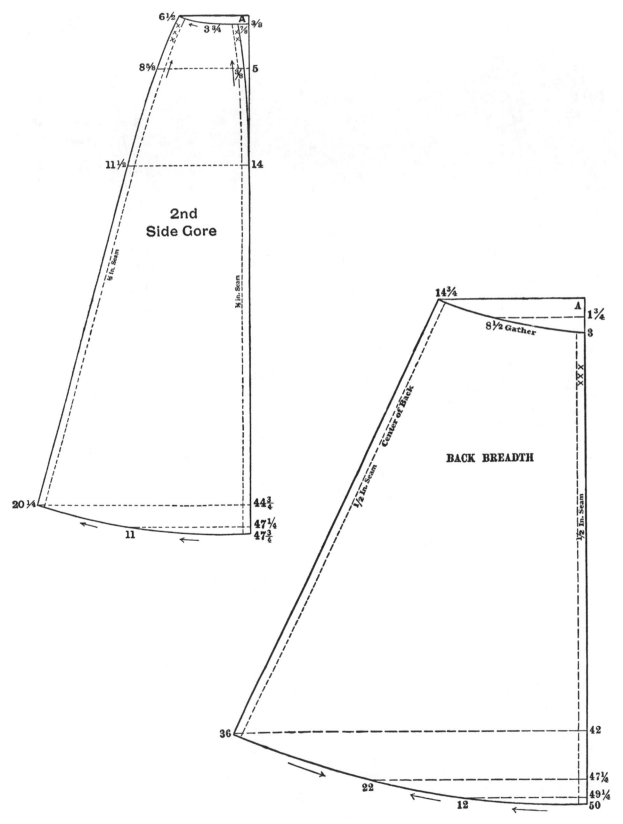

2nd
Side Gore

BACK BREADTH

 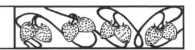

Ladies' Dressing Sacque with Skirt

This sacque may be made in a loose or a fitted style. Draft using the scale corresponding to the bust measure. Use the scale corresponding to the waist measure to draft the skirt. Regulate all lengths by the tape measure.

To make the sacque with the loose front, use the back, side back, underarm gore, both fitted and loose fronts, the sailor collar, the small collar, and the pointed sleeve. Join the back, side back, and underarm gore. Take up darts in the front. Gather the full front at the neck to fit the under front. Hem the fronts of the upper and fitted lining separately. Finish the neck with a narrow band. Make the small collar and tack over this band. The sailor collar may or may not be lined, is finished at its edges before being adjusted to the sacque, and is sewed across the back of the neck and just back of where the fullness hangs from the neck.

The fitted lining may be omitted if desired, and straps set at the underarm seams, at the waistline, and fastened in back to hold the back in place. But the fitted lining gives a more satisfactory ad-justment. The small sleeves may also be used underneath the loose sleeve, and should be made of silk or some light material to suggest an undergarment finished in some pretty way at the wrist.

To make the fitted sacque, join the back, side back, and underarm gore. Take up darts and join the fronts and back in the usual way. Slope the fronts to form a low V-shaped neck by commencing at the shoulder seam at the side of neck, cutting off the corner that forms the high neck. When cutting the rolling collar regulate the length to fit the front; the collar should be lined. The small sleeve is used, and the cuff is sewed on and turned up. Line the cuff the same as the rolling collar.

In the illustration the skirt has a straight gathered flounce, decorated with a ribbon gathered through the center.

This costume was developed in a soft wool novelty goods. To make the loose-front sacque for a medium-sized lady requires 3 3/4 yards of 36-inch material, or 3 for the fitted front. The skirt requires 7 yards of 36-inch material.

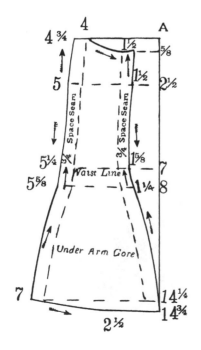

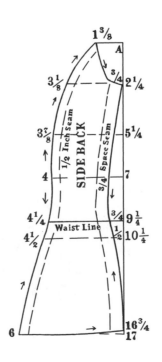

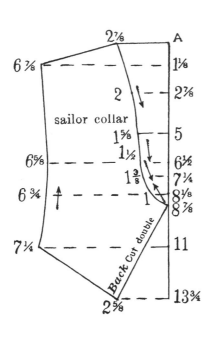

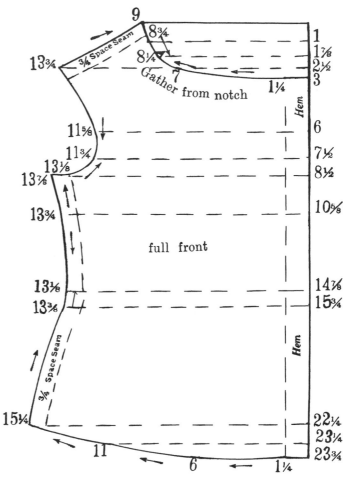

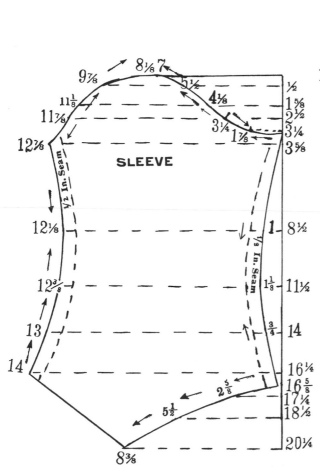

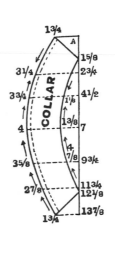

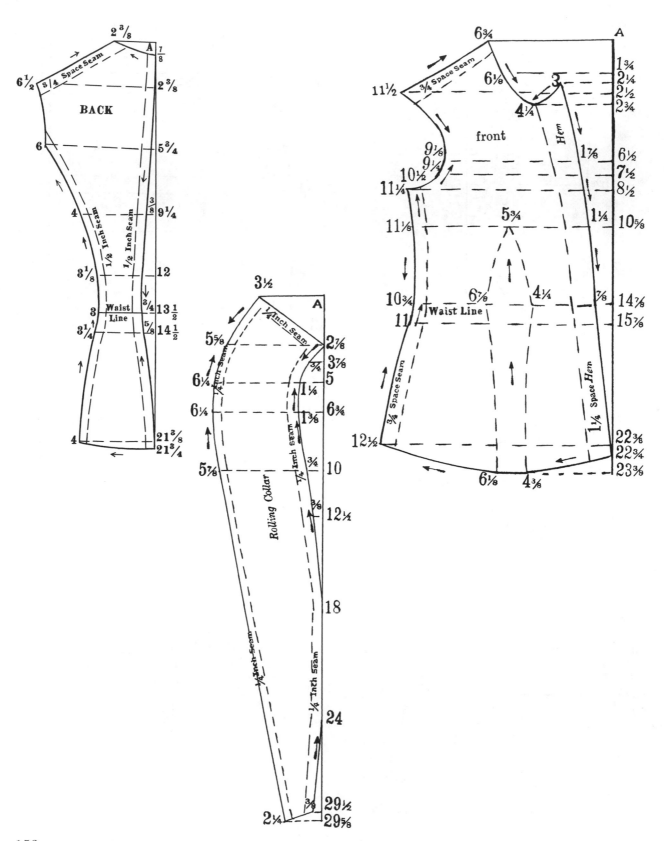

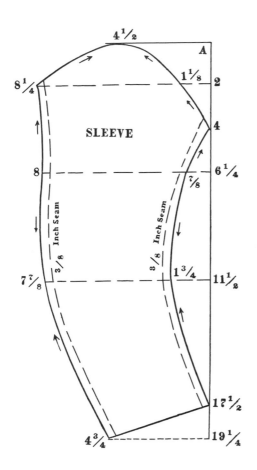

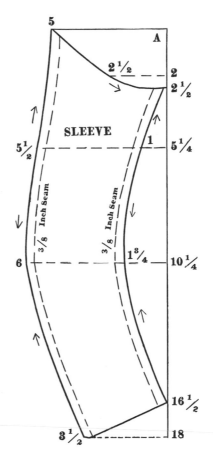

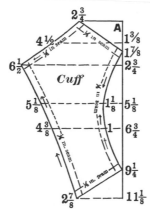

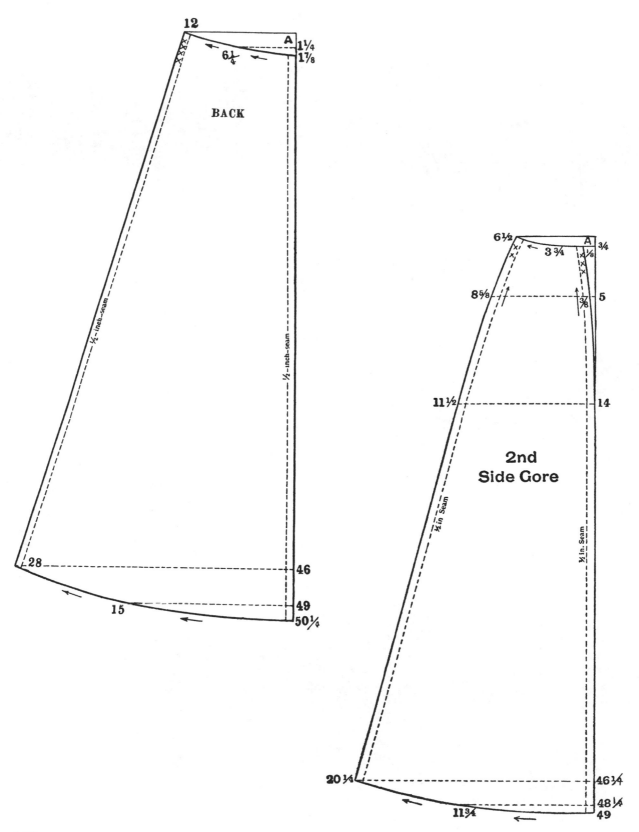

BACK

2nd
Side Gore

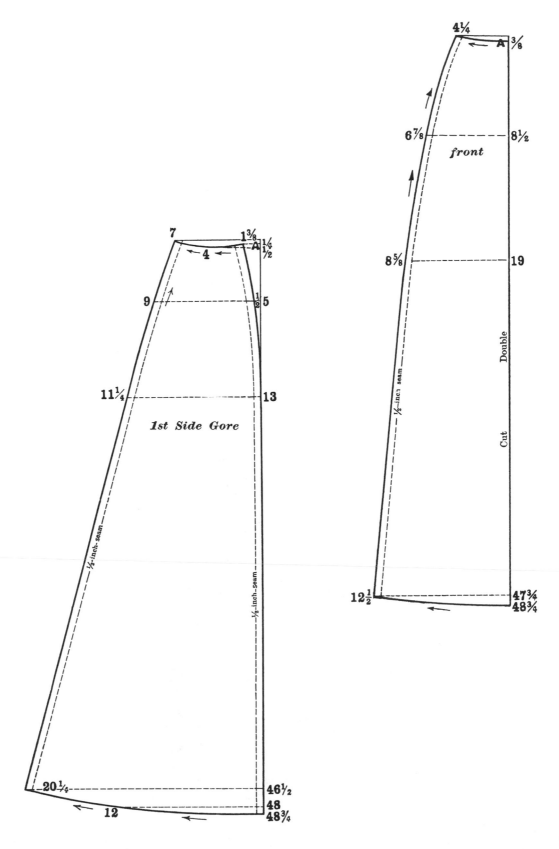

1st Side Gore

front

159

Ladies' Empire

Use the scale corresponding to the bust measure to draft the waist, which consists of seamless waist, fichu collar, two small sleeve parts, and one full sleeve. Use the scale corresponding to the waist measure to draft the skirt. Regulate all lengths by the tape measure.

In cutting the fichu cut the left side off on the dotted line. Gather the end to about 1/3 its width and fasten to the front of waist. Leave the right side long. Bring it over to the left side as illustrated, lay it in three upward-turning pleats, and fasten it just over the waistline, its end being concealed by the bow of the sash. Gather and sew skirt to waist.

This handsome gown is made of a very soft silk and wool material, in light heliotrope with bright green bow knots in silk. To make it for a lady of medium size requires 6 yards of 42-inch goods, or 8 yards of 36-inch material. The sash, fichu, full sleeves, and skirt trimming are of cream silk; 6 yards are required. The skirt at the foot is finished with several rows of narrow velvet ribbon in black. Black velvet cuffs and belt complete the decoration of this pretty house gown.

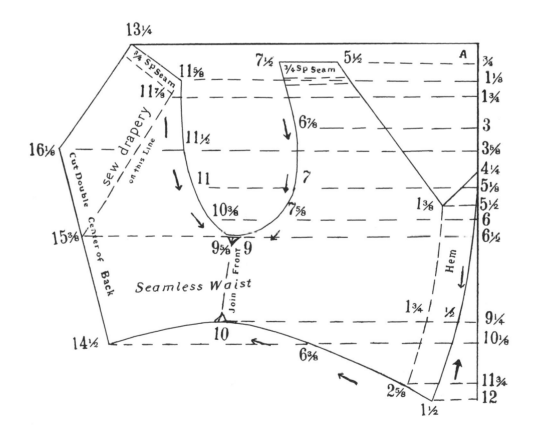

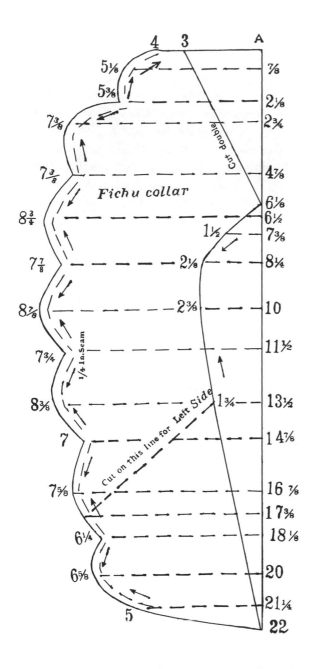

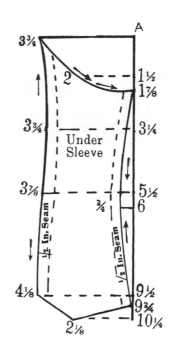

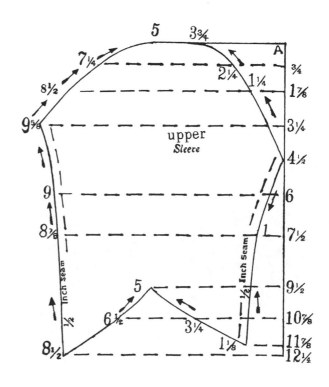

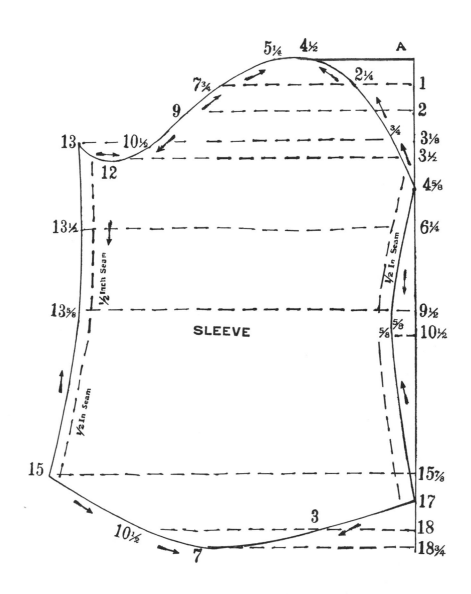

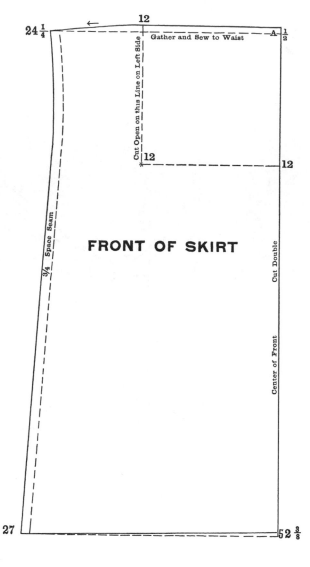

FRONT OF SKIRT

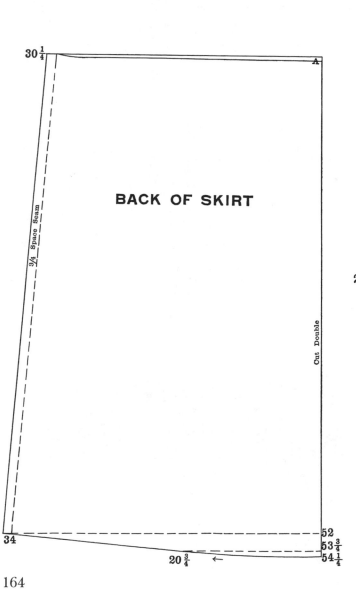

BACK OF SKIRT

Ladies' Evening Costume

Ladies' Evening Costume

Use the scale corresponding to the bust measure to draft the waist, which consists of lining back, side back, underarm, and front; upper back and upper front; back and front jacket parts; two upper sleeve parts; sleeve puff and puff lining; and cuff. Use the scale corresponding to the waist measure to draft the skirt and drapery. Regulate all lengths by the tape measure.

Join the back and side back. Adjust the upper back to them and gather the extra fullness from the notches at the top and bottom, to the back. Take up darts in the front lining. Adjust the full front, first hemming the different parts separately. The jacket parts are finished at the top and bottom before be-ing adjusted to the waist. The jacket at the left side in front is finished with a facing and fastened with hooks and eyes. Gather the puff to fit puff lining, both at top and bottom, and join them to the lower edge of the sleeve. Line and interline the cuff. Set it over the line where the sleeve and cuff join, and turn it back. The puff may be faced at the bottom. Or it may be finished with a fancy band of velvet, satin, or any material the fancy may suggest; or a frill of lace is pretty.

Cut the skirt drapery as instructed on the diagram and lap the fronts as shown in the illustration. Gather or pleat the drapery at top. Each width of flounce is cut out in a V at top, caught down to where the straight part of the top is also gathered into a very narrow space, and covered with a bow or rosette.

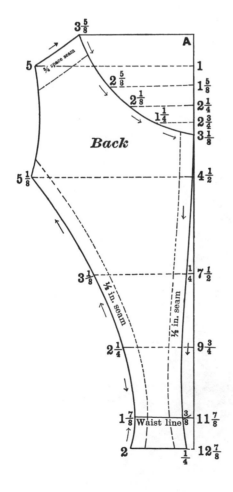

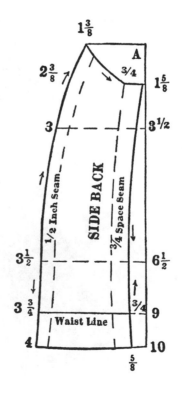

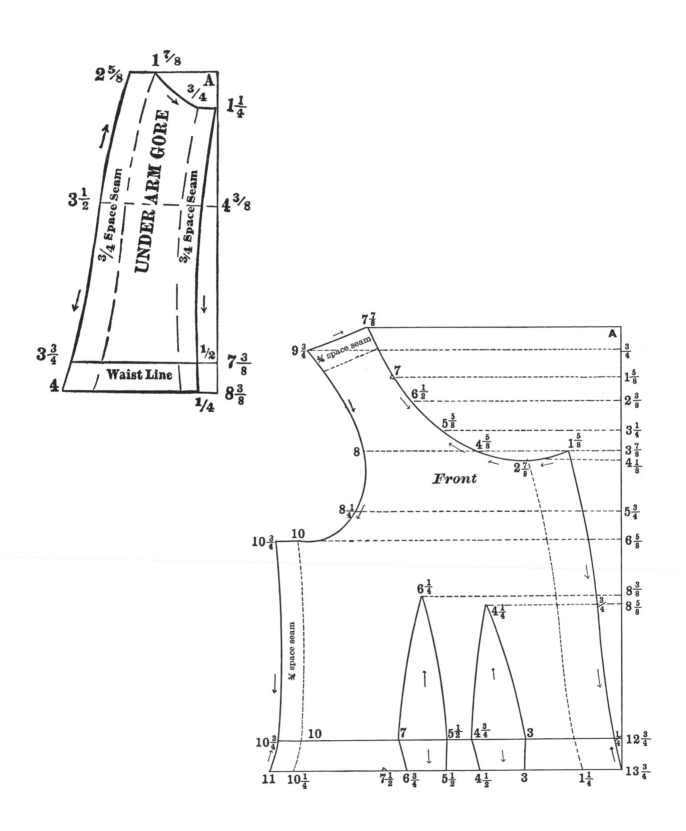

UNDER ARM GORE

2⅝ 1⅞ A ¾ 1¼

3½ ¾ Space Seam ¾ Space Seam 4⅜

3¾ ½ 7⅜

Waist Line

4 ¼ 8⅜

7⅞ A

9¾ ¾ space seam ¾

7 1⅝

6½ 2⅜

5⅝ 3¼

4⅝ 1⅝ 3⅞

8 2⅞ 4⅛

Front

8¼ 5¾

10¾ 10 6⅝

¾ space seam

6¼ 8⅜

4¼ ¾ 8⅝

10¾ 10 7 5½ 4¾ 3 ¼ 12¾

11 10¼ 7½ 6¾ 5½ 4½ 3 1¼ 13¾

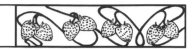

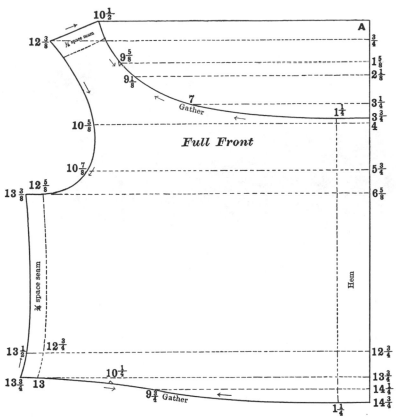

Full Front

¾ space seam

10½
12⅜
9⅝
9⅛
7 Gather
1¼

A
¾
1⅝
2⅛
3¼
3¾
¾

Full Front

10⅝
10⅞
12⅝
13⅜
5¾
6⅝

¾ space seam

Hem

13½   12¾
13¾   13
10¼
9¾ Gather
1¼

12¾
13¾
14⅛
14¾

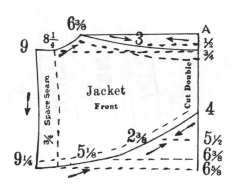

9   8¼   6⅜   3
Space Seam ¾
Jacket Front
Cut Double
9¼   5⅛   2⅜

A
½
¾
4
5½
6⅜
6⅞

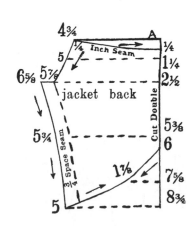

4¾   A
¼ Inch Seam   ¼
5   1¼
6⅝ 5⅞   2½
jacket back
Cut Double
5¾   5⅜
¾ Space Seam   6
1⅛   7⅝
5   8¾

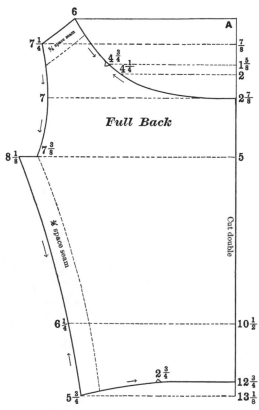

6   A
7¼ ¾ space seam   ⅞
4¾   1⅝
4¼   2
7   2⅞

Full Back

8⅛   7⅜   5
¾ space seam
Cut double

6¼   10½

5¾   2¾   12¾
13⅛

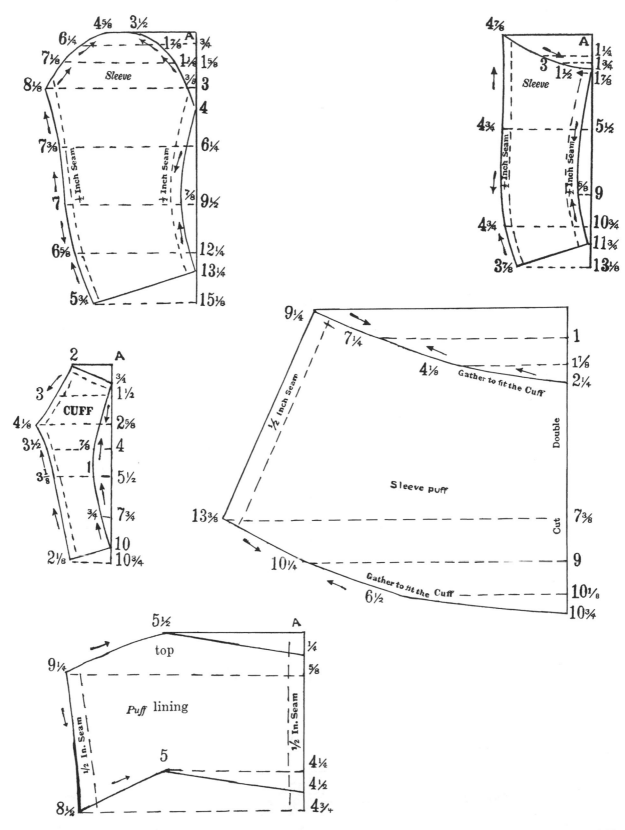

169

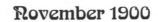

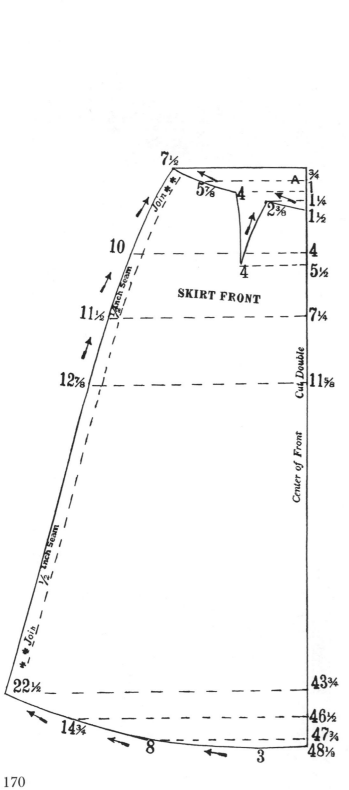

SKIRT FRONT

Center of Front

Cut Double

½ inch Seam

Join

7½
5⅞
4
2⅜
10
11½
12⅞
22½
14¾
8
3

¾
1¼
1½
4
5½
7¼
11⅝
43¾
46½
47¾
48⅛

A

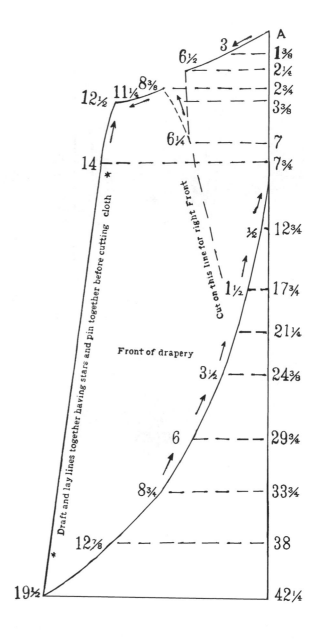

Front of drapery

Draft and lay lines together having stars and pin together before cutting cloth

Cut on this line for right Front

A
3
6½
8⅜
11¼
12½
6¼
14
½
1½
3½
6
8¾
12⅞
19½

1⅜
2⅛
2¾
3⅜
7
7¾
12¾
17¾
21¼
24⅜
29¾
33¾
38
42¼

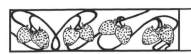

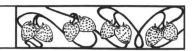

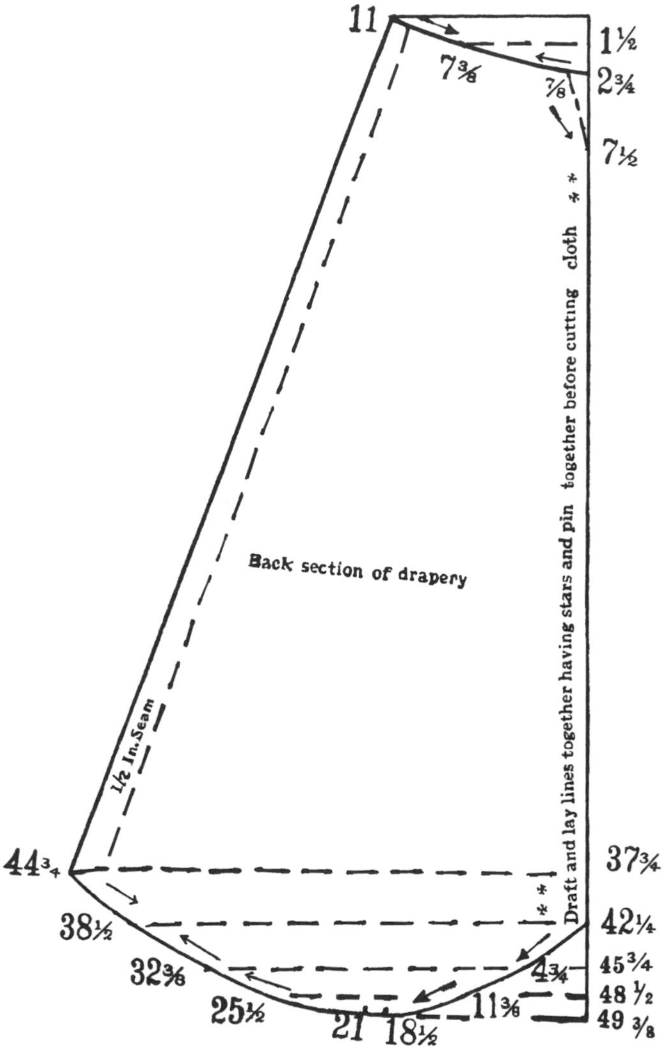
11
1½
7⅜
2¾
⅞
7½
Draft and lay lines together having stars and pin together before cutting cloth
Back section of drapery
½ In. Seam
44¾
37¾
38½
42¼
32⅜
45¾
4¾
25½
48½
21
18½
11⅜
49⅜

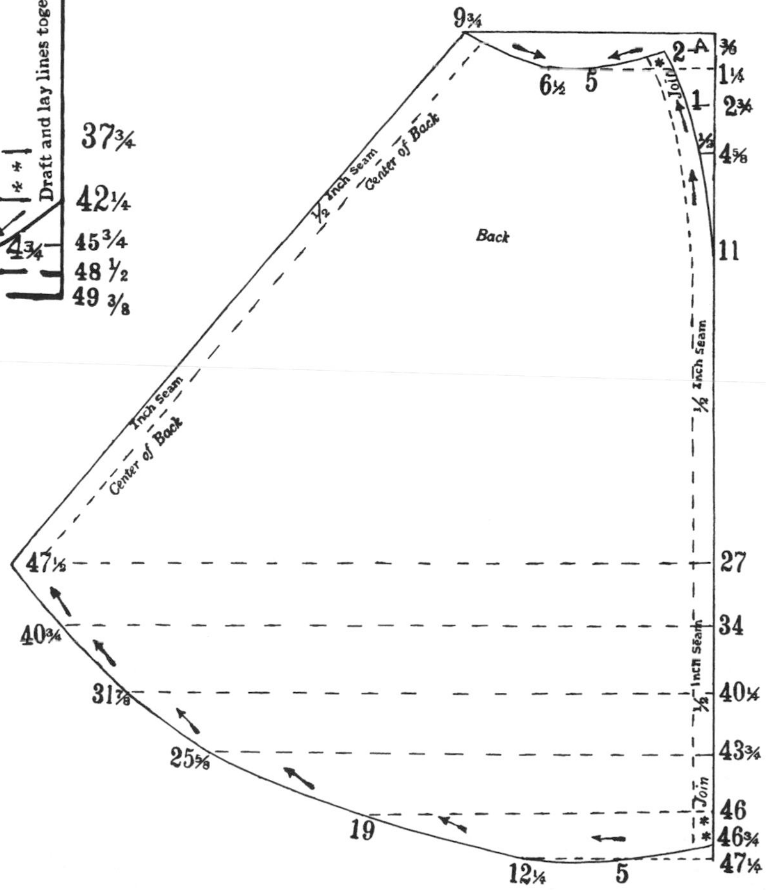
9¾
2-A
⅜
6½
5
1¼
Join
1
2¾
½
4⅝
½ Inch Seam
Center of Back
Back
11
½ Inch Seam
Inch Seam
Center of Back
47½
27
40¾
34
31⅞
½ Inch Seam
40¼
25⅝
43¾
Join
46
19
46¾
12¼
5
47¼

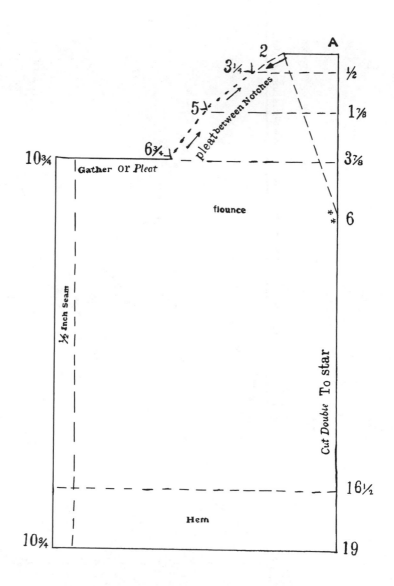

Ladies' Golf Cape

Use the scale corresponding to the bust measure to draft the entire garment, which consists of half of large cape, yoke, upper and under drapery sections, and three collar portions. Regulate the length by the tape measure.

Cut cape yoke and two drapery pieces on a lengthwise fold of the material. Join cape to yoke with 1/4-inch seam. Place the right sides of the drapery sections together and sew them in 1/4-inch seam at outer edge. Join small or upper curved side of

the small drapery section to cape around the edge of the yoke. The drapery is lined, or the heavy material may be finished at its upper edge by a narrow hem neatly stitched. Join the seams of the collar as indicated by the stars. Interline with canvas and line. Join to the neck in the same manner as you would a jacket collar.

This garment is of heavy two-faced cloth. For a lady of medium size it requires 2 yards of 42-inch material, or 1 1/2 yards of 54-inch goods.

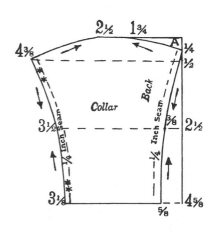

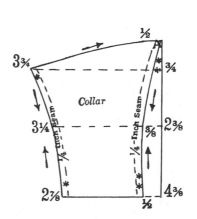

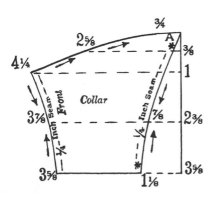

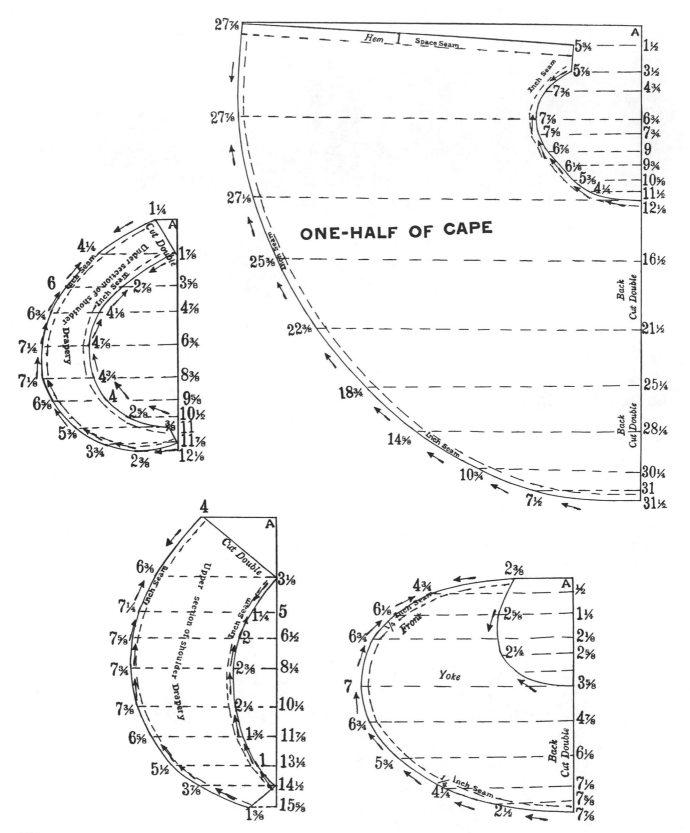

ONE-HALF OF CAPE

February 1901

Already the stores and shops are displaying all manner of sheer materials for spring and summer. Among the St. Gall swisses are some of the most beautiful patterns imaginable. On many their dots are placed to form floral or other designs, and over all some beautiful color scheme, sometimes in a floral design, often in shadings and irregular tracings, six or seven colors being seen in one pattern. There are also innumerable patterns in transparent grenadines. Some patterns in crepe de chine have large floral designs in very rich and bright colors; others are seen in oriental effects. Taffeta will continue to be a favorite material for waists, as well as entire costumes.

For heavier wear plain and fancy velveteens and velvets are used in great quantities. Some of the most fashionable people are wearing velvet for their best dresses, even for dinner and reception costumes, and a great many outdoor costumes are made from these substantial materials.

Velvet cords will continue to be much worn till near the advent of warm weather. This material is an imported corduroy, and is used for separate skirts and jackets, as well as for entire costumes; it is made in every instance severely plain. The cords run from 1/8 to 5/8 inch wide. This corduroy and some of the lighter materials will to a great extent take the place of the extremely heavy materials that have been used so extensively for short skirts. One material to be used in these walking skirts is a double-faced cloth with a worsted face and a mercerized cotton back. It comes in browns, blues, grays, and blacks for fronts, and a plain, striped, or plaid back. This mercerized back makes a lining unnecessary and therefore takes from the weight of the garment.

The great number of waists of cloth for tailor-made costumes, and even the ones for evening wear and more dressy occasions, make more of an attempt to match the skirt. Broadcloth is still a prime favorite, as are fancy tweed, zibeline, thibet, and also galway frieze. There is also a handsome mixed cloth, usually in a solid color, but has a long, white hair very fine, which gives it the effect of a two-toned cloth.

On all manner of dresses, wraps, and bonnets we see the flash of gold, tinsel, and metal. These trimmings are especially suitable for plain cloths, and all manner of plain materials. Stitched strappings are still wonderfully popular, and are no longer confined to the seams and edges of garments but are put on in all manner of fanciful designs. One way of treating fancy straps is to stitch them at either edge, slash them crosswise at short and regular intervals, and run a ribbon or fancy gilt or colored braid through these openings.

One novelty is that of lining the cloak with lace. Of course these are only for evening wear. These garments are made of the light cloths and have an interlining of satin, and the effect is very rich.

Boas will be much longer. Fichus of lace, net, chiffon, mull, etc., very much trimmed, will be worn. They are a pretty addition to an otherwise plain waist, or thrown over a tea gown or house dress.

Very new and pretty are the shirtwaist sets of bands, for trimming the collar, waistband, and front. Some have enough for strappings on the yoke. They are known as persian bands and come in all colors and all manner of floral designs. Some designs are outlined in gilt or gold trimmings, while others are of embroidery. Perforated cloths are employed in various ways over gold cloth for collars, cuffs, revers, vests, girdles, belts, panels, and even flounces and wide bands on skirts. Also boleros are made of these perforated materials.

The chatelaine bag is considered an almost absolute necessity. Some are of suede with mountings of silver, gold, or gunmetal.

Some of the most beautiful imported millinery is made entirely of autumn leaves, in all their rich and varying shades, with perhaps a touch of panne formed into a rosette in the shade that predominates, and perhaps a rose under the brim at the point where it is upturned. Tam-o-shanter crowns and double brims are very stylish. Then there are the turbans, made stylish by the use of pheasant and impeyan breasts, soft folds of velvet, or masses of any soft material. The fancy for gold and metal trimmings is expressed in many hats. White and gold is a favorite combination. Gold lace is employed over white tulle, and is used to some extent on hats for general wear, though more sparingly than on those for dressy occasions. Gold lace over velvet of any color produces a striking effect. Buckles are larger than ever before. Fur is used on all manner of hats and bonnets, in every conceivable way.

Lingerie is almost all of the unstarched variety, very soft and clinging. It is almost wholly—in some instances—of lace and soft fine embroideries. Some petticoats are plain gored styles and some have close-fitting yokes. Some have two or three flounces, the upper one very deep, and the yoke petticoats sometimes have two skirts set on one yoke. This prevents the clumsy effect that wearing many full skirts gives about the waist, and also gives the desired flare at the foot. Sometimes the waist and skirt are combined, the waist forming the corset cover. The chemise, though not strictly up-to-date, is useful for this purpose, worn over the corset. Valenciennes and point de paris are the laces most extensively used for trimming underwear.

Stockings are very gay in both color and design. A novelty, or rather a fad, is to have the monogram embroidered on the instep.

Ladies' Dinner Dress

Use the scale corresponding to the bust measure to draft the waist, which consists of back and front lining, upper back, upper front, vest front, collar, and six sleeve parts. Use the scale corresponding to the waist measure to draft the skirt. Regulate all lengths by the tape measure.

Adjust the upper back to the lining back. Take up the darts in the front lining and adjust the upper fronts. Cut on line as instructed on the diagram for the left upper front. The vest front may be cut about 1 space wider than the diagram, to ensure its edge being concealed at the left side. Tack vest to the lining at the right side and fasten it to the lining at the left side with hooks and eyes. The upper back is cut away to form a square yoke, the same as the front. Gather the puffs and sew them to the lines on the foundation sleeves as instructed on the diagram. Cut the upper sleeves away on the lines marked, in points on the upper sleeve and on the dotted lines on the short undersleeve. The edges of the sleeves and upper parts of the waist are finished with a narrow piping. Try the sleeve on before it is stitched in securely, to ascertain if it sets properly, as the sleeve is apt to twist if either seam is set too high. Finish the neck with a narrow band, over which the collar is adjusted. Make the collar in the usual way. If it is to fasten in back, cut double on the line for center of front and cut off on the line marked center of back.

Make skirt in the usual way. Lay the edges of the side gore and the back that is next to the baseline on the selvage, or a straight edge of the goods. The skirt is finished at the foot with an inner lining of canvas from 6 to 10 inches wide and a velveteen facing.

This dress is of very dark green appliquéd in black and white, with a white silk vest, collar, and sleeve puffs. Small brass buttons are tacked on the edges of the upper fronts, over which is caught a silk cord to form a facing. A white velvet belt is fastened with a brass buckle. For a lady of 34- to 36-inch bust measure, it will require 7 to 8 yards of 36-inch material, or 12 yards of silk 24 inches wide, with 2 for vest front and sleeve puffs, or 5 yards of 42-inch material.

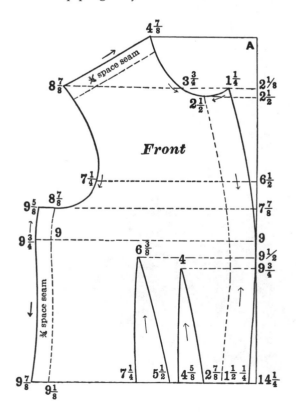

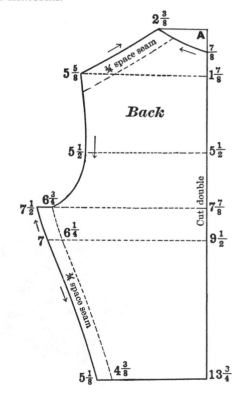

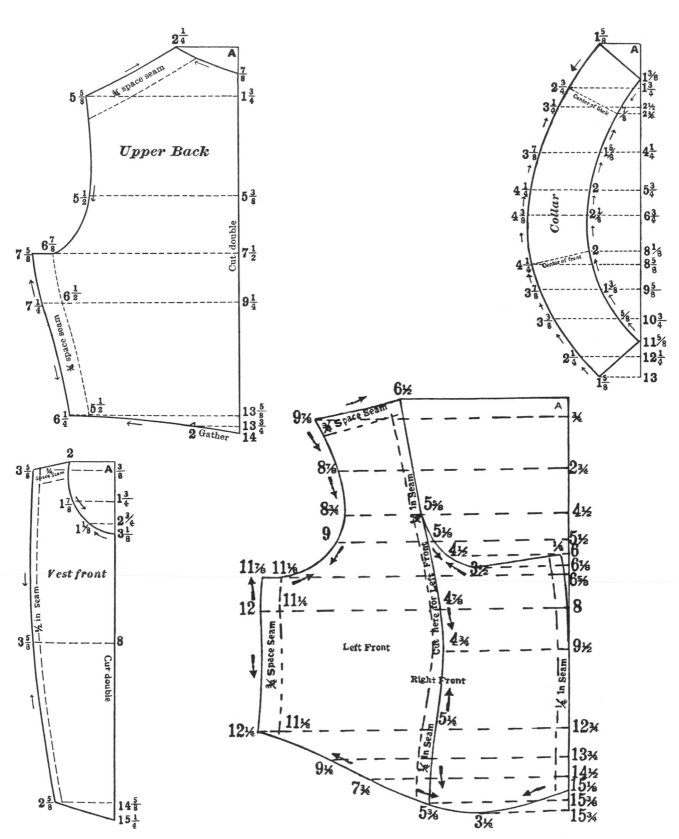

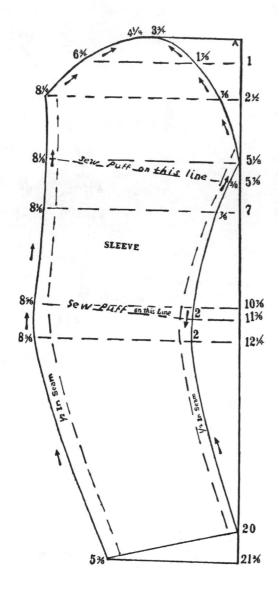

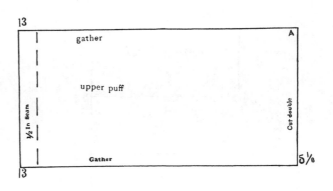

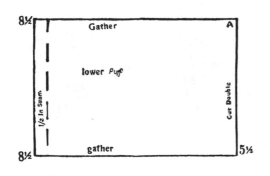

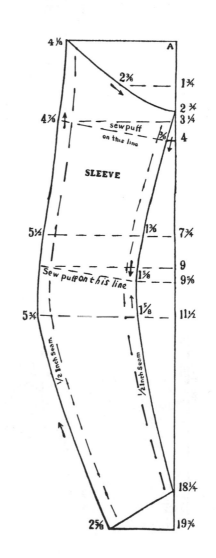

 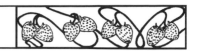
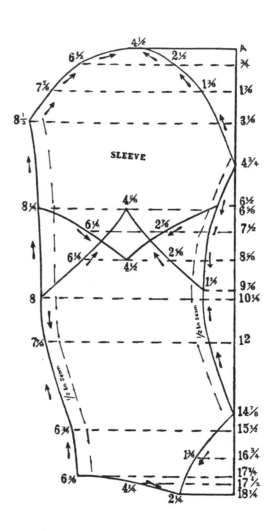

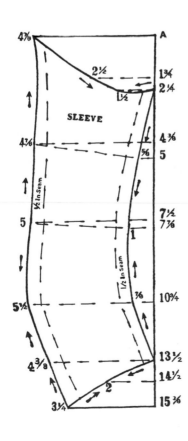

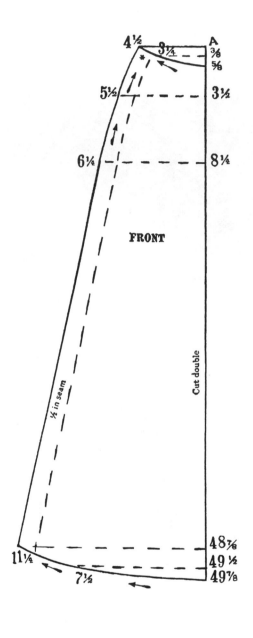

FRONT

Cut double

½ in seam

A
4½ 3¼ ⅜
5⁄8
5½ 3½
6⅛ 8½

48⅞
49 ½
11¼ 49⅞
7½

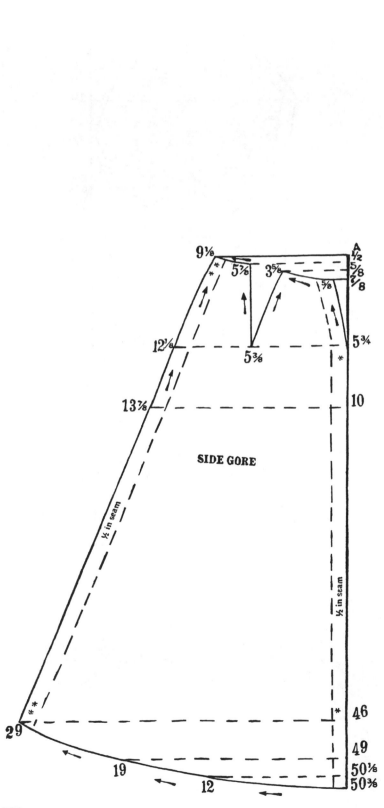

SIDE GORE

½ in seam

½ in seam

9⅛ A
5⁄8 3⅝ ½
5⅛ 5⁄8 5⁄8
5¾
12⅛ 5⅜
13⅞ 10
29 46
49
19 50⅛
12 50⅜

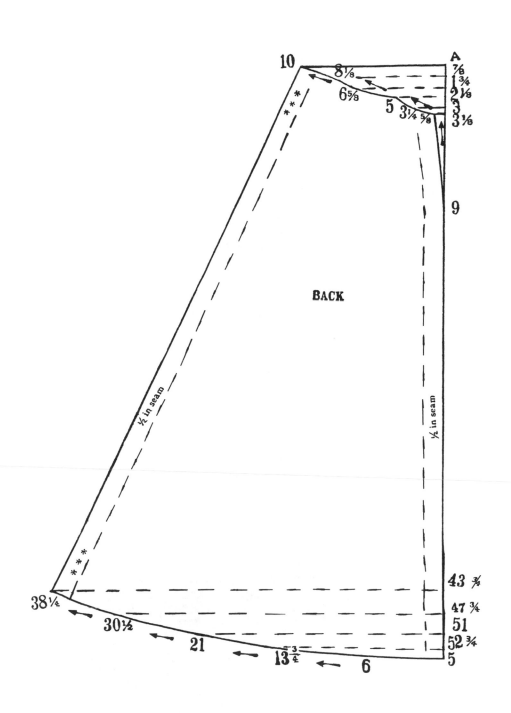

Ladies' Evening Dress

Use the scale corresponding to the bust measure to draft the waist, which consists of back and front lining, upper back and front, full front, two draped jacket parts, and sleeve. Use the scale corresponding to the waist measure to draft the skirt. Regulate all lengths by the tape measure.

Cut an upper and a lining section from the back. Pleat the full front according to the stars and notches. Gather the extra fullness at the bottom to fit the lining fronts. Lay the pleats in the draped jacket parts according to the stars and notches, and adjust them to the waist as illustrated. Cut the lining for the sleeve the full size of the pattern. The puff may be cut as full and short as desired. The

upper sleeve is then cut long enough to insure its lower edge, covering the upper edge of the puff and finished in any way the fancy may dictate.

On the skirt, the accordion-pleated ruffle is cut out in points at the top and outlined with appliqué, the two bands being crossed and carried down onto the flounce to form diamond shapes.

This handsome costume is developed in silk foulard, lace, and chiffon, with ribbon velvet, lace, and appliqué for trimming.

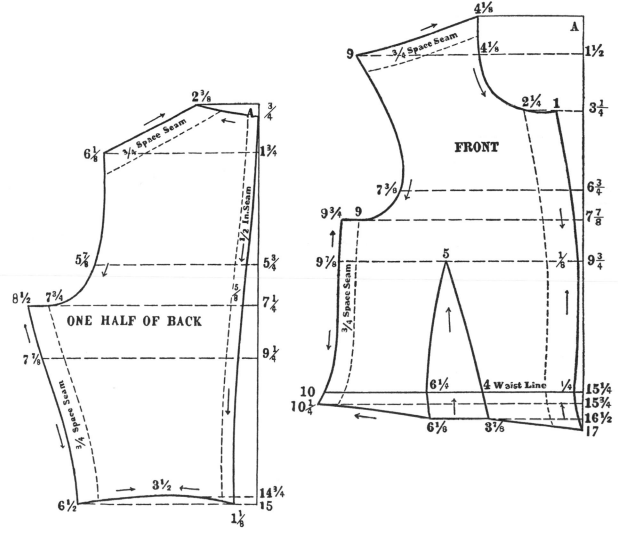

185

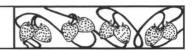

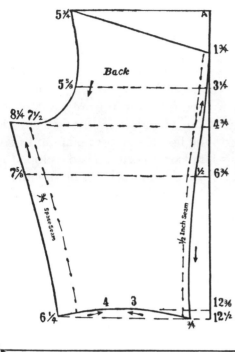

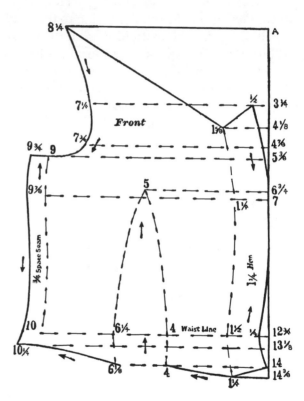

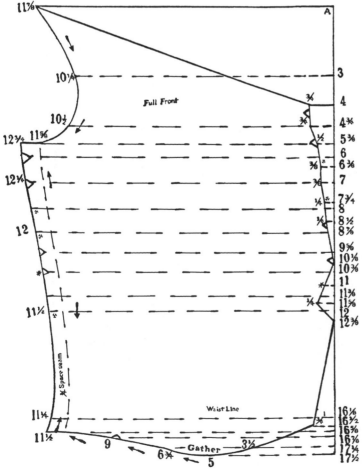

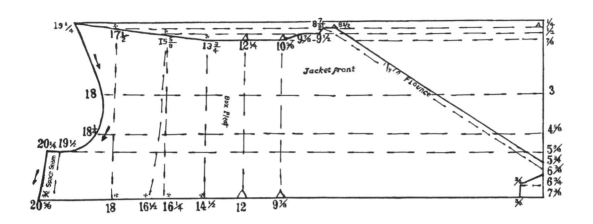

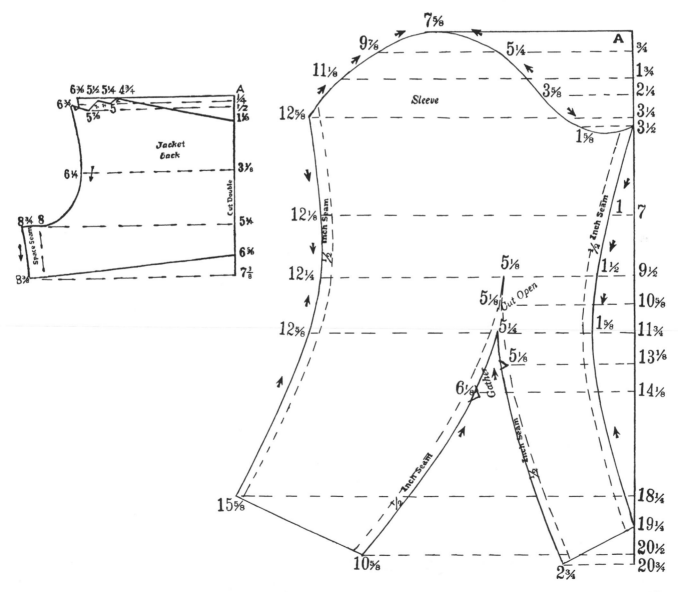

187

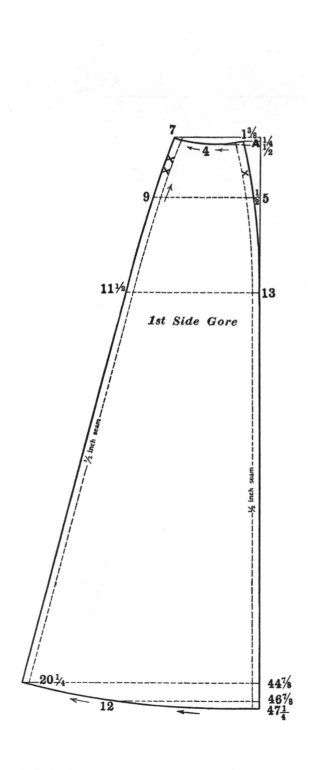

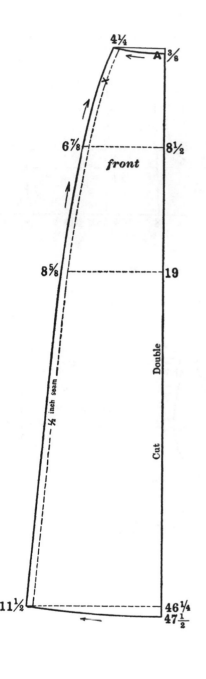

1st Side Gore

½ inch seam

½ inch seam

7   1³⁄₈
A 1¼
     1½
4
9   ½ 5
11½   13
20¼   44⁷⁄₈
12   46⁷⁄₈
       47¼

front

4¼
A ³⁄₈
6⁷⁄₈   8½
8⁵⁄₈   19
½ inch seam
Double
Cut
11½   46¼
       47½

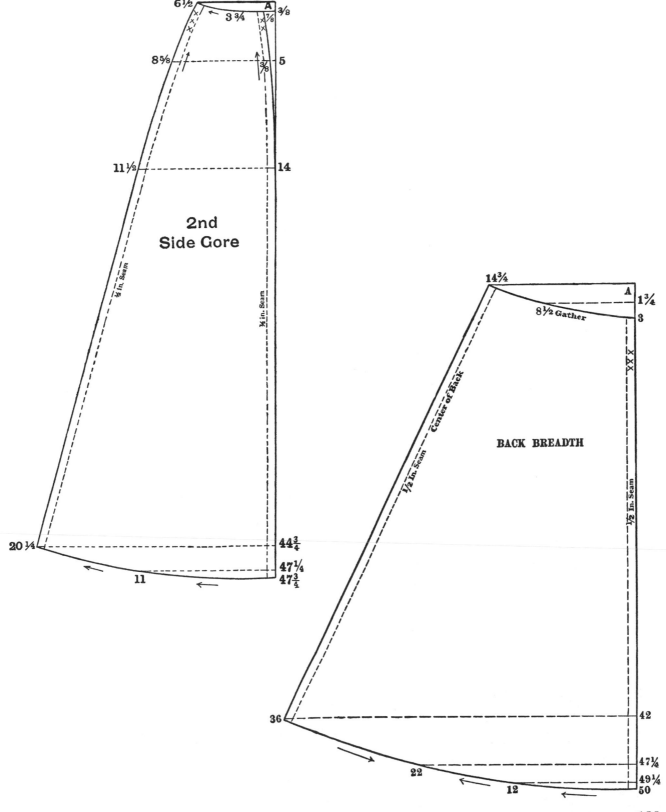

2nd
Side Gore

BACK BREADTH

Ladies' or Misses' Petticoat

Use the scale corresponding to the waist measure to draft this garment, and regulate the length by the tape measure. The top is finished with a narrow facing through which a tape is run to draw the fullness to the waist. The wide flounce is cut 1 1/3 times as wide as the skirt at the point where it is to be sewed on. The lower flounce is cut 1 1/2 times as full as the wide flounce. The petticoat also has a flounce set underneath at the foot.

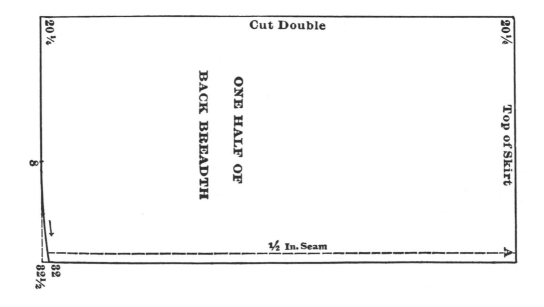

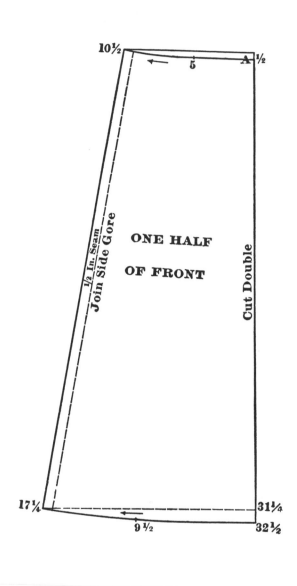

One half of Front — Cut Double. Measurements shown: 10½, A ½ (top), 5, ½ In. Seam, Join Side Gore, 17¼, 9½, 31¼, 32½.

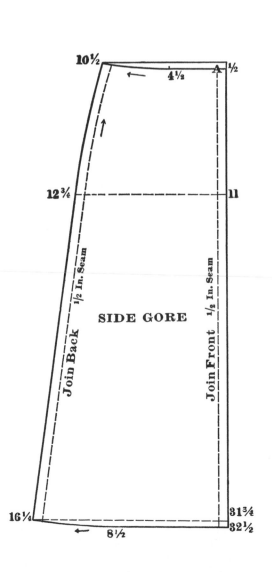

Side Gore. Measurements shown: 10½, 4½, A ½ (top), 12¾, 11, Join Back ½ In. Seam, Join Front ½ In. Seam, 16¼, 8½, 31¾, 32½.

191

Ladies' or Misses' Corset Cover

Use the scale corresponding to the bust measure to draft the waist, which consists of back, side back, underarm, and front. Regulate the length by the tape measure. The garment may be cut as long as desired. Join all the different parts in the usual way. Trim the upper part as illustrated, and cut the material away underneath.

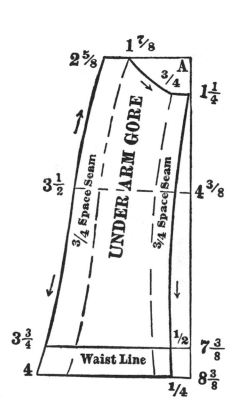

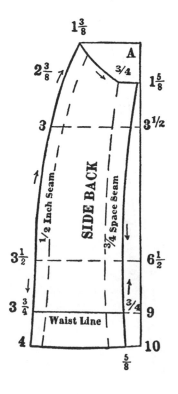

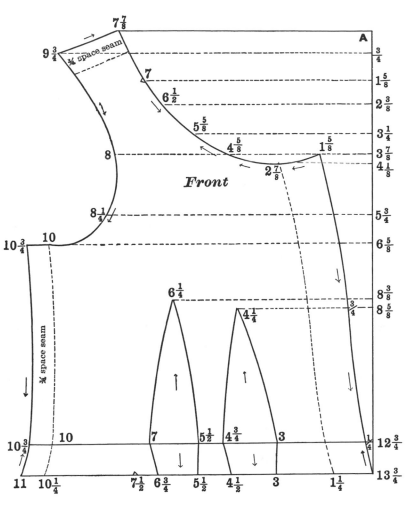

Front

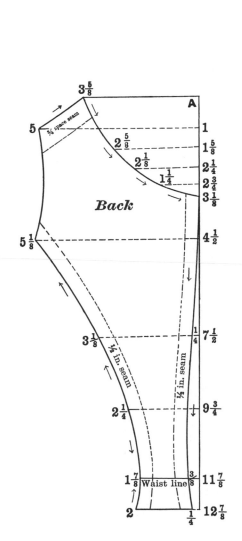

Back

Ladies' or Misses' Nightgown

Use the scale corresponding to the bust measure to draft the entire garment, which consists of back, shirring for the front, yoke, and one sleeve part. Regulate the length by the tape measure. To make the V-shaped yoke, cut on the dotted line from side of neck to center of front. Join the back and front in the usual way. Gather the sleeve at the top to fit the armseye. Gather it at the bottom to fit the hand.

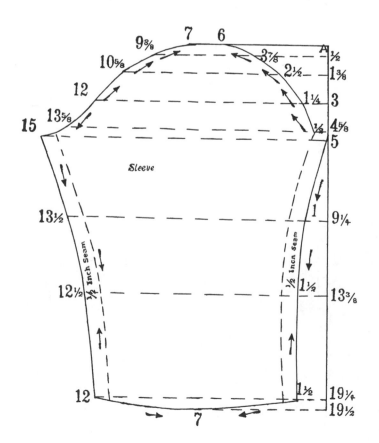

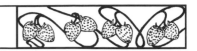

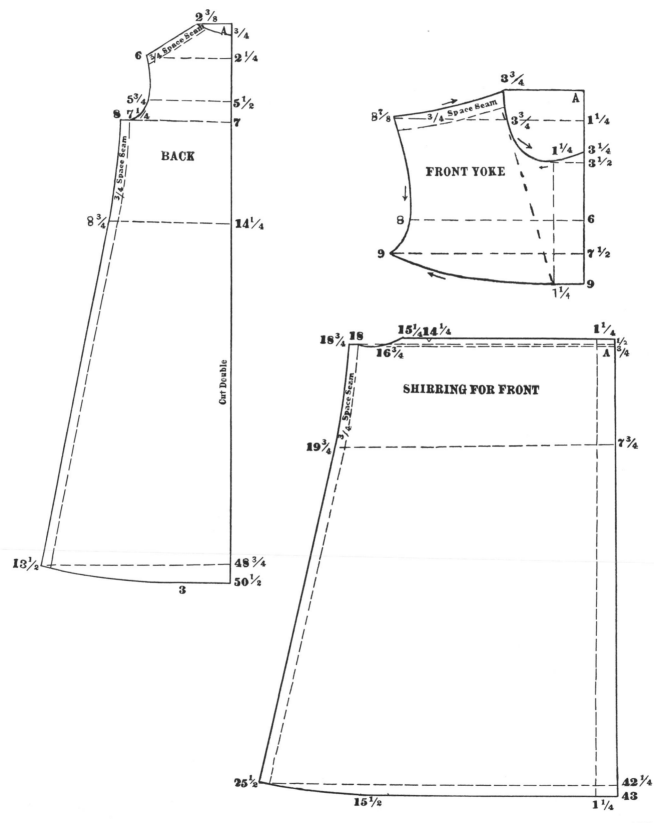

BACK

FRONT YOKE

SHIRRING FOR FRONT

Ladies' Chemise

Use the scale corresponding to the bust measure to draft the entire garment, and regulate the length by the tape measure. Gather the back and sew to the small back yoke. Gather the front to fit the front yoke, and trim in any way the fancy may dictate.

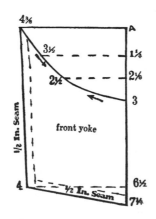

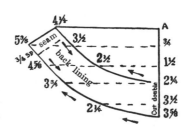

 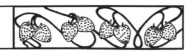

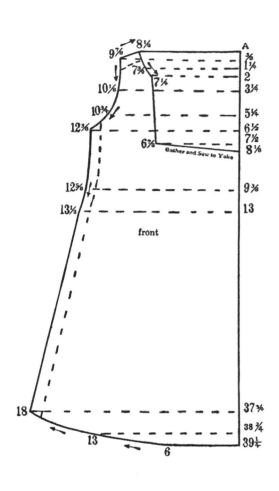

front

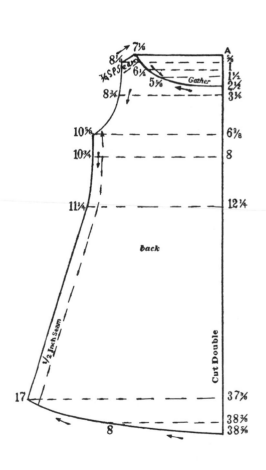

back

197

Ladies' Drawers

Use the scale corresponding to the waist measure to draft this one-piece garment. Regulate the length by the tape measure. Hem the front and back. Make band to fit the waist; cut two thicknesses, to make it strong. Gather front and back at the top and sew to band. Trim the bottom to suit.

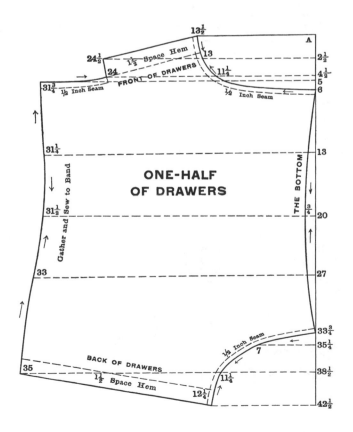

August 1901

As the traveling season is now at its height it is a question as to what kind of material to select for a traveling costume. The first essential is one strong enough to endure the wear and tear of travel, and at the same time not so heavy as to be burdensome. Homespuns, mixed woolens, tweeds, friezes, serges, mohairs, and doublestuffs are therefore principally made up for traveling costumes. Then as to color, it is of course important to select that which will not too plainly show dust and travel stains. All shades of brown seem to be very much in favor, as also are blues, grays, and fawn. Large plaid patterns have given place to smaller checks. As to length, the usual walking toilet is a good guide.

Flat braids are much in favor; also bias bands of silk, satin, or any desirable material, contrasting with the goods of which the garment is made. These bands may be of any width desired, and put on according to the artistic taste of the designer. If made of the same material as the dress, they may be edged with a narrow cord of some contrasting shade.

Flounces are still in favor and the side-pleated flounce is shown on many skirts. This gives the desired flare at the foot. Stiffening is again being used in flared skirts, which gives them a degree of firmness instead of the soft, clinging effect of the past season. Separate skirts of linen, either white or colored, are to some extent taking the place of those of piqué or duck.

A very pretty and stylish costume for the seaside is made of white serge or flannel. It may be trimmed with gold braid, or narrow bands of velvet ribbon of some bright shade.

Some of the most stylish summer costumes for dressy affairs are made of satin foulard. This is much more exquisite than ordinary foulard, owing to its luster and its almost unlimited variety in coloring and design. Green is the favorite background, although it may be obtained in any of the prevailing shades. The most desirable trimming for this material is antique lace, either white or ecru.

Many dressy summer costumes are of etamine, made over silk or a fine quality of percaline. Cretonne appliqué is a favorite decoration. Some jackets show vests and cuffs of embroidery. Some are decorated with stitching in elaborate designs, while others are trimmed with buttons.

Embroidered swiss is among the favorite fabrics for summer wear. Many simpler gowns are made of the numerous pretty and inexpensive wash materials. Narrow ribbon, shirred in the center, put on in ruffles, or sewed on plain, is a favorite trimming. Lace and insertion are also used abundantly, including embroidered applications of every color and style.

Blouses as usual are in great demand. They are made of silk batiste, washing silk, or linen, and look well with a cravat and a high elastic belt. Shirtwaists are made with so much decoration that the name hardly seems fitting. Chambray, lawn, percale, and duck are among the favorite materials.

Belts are in many different styles and materials, from the narrowest band of ribbon or beaded material to the wide pointed girdle, which is laced in front with a ribbon or silk cord. This girdle gives a dressy effect to an otherwise plain waist. It may also be worn with an eton or bolero with a simple vest. The point in back may be made deep enough to meet or extend a little above the lower edge of the jacket. Another novelty is the pointed leather belt having the dip portion separate from the rest, and attached by a buckle at each side.

Sleeves are still elaborately trimmed. Puffs are used a great deal, and are usually in some material contrasting in color and texture with the foundation goods.

The coat or the half-loose jacket may be worn either open or closed; the advantage being that the merest corset is sufficient. Jacket costumes of brown, gray, or black brilliantine with decoration of stitched silk bands are popular for general wear. So, too, are tailor-made costumes of basket-weave scotch cheviot with silk braid trimmings.

Sunshades are shown in polka-dot silk, and other fancy and popular shades. White and other delicate shades of silk gloves are worn.

In fall, velveteens and dress cords will take the place of cloth to a great extent. Black velveteen will be used for wraps.

The shirtwaist hat is quite popular, but the short-backed sailor still holds its own. For a large hat the gainsborough is a favorite. Plumes, wings, and other feather trimmings are used much more extensively than flowers. Black and white predominates in many of the most artistic designs. Narrow velvet ribbon is used in abundance.

Ladies' Princess Gown

Use the scale corresponding to the bust measure to draft the waist and jacket. The waist consists of yoke lining, full waist, collar, and full sleeve. The jacket consists of a main portion and two sleeve portions. Use the scale corresponding to the waist measure to draft the skirt front and back. Regulate all lengths by the tape measure.

Sew up the shoulder seams of the yoke. Gather the full waist to fit the neck and armseye. Baste to the yoke at neck and armseye and shirr as many times as desired. The waist should be gathered at the waistline and stitched to a belt the size of the waist. The sleeves are gathered to fit a band just large enough to slip over the hand. Gather the full-

ness at the top to fit the armseye. The seam of the jacket and lining are sewed separately; the jacket has an interlining of scrim. The sleeve and sleeve lining are also sewed separately.

The foundation skirt is cut full length. It is interlined at the foot with canvas, about 6 inches deep, and has a tucked or accordion flounce 18 inches deep. The upper skirt is cut the same as the foundation to the lines forming points.

Silk, velvet, liberty satin, panne cloth, crash linen, or silk gingham may be used for this design.

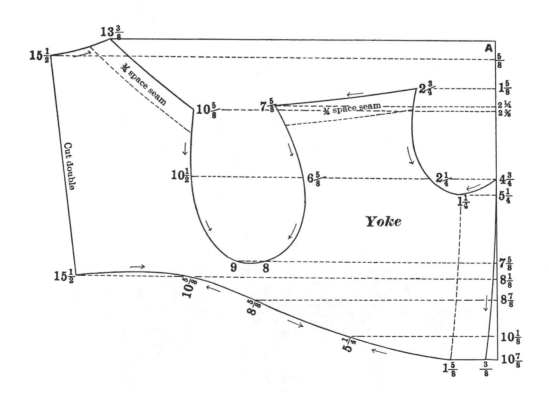

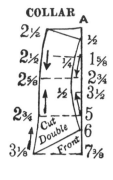

COLLAR A

2½	½
2½	1⅝
2⅝	2¾
2¾	3½
	5
	6
3⅛	7⅜

Cut Double — *Front*

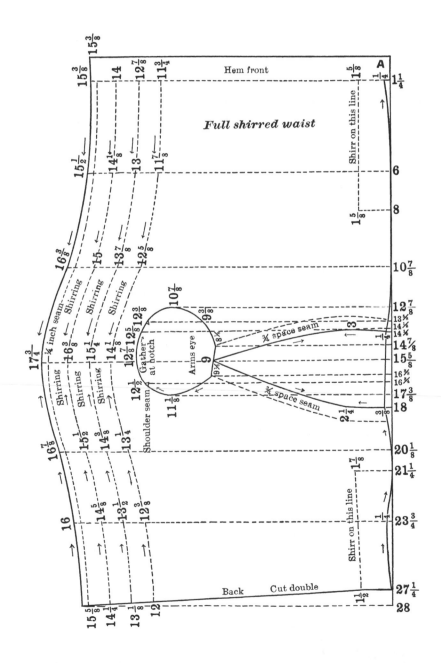

Full shirred waist

Hem front

Shirr on this line

Arms eye

Gather at hotch

Shoulder seam

¾ space seam

¼ inch seam

Shirring

Back   Cut double

Shirr on this line

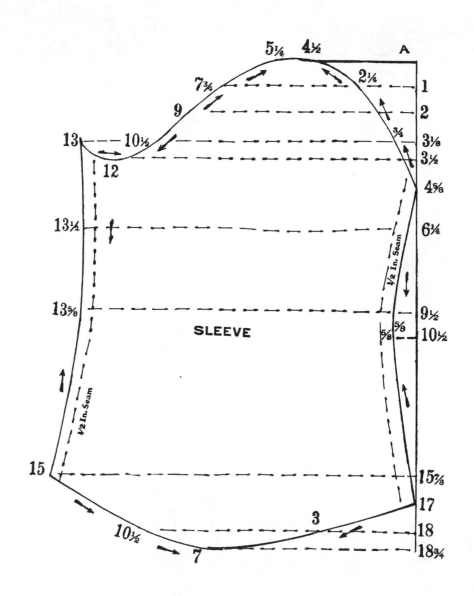

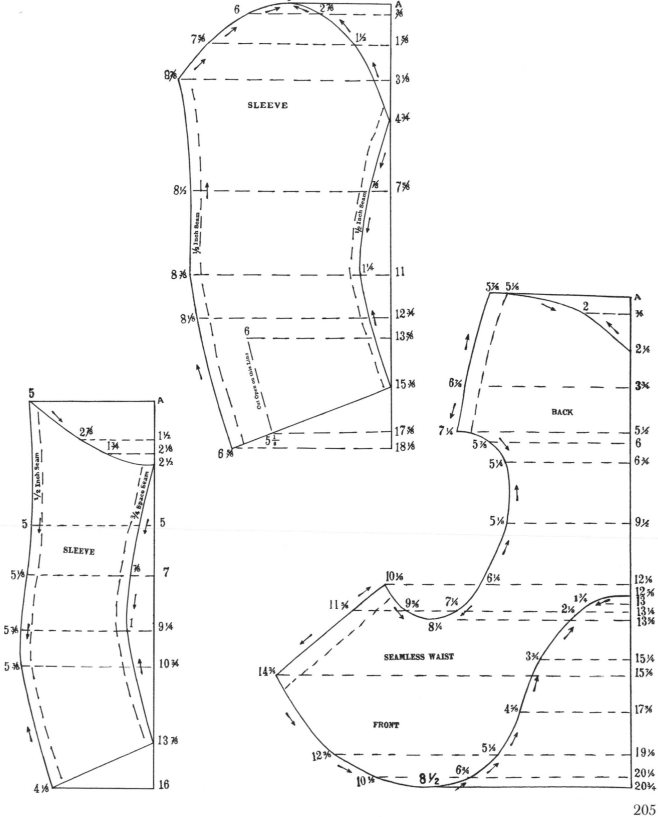

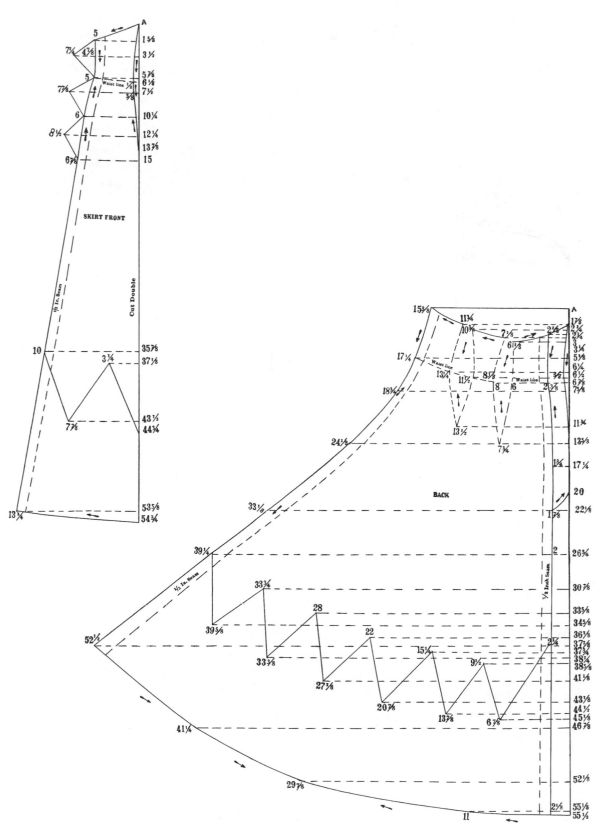

Ladies' Calling Costume

Use the scale corresponding to the bust measure to draft the waist, which consists of the foundation back, side back, and front; upper back and front; two collars; sleeve; vest; and vest front. Use the scale corresponding to the waist measure to draft the skirt. Regulate all lengths by the tape measure.

Join the back and side back linings and adjust the upper back. Take up darts in front lining. Fasten center of front with hooks and eyes. Adjust the upper fronts. Close separately with hooks and eyes. Join shoulder seams separately. Place center of vest on edge of right front. Sew right side of collar to vest. Fasten left side with hooks and eyes. The small collar is finished and sewn on with the large one. The vest front is lined and finished at the neck with the collar. The sleeves are gathered at the hand to fit the cuff. Gather the fullness at the top to fit the armseye.

Join the different skirt gores according to the Xs. Interline the gores at the foot with canvas, or omit the canvas and use featherbone.

This dress is made of pearl gray cashmere, with vests and small collar of white silk covered with lace. Large collar, skirt, and sleeves are trimmed with black ribbon velvet and pearl buttons.

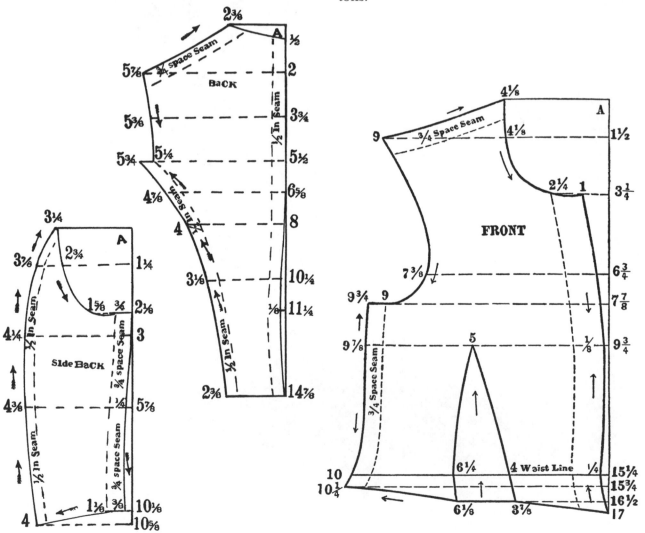

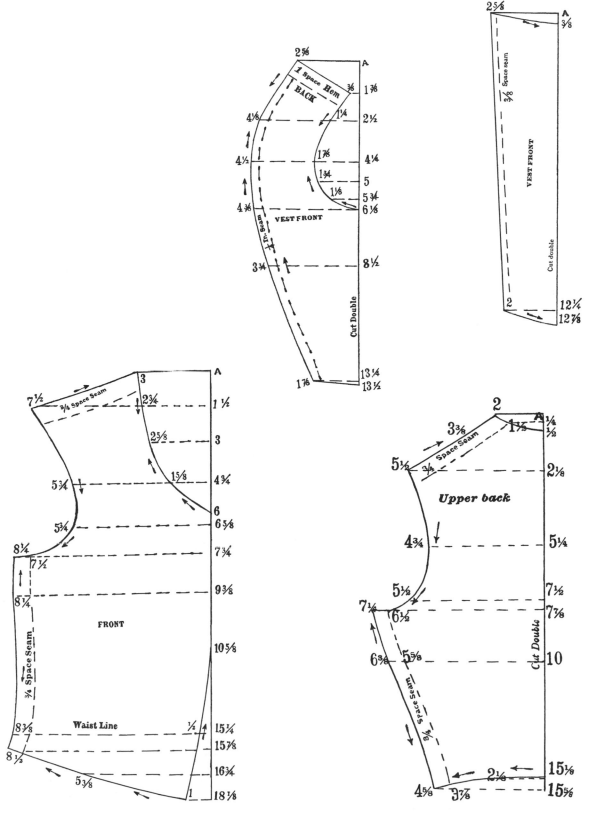

209

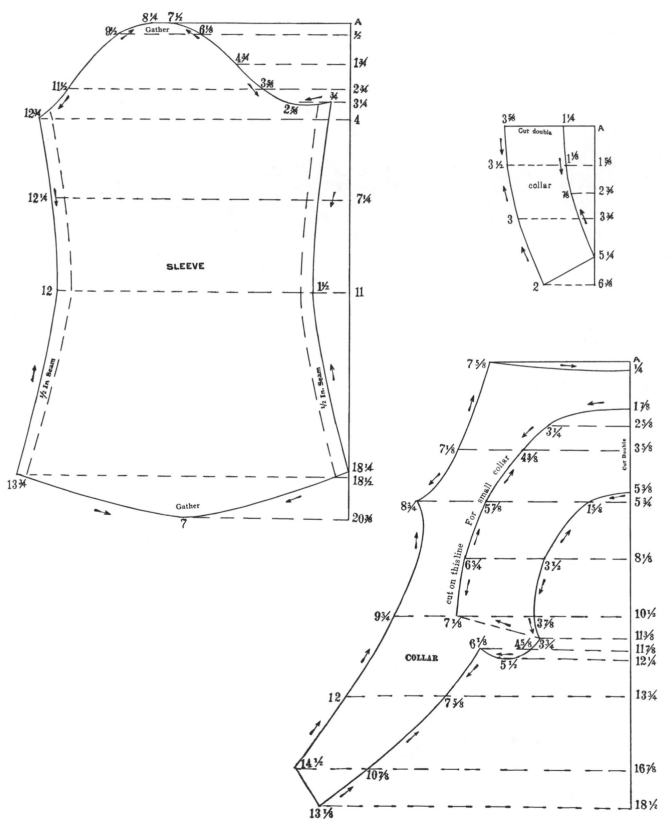

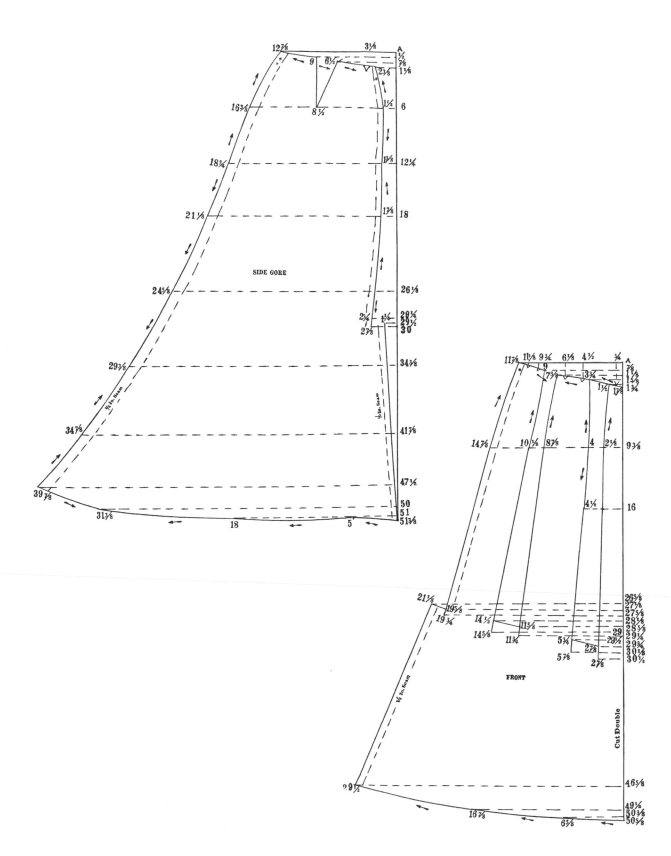

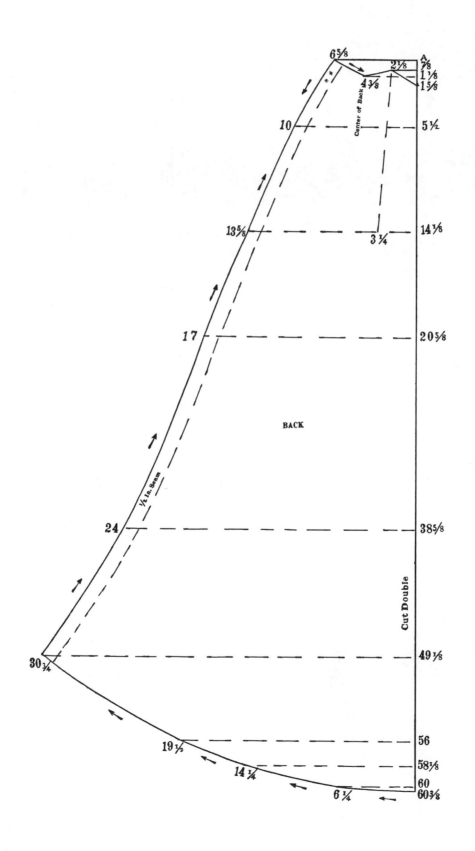

 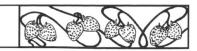

Ladies' Toilet

Use the scale corresponding to the bust measure to draft the waist, which consists of the lining back, side back, underarm gore, and front; upper back and front; full front; two collar portions; and sleeve. Use the scale corresponding to the waist measure to draft the skirt. Regulate all lengths by the tape measure.

Join the back and side back linings and adjust the upper back. Take up darts in front lining. Place the upper fronts on the lining fronts and join the underarm seams together. Join shoulder seams separately. The full vest may be gathered or tucked. It is tacked to the lining at the right side and fastened to the left lining with hooks and eyes. Finish the neck of the dress with a narrow band. Make collar and tack over this band. Finish the large collar and sew to the upper back and upper fronts. Gather the sleeve to fit a band just large enough to slip over the hand. Gather the extra fullness at the top to fit the armseye. Join the different skirt gores according to the Xs.

This dress may be made of taffeta, foulard, panne, louisine, lansdowne, lawn, chambray, or silk gingham. Lace, insertion, braid, gimp, or ribbon would be suitable for trimming.

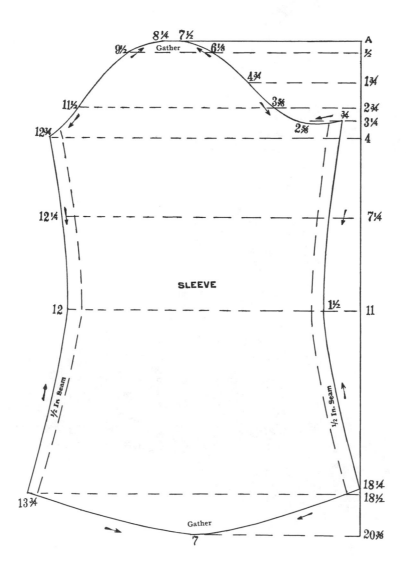

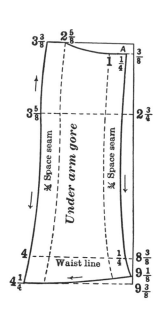

Under arm gore

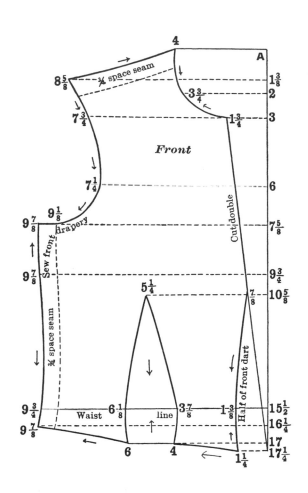

Front

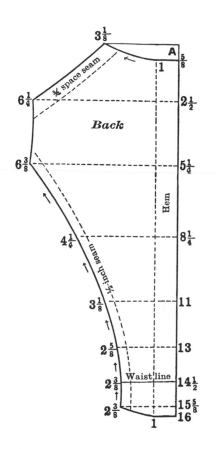

Back

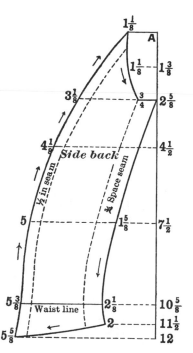

Side back

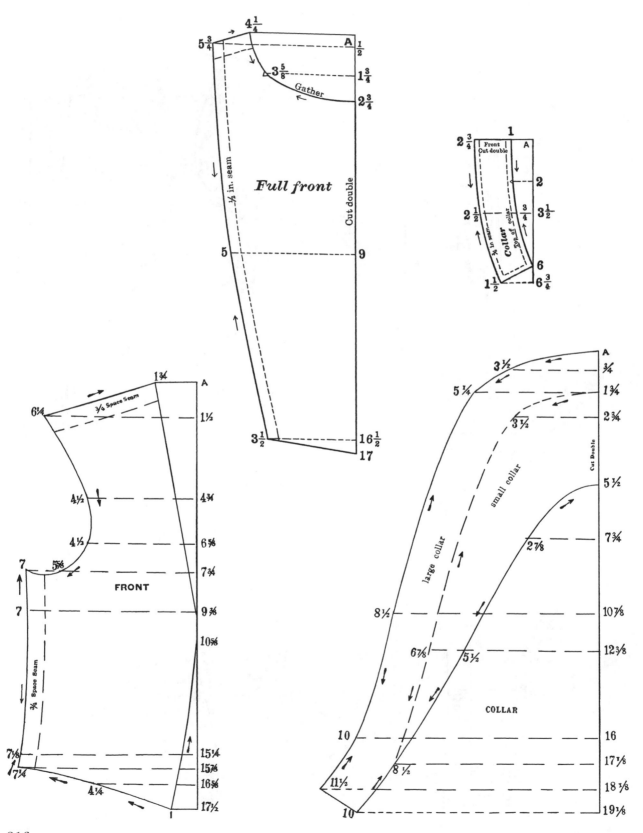

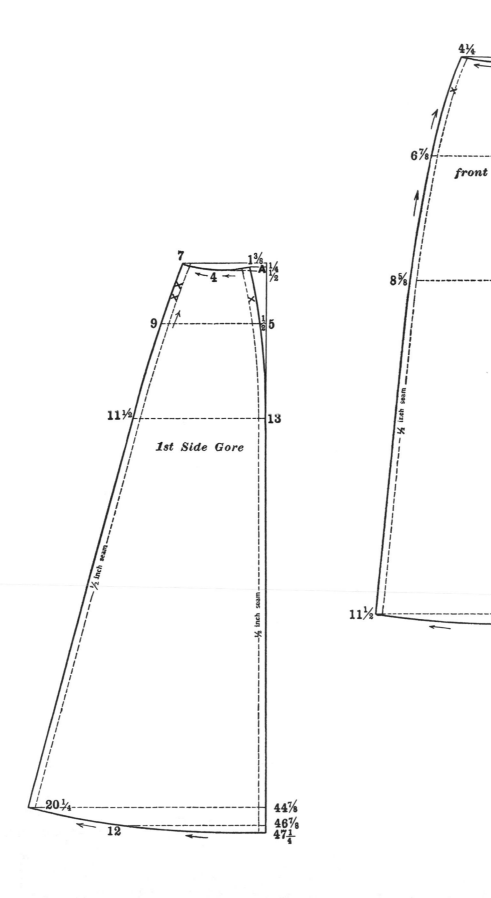

1st Side Gore

front

217

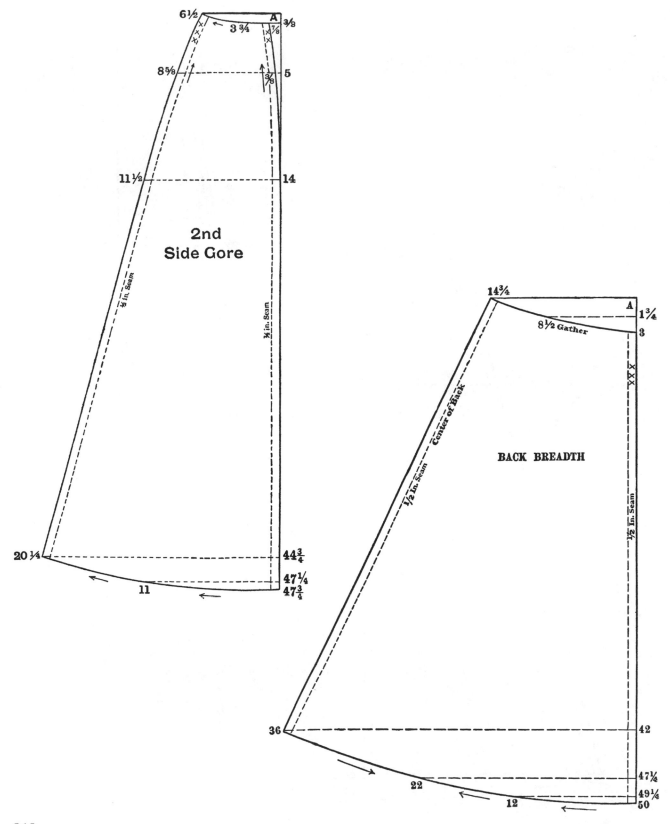

2nd
Side Gore

BACK BREADTH

Ladies' Summer Dress

Use the scale corresponding to the bust measure to draft the waist, which consists of back, front, upper back, upper front, full back and front, collar, and sleeve. Use the scale corresponding to the waist measure to draft the skirt. Regulate all lengths by the tape measure.

The yoke is cut by the back and front lining down far enough to finish with the upper back and front. Close the underarm seams of the upper back and fronts. Gather and adjust the full back and fronts upon the upper back and fronts, placing them on the fitted lining. Close the lining fronts with hooks and eyes. Finish neck with a narrow band. Make collar and tack over this band. Tuck goods for sleeves before cutting out, except the bottom of sleeve which is tucked to fit the hand.

The skirt may be tucked or gathered to fit the waist measure. The flounce may be straight or circular.

Amount of foulard required for a lady of medium size, 15 yards 27 inches wide.

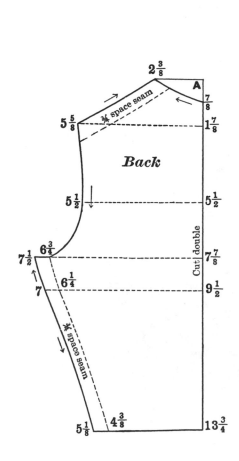

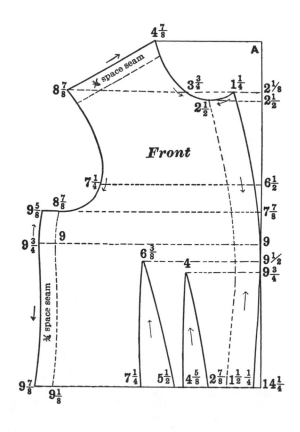

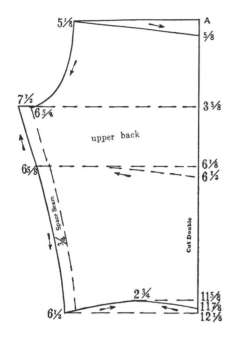

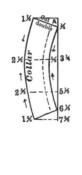

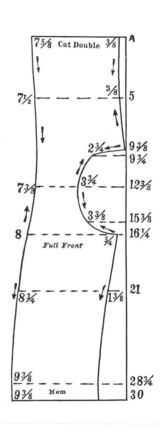

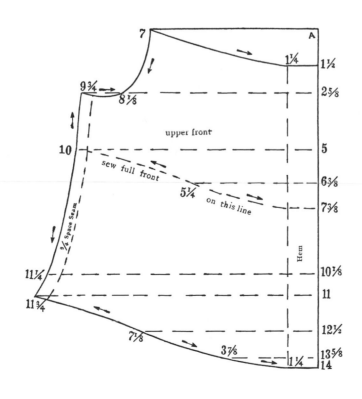

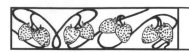

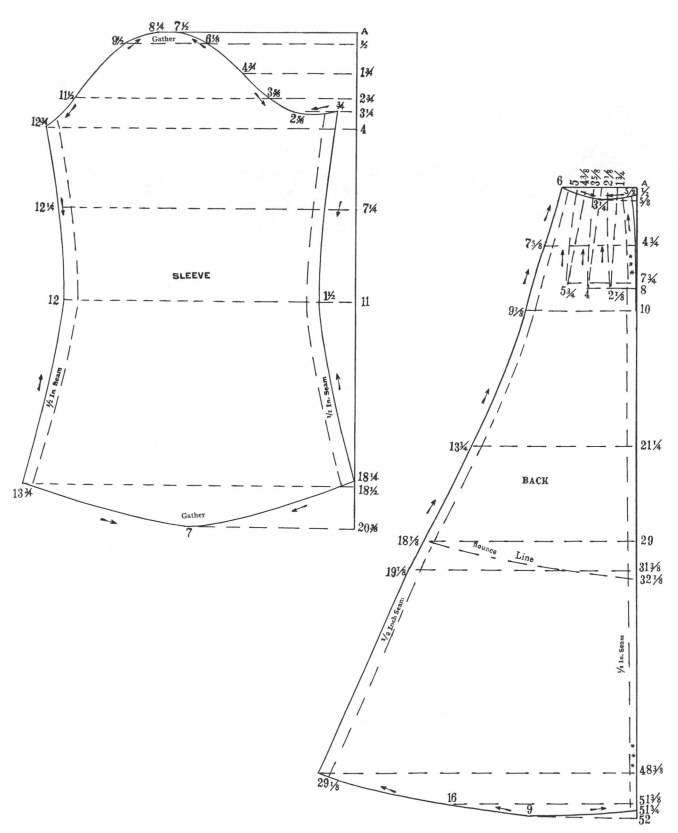

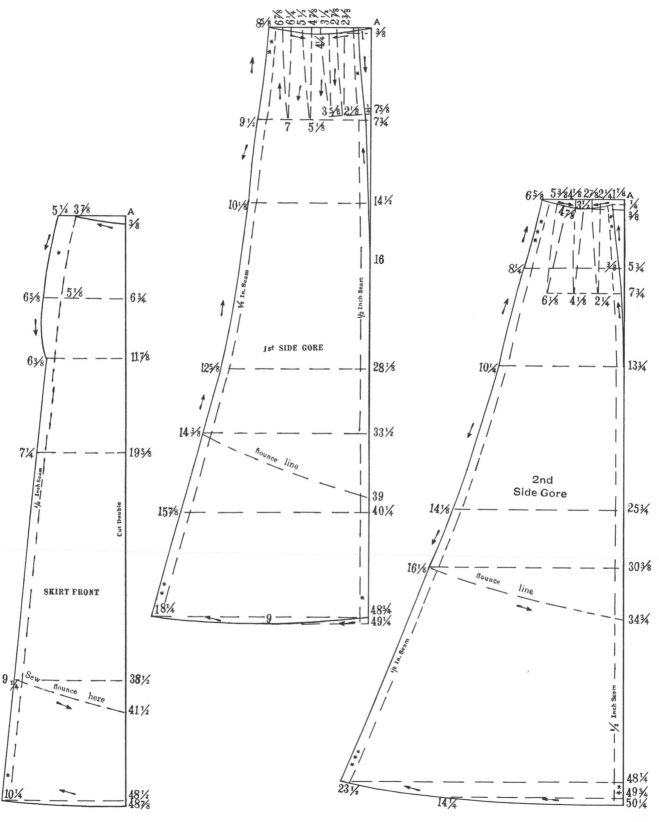

SKIRT FRONT

1st SIDE GORE

2nd Side Gore

flounce line

Sew flounce here

Ladies' Jacket

Use the scale corresponding to the bust measure to draft the jacket and vest. The jacket consists of back, side back, underarm, front, collar, sleeve, and cuff. The vest consists of back and front. Regulate all lengths by the tape measure.

The vest is faced all around the edges and armseye. It closes with buttons and buttonholes.

The jacket is fitted by the center back, side back, underarm, and shoulder seams; also bust darts. Interline the fronts with linen canvas to within

2 1/2 inches of the underarm seam. If the goods are thin and likely to pull out of shape, interline throughout. Make collar in the usual way. The sleeves are finished at the wrist by shaped cuffs, which may be narrower if so desired.

The vest is cut from brocade material. For the jacket, cheviot, panne cloth, drap d'ete, henrietta, duck, piqué, or linen may be used.

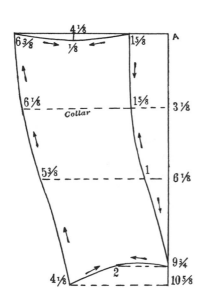

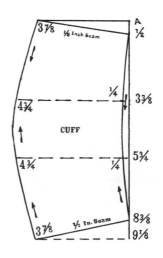

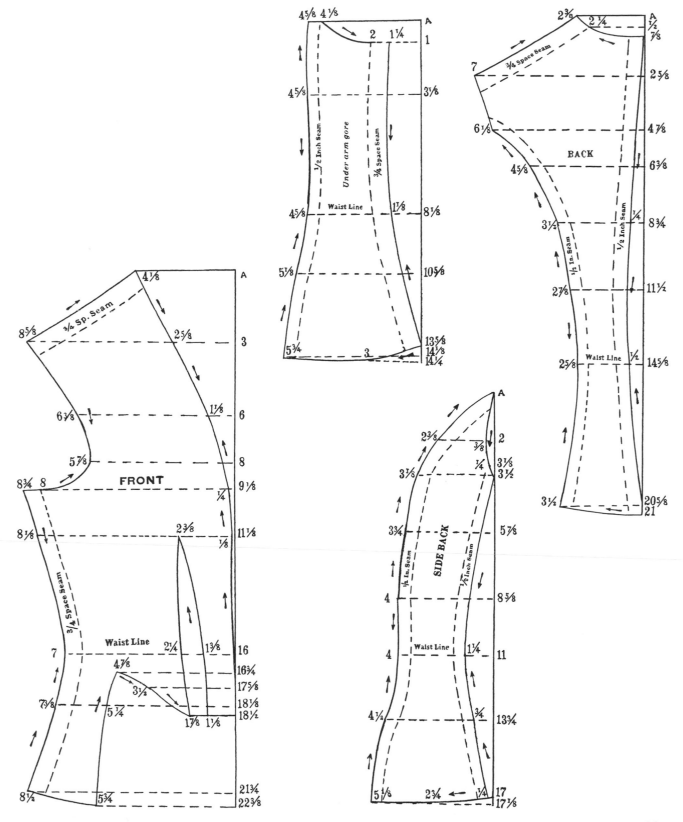

225

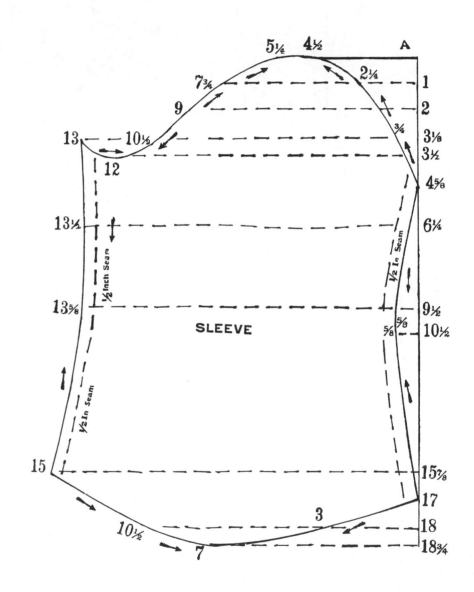

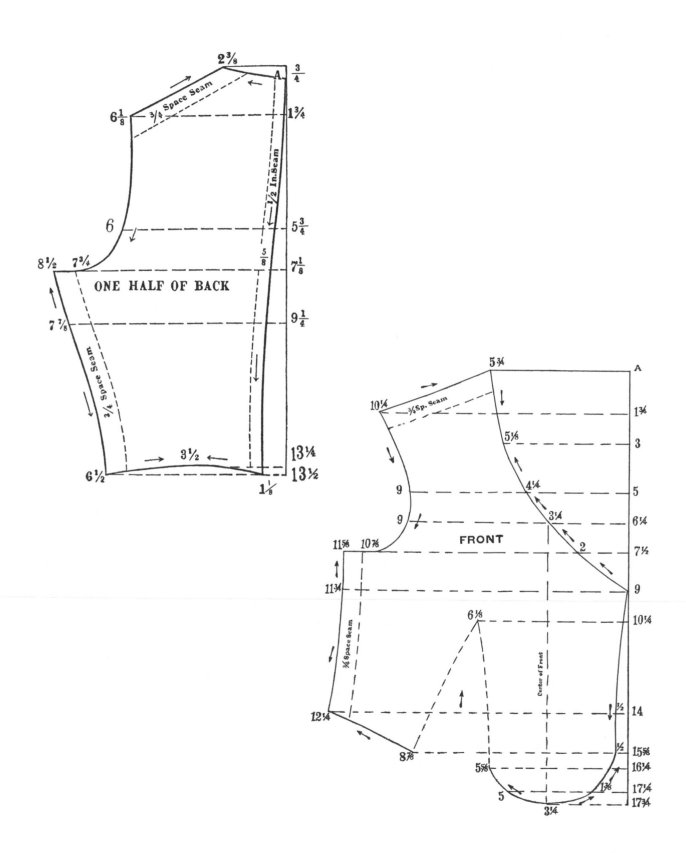

November 1901

Skirts to be stylish must fit closely around the hips with a graceful flare at the feet, and finish with a sweep. The flare may be attained in various ways. A pleated skirt with the pleats running lengthwise is very soft and pretty for slender forms. Like the tucked skirt, it fits neatly around the waist and hip, the fullness from the pleats making the desired sweep at the bottom. Next comes the flounced skirt with as many or as few flounces as you desire. They may be narrow and wide and may be all around alike, or graduate toward the back of the skirt. In softer materials ruffles may take the place of a fitted flounce. In a tailor-made garment the skirt may be simply flared, and stitching and trimming arranged to give the appearance of a flounce. Lined skirts are more in favor again as the unlined ones do not retain their shape so well.

Waists are simple but elegant, the more elaborate ones being mostly for evening wear. The bolero is in great evidence. Some of them consist almost entirely of trimmings, laces, and tucks. Sleeves form an important part of the plainer bolero, and it is used as an outside garment for cooler days.

Laces, painted flowers, velvet roses, and spangled effects are much in vogue. Persian and oriental trimmings will continue in good standing. Velvet and velvet ribbon will be extensively used. Braids are in great demand, the narrow being most popular, while the broader ones are so loosely woven that they can be used quite advantageously in designing. Buttons of every size, color, and description are arranged on waists in every conceivable shape and form. Cut-out cloth will be used on both silk and velvet.

The great beauty of the shirtwaist is its neat and pretty effect attained without a lining. Tucks are used very much, varying from very small ones up to 1 inch. The larger ones have several rows of stitching to each tuck. Broad-shoulder effects are aimed at. Sailor collars are quite popular.

The conventional waist dip is still in force, but not to such extremes. The lady who extends the front of her waist more than 2 inches below the waistline is bordering on the passé.

Fancy stocks and neckwear grow more elaborate and are considered the "swagger" thing with flannel and silk waists. The barb tie is much worn. It may be tied in a small bow or left with long ends. Lace collars are not on the wane.

As to colors, black still leads, and black and white are in great evidence. Green and brown are smart; the latter being seen in all shades from fawn, copper, castor, and beaver on down. Wedgwood blue is much seen among fall fabrics. Blue serge with no trimming but strappings of blue makes a very stylish costume. Red and brown is in force among tailors. White will be carried into the winter, especially for evening and house gowns.

The new material for street wear is corduroy or corded velvet. After the velvet come plain cloths, serges, twills, whipcords, venetians, and canvas weaves. Many combination goods are seen—soft, rough, hairy goods made up with plain materials.

Outside garments are divided into three lengths—the short coat coming a little below the waist, the three-quarter length extending halfway down the skirt, and the full-length coat. Most short coats are double-breasted or have box effects. Some are severely plain; others are trimmed with stitching or velvet. All coats fasten with handsome buttons. Small fur neckpieces will be the correct thing.

The prevailing style of hats will be the kind that shades the eye, principally in soft draped effects. English walking hats are very popular. The gainsborough still survives, also the low flat effects so popular during the summer season. Tan and

 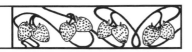
brown will be modish colors, especially for early winter wear. As to trimmings, feathers will be used extensively, while the plume, so long in oblivion, will once more struggle for supremacy. Wings, birds, and flowers will all come in for their share of attention. For the very dressy hat, velvet and real lace will be the correct thing.

 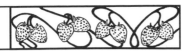

Ball Dress

Use the scale corresponding to the bust measure to draft the waist, which consists of lining back, side back, underarm, and front; outside back and front; two sleeve portions; fichu; and girdle. Use the scale corresponding to the waist measure to draft the skirt. Regulate all lengths by the tape measure.

Take up darts in waist lining. Join back, side back, and underarm gore. Place outside back on this lining back, and lay fullness at waistline in two inward-turning pleats as indicated. Arrange the pleats in the fronts as indicated, via three upward-turning pleats at underarm seam, four at front, and two forward-turning pleats at waistline. Face the center of fronts and arrange this on front lining with corresponding seams together. Join waist at underarm seam. Fasten at front and cover opening with a pleat. Join sleeve portions. Join under portions to armseye and around on each side to edge of neck. Finish upper portion of sleeve and hold in place with ribbon straps over shoulder. Finish lower portion with a ruffling of any soft material. Finish neck and arrange fichu around it, shirring fichu at shoulder and center.

The skirt is all in one piece and should be lined with a drop lining. Take up the darts and join seam at back, leaving an opening sufficient for the placket. Finish placket with an underlap and join the whole to skirt band.

This costume may be made of any soft material suitable for evening wear. The one shown is made of gaslight green china silk, trimmed with chiffon and black velvet ribbon. The skirt is trimmed with red velvet roses, and these are also intermingled in chiffon at neck and on sleeves. Black velvet straps are arranged over shoulder and a rosette of same where straps terminate. Straps of velvet are also arranged over pleat at waist front, each terminating with a black velvet button. The whole garment is made over a white taffeta silk lining. Ruffling or pleating of same on skirt lining will give the skirt a more graceful effect.

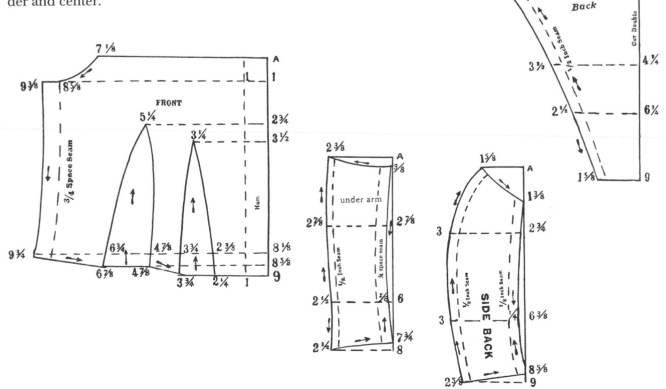

231

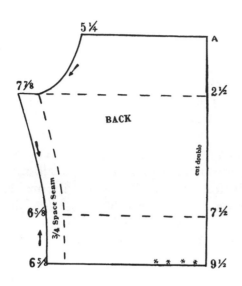

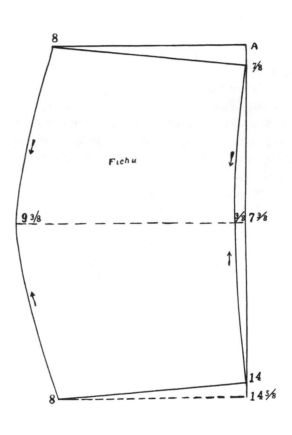

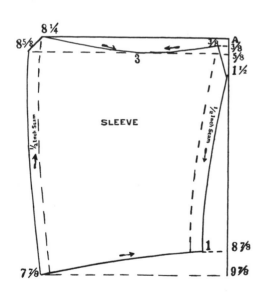

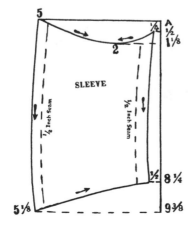

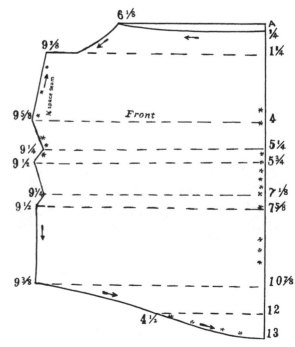

232

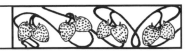
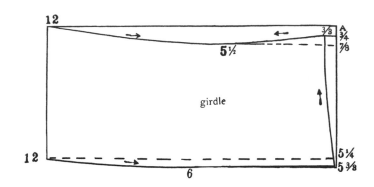

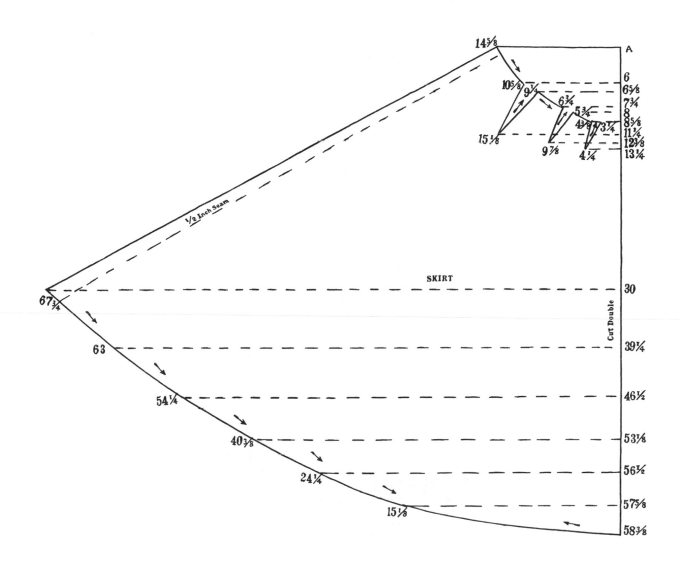

Reception Dress

Use the scale corresponding to the bust measure to draft the waist, which consists of front and back lining, bolero, bertha, yoke, collar, peplum, two sleeve lining portions, two sleeve lining cuff portions, outer sleeve, and outer cuff. Use the scale corresponding to the waist measure to draft the skirt, which has two skirt and four flounce portions. Regulate all lengths by the tape measure.

Take up darts in front lining. Place bolero on the front, putting corresponding seams together and arranging two backward-turning pleats in top as indicated by stars. Lay yoke on lining back, placing center to center back. Cut outside back from lining, extending it only to yoke. Remove yoke, place this back to lining back, and join shoulder and underarm seams. Again place yoke in position, extend it on around to front, and fasten. Position bertha center back to center back of yoke, and join it to bottom of yoke. Join peplum to bottom of waist, placing center to center back, and finish with a belt. Use any soft material for full front. Join the crush collar in the usual way. Place upper and un-der cuff on corresponding sleeve linings and join. Take up tucks in outer sleeve as indicated. Gather fullness at bottom to fit sleeve. Place the turn-back cuff on lower edge of sleeve and join the whole to sleeve lining where lower cuffs terminate. Gather surplus fullness at top to fit sleeve lining and join to armseye.

Each skirt flounce should be cut all in one piece. Join diagrams at points indicated by stars, and place this as a whole on material before cutting. Join seams in skirt. Place flounces on it at points indicated.

This costume may be made of any desired material. The one shown is of black and white velvet. The yoke, collar, and lower cuffs are of cream taffeta silk covered with black and white net lace. The bertha is also covered with this net. Wide satin ribbon in two shades of lavender forms the full front, with loop of same at bust. Braid finishes the edges of the bolero and flounces.

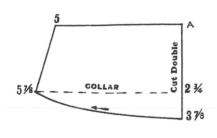

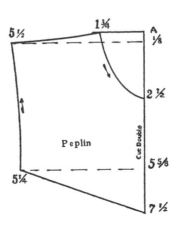

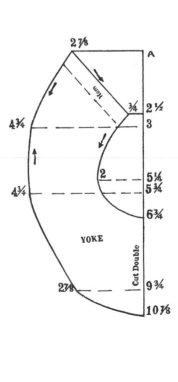

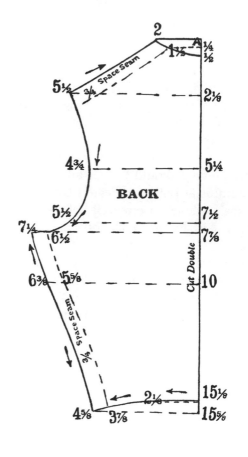

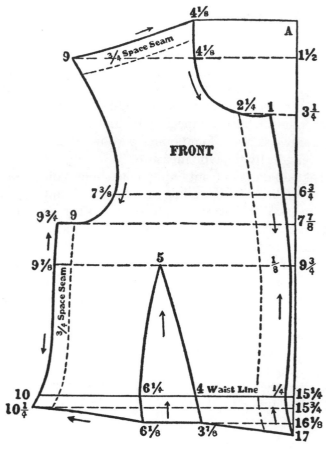

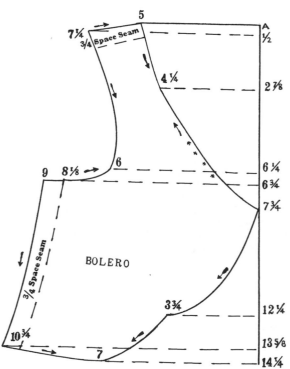

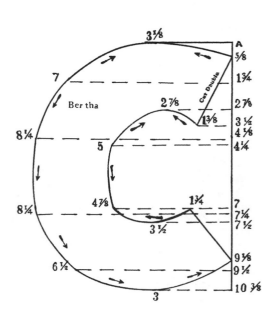

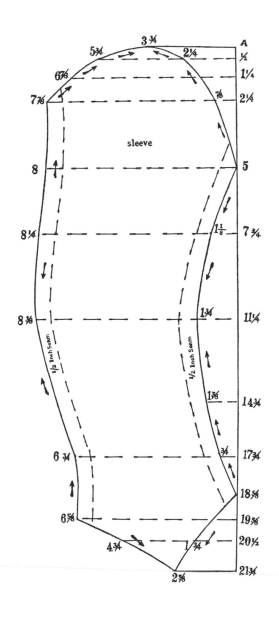

sleeve

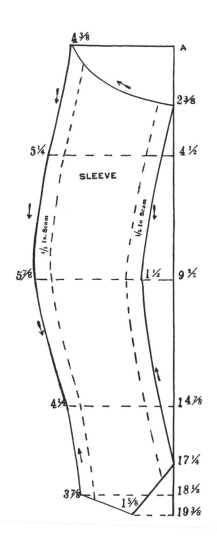

SLEEVE

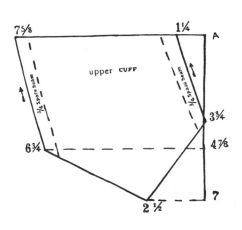

upper CUFF

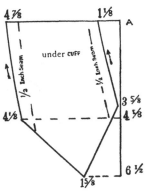

under CUFF

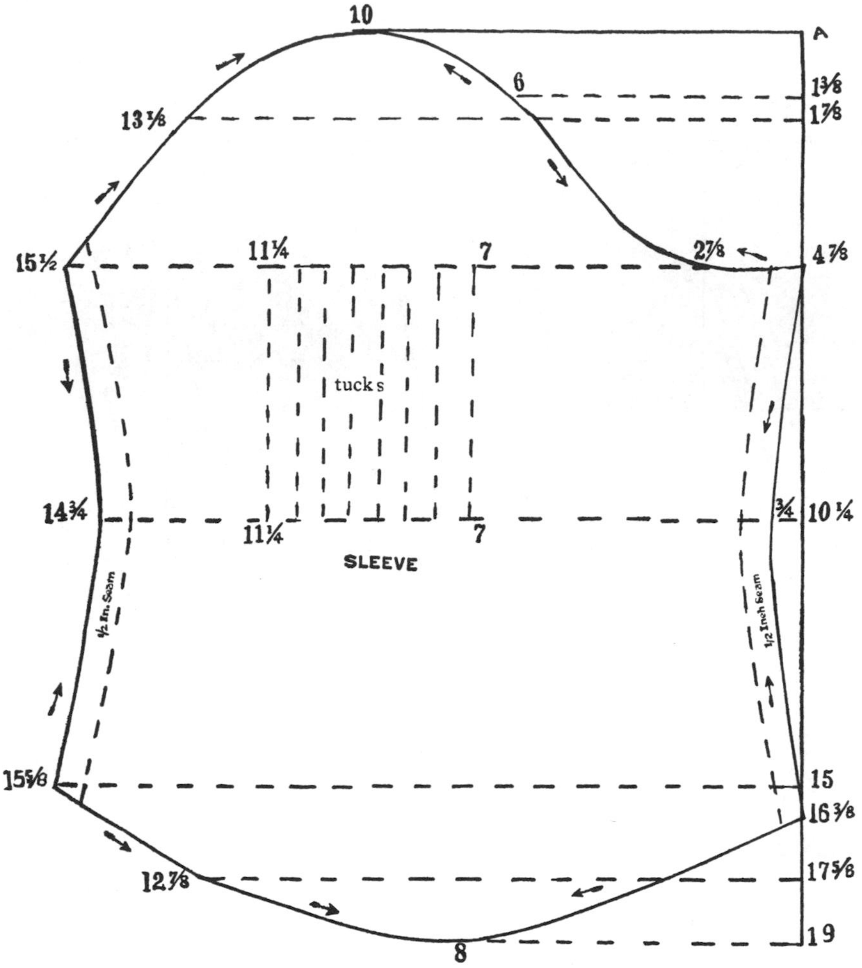

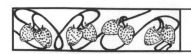

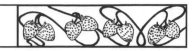

10
A
6
1⅜
13⅛
1⅞
15½
11¼
7
2⅞
4⅞
tucks
14¾
11¼
7
¾
10¼
SLEEVE
½ in. Seam
½ Inch Seam
15⅝
15
16⅜
12⅞
17⅝
19
8

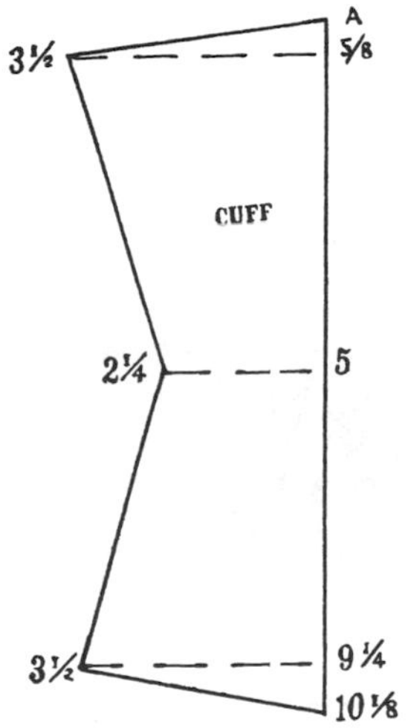

A
3½
⅝
CUFF
2¼
5
3½
9¼
10⅛

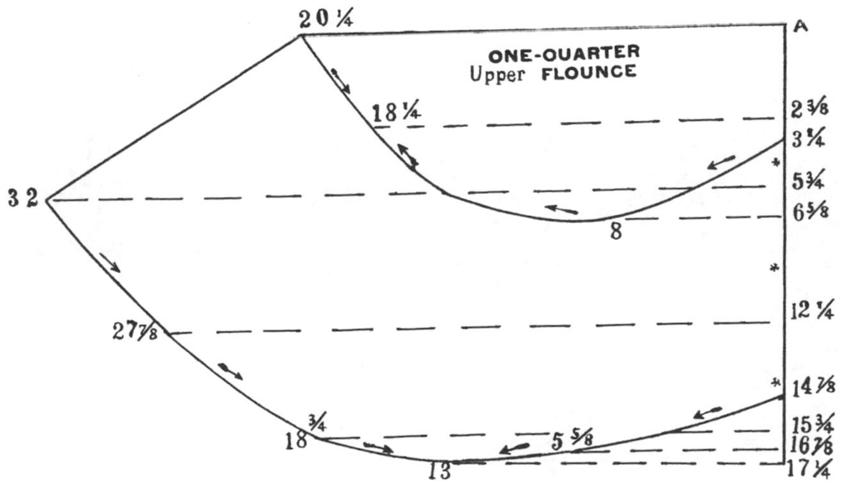

20¼
A
ONE-QUARTER
Upper FLOUNCE
18¼
2⅜
3¼
5¾
32
8
6⅝
27⅞
12¼
14⅞
15¾
18¾
5⅝
16⅞
13
17¼

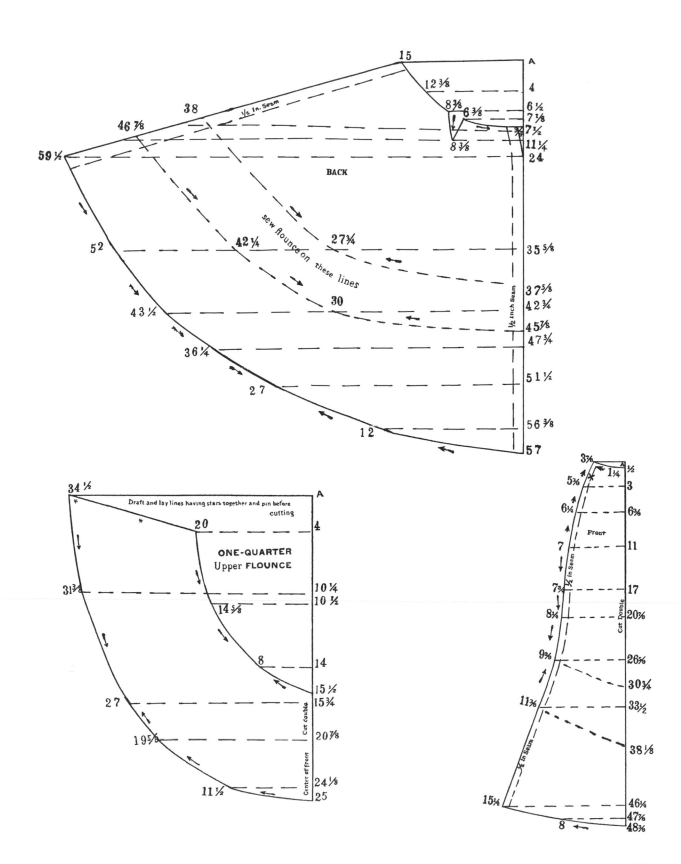

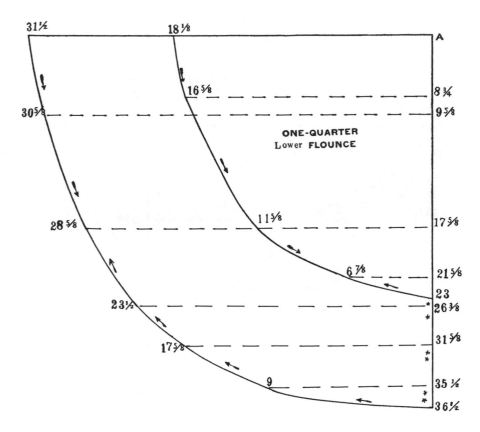

31½   18⅛   A

16⅝   8¾

30⅝   9⅝

ONE-QUARTER
Lower **FLOUNCE**

28⅝   11⅝   17⅝

6⅞   21⅝

23

23½   * 26⅜
*

31⅝

17⅝   *
*

9   35¼

* 36½
*

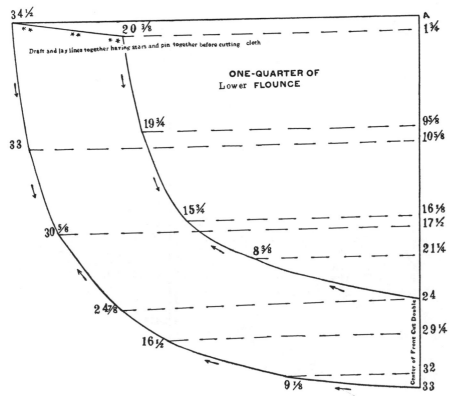

34½   A
**   **   20 ⅜   1¾
**

Draft and lay lines together having stars and pin together before cutting cloth

ONE-QUARTER OF
Lower **FLOUNCE**

19¾   9⅝

10⅝

33

15¾   16⅛

17½

30⅝   8⅜   21¼

24

2 4⅞   29¼

16½

32

9⅛   33

Center of Front Cut Double

240

Calling Costume

Use the scale corresponding to the bust measure to draft the waist, which consists of back and front lining, outside back and front, vest, lay-down and standing collars, and sleeve. Use the scale corresponding to the waist measure to draft the three skirt portions. Regulate all lengths by the tape measure.

Take up dart in lining front and place outside front on it. Place outside back on lining back and join at shoulder seams. Join underarm seam separately. Arrange fullness at front and back, at bottom of waist, and finish with a belt. Place vest on right front lining and extend underneath left outside front. Place lay-down collar around neck; extend down fronts underneath revers. Arrange standing collar to neck in the usual way. Join sleeve. Gather any surplus fullness at top to fit armseye.

Join the skirt and arrange the pleats according to the notches. The skirt is laid in forward-turning pleats in front and backward-turning pleats in back. A small box pleat is thus formed at the back seam of the side gore.

This costume may be made up in any of the smoother weaves, the softer effects being more desirable. The one illustrated is brown henrietta cloth, with a deep shade of ecru appliquéd braid and narrow velvet ribbon for trimming.

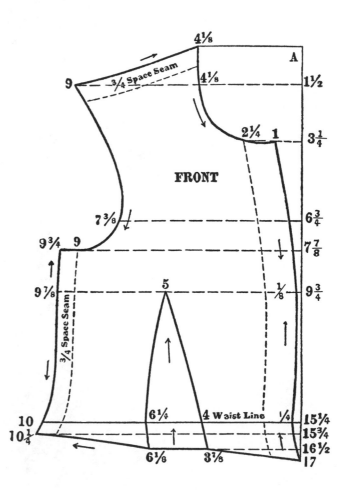

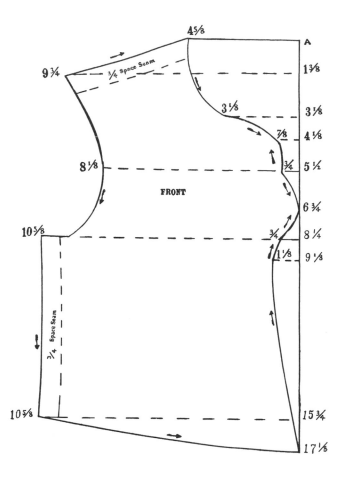

FRONT

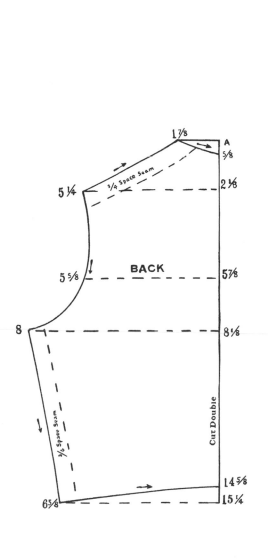

BACK

Cut Double

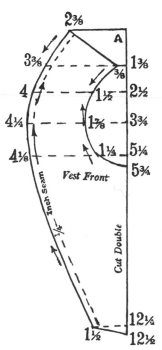

Vest Front

Cut Double

243

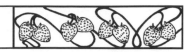

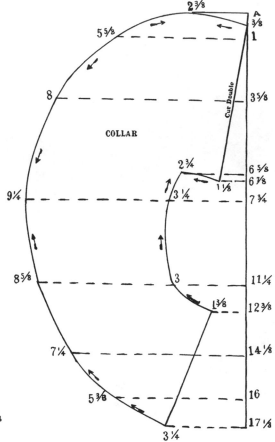

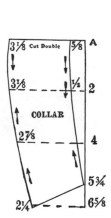

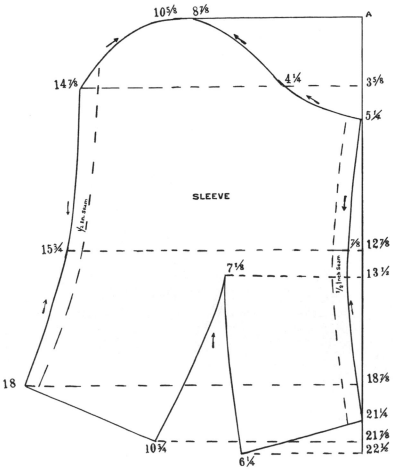

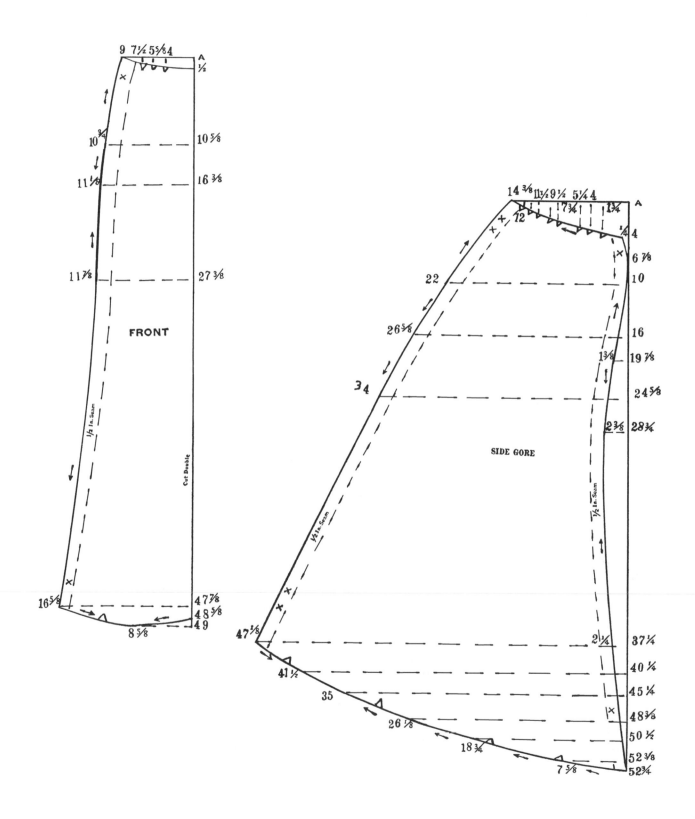

FRONT

SIDE GORE

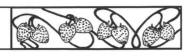

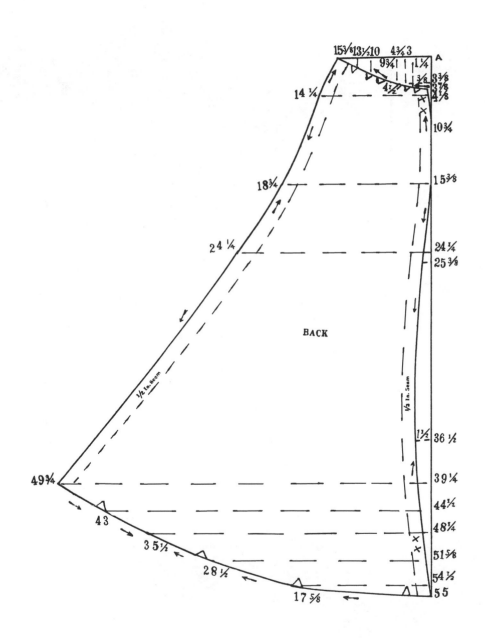

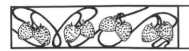

Traveling Suit

Use the scale corresponding to the bust measure to draft the waist, which consists of back, side back, and front lining; outside back and front; vest; collar; and sleeve. Use the scale corresponding to the waist measure to draft the four skirt portions. Regulate all lengths by the tape measure.

Take up darts in outside front and place on front linings. Join lining back and side back and place outside back on same. Join at shoulder and underarm seams. Place vests on lining underneath outside edge of fronts. Stitch straps to same. Arrange collar to neck and interline it heavily. Join sleeves and fit to armseye. Fasten waist at center of front, lapping right front over left at lower vest.

Join seams of skirt and arrange fullness at back in an inverted pleat. Trim in any desired way.

This suit is made of dark blue broadcloth. The vest is blue velvet. Straps are of the same material as the dress. Bands of stitched black satin on waist, skirt, and sleeves furnish the trimming.

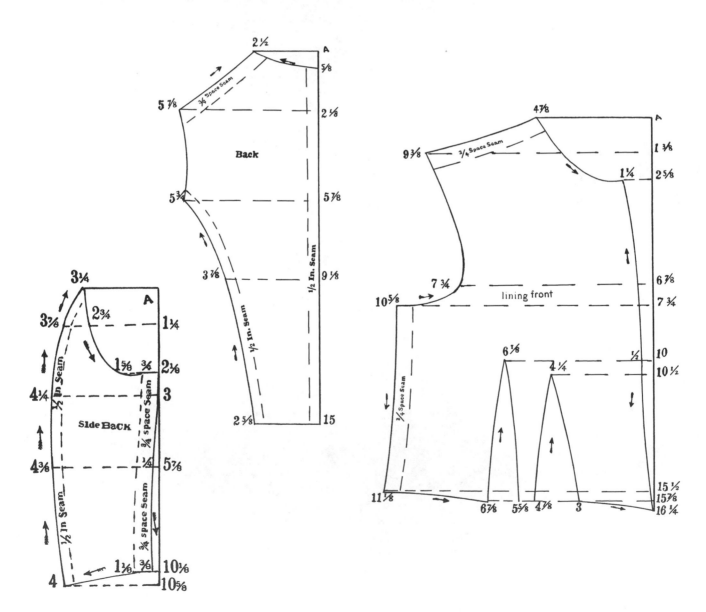

 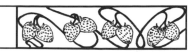

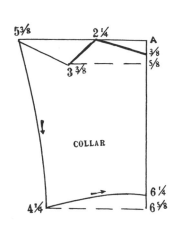

COLLAR

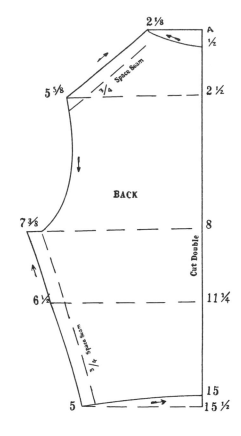

BACK

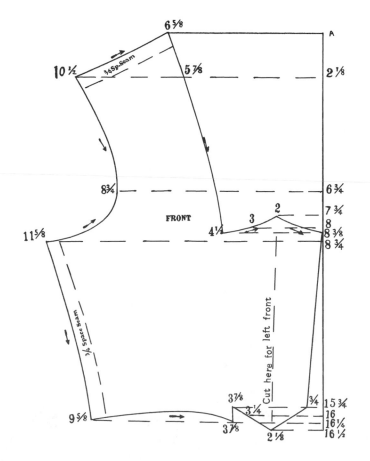

FRONT

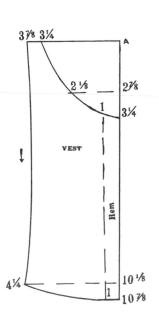

VEST

249

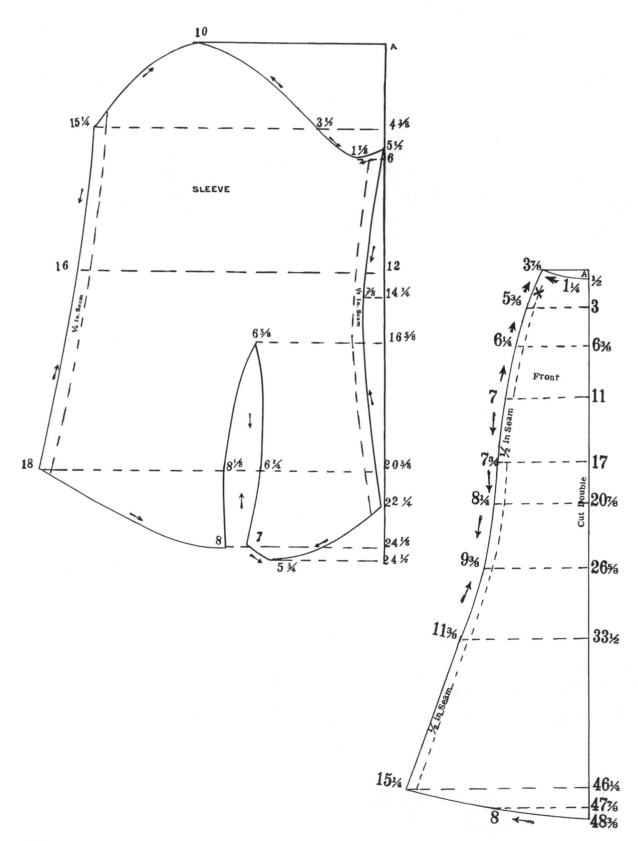

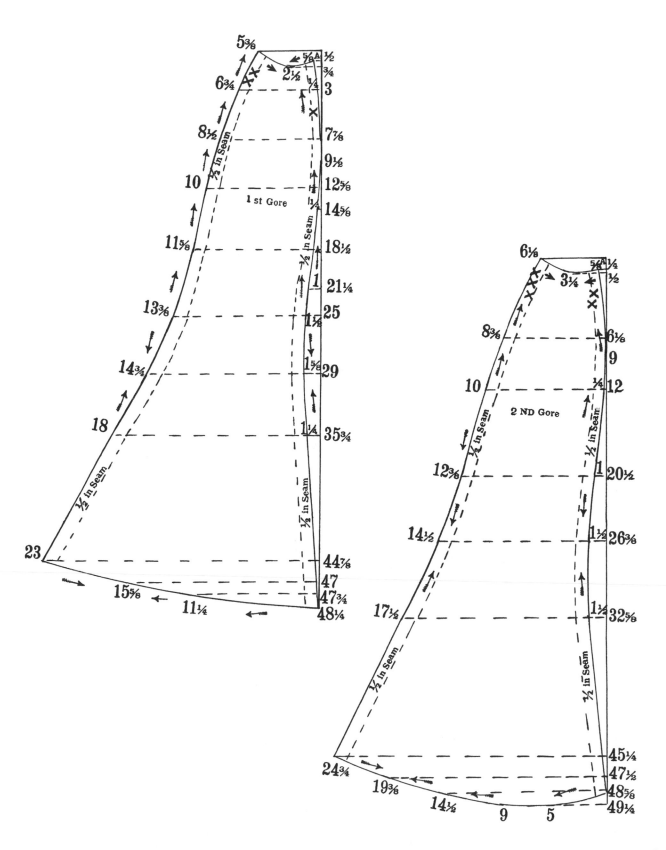

251

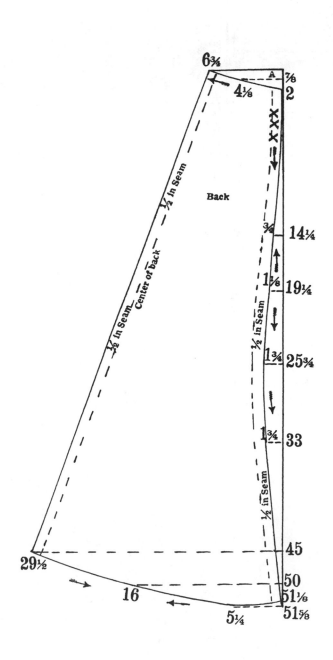

Ladies' Shirtwaist

Use the scale corresponding to the bust measure to draft this waist, which consists of back, front, full front, yoke, collar, strap, and sleeve. Regulate the length by the tape measure. This waist may be made with or without a lining. If lining is desired select any suitable one.

Take up the tucks as indicated in front and join to full front. Arrange straps over this front and fasten to left side. Place yoke over full front at neck and join collar. Join sleeve. Gather fullness at bottom to fit wristband and at top to fit armseye.

Any shirtwaist material may be used. The one designed is of flannel, with lace yoke, collar, and cuffs, and a contrasting material for front.

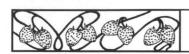
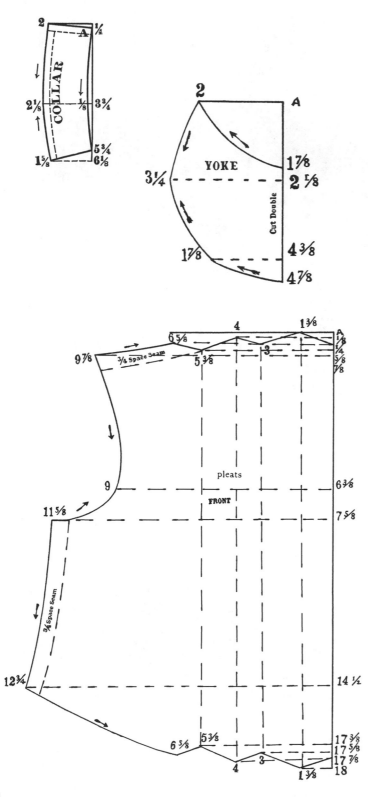

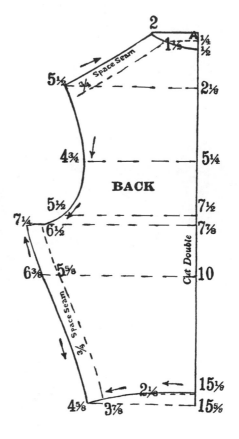

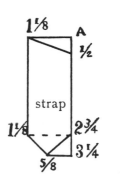

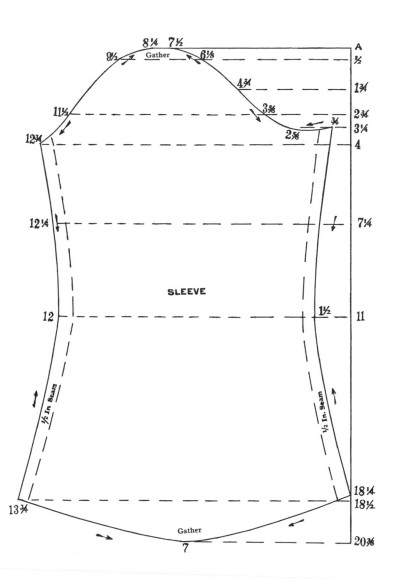

SLEEVE

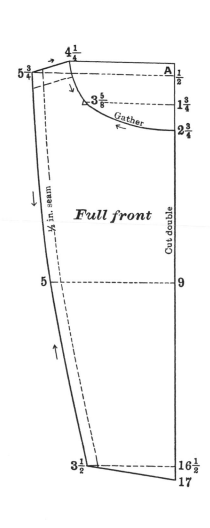

Full front

Ladies' Shirtwaist

Use the scale corresponding to the bust measure to draft this waist, which consists of back and front lining, outside front, collar, sleeve puff, and two sleeve portions. Regulate the length by the tape measure.

The back and back lining are the same. Lay pleats in material before cutting. Arrange fronts on lining fronts and join garment. Join collar in the usual way. Join sleeve lining. Arrange pleats in upper sleeve before cutting, join seam, and arrange this on sleeve lining. Gather sleeve to fit armseye. Arrange cuff on bottom of sleeve.

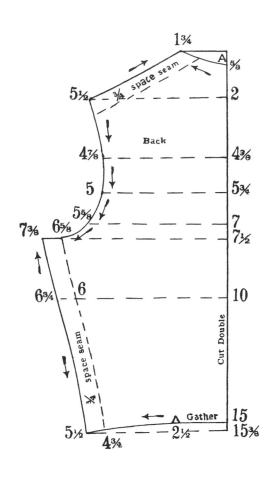

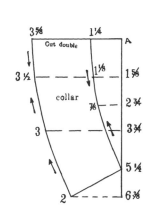

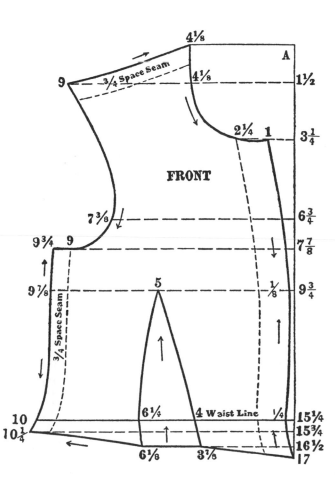

257

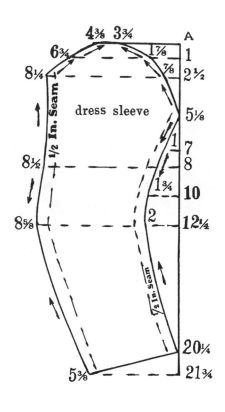

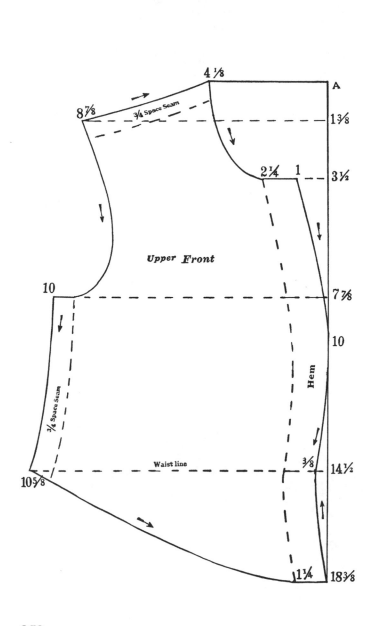

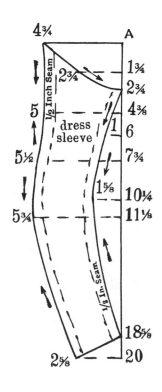

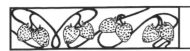

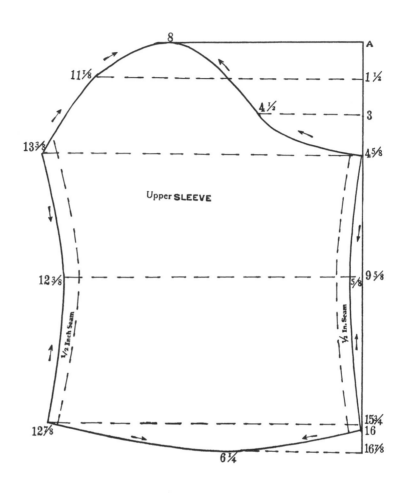

Upper SLEEVE

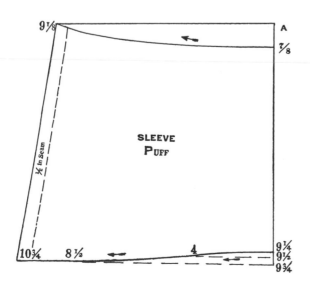

SLEEVE PUFF

259

August 1902

To be really chic, you must have a blouse effect. It may be a plain blouse, a tucked blouse, or a yoke effect; it may have revers, a vest front, or a collar of any shape or design.

Yokes are very popular. They do not form the foundation for the chief decoration but are made of one unlined thickness, lace and one-piece appliqué effects being greatly used. Insertion and tucks are also greatly used, especially for thinner materials. In many instances the bodice below the yoke is elaborately tucked and joined to it by means of beading, insertion, etc.

The greater part of the new silks are made to correspond with the ever-increasing demand for blouses. There are many pretty materials in wool, as well. Voile is on the transparent order and comes in all shades. Mohair is especially elegant in black and white. We still have zibelines and etamines in the lighter weights.

Trimmings are superb. Velvet ribbon interlaced, fringes and hand-painted ribbon, silk bands, and tastefully designed braids with complicated patterns are much used. Gowns are massed with trimmings both as to bodice and skirt.

Outdoor costumes find a charming completion in boas, ruchings, and scarves.

The most popular up-to-date shirtwaist effect is the Gibson, which consists of broad shoulder lines. This effect may be obtained in various ways, by pleats extending over the sleeve, or with a short yoke extending out over the sleeve with pleats extending to the bust. This widened effect may also be obtained by the cape collars, which also appear on simple and dressy gowns. These collars may be put on almost any shaped bodice.

Pretty ties and stocks are one of the most important features of the shirtwaist outfit. There are plain stocks, stocks with fluttering ends, and all sorts of soft fluffy creations of lace and chiffon. The simple bow knot with two loops and two ends is the accepted method of fastening. There are some very smart handkerchief stocks with pronounced patterns and dots.

Buttons, large fancy ones, are a modish and effective trimming for shirtwaists. Then there are the innumerable fancy accessory buttons and pins.

While tailor-made suits become more elaborate, the plainer ones with stitched straps and bands seem more suitable for office and business wear. Jackets are worn, but those en suite are most popular. In thinner wraps for summer and fall, long silk coats and fancy jackets are the correct thing.

Cape collars indicate the return of the shoulder cape, a few of which are already in sight. They are made mostly of lace and jetted net, with ruffles of lace and ribbon. A few silk ones are trimmed with white and black lace.

Many hats seem to be practically all brim. We have the shirtwaist hat in its many shapes and designs, the sailor, and for more dressy occasions the lace or chiffon hat. The last mentioned, of course, is large. It may be trimmed elaborately with flowers, or a long curling plume resting gracefully on the brim. Feathers, paradise plumes, wings, and quills are much in vogue. Scarf-adorned hats are seen in great numbers.

Promenade Costume

Use the scale corresponding to the bust measure to draft the waist, which consists of lining back and front, outside front, full front, collar, standing collar, sleeve, and cuff. Use the scale corresponding to the waist measure to draft the four skirt portions. Regulate all lengths by the tape measure.

Tuck front, back, and sleeve before cutting goods. Cut outside back the same as lining back. Place on lining back with corresponding seams together. Place full front on right lining front. Gather at neck to fit lining neck, allowing same to overlap left front and fasten at left side. Take up darts in lining fronts and place on outside fronts. Join waist

at shoulder and underarm seams. Place center of collar to center of back and allow it to fall into place down fronts. Join standing collar in the usual way. Join sleeve and lay fullness at wrist in small tucks instead of gathering. Adjust cuff and join to sleeve. Adjust sleeve in armseye, gathering surplus fullness at top to fit armseye. Finish at waist with sash effect, as illustrated.

This skirt is to be made over a drop lining. Take up darts in skirt yoke. Join skirt portions and lay tucks as indicated on draft. Join skirt to yoke and finish in the usual way.

This suit would be very pretty developed in sicilienne cloth, of a wedgwood blue color, with a bright shade of red as a contrasting color.

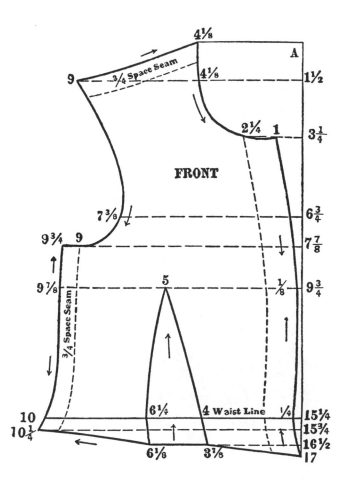

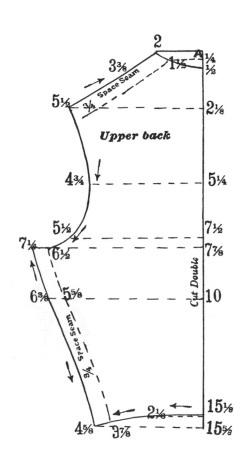

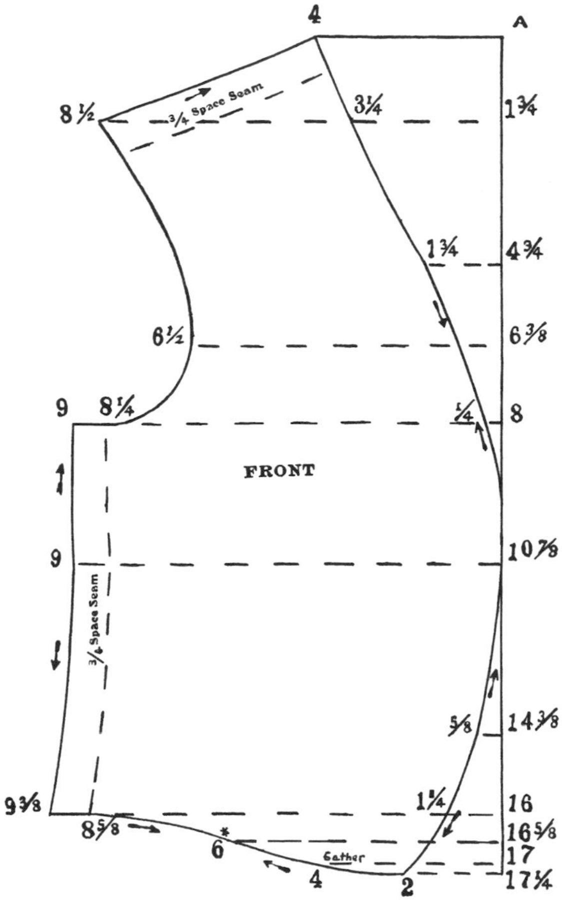
4
A
8½
¾ Space Seam
3¼
1¾
1¾
4¾
6½
6⅜
9
8¼
¼
8
FRONT
9
10⅞
¾ Space Seam
⅝
14⅜
9⅜
1¼
16
8⅝
16⅝
6
17
Gather
4
2
17¼

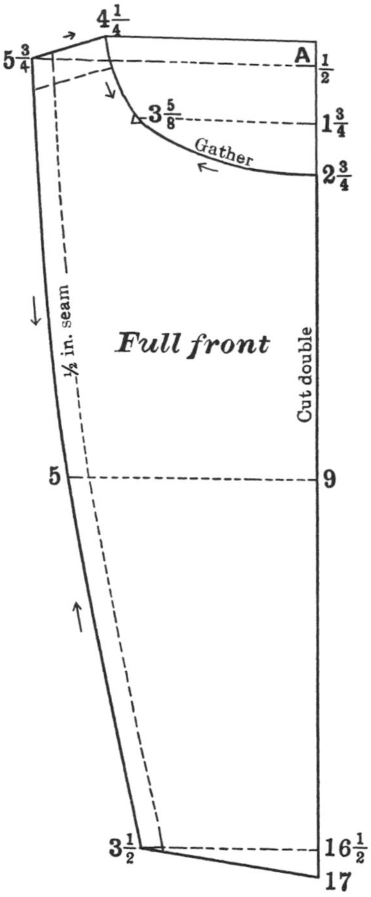
4¼
5¾
A
½
3⅝
1¾
Gather
2¾
½ in. seam
Full front
Cut double
5
9
3½
16½
17

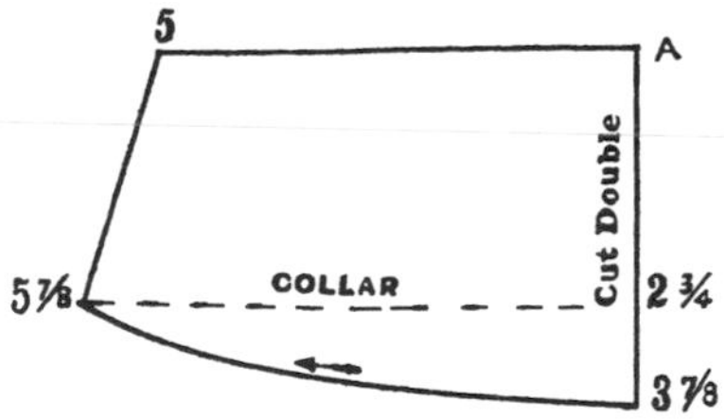
5
A
Cut Double
5⅞
COLLAR
2¾
3⅞

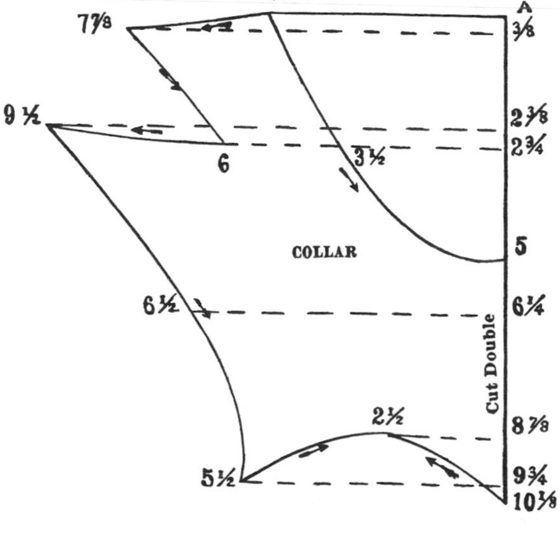
4⅞
A
7⅞
⅜
9½
2⅜
6
3½
2¾
COLLAR
5
6½
6¼
Cut Double
2½
8⅞
5½
9¾
10⅛

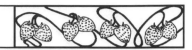

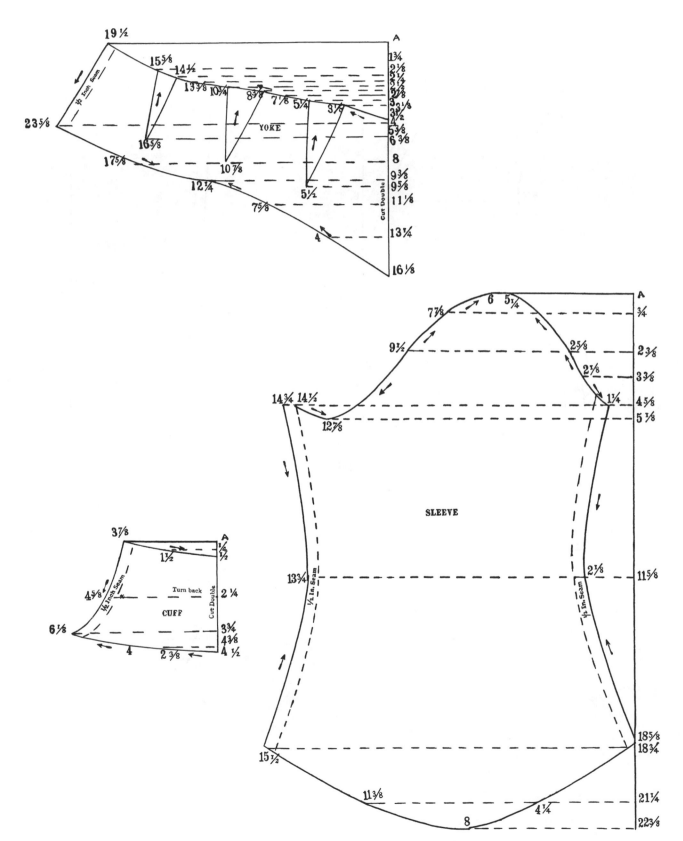

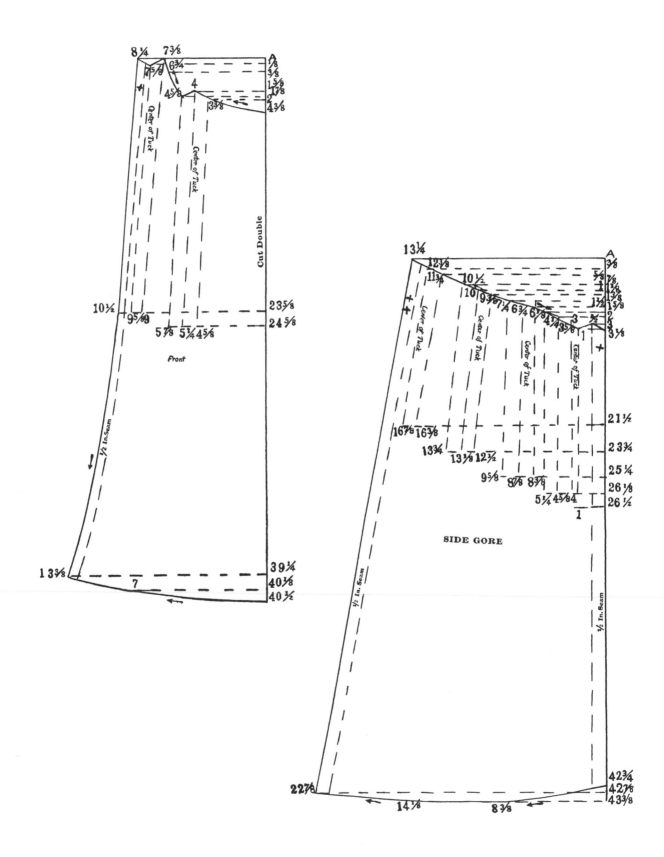

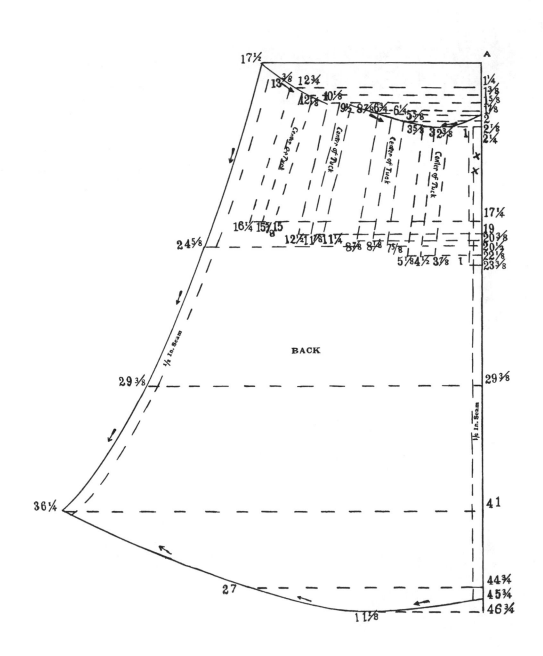

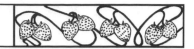
Afternoon Toilet

Use the scale corresponding to the bust measure to draft the waist, which consists of lining back and front, outside front, rever, vest, peplum, collar, two sleeve portions, sleeve puff, and cuff. Use the scale corresponding to the waist measure to draft the two skirt portions. Regulate all lengths by the tape measure.

Take up darts in lining front. Place outside front on it with corresponding seams together. Place vest front on right lining front underneath outside front, and allow same to overlap left front and fasten at left side. Cut outside back the same as lining back. Join waist at shoulder and underarm seams. Join revers to front. Join collar in the usual way. Join peplum to waist, placing center of back to cen-

ter of peplum. Cut outside sleeve portions the same as the lining portions, extending same only to upper edge of puff. Join sleeve and arrange puff on it. Join cuff to lower edge of upper sleeve. Adjust sleeve in armseye, gathering surplus fullness at top to fit armseye. Finish with band at wrist.

Join skirt portions. There is a seam down center of front. Join flounce to bottom of skirt, placing center of flounce to center of front. Arrange fullness at back in an inverted pleat. Finish at bottom in the usual way.

The suit illustrated is linen, polka dotted in black, and trimmed with black ribbon.

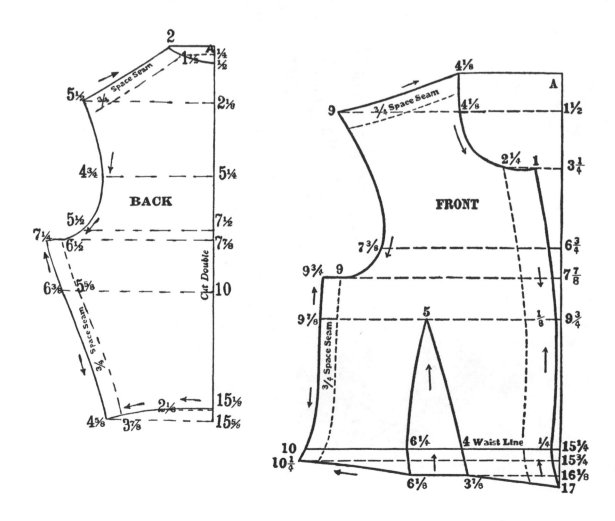

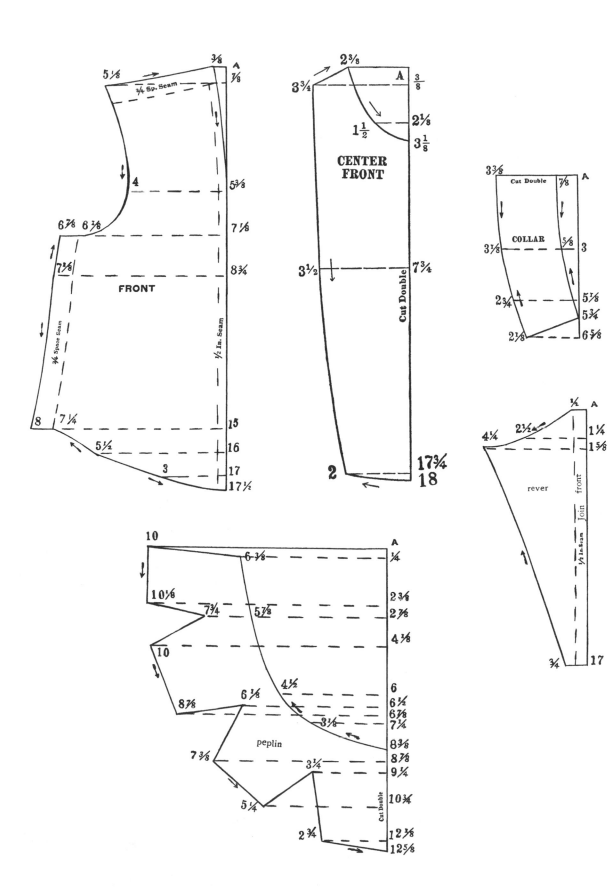

269

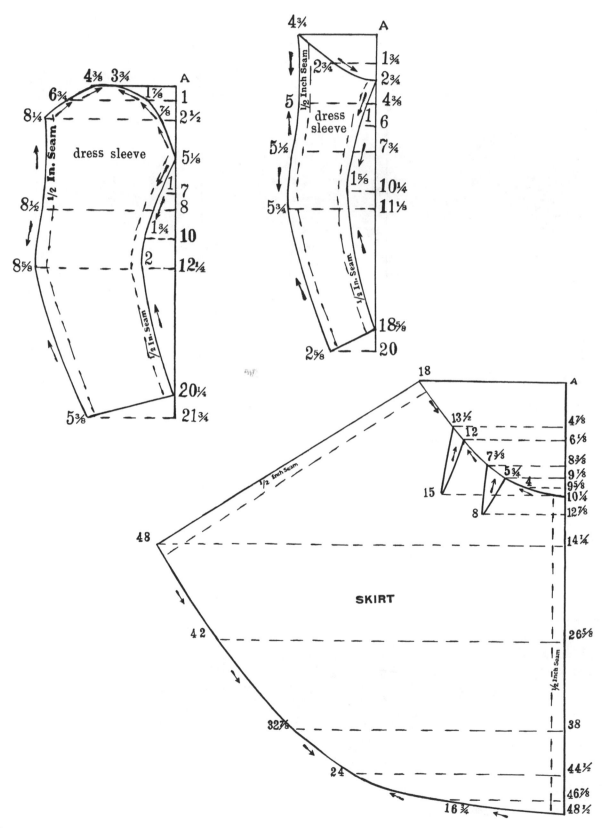

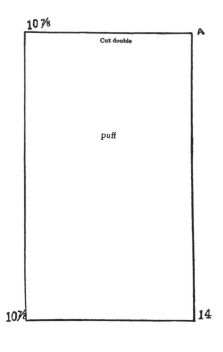

10⅞

A

Cut double

puff

10⅞   14

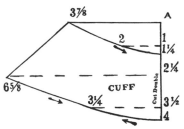

3⅞

2   A

1
1¼

2¼

CUFF

6⅝

3¼   3½

Cut Double

4

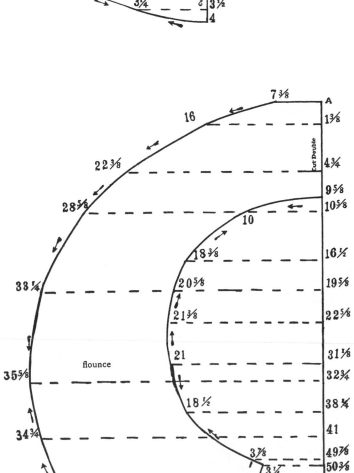

7⅜ A

16   1⅜

22⅜   4¾

28⅝   9⅝

10   10⅝

18⅜   16½

20⅝   19⅝

33¼   21⅜   22⅝

21   31⅛

flounce   Cut Double

35⅝   32¾

18½   38¾

34¾   41

3⅞   49⅞

3¼ 50⅜

29¾   52

½ in. Seam

24⅝   57⅛

13⅜   65½

271

 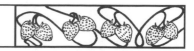

Jacket Suit

Use the scale corresponding to the bust measure to draft the jacket, which consists of front, back, peplum, collar, and two sleeve portions. Use the scale corresponding to the waist measure to draft the one-piece skirt. Regulate all lengths by the tape measure.

Join jacket at back, shoulder, and underarm seams. Take up darts and interline fronts with canvas. Join sailor collar to neck as illustrated, placing center of collar to center of back. Join sleeve por-

tions and adjust in armseye, gathering fullness at top to fit armseye. Arrange peplum at bottom of jacket as illustrated.

Join skirt seam at back, leaving sufficient opening for placket. Arrange fullness at back in an inverted pleat and join to band. Finish bottom in the usual way.

This suit was developed in black corded silk, with velvet collar. Smooth, pliable silk braid was stitched on for trimming.

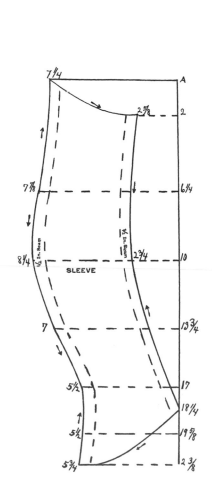

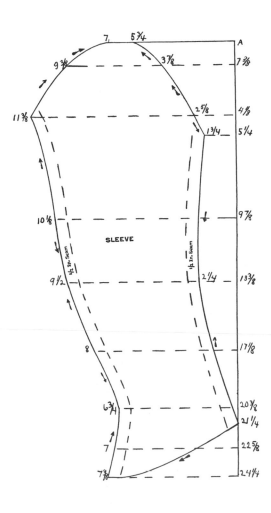

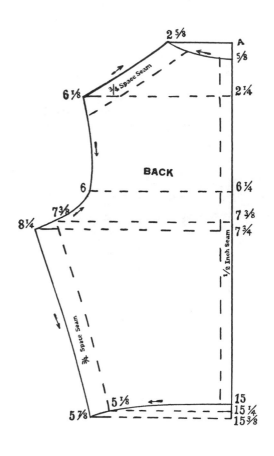

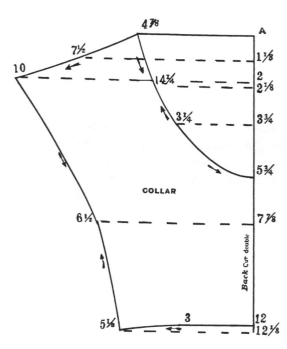

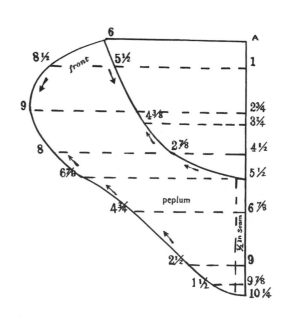

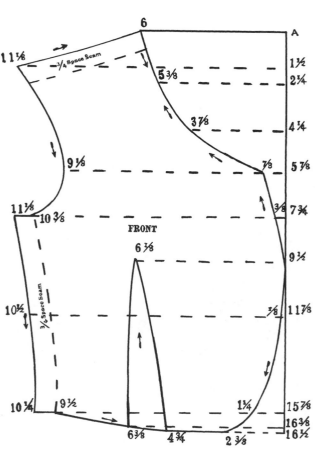

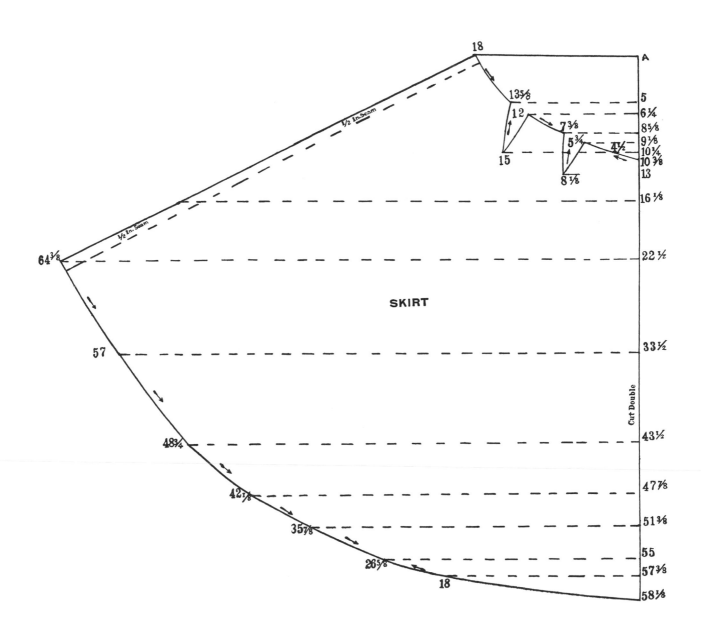

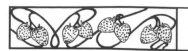
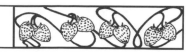

Shirtwaist

Use the scale corresponding to the bust measure to draft this pattern, which consists of front, back, collar, and sleeve. Regulate all lengths by the tape measure.

Join waist at shoulder and underarm seams. Lay pleats in back as indicated. Tuck goods for front before cutting. Join sleeve and arrange in armseye, gathering fullness at top to fit armseye and at bottom to fit wristband. Finish neck with band. Tuck collar and adjust in the usual way.

This waist would be very pretty developed in silk, with velvet ribbon for trimming.

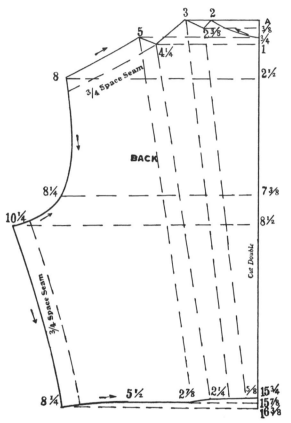

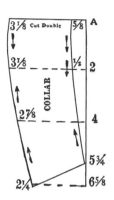

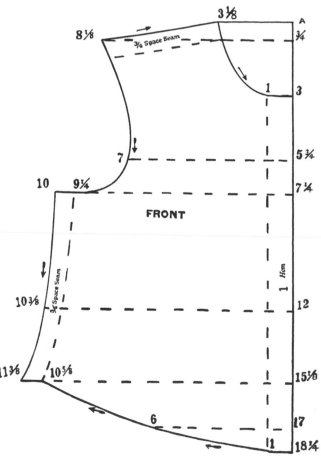

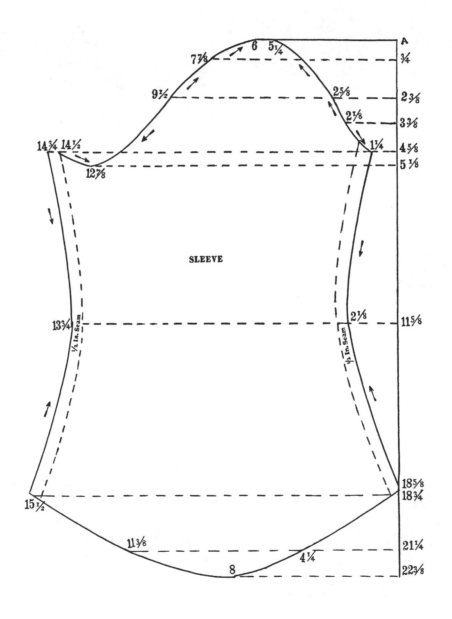

Corset Waist

Use the scale corresponding to the bust measure to draft this pattern, which consists of waist and peplum. Regulate all lengths by the tape measure. Join at shoulder seams. Gather fullness at waist to fit peplum and join same, placing center of back to center of waist back. Gather at top, by tape or ribbon, to fit bust. Trim in any desired way.

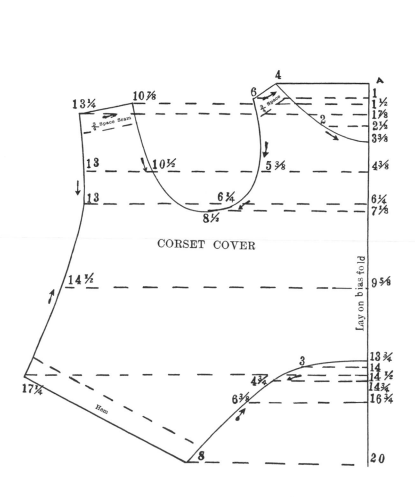

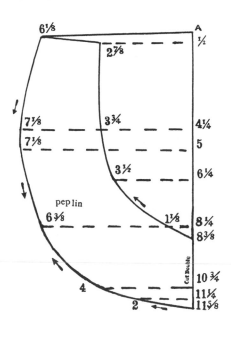

279

August 1903

The pelerine, or cape collar, is a great feature of the up-to-date costume. They are cut rather low and are wider than ever. Some fall in folds over the arm as far as the elbow, others are rounded in back and come down to the waist in a point at front, while others are pointed both front and back. Lace collars are very much worn. They must not appear put on as an afterthought, but must coincide with the other trimmings. Preference now seems given to collars made of the same material as the gown. All stole collars are made deep on the shoulder with the ends falling at least to the knees.

Dress sleeves are gradually getting larger and more fussy, while some coat sleeves are of immense proportions. Once noticeable feature of the dress sleeve is that it fits more closely at wrist to elbow, thus bringing the greatest fullness at the elbow and above.

In bodice effects the short jacket is a favorite. The blouse will continue in favor, with a shorter waistline than ever at back. Deep girdles are an addition to the more dressy waists.

Skirts are arranged in all sorts of tucks, pleats, and shirrings, and the fullness at bottom becomes greater. These skirts need a great amount of support, therefore much attention should be given to the construction of the underskirt to produce that graceful flare at bottom. Many skirts have panels both back and front, while the box pleat, as well as the double box pleat at back, is revived. The yoke and panel front combined is also a favorite model. Except for dressy occasions, short or round skirts, just clearing the ground, are the accepted thing. Very few trailing gowns are now seen on the street. Strapped effects with the double flounce are also used, but these double skirts can be worn only by the most stately.

Softer and lighter materials, such as voile, etamine, and soft silks, are most utilized for elaborately tucked and shirred costumes. Washing satin, Japanese silk, muslin, foulard, and chiffon voile, all are charming materials for late summer wear. For early fall and cooler days delaine will, in many instances, take the place of flannel. Delaines are produced in many old-fashioned patterns and nothing washes better. They are particularly adapted for outing and sporting frocks.

Snowflake and small-checked cloth will be greatly in vogue for early fall. The snowflake cloth differs from last season's inasmuch as the little white tufts are much smaller and softer and set closer together. The fabric is also lighter in color. In the checked cloth the squares are so small as to be almost invisible; at a distance the cloth has the appearance of plain material. All shades of rather deep blue, in the plain cloths, are very popular.

There is nothing quite so cool and attractive as the shirtwaist suits made out of white linen. These may be hand embroidered or trimmed with insertions of linen lace. In all cases they are made up very simple, the skirts pleated or with a flounce and the bodice developed on shirtwaist lines. The shirtwaist proper has, to some degree, been supplanted by the more fancy waist. These, in many instances, follow shirtwaist lines, but their identity is almost lost in the mass of trimmings, tucks, and shirrings which adorn them.

Coats are of every length, from the short jacket barely reaching the waistline, to the long coat completely covering the costume. Many tight-fitting jackets are prophesied for the coming season. Loose coats with large sleeves are holding their own.

In shapes hats vary but little from those for earlier summer wear. Flat effects, with perhaps more tilt at the side, will still be worn. We still have the ever-present turban, with a more pronounced desire for toques. This new toque has a brim turned up vertically against a rather wide crown, which sets well on the head. These hats are made of fanciful braids.

A great quantity of red is being worn. A white straw spotted with red is very picturesque worn with a red gown; while white spotted with black, navy blue with white, and tan with black are all favorite mixtures. The better style of hats, however, are chiefly kept to one color. Black bravely holds its own, while some of the white hats, with their large white plumes, are dreams of beauty. A white chip hat trimmed with pink roses with a touch of black, introduced by a row of black velvet daisies, makes a very stunning effect. Hats of mohair braid with lace and chiffon will be introduced late into the season. Felts in very light colors will be very noticeable for early fall wear. We also have the felt braid, which with velvet ribbon makes up very artistically.

This hat is made of fancy braid and trimmed with a lace drape and flowers.

This is a chiffon hat trimmed with velvet ribbon, lace, and flowers.

This is a flat felt hat trimmed with velvet ribbon and ornamented with fancy buckles.

This hat is made of Neapolitan braid and trimmed with flowers and ribbon.

Hat of light-colored felt with a dark velvet binding trimmed wih foliage.

This hat is made of felt braid trimmed with silk and velvet ribbon, a fancy buckle being the only ornament.

Reception Gown

Use the scale corresponding to the bust measure to draft the waist, which consists of lining back and front, outside front, collar, sleeve cap, undersleeve, and cuff. Use the scale corresponding to the waist measure to draft the five skirt portions. Regulate all lengths by the tape measure.

Tuck all goods before cutting. Cut outside back the same as lining back. Place on lining back with corresponding seams together. The front is cut all in one piece, the yoke effect being obtained by the use of trimming. Place outside front on lining front with corresponding seams together. Gather fullness in front at waistline to fit waist lining. Join the whole at shoulder and underarm seams. Gather fullness at top of undersleeve to fit the lower edge of sleeve cap and join. Join the sleeve. Gather fullness at wrist into cuff, and at top to fit the armseye. Adjust sleeve in armseye in the usual way. Bind neck and adjust collar.

Join the skirt portions according to the Xs. Finish in the usual way. Leave sufficient space at back for placket. Finish at top with band.

This gown is made of etamine and trimmed with lace, velvet, and fagoting. A drop silk lining completes the costume.

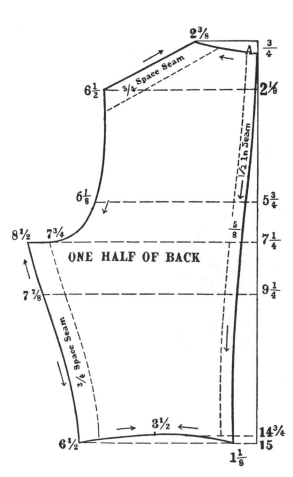

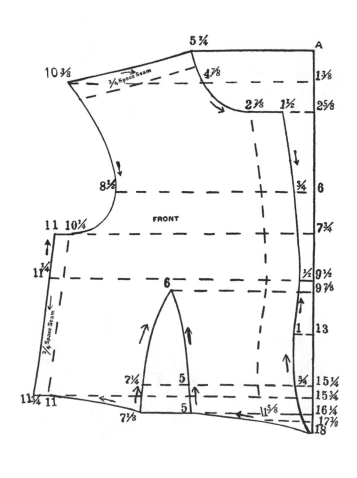

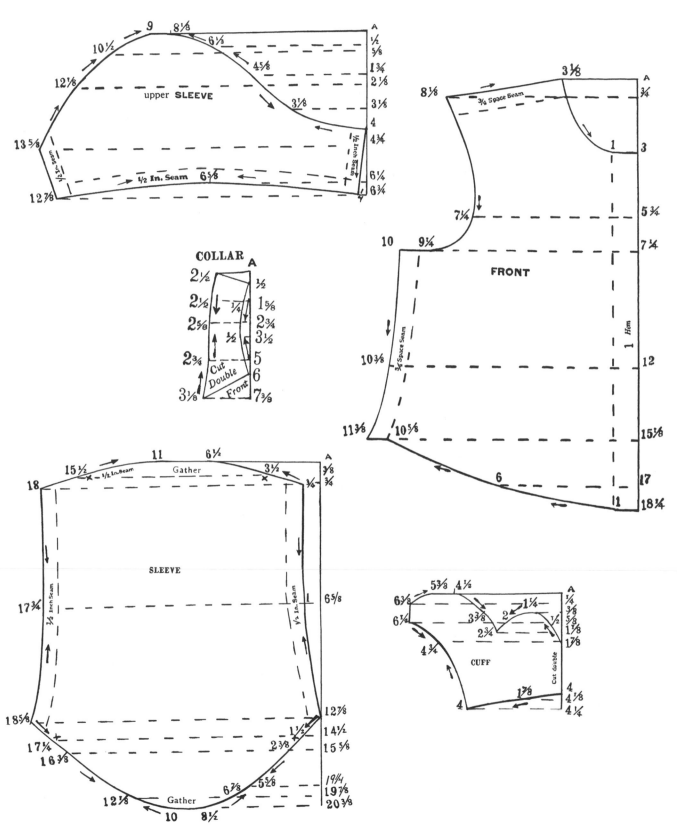

285

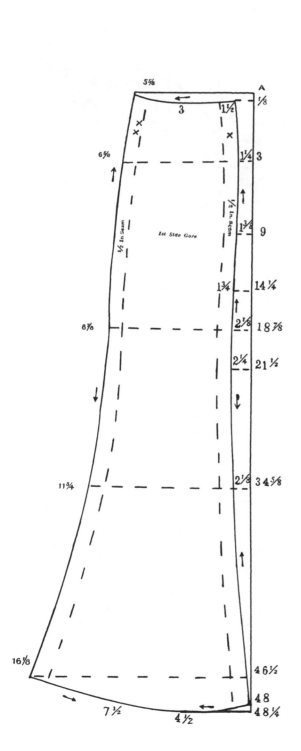

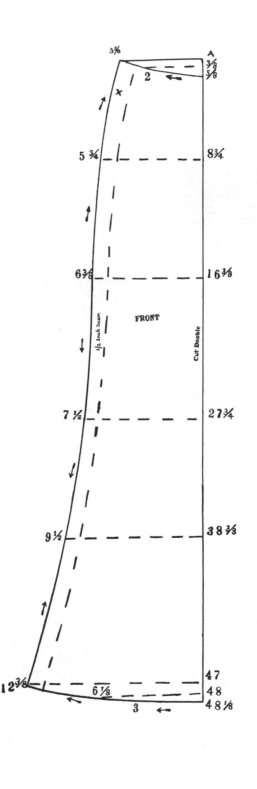

286

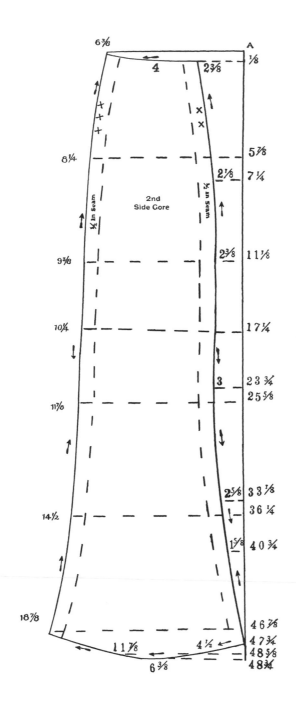

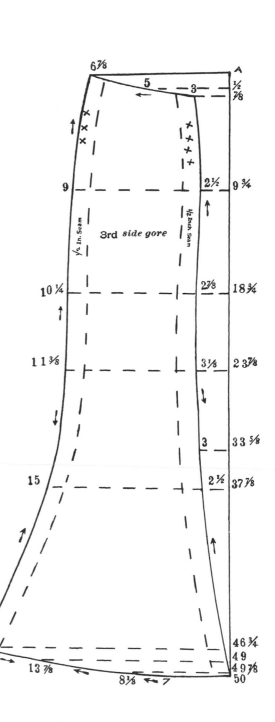

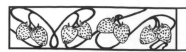

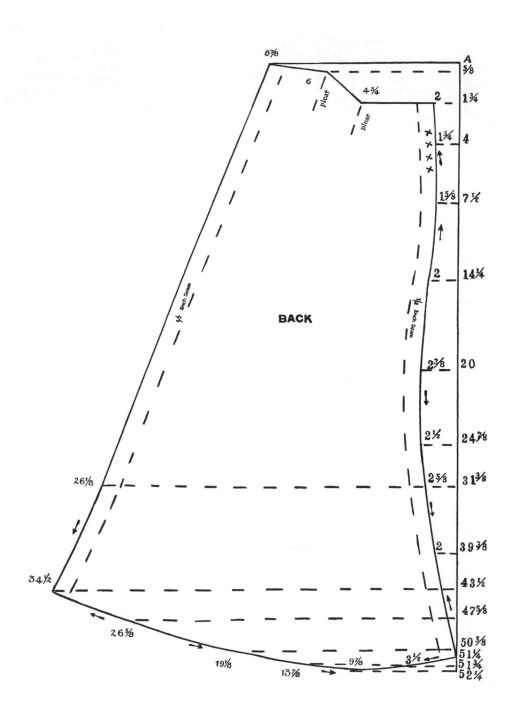

Afternoon Gown

Use the scale corresponding to the bust measure to draft the waist, which consists of back, front, yoke, collar, and sleeve. Use the scale corresponding to the waist measure to draft the two skirt portions. Regulate all lengths by the tape measure.

Use your own taste and the illustration to determine the amount of shirring on both the bodice and the skirt. The yoke is made of alternate rows of shirring and insertion. Arrange this on the yoke. Gather the fullness in front to fit front yoke and join it to lower edge of yoke. Gather the fullness in back to fit back yoke and join it to lower edge of yoke. Join whole at underarm seam. The fullness at bottom of both back and front is shirred and gathered to fit the waist measurement. Shirr top of sleeve and join. The fullness at the bottom of the sleeve is gathered into a straight shirred cuff and at top to fit the armseye. Adjust sleeve in the usual way. Bind neck and adjust collar.

Join the skirt portions according to the Xs, leaving sufficient space at back for placket. Shirr the fullness at the top to fit the waist measurement.

This gown is made of silk lansdowne and trimmed with ribbon, appliqué lace, and insertion. It can be made prettily of any soft material.

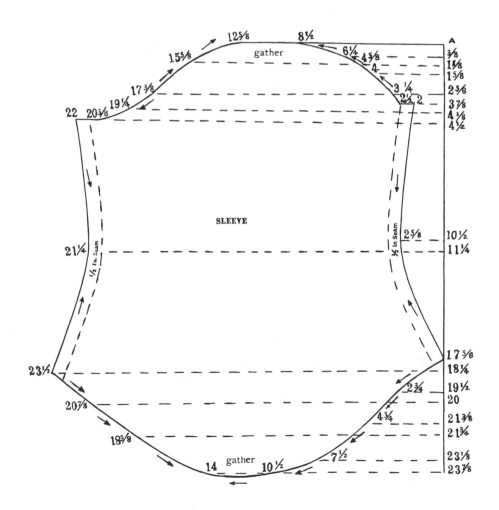

 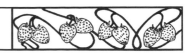

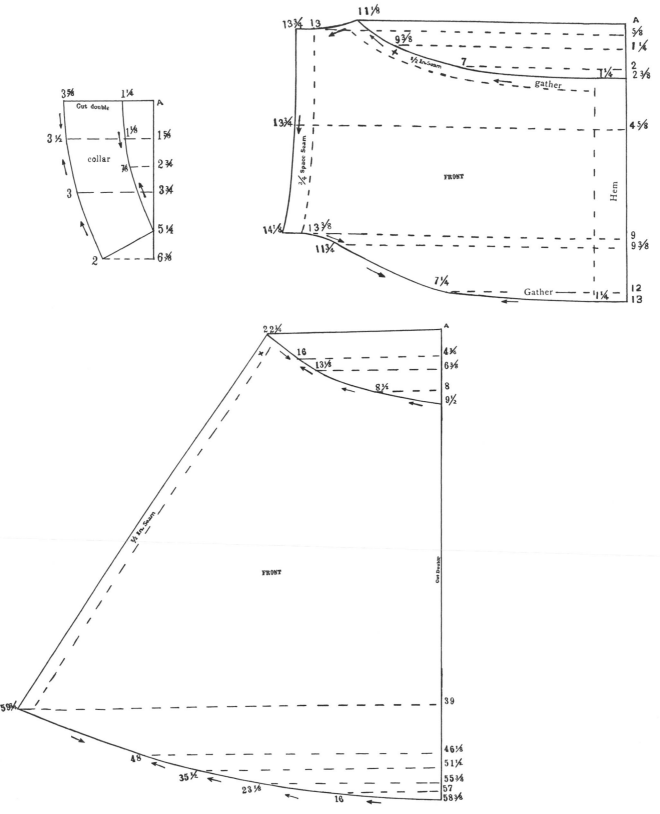

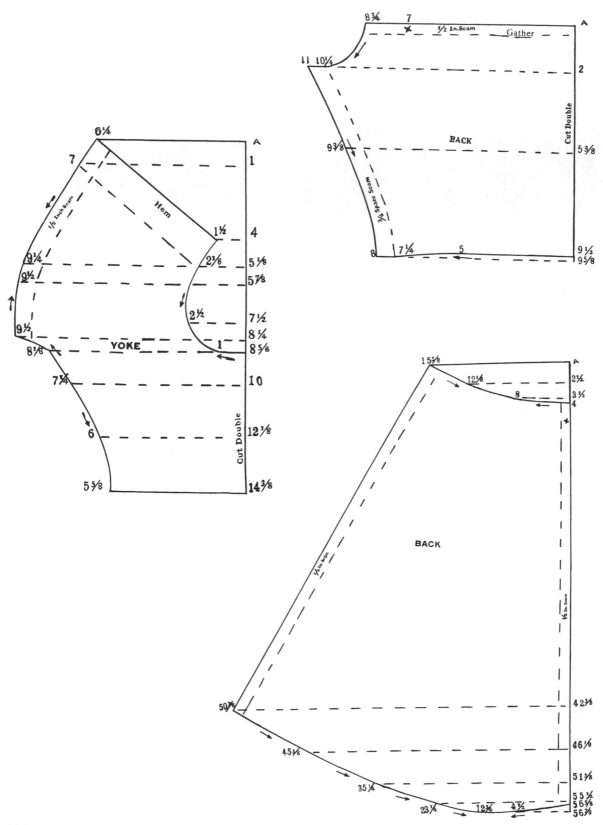

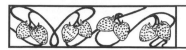

Calling Costume

Use the scale corresponding to the bust measure to draft the waist, which consists of lining back, side back, and front; outside back and front; full front; collar; sleeve; and cuff. Use the scale corresponding to the waist measure to draft the seven skirt portions. Regulate all lengths by the tape measure.

Join lining back and side back. Place outside back on them with corresponding seams together. Lay a box pleat in goods as illustrated before cutting side fronts. Take up darts in lining fronts. Place outside fronts on them with corresponding seams together. Shirr fullness in full front to any depth desired. Place it on right lining front underneath outside front, allowing it to overlap left front, and fasten at left side. Gather fullness in fronts at waist-

line to fit waist lining. The collar is a fancy lace collar (no draft is provided). Bind neck and adjust standing collar in the usual way. Join sleeves at their respective seams and join to cuff as illustrated. Adjust sleeve in armseye and gather surplus fullness at top to fit armseye.

The skirt has an extra pleat at the back. Join it to skirt, and arrange, according to the directions on the draft. Join skirt portions according to Xs and finish in the usual way.

This suit is made of cloth with embroidery down every other skirt gore, and on the waist and cuff. The skirt seams are strapped with bias folds of the goods. A white chiffon front, strapped across with black velvet ribbon, and a large fancy lace collar complete the costume.

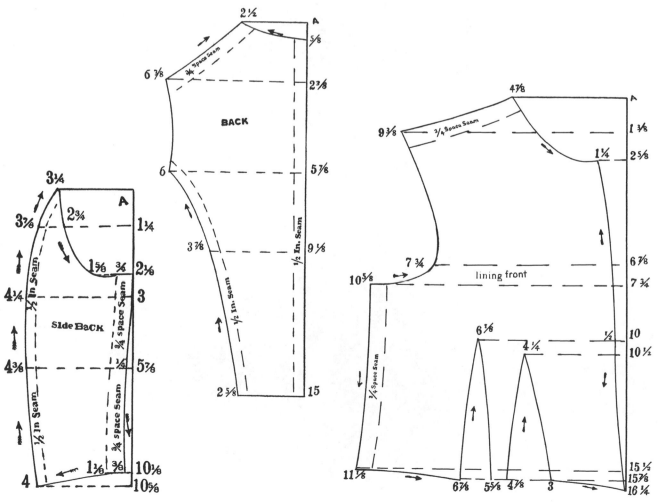

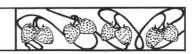

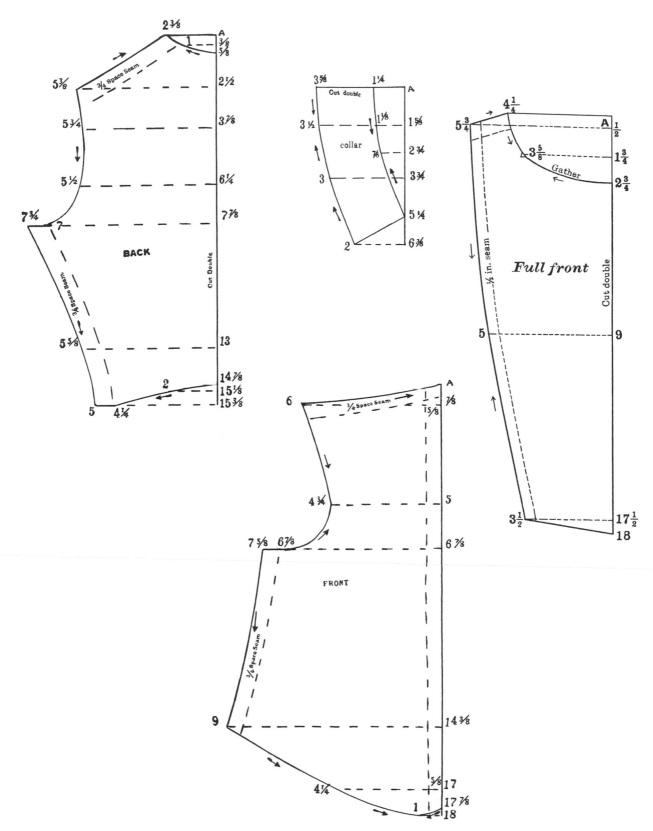

295

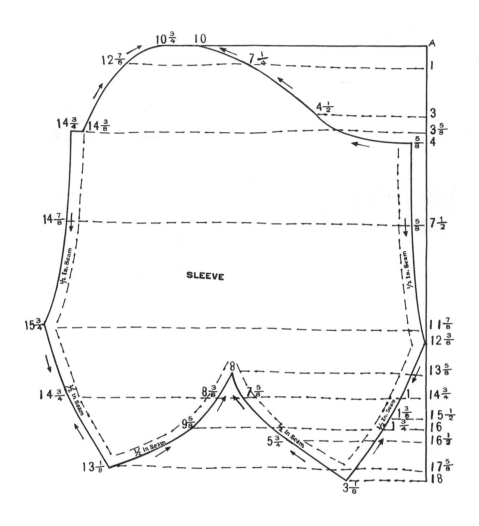

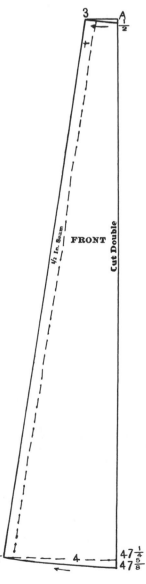

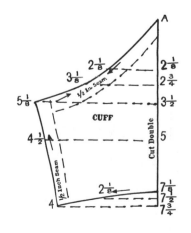

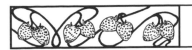 

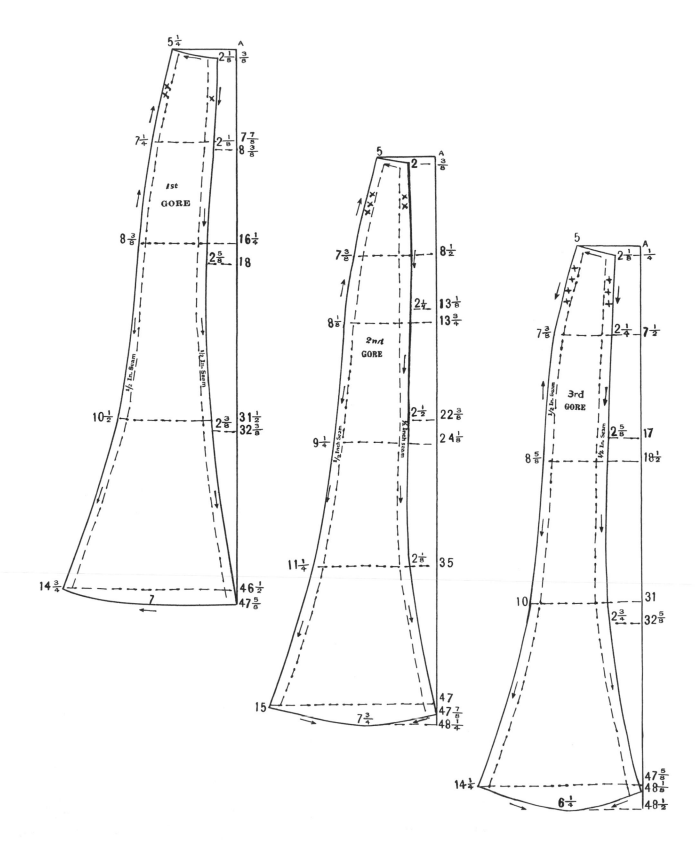

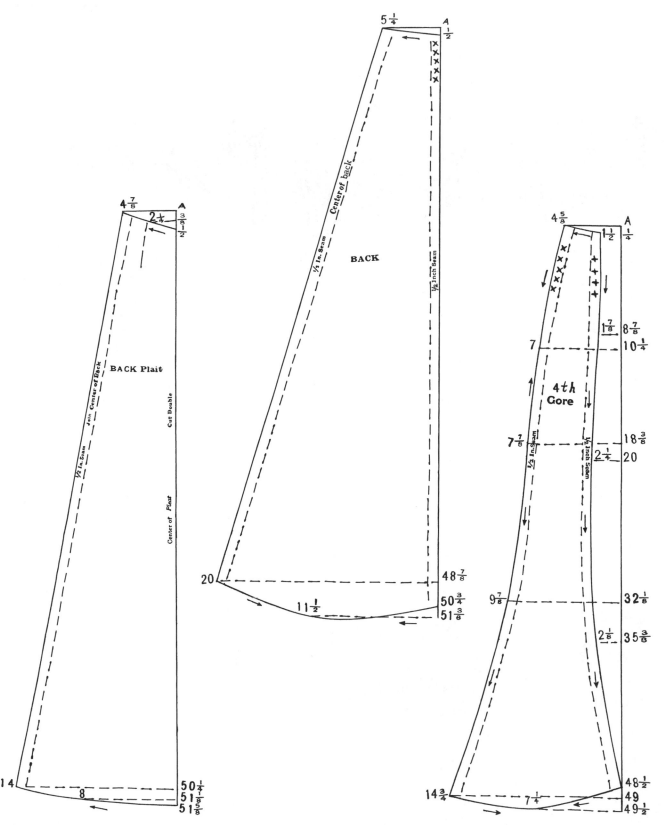

Ladies' Toilet

Use the scale corresponding to the bust measure to draft the waist, which consists of lining back and front, side front, vest, collar, shoulder cap, sleeve, upper sleeve, and cuff. Use the scale corresponding to the waist measure to draft the four skirt portions. Regulate all lengths by the tape measure.

Tuck all goods, or allow space for tucks in your goods, before cutting. The vest is tucked in small tucks arranged diagonally, while the front, back, and upper sleeve have the same small tucks running to the yoke line. Wider tucks finish the bottom of skirt side gore and flounce. The shoulder cap is made of alternate rows of insertion and the goods, while the same insertion extends down each edge and center of front.

Take up darts in lining fronts. Place side fronts on them with corresponding seams together. Place vest front on lining front underneath outside fronts. Cut outside back the same as lining back. Place on lining back with corresponding seams together. Join

the whole at shoulder and underarm seams. Gather fullness in front to fit the waist measurement. Finish waist in the usual way. Bind neck and adjust standing collar in the usual way. Join outside sleeve and undersleeve in one seam. Gather the fullness at the bottom of the undersleeve to fit the cuff. Allow outside sleeve to fall loose at bottom as illustrated. Adjust in armseye, gathering fullness at top to fit armseye. Tack shoulder cap in the desired position before finishing neck. Finish waist at waistline with belt.

Be very careful to lay skirt pleats in the front and back as indicated on the drafts. Pleats are stitched in place to flounce line in front and within a short distance of bottom at back. Join the skirt portions as indicated on the drafts. Shirr the flounce two or three times at top. Join it to bottom of side gore only, joining ends of flounce to back and front pleats in seam with side gore.

This suit is made of voile over a silk foundation skirt. It may be developed in any soft or lightweight material.

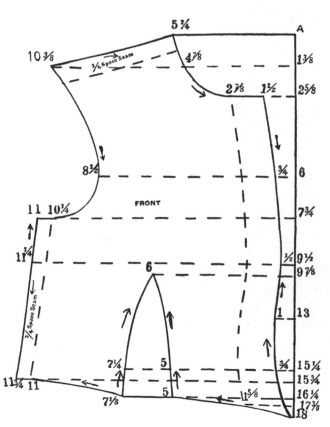

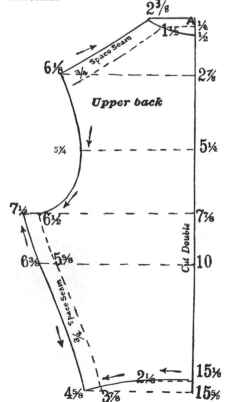

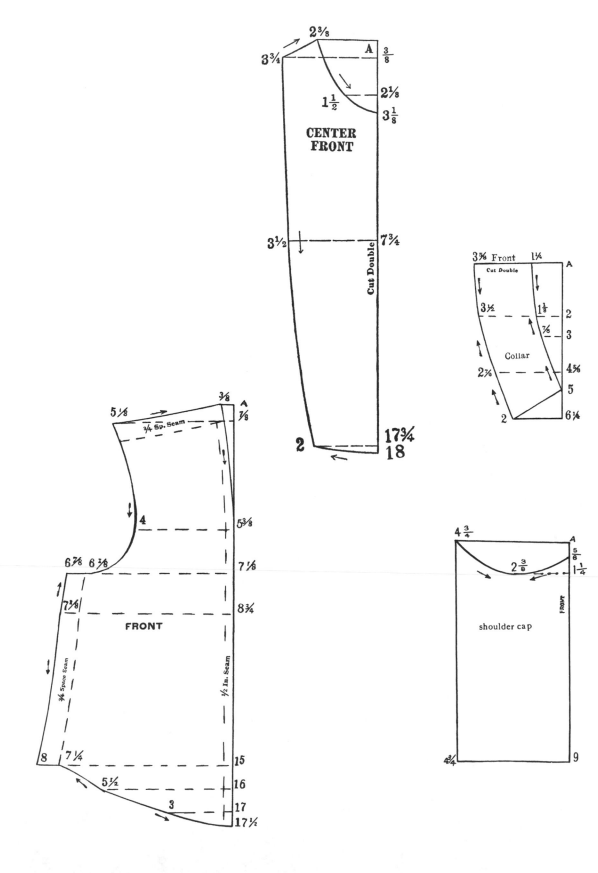

301

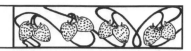

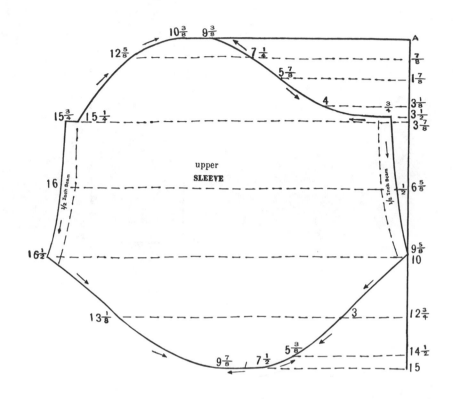

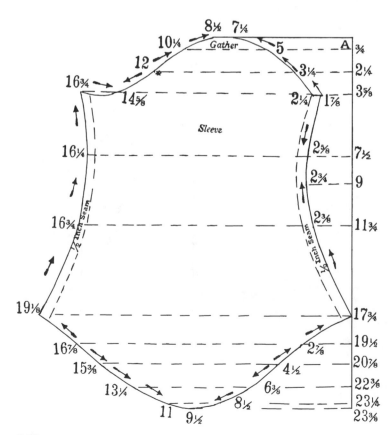

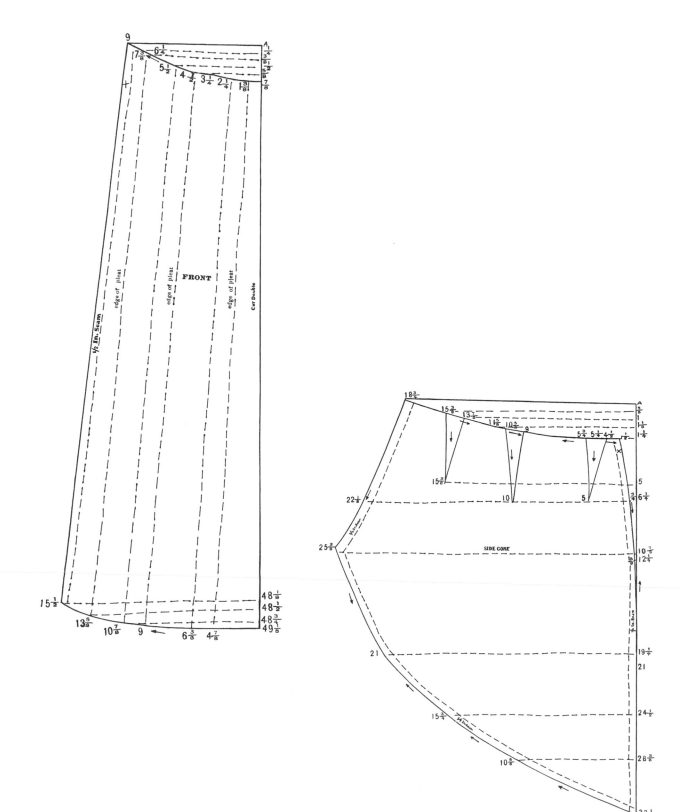

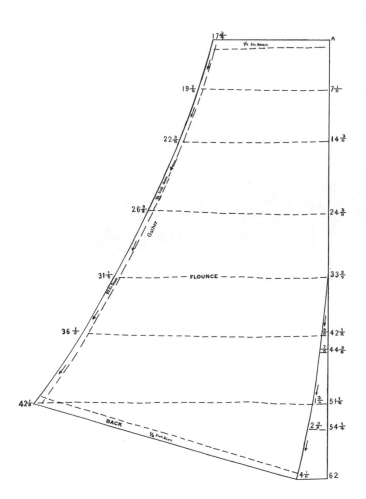

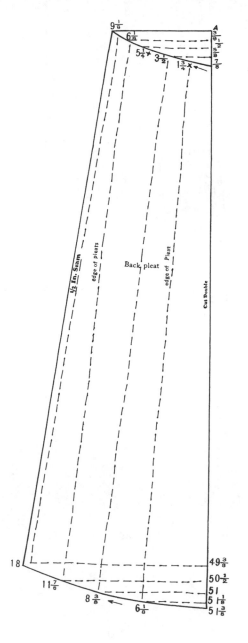

Jacket Suit

Use the scale corresponding to the bust measure to draft the waist, which consists of waist back and front, jacket back and front, collar, and sleeve. If a lining is desired, use any of the standard linings. Use the scale corresponding to the waist measure to draft the six skirt portions. Regulate all lengths by the tape measure.

Join jacket and waist separately. Join waist front at shoulder and underarm seams. Gather the fullness at front and back to fit the waist measurement. Join the front and back of jacket at shoulder and underarm seams. Place same on waist with corresponding seams together. Join sleeve and adjust in armseye, gathering fullness at top to fit armseye.

Bind neck of waist and adjust standing collar in the usual way. The suit illustrated has a full skirt yoke. To obtain this arrange your material on skirt yoke the desired fullness, in pleat form or any way you wish. Then cut out in the form of the yoke lining. Join all skirt portions according to the Xs. Lay your slot seams as indicated on drafts, to within any desired distance of skirt bottom (see illustration). When all seams have been arranged join skirt to skirt yoke as indicated. Finish at top and bottom in the usual way.

This suit is trimmed with braid and appliqué lace.

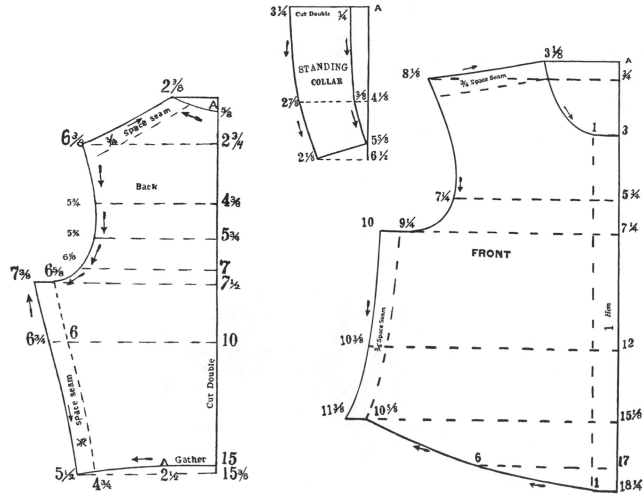

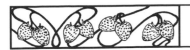 

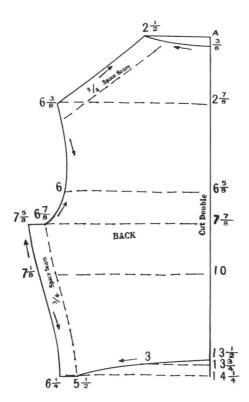

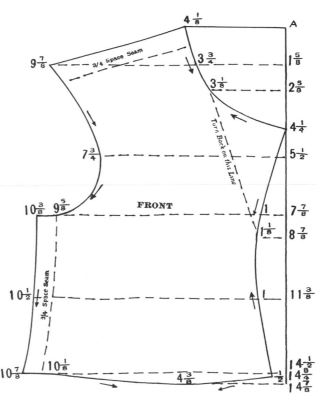

307

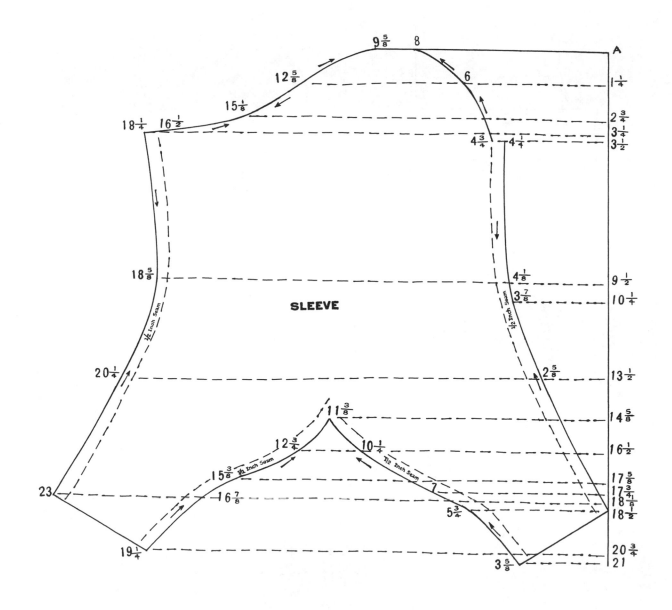

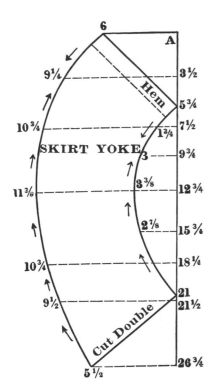

6 **A**

9¼ 3½

Hem

10¾ 5¾

7½

1¾

SKIRT YOKE 3 9¾

3⅜ 12¾

11⅜

2⅞ 15¾

10¾ 18¼

21
9½ **21½**

Cut Double

5½ 26¾

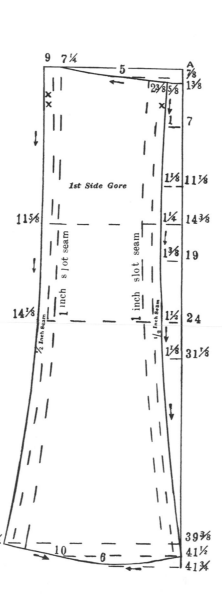

9 7¼ 5 **A**
7/8
2⅜ 5⅝ 1⅜
X X
X X X 1 7

1⅛ 11⅛

1st Side Gore

1¼ 14⅜

11⅝

1⅜ 19

1 inch slot seam 1 inch slot seam

14⅛ 1½ 24

½ Inch Seam ½ Inch Seam

1⅛ 31⅛

19¾ 39⅜
10 6 41½
41¾

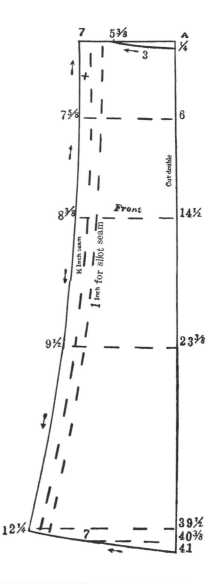

7 5⅜ **A**
¼
3

7⅝ 6

Cut double

8⅜ Front 14½

¾ Inch seam
1 inch for slot seam

9½ 23⅜

12¼ 7 39½
40⅜
41

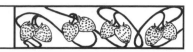

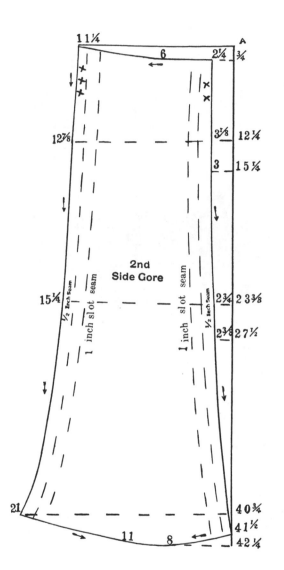

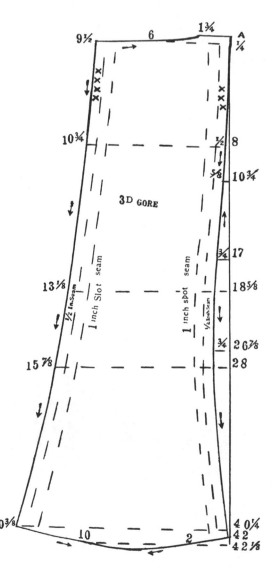

Jacket Suit

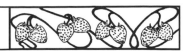

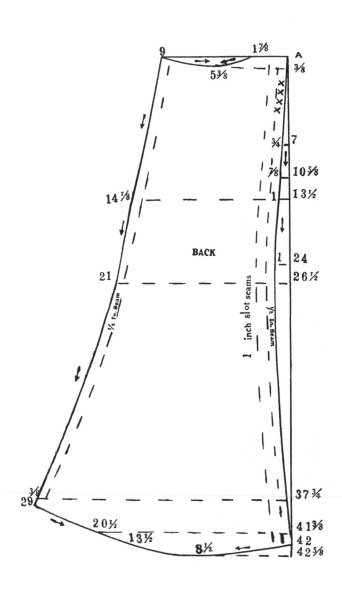

311

Fall Suit

Use the scale corresponding to the bust measure to draft the jacket, which consists of back, front, collar, stole, neckpiece, sleeve, and cuff. Use the scale corresponding to the waist measure to draft the four skirt portions. Regulate all lengths by the tape measure.

Join the jacket back and front at the shoulder and underarm seams. Join the sleeve and gather the fullness at bottom to fit cuff. Adjust sleeve in armseye, gathering fullness at top to fit armseye.

Place center of collar to center of jacket back, and allow it to fall in position around neck. Finish neck with neckband. Finish the stoles and tack them in position as illustrated.

Join the skirt portions according to the Xs. Arrange the fullness at top in back in an inverted pleat. Finish skirt in the usual way.

This suit can be developed very elegantly in taffeta silk. The jacket has a large fancy lace collar and lace cuffs. Fancy silk braid adorns both skirt and jacket.

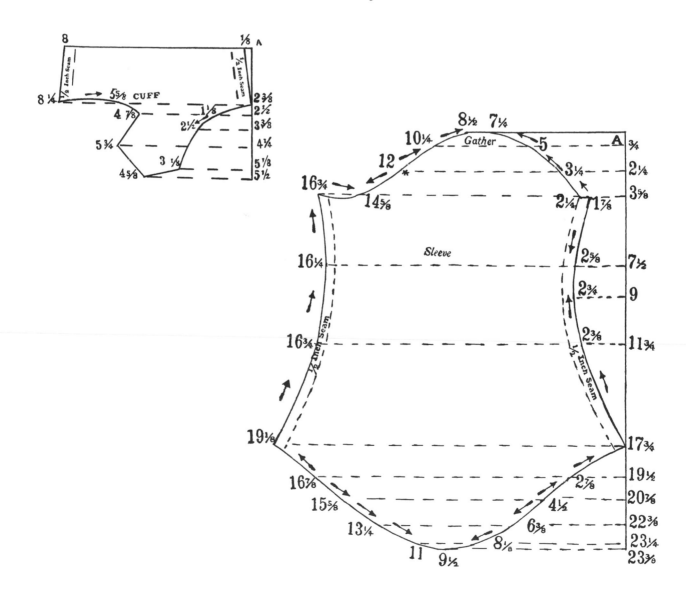

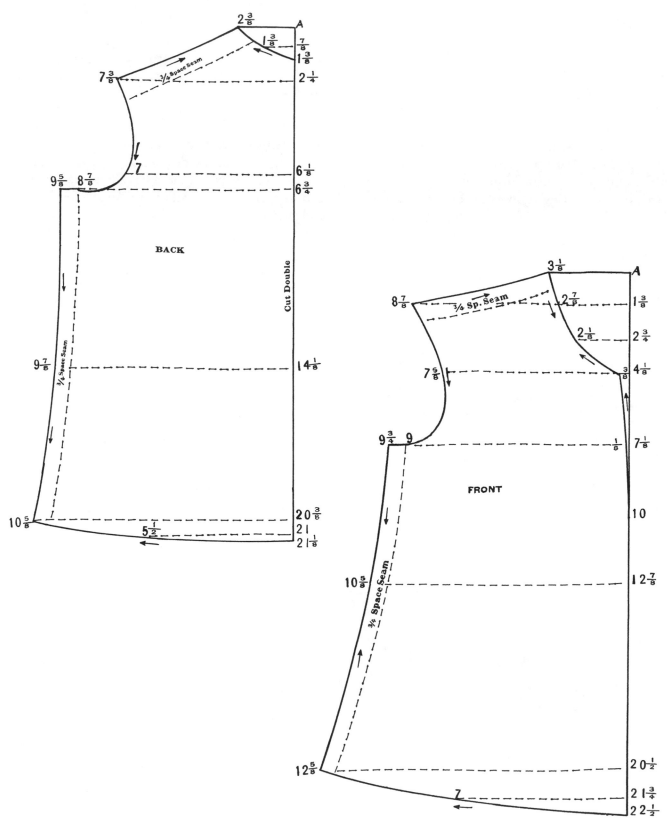

314

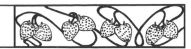
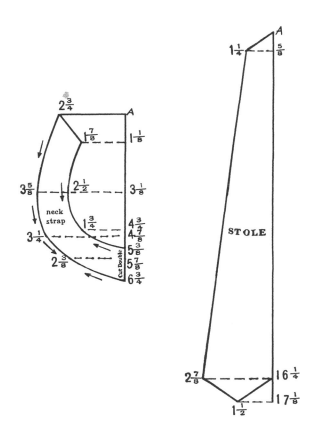

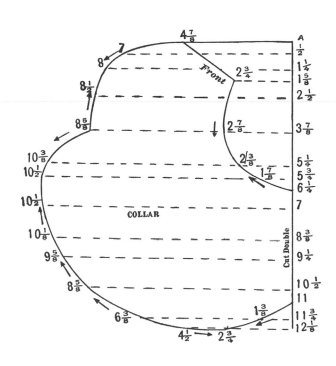

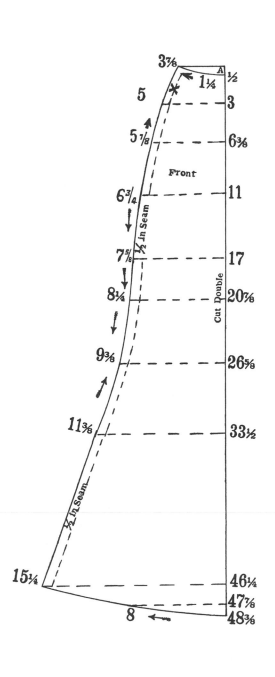

STOLE

Front

neck strap

Cut Double

COLLAR

Front

Cut Double

½ In Seam

½ In Seam

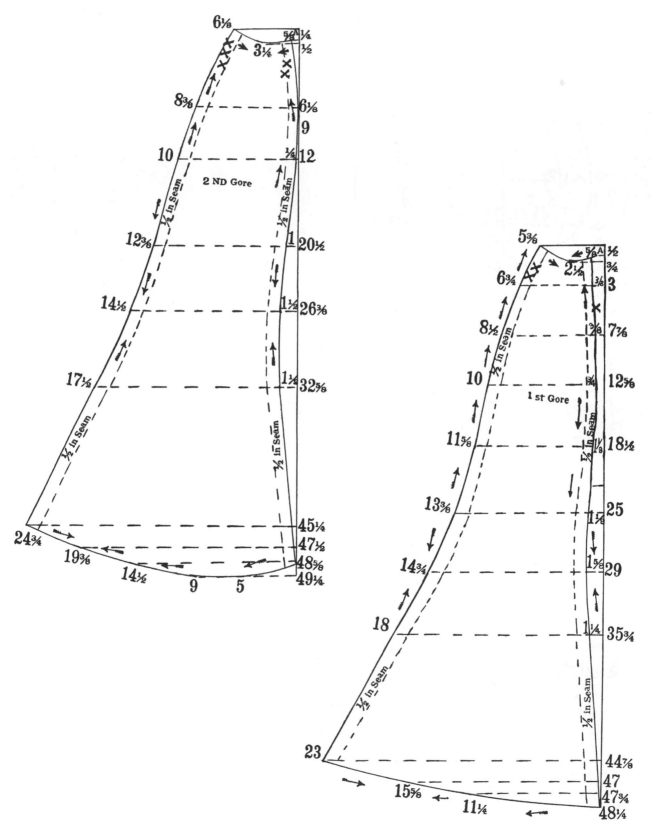

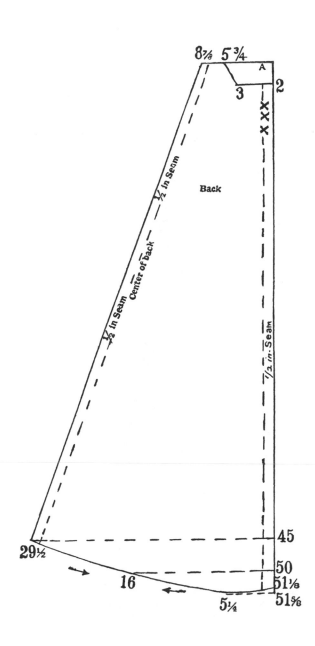

Equestrian Suit

Use the scale corresponding to the bust measure to draft the waist, which consists of back, side back, underarm gore, front, peplum, collar, and two sleeve portions. Use the scale corresponding to the waist measure to draft the four skirt portions and two bloomer portions. Regulate all lengths by the tape measure.

Take up the darts in front. Join back, side back, underarm gore, and front at their respective seams. Join remainder of waist at shoulder seam. Turn revers on fronts; bind neck and adjust standing collar in the usual way. Take up the darts in the peplum. Join it to bottom of waist, placing center of back to center of waist back, and allow peplum to fall into position around to front. Join sleeve portions. Adjust sleeve in armseye, gathering any surplus fullness at top to fit armseye.

The skirt is a divided skirt. Notice the markings on each draft indicating which edge is to be placed on a selvage of the cloth. Pay attention to this and the skirt will set properly. Join the under front, side gore, and back as indicated by the Xs. Join back width together down to lower point of curve. Now take back edge of the back breadth below curve and front edge of front breadth below the fly, and sew them in seam together. Lay two forward-turning pleats in front, and two backward-turning pleats in back, according to stars and notches. The upper front is set on to come to side seams, giving the appearance of a round skirt. For convenience when riding astride, one side of upper front is finished and left loose.

Take up darts in bloomers as indicated, or gather if preferred. Join one fly to the front edge of the left front. Underface the front edge of the right front and place the remaining fly underneath the right front. Close the leg seams, and the center seams from the top to the fly. Turn lower edge of each leg under 1 1/4 inches for a casing. Insert elastic to regulate the fullness. Arrange fullness at back in an inverted pleat. Finish top with an underfacing. Close garment with buttons and buttonholes.

Make suit of any suitable material.

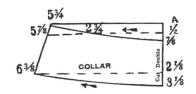

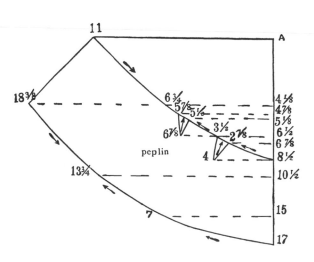

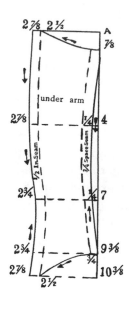

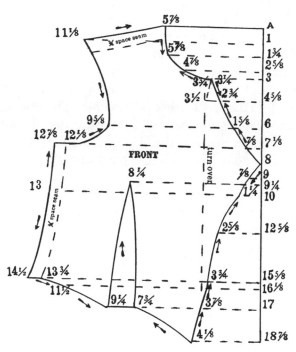

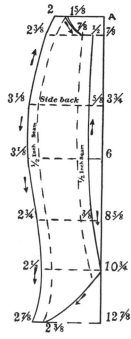

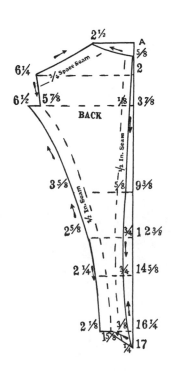

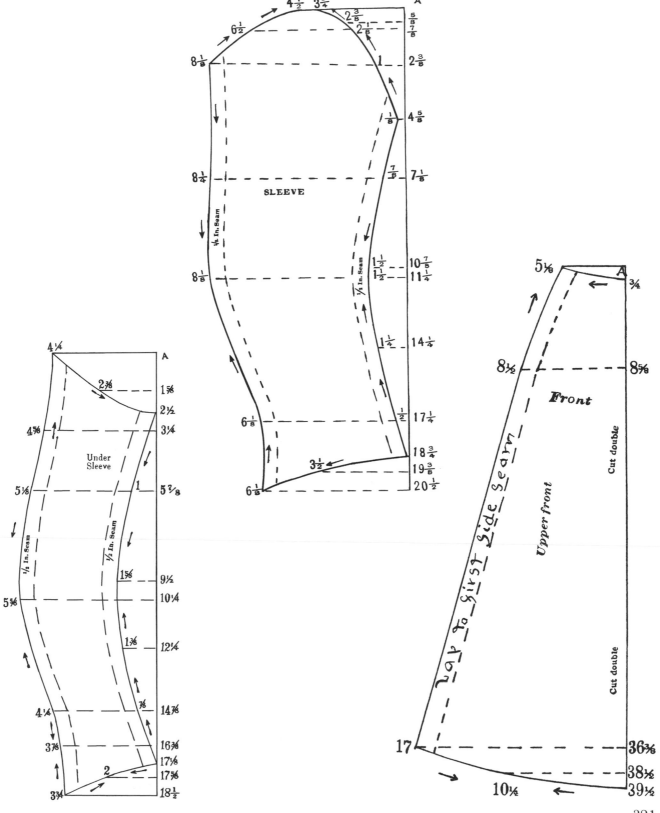

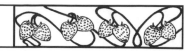

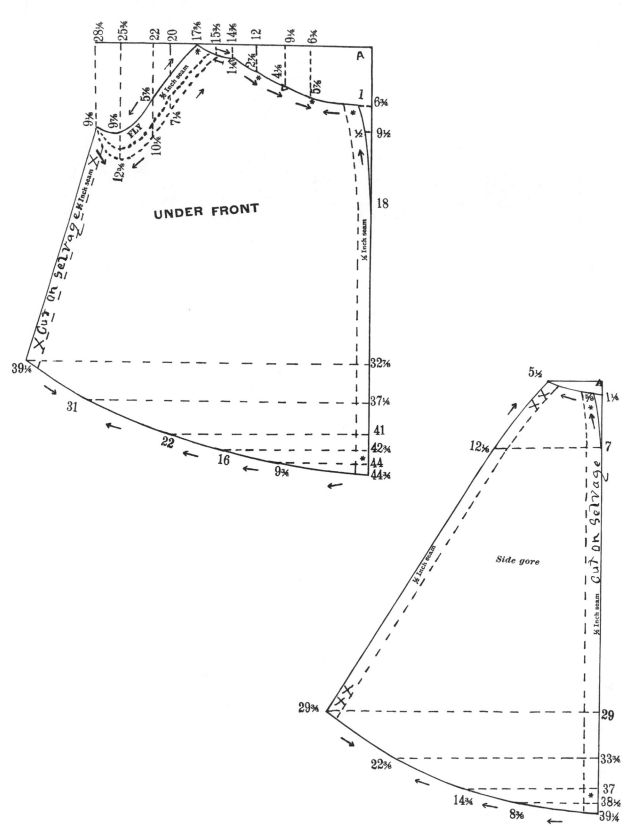

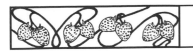

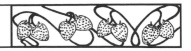

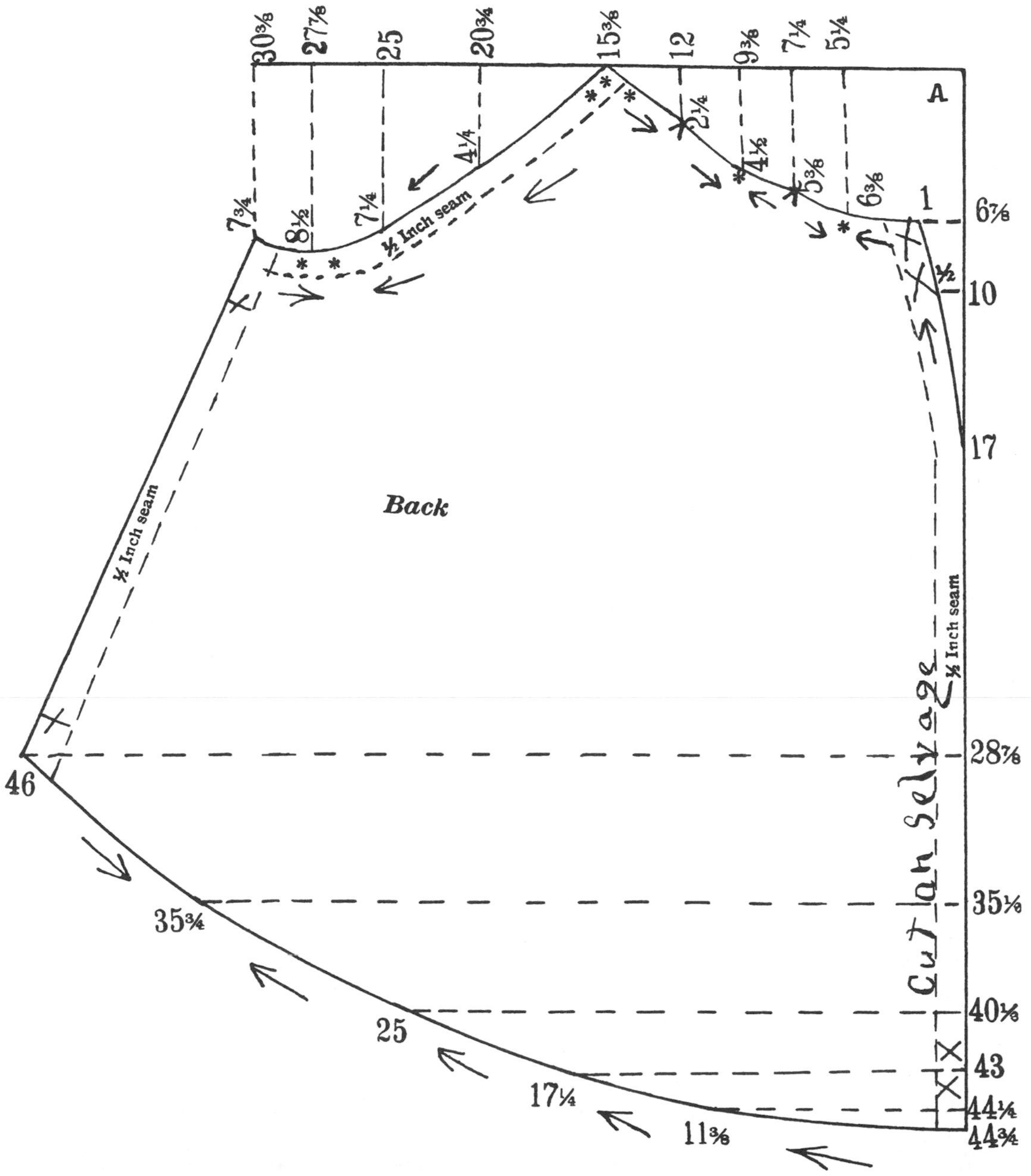
30⅜
27⅞
25
20¾
15⅜
12
9⅜
7¼
5¼
A
2¼
4¼
4½
5⅜
6⅜
7¾
8½
7¼
½ Inch seam
1
6⅞
½
10
17
Back
½ Inch seam
½ Inch seam
Cut on selvage
28⅞
46
35¾
35⅛
25
40⅛
43
17¼
44¼
11⅜
44¾

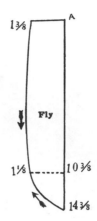

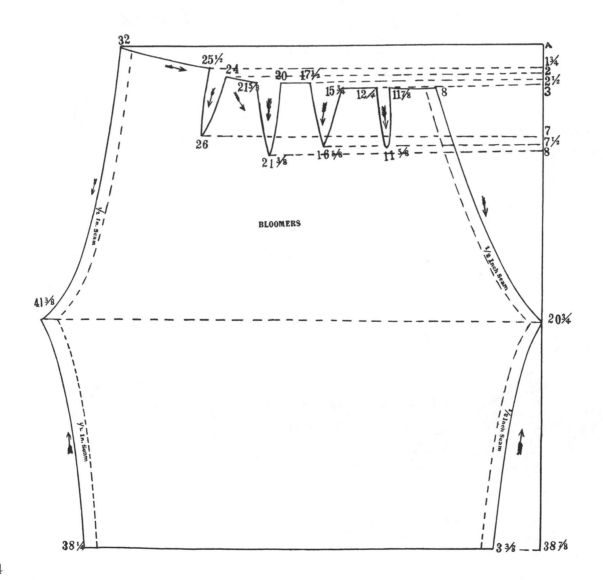

November 1903

At present the tight skirt flaring at the bottom, the sun-pleated skirt, the tucked skirt with flounce, and now the full skirt, all seem equally correct.

For fall and winter street wear, suits will be made with skirts of instep length, with a long fitted jacket. The drop skirt has been found very unsatisfactory worn with these short skirts, and there is a decided tendency to the return of the lined and slightly stiffened skirt. Great care should be exercised in hanging these short skirts to avoid that dip in the back so often noticeable. Rather make the measurement in back the least bit shorter than the front, as everything tends to length in front and shortness at the back. Since these suits are mostly for business and professional wear the greatest interest settles on the fabrics. Novelty goods, almost invariably in zibelines, seem the most popular, while we have heavy homespuns, mixed cheviots, tweeds, and men's suitings as well. The snowflake effects and plaids of the zibelines are most beautiful.

The material for full skirts and for evening wear is softer, such as crepe de chine, chiffon, net, lace, and the softer silks. Following these comes voile and a few of the wool crepe weaves.

Princess gowns are extremely fashionable both for street and evening. It is a great mistake to overload them with trimmings, for thereby all simple lines, their greatest beauty, are lost. The most approved styles are made with trains, yet many round lengths are made. Broadcloth, velveteen, and soft-finished silks make up most appropriately in these gowns.

Sleeves are becoming more voluminous. The deep, tight cuff is very popular, thereby causing the greater amount of fullness to puff at the elbow or just below.

Girdles are very popular. The correct girdle does not lengthen the waistline unduly, but adapts to the curves of the hip. It may extend in a straight line across the back or slope downward to form a point. Velvet seems the chosen material, yet ribbon makes up very nicely, especially when bows and loops are desired.

We are still favored with the large cape or collar in all its varied shapes and designs. Long-shouldered, sloping effects are still our aim. Fancy stocks of all descriptions, with their elongated tabs, together with the little turnovers so popular, will continue to be worn.

White in the various wool textures, together with the lighter-weight materials, will be worn all winter. Nothing seems more beautiful or appropriate for evening wear than these all-white costumes. Lace will form an important part in their makeup. Straps and buttons will be the main trimming for street and tailored gowns.

Coats are mostly of three-quarter length and some are even longer. Their tendency is to be tight fitting. We also have the tight-fitting jacket, with a plain tailored sleeve; while the coat with the long skirt attached has come to stay.

Stoles and muffs are at the height of their popularity.

There is great variety in winter millinery. Soft white and light-colored felts will be much worn. The tendency for smaller shapes is noticeable, but low crowns still prevail. Turbans are constructed in so many varied shapes as to adapt themselves to all faces. These hats are simply trimmed with quills and egrets and are very becoming with street costumes. For more dressy hats ostrich and osprey plumes will continue to be favorites. Birds of the manufactured kind are to be worn more than ever.

Ladies' Evening Costume

Use the scale corresponding to the bust measure to draft the waist, which consists of lining back and front, outside back and front, vest, bertha, collar, and sleeve. Use the scale corresponding to the waist measure to draft the four skirt portions. Regulate all lengths by the tape measure.

Take up the darts in lining front. Place outside front on it with corresponding seams together. Gather the fullness at bottom to fit the lining. Place vest on front and allow bertha to fall into position covering the seam where vest joins front. The bertha is attached only at the vest line and allowed to fall loose the remaining distance, as illustrated. Place outside back on lining back with corresponding seams together. Gather any surplus fullness at bottom of back to fit the lining at the waistline. Join waist at shoulder and underarm seams. Bind neck

and adjust collar in the usual way. Join sleeves and adjust them in armseye, gathering any surplus fullness at top to fit the armseye. The sleeve has no cuff; the fullness at the bottom is gathered to fit the forearm and finished at the bottom with a ruffle of lace. A deep ruffle of lace finishes the edge of the bertha. The waist is finished at the waistline with a sash.

Join skirt portions at their respective seams according to notches. Gather the fullness at the top to fit the waist, pushing the greater amount of fullness toward the back. Finish skirt at the bottom in the usual way.

This costume is made of soft silk and trimmed with ribbon and appliqué lace.

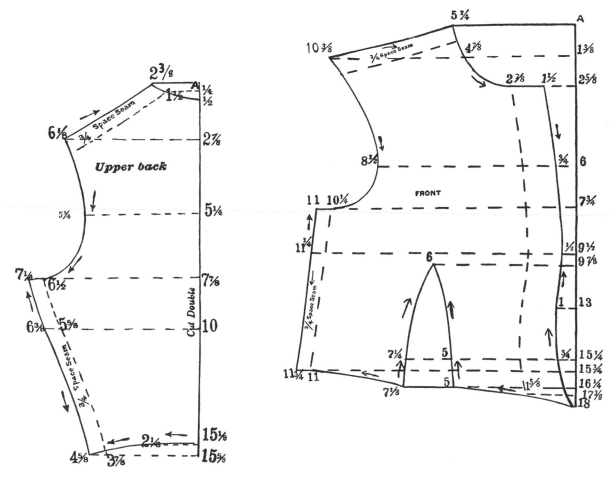

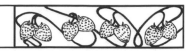

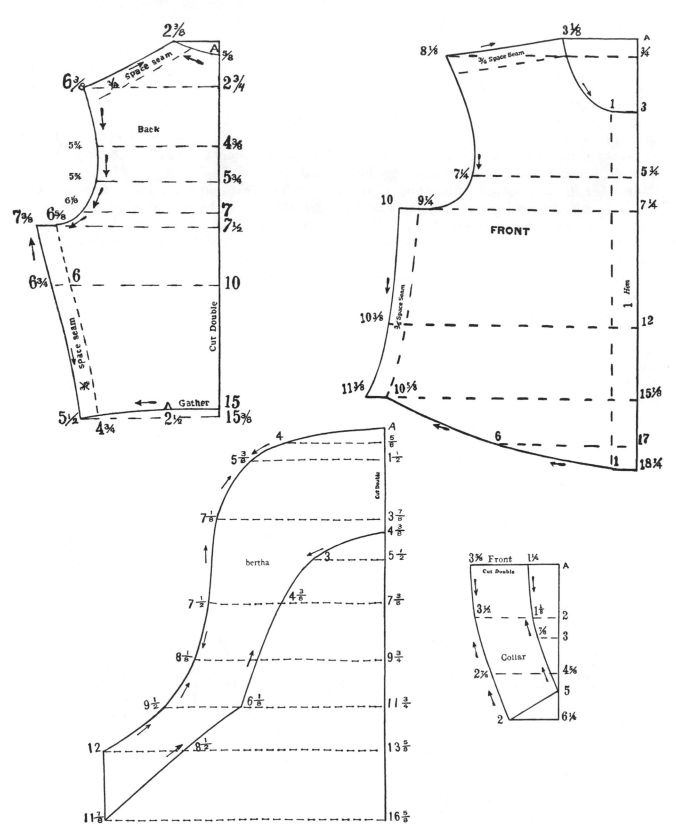

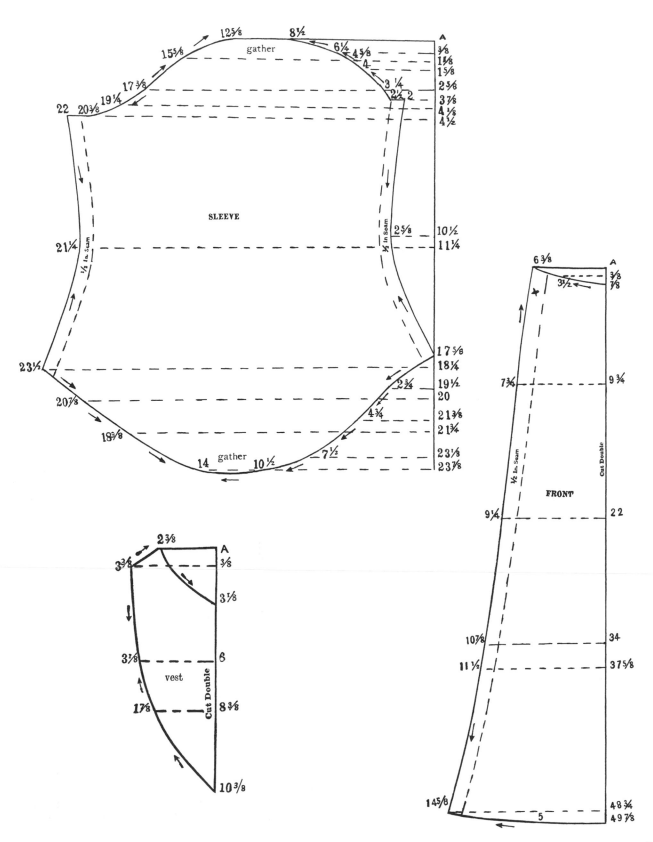

SLEEVE

FRONT

vest

329

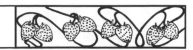
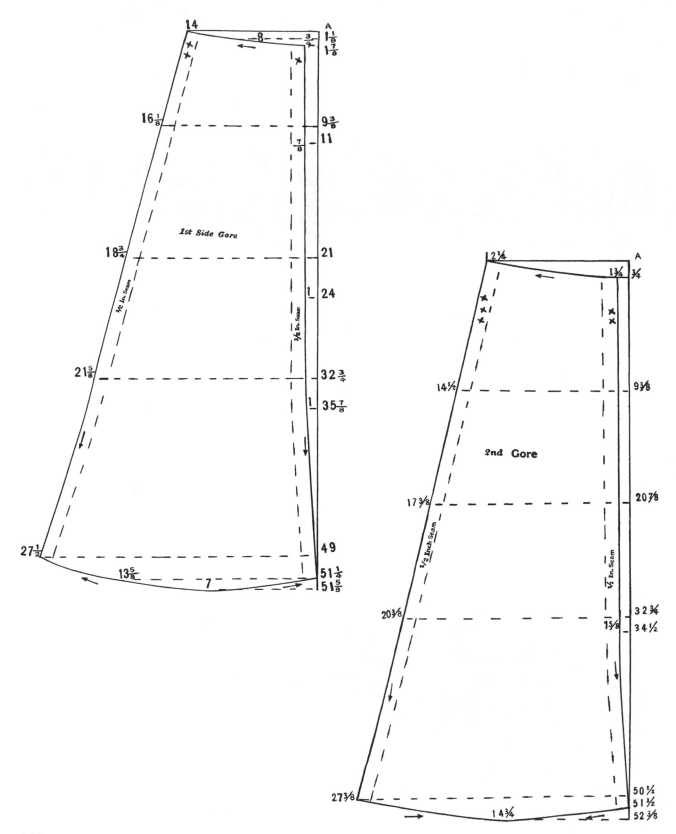

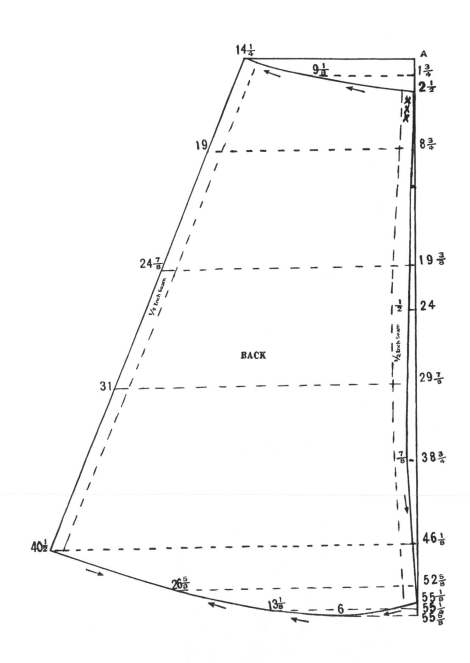

 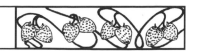

Promenade Costume

Use the scale corresponding to the bust measure to draft the waist, which consists of lining back, side back, and front; outside back and front; yoke; bertha; collar; girdle; and sleeve. Use the scale corresponding to the waist measure to draft the seven skirt portions. Regulate all lengths by the tape measure.

Take up the darts in the lining fronts. Cut left outside front on dotted line. Place the outside fronts on the lining with corresponding seams together. Place the outside back on lining back with corresponding seams together. Join the waist at the shoulder seams. Then position center of yoke back to center of lining back. Allow yoke to fall around on right front, overlapping left front and fastening at left side. Allow right front to overlap left front and

fasten at left side. Join the waist at the underarm seam, but join the lining and the outside separately. Gather the fullness in back and front to fit the waistline. Place center back of bertha to center of waist back and allow to fall into position down side fronts, as illustrated. Finish bottom of waist with girdle. Bind neck and adjust collar in the usual way. Join the sleeve and the cuff at wrist up to the point indicated by the X. Then gather the fullness at the bottom of the sleeve to the remaining portion of the cuff. Adjust sleeve in armseye, gathering fullness at top to fit the armseye.

Join all skirt portions according to the Xs and instructions on drafts. Finish bottom of skirt in the usual way.

This suit is made of novelty goods and trimmed with silk cord and buttons. The yoke is of soft silk, shirred many times.

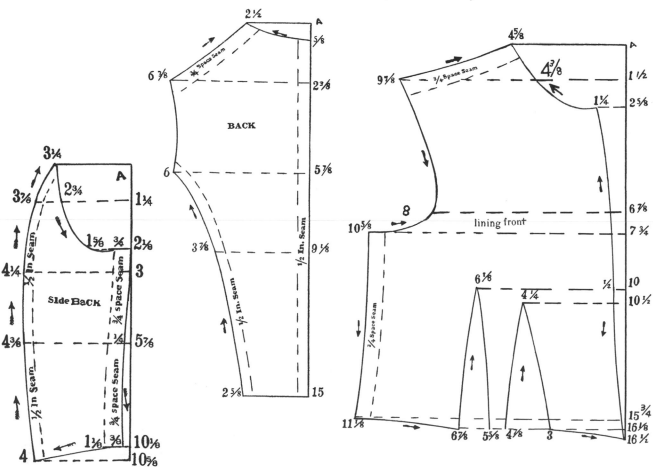

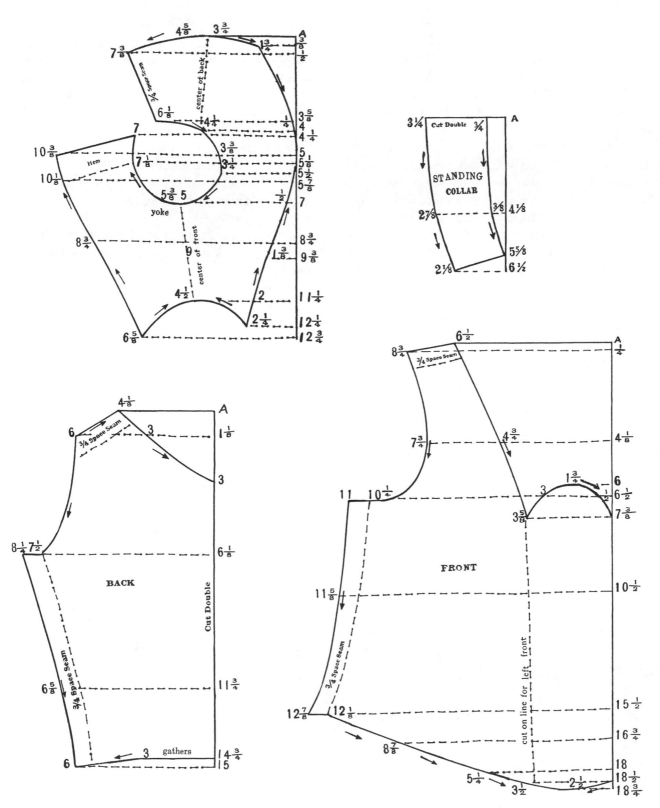

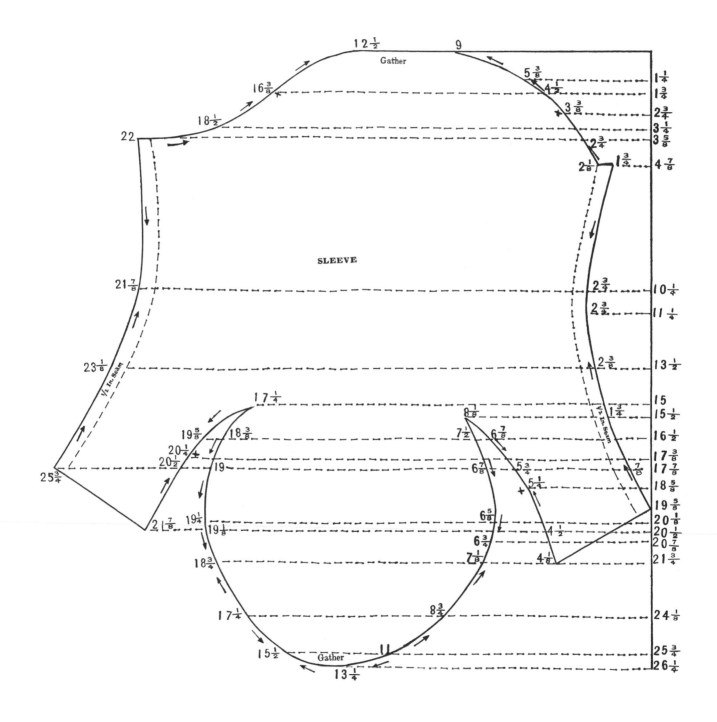

335

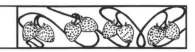
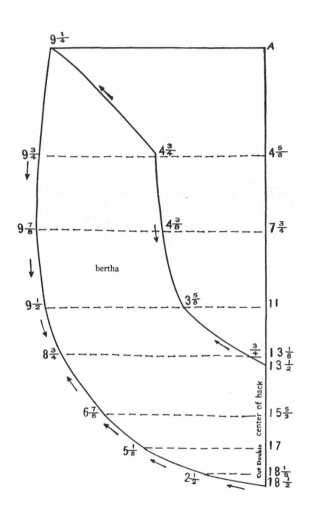

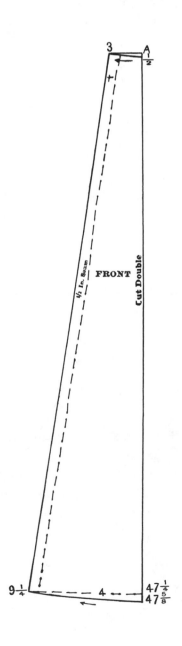

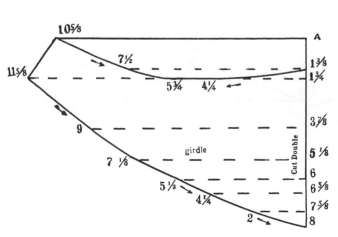

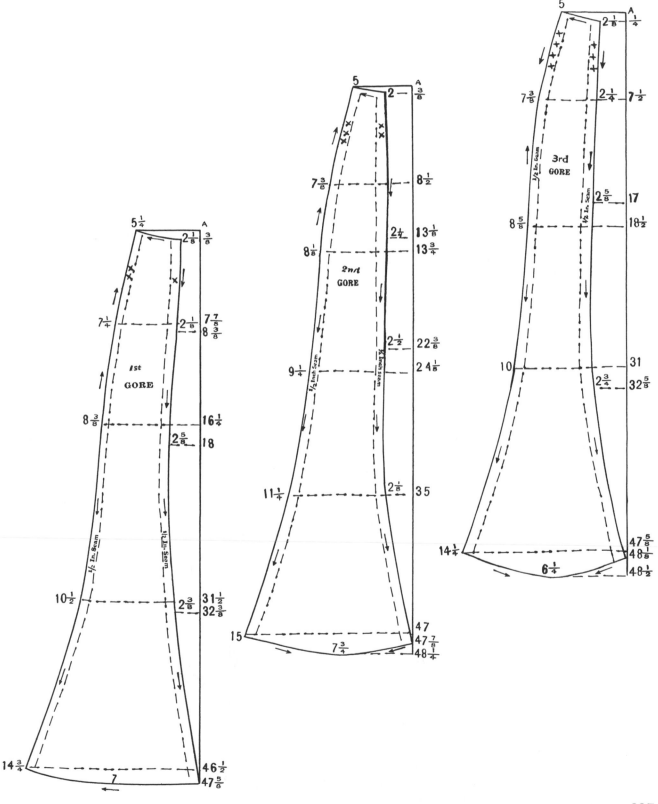

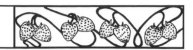

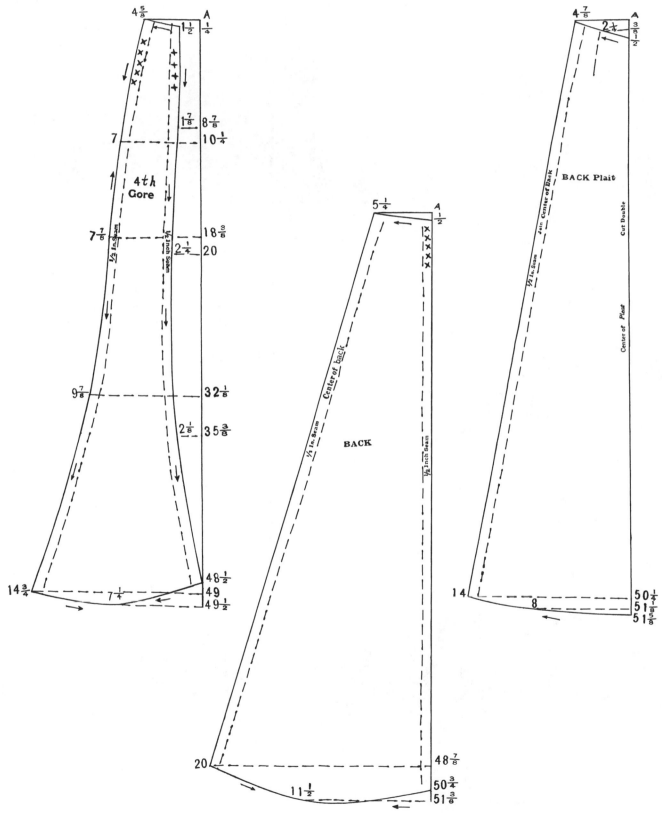

Shirtwaist

Use the scale corresponding to the bust measure to draft this pattern, which consists of back, front, collar, sleeve, and cuff. Regulate the length by the tape measure.

Gather the fullness in front at shoulder and neck to fit the shoulder and neck measurements. Join back to front at shoulder and underarm seams. Waist opens in the back. Fold the hem in the back draft. Gather any surplus fullness in front and back to fit the waist measurement. Join the sleeve and adjust in armseye, gathering any surplus fullness at top to fit the armseye and at bottom to fit the cuff. Bind neck and adjust collar in the usual way.

This waist is made of soft material and trimmed with heavy lace, as illustrated.

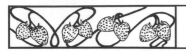

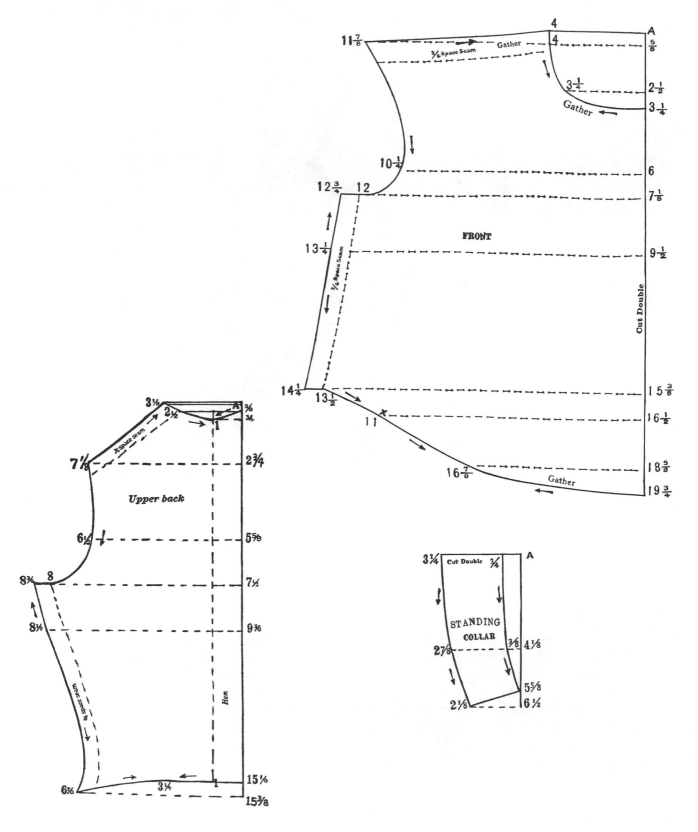

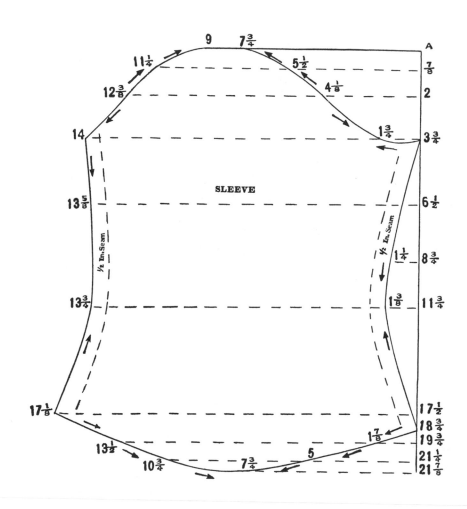

SLEEVE

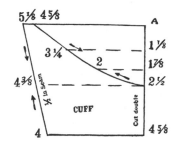

CUFF

Shirtwaist

Use the scale corresponding to the bust measure to draft this pattern, which consists of back, front, collar, two sleeve portions, and cuff. Regulate the length by the tape measure.

Tuck all goods before cutting. Waist opens in the back. Join waist at shoulder and underarm seams. Gather fullness in front to fit the waist measurement. Bind neck and adjust collar. Gather the fullness of the lower portion of sleeve to fit the sleeve cap and join. Join the sleeve thus formed and adjust in armseye, gathering fullness at top to fit the armseye and at bottom into cuff.

This waist is made of silk and trimmed with medallions of lace.

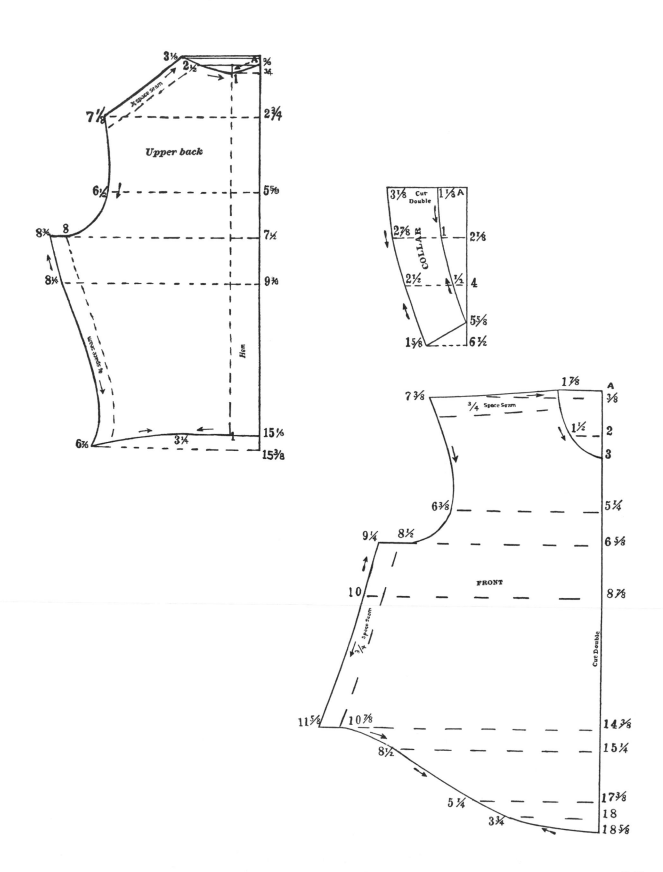

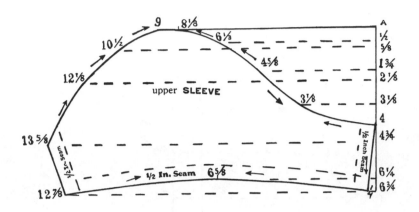

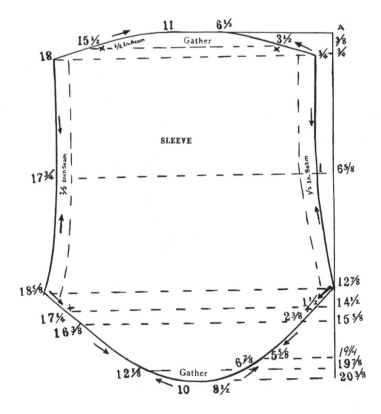

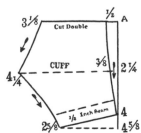

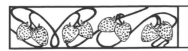 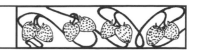

Afternoon Gown

Use the scale corresponding to the bust measure to draft the waist, which consists of back and front lining, outside back and front, yoke, two sleeve lining portions, sleeve, and cuff. Use the scale corresponding to the waist measure to draft the three skirt portions. Regulate all lengths by the tape measure.

Join the backs and place outside back on lining back with corresponding seams together. Gather the fullness in back at top and bottom to fit the lining back. Take up the darts in the lining fronts. Place outside fronts on them with corresponding seams together. Gather the fullness in fronts at top and bottom to fit the lining. Join the waist at the shoulder seam. Then place center of yoke back to center of waist back and allow it to fall into position around the front. Join waist at underarm seam. Adjust collar in the usual way. Join sleeve lining and place outside sleeve on it with corresponding seams together. Gather the fullness at top to fit the armseye and adjust sleeve in armseye. Join sleeve lining and outside sleeve separately. Place cuff on sleeve lining and gather the fullness at bottom of sleeve to fit the cuff.

This waist can be very readily made without the lining. Join the front and back waist portion to the yoke and the cuff to the outside sleeve. Join the remainder of the waist the same. Instead of gathering the fronts to the yoke, the fullness can be laid in pleat effects and then fagoted together a short distance as illustrated.

Join the skirt portions at their respective seams according to the stars. Lay the pleats at the bottom in inverted box pleats and tack in place. Arrange fullness at back in an inverted box pleat. Finish at waist and bottom in the usual way.

This gown is made of tan cashmere and trimmed with brown taffeta silk bands. The yoke is also outlined with appliquéd lace.

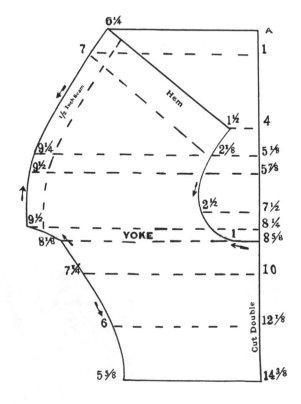

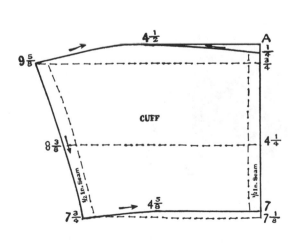

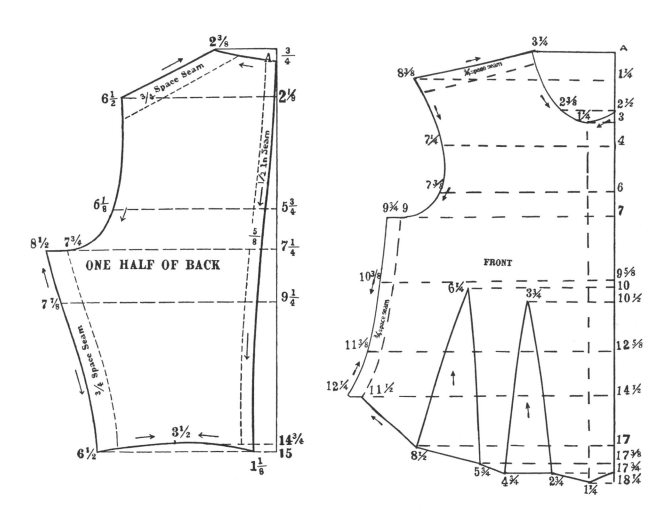

ONE HALF OF BACK

FRONT

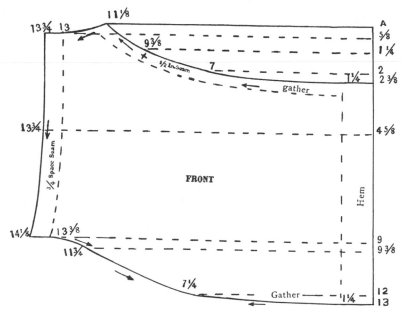

FRONT

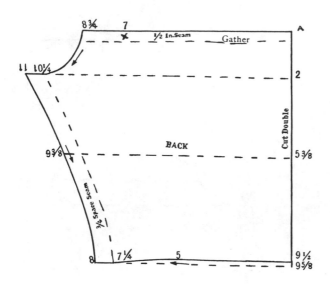

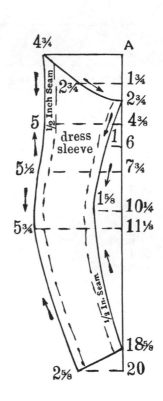

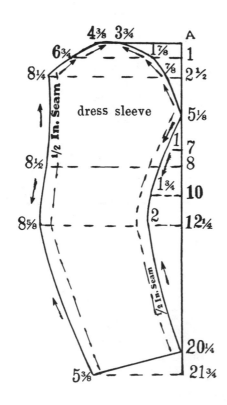

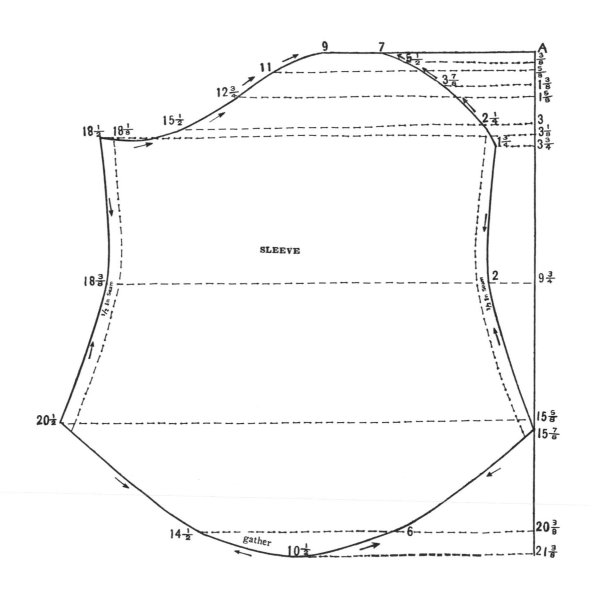

SLEEVE

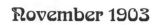

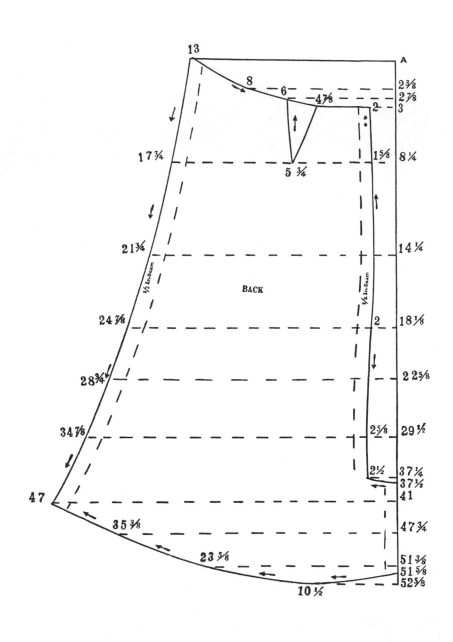

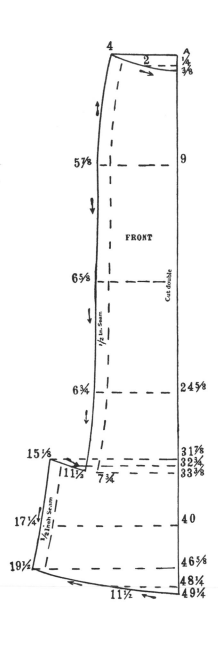

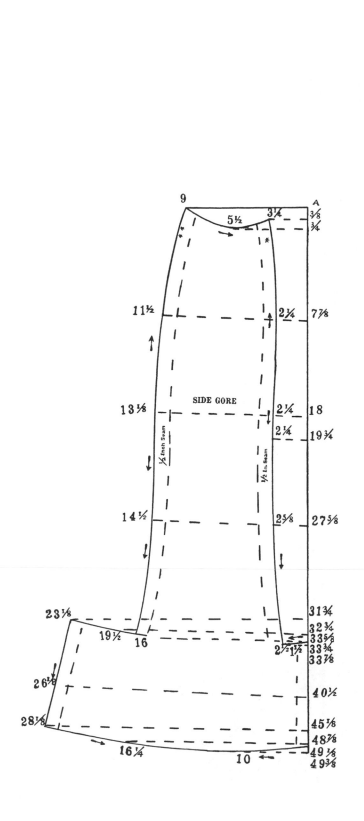

 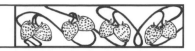

Jacket Suit

Use the scale corresponding to the bust measure to draft the jacket, which consists of back, side back, underarm, front, vest, peplum, collar, and sleeve. Use the scale corresponding to the waist measure to draft the five skirt portions. Regulate all lengths by the tape measure.

Place vest on outside front, allowing the outer edge of vest to fall along line of dart in front, and take up front dart. Join back and side back at their respective seams. Join the whole at the shoulder and underarm seams. Lay pleat in peplum at back as indicated on the draft. Join peplum to lower edge of jacket, placing center of peplum to center of back and allowing peplum to fall into position toward front. Make and join collar in the usual way. Join sleeve and adjust in armseye, gathering fullness at top to fit the armseye.

Join the skirt portions according to the Xs. Finish at top and bottom in the usual way.

This suit may be prettily developed in any of the novelty or heavy woolly goods now so popular. The one illustrated is made of novelty goods and has a vest of contrasting color. The suit is trimmed with braid.

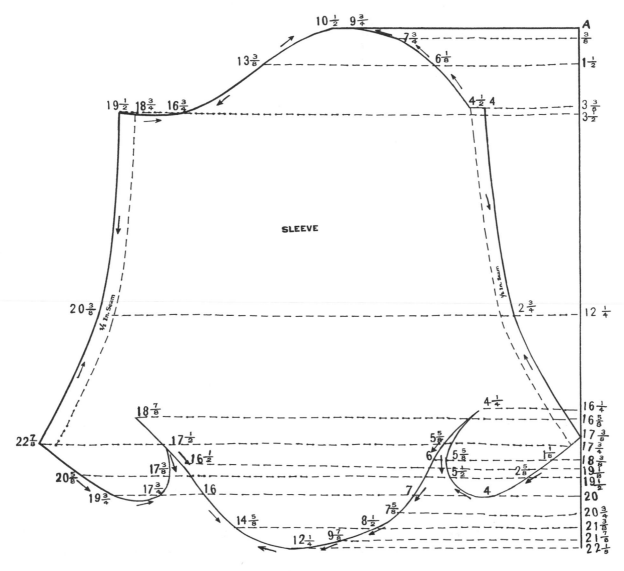

353

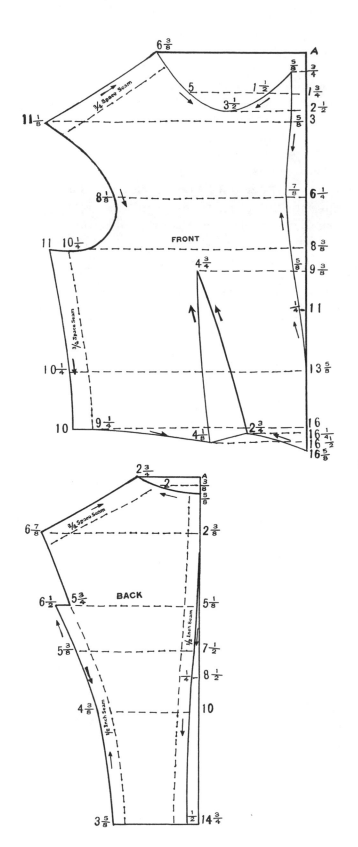

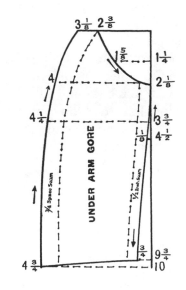

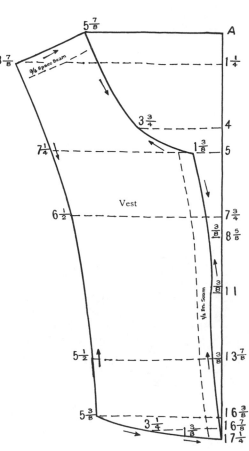

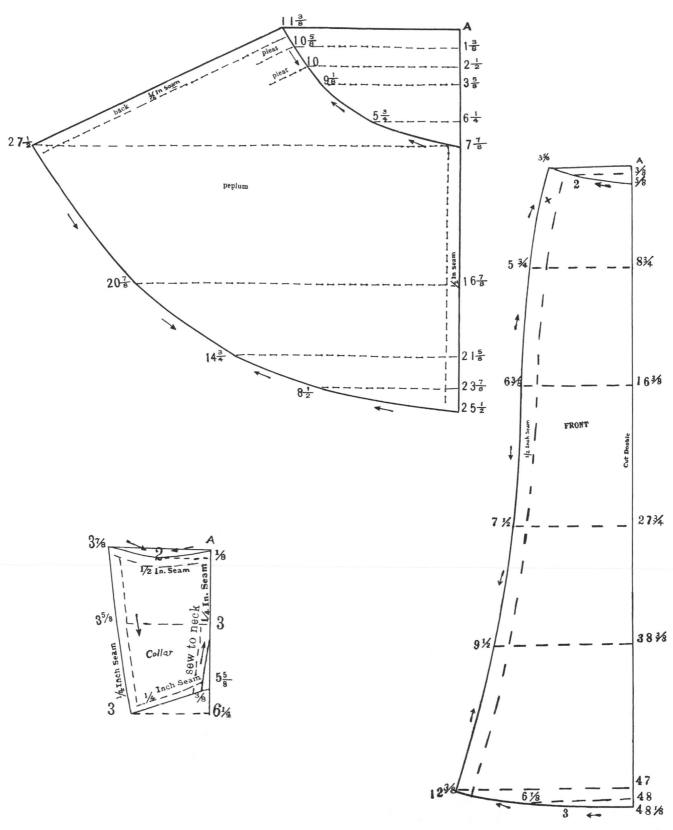

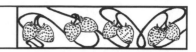

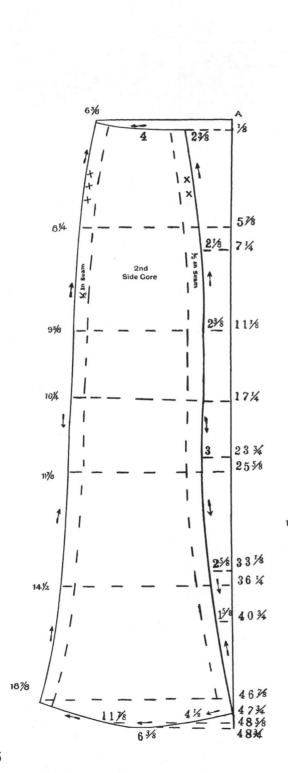

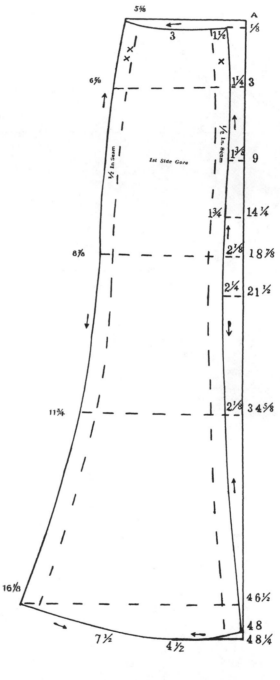

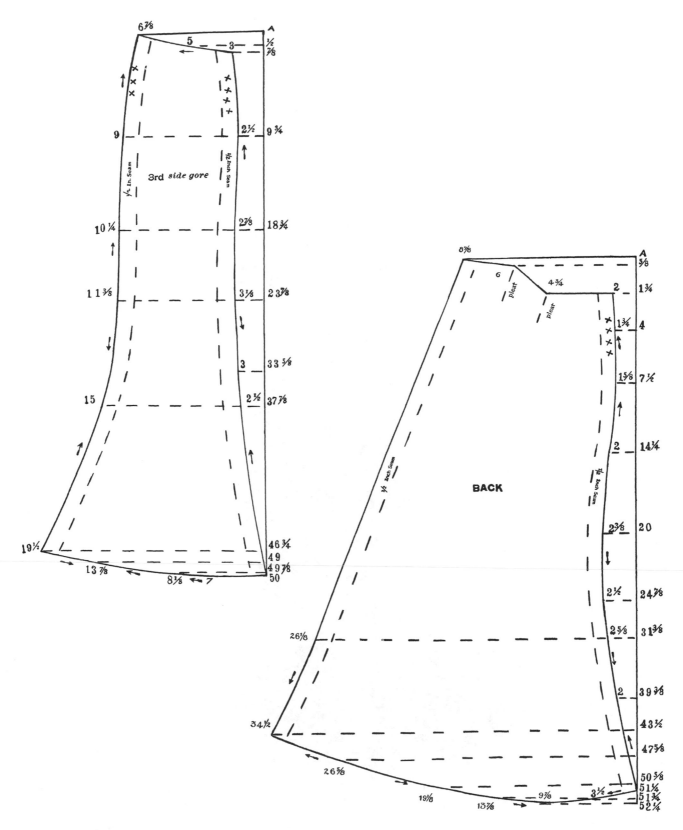

357

Ladies' Coat

Use the scale corresponding to the bust measure to draft this coat, which consists of back, front, collar, cape, sleeve, and cuff. Regulate all lengths by the tape measure.

Take up the darts in the fronts. Join fronts to the back. Join the whole at shoulder seam. Join sleeve and adjust in armseye, gathering fullness at top to fit the armseye and at bottom into cuff. The cape collar extends over the shoulder and terminates in a narrow strap in back, which extends be-low the waistline. Place the collar in front and allow it to fall into position down the back. When properly adjusted the straps will fall about midway on each side of the back seam. This straplike portion of the cape should be stitched in position, but the remainder should fall loose. Adjust standing collar in the usual way.

This coat is made of one of the new weaves of zibeline. Stitching and buttons form the trimmings.

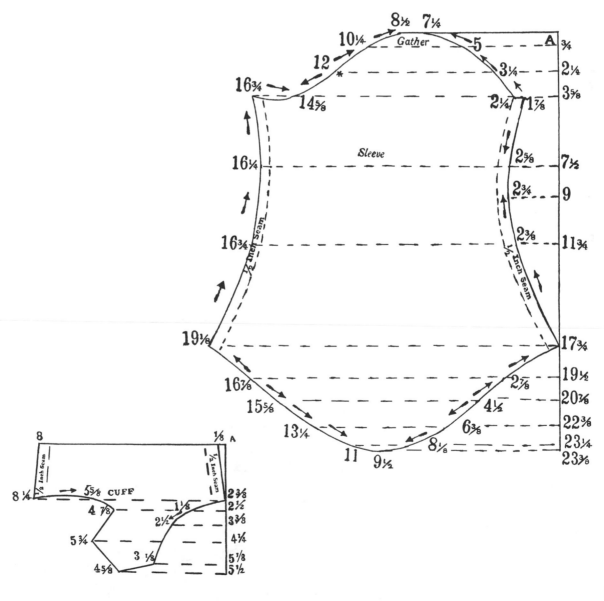

359

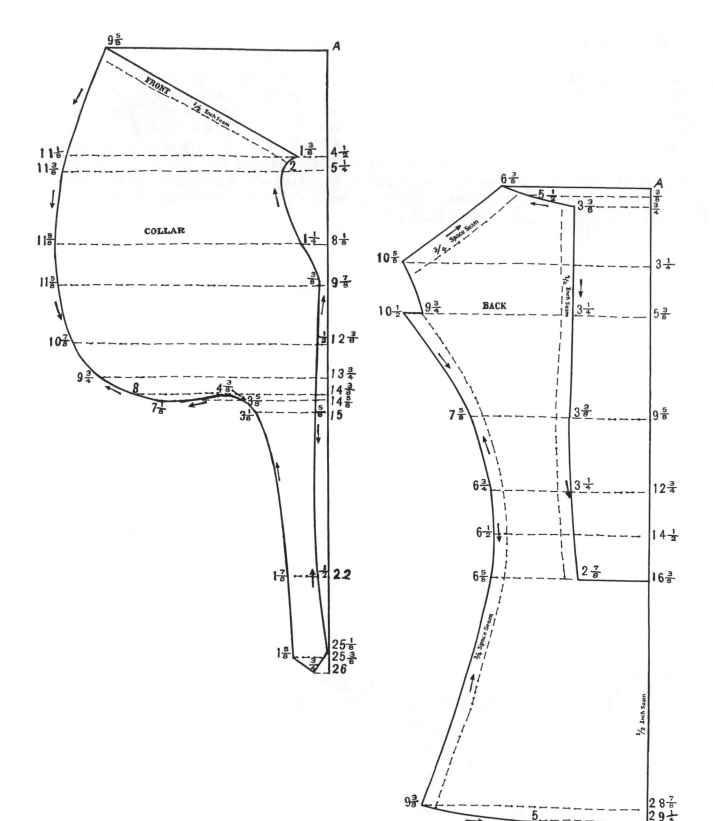

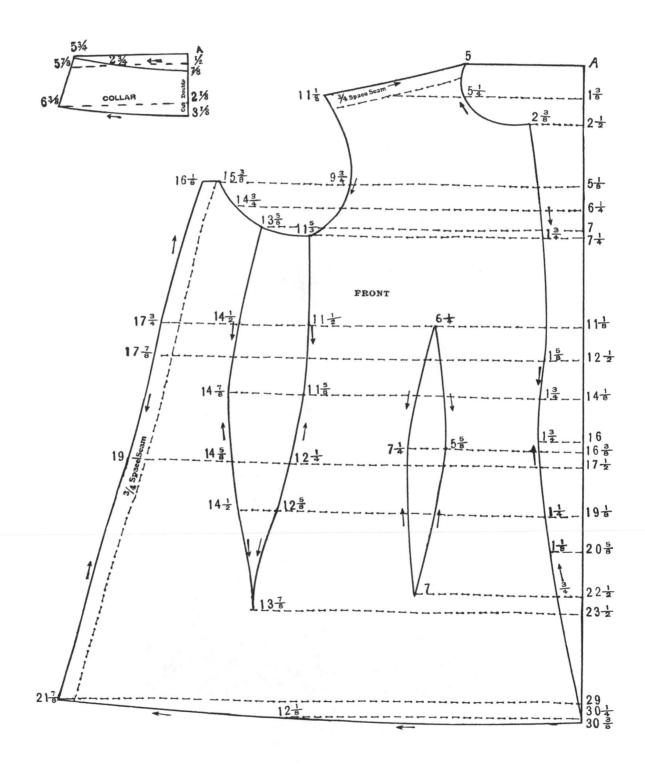

COLLAR

Cut Double

FRONT

¾ Space Seam

¾ Space Seam

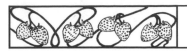 

Tea Gown

Use the scale corresponding to the bust measure to draft all waist portions, which consist of front and back yoke, three sleeve portions, and collar. Use the scale corresponding to the waist measure to draft the two skirt portions. Regulate all lengths by the tape measure.

The fullness in the skirt portions is arranged in small tucks terminating at the waistline. Take them up in front and back. Join the skirt portions to the yokes. Join the shoulder and underarm seams. Tuck goods for the sailor collar before cutting. Place center back of collar to center of yoke back and allow collar to fall in position around to front. This forms a V at the neck which can be filled in with any desired material. Join the sleeve peplums to the sleeve proper. Join the whole and adjust in armseye, gathering any fullness at top to fit the armseye.

Make this garment of any soft material. The one illustrated is trimmed with small ruffles, soft lace, and lace appliqué.

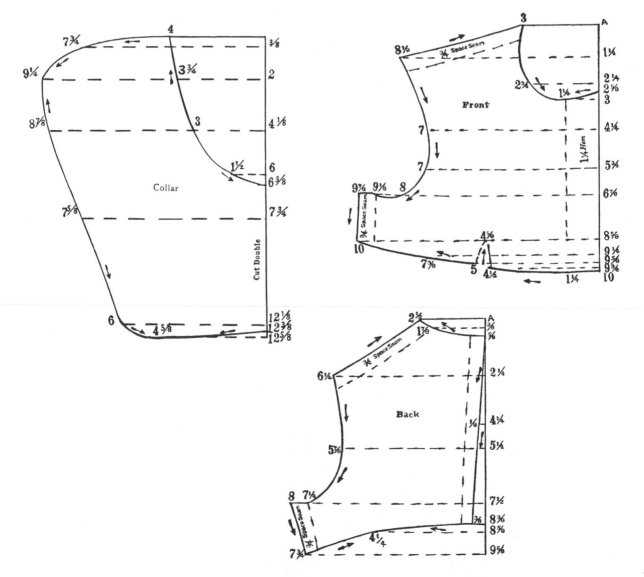

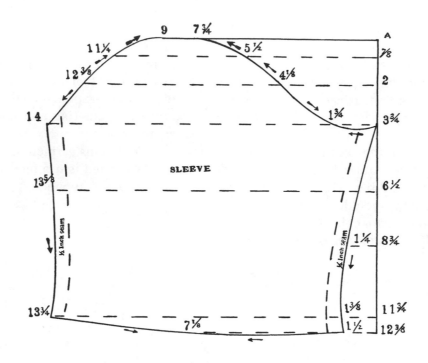

9   7¾

11¼   5½

12⅜   4⅛

A
⅞
2
3¾

14   1¾

SLEEVE

13⅝   6½

½ Inch seam   ½ Inch seam   1¼   8¾

13¾   1⅜   11¾

7⅛   1½   12⅜

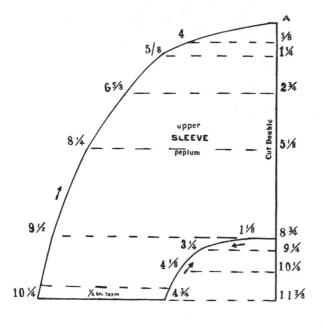

4   A
⅝
5/8   1¼

6⅝   2¾

upper
SLEEVE
peplum   5⅛

Cut Double

8¼

1

9½   1⅛   8¾
3¼   9¼
4⅛   10⅛
10¼   ½ In. Seam   4¾   11⅜

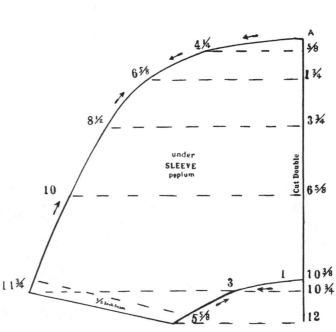

4¼   A
⅝
6⅝   1¾

8½   3¾

under
SLEEVE
peplum   6⅝

Cut Double

10
1

11¾   3   1   10⅜
10¾
5⅝   12

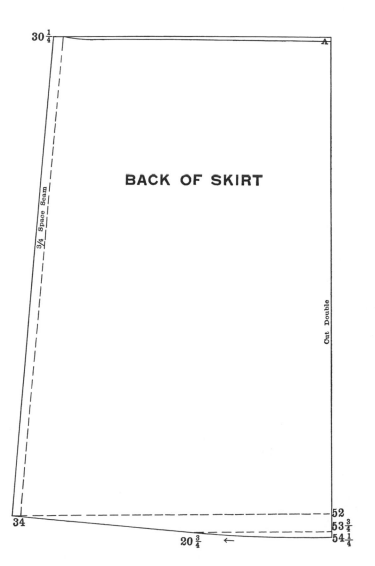

BACK OF SKIRT

$30\frac{1}{4}$ A

3/4   Space Seam

Cut Double

34   52
      $53\frac{3}{4}$
$20\frac{3}{4}$ ← $54\frac{1}{4}$

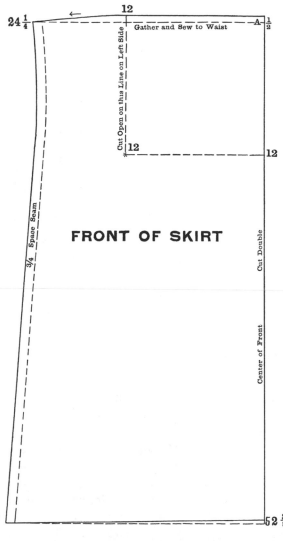

FRONT OF SKIRT

$24\frac{1}{4}$ ←   12   A $\frac{1}{2}$

Gather and Sew to Waist

Cut Open on this Line on Left Side

3/4   Space Seam

12   12

Center of Front

Cut Double

27          $52\frac{3}{8}$

365

Shirtwaist

Use the scale corresponding to the bust measure to draft this waist, which consist of back, front, vest, collar, sleeve, and cuff. Regulate all lengths by the tape measure.

Lay the tucks in the fronts before cutting goods. Join vest to right front and allow it to underlap left front and fasten at left side. Join front to back at shoulder and underarm seams. Gather fullness in front and back to fit the waist measurement. Join sleeve and adjust in armseye, gathering fullness at top to fit the armseye and at bottom to fit the cuff. Adjust collar in the usual way.

This waist is made of flannel trimmed with persian bands and ornamented with buttons. It is completed by a collar and vest of allover lace.

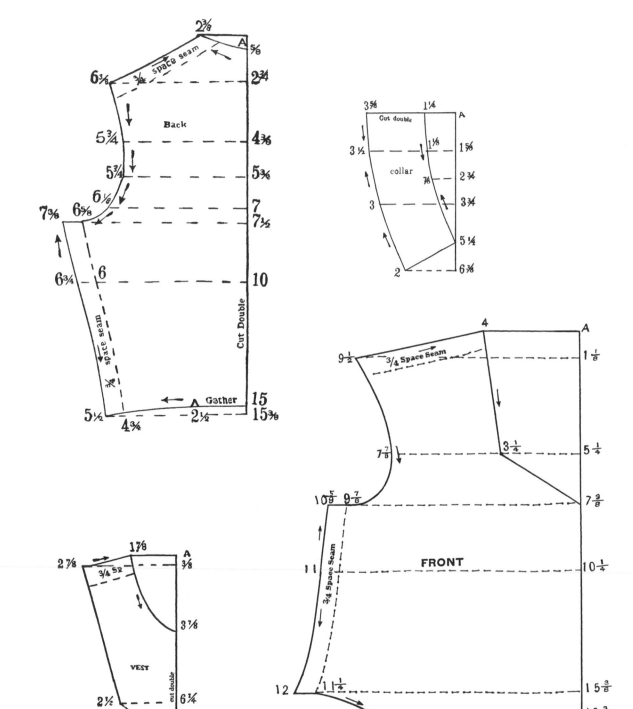

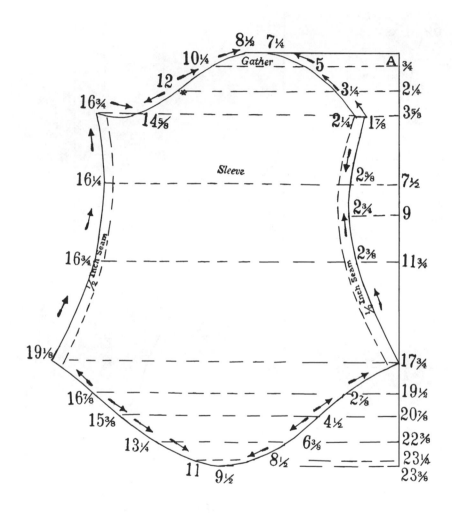

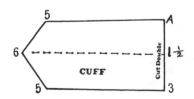

May 1904

The planning and scheming of every gown now hinges upon the style of its skirt. Some skirts measure from 6 to 7 yards around and are as large at the top as at the bottom. All skirts, however, are not cut on these lines. One may wear a skirt far less extreme, and all else being correct, feel correctly gowned. Full skirts are becoming to the more slender figure, the fullness adding grace to the hips. For stout people they should be cut with much less fullness about the hips, and what fullness there is should be arranged in lengthwise folds or closely drawn shirrings. These skirts do not possess possibilities for trails and long effects as the closely fitting skirt has in the past. Hence we must be content with the more rounding lengths.

We still have the short skirt, which will be more for shopping and walking. It is made almost entirely round and either just clears the ground or just touches the shoe. It should be very wide at the bottom, while above it is closely fitted to the figure, and may be attached to a fitted yoke or arranged in closely fitted pleats.

Worn with these skirts are jackets of every description, from eton to three-quarter length. The eton seems most preferable, however, and may be treated in many different styles. Inserted vests are popular and chic. Sleeves are large and full and attached to a long and sloping shoulder.

With bolero and jacket costumes the blouse is indispensable. A costume with the skirt and jacket in different materials is not considered strictly elegant. So also is good taste applied to blouses. The blouse should be in the exact shading of the skirt, or the trimming should show the connection. This applies to costumes en suite for evening and society wear. Skirts and blouses of contrasting colors are much more practical, and very common for traveling and outdoor wear. More fancy blouses are a mass of costly details, with layers of lace upon lace.

Sloping shoulder effects are attained in many ways. Large collars extending wide over the shoulders are most popular. Sleeves are very fancy and becoming larger and larger.

English woolen goods, fine and coarse textures, are suitable for everyday wear, for walking and traveling costumes, in mixed grays and browns. Striped and checked designs are most fashionable.

The new silks are distinguished by their softness and suppleness. These are especially adapted to the shirrings, smockings, and tuckings that characterize the present costume. Since soft effects are the principal aim, taffeta is not so popular for lining, the softer silks being also used for this purpose. The popular shades are gray, in all its pale tones, dark blue, raspberry, and bread crust brown.

Girdles form a very important feature. There are many designs, such as suede girdles with long buckles back and front. The draped girdle of satin, silk, or cloth has buckles on each side as well as front and back. These buckles are connected with tiny chains which reach from one to the other. Many handsome buttons are used instead of buckles. These girdles, while in most instances very wide, conform to the figure. Belts of every width are also seen. They may be leather in various shades, also kid, which may be hand painted or embroidered.

Fancy stocks are very much worn, as are little turnover collars and cuffs.

The simple toque of coarse fancy straw, whose only ornament may be a straw buckle, goes nicely with walking suits. With the more elegant costumes, fluffy creations are worn draped with lace veils or scarves arranged to fall deeply into the neck behind, while in front they cover the hat brim or may be drawn over the face. Violets, cowslips, daisies,

and lilies of the valley are among the small flowers seen on hats. Artificial fruits are also finding great favor, especially huckleberries and tiny grapes. Ribbon is used, also lace very extensively.

The hat does not match the costume in color, but generally accords in tone with some part of the trimming. Shoes and gloves must harmonize with the general color of the toilet.

Princess Gown

Use the scale corresponding to the bust measure to draft the lining back, side back, underarm gore, and front; outside back and front; yoke; sleeve; and cuff. Use the scale corresponding to the waist measure to draft the flounce. Regulate all lengths by the tape measure.

Take up the darts in the front lining. Join all lining portions at their respective seams. Join the outside front and back separately from the lining at the underarm seam. Only one line for shirring is indicated on the drafts and that is at the waistline, allowing for a slight dip in front. Gauge the remainder of your shirrings above and below this line in as many rows as you desire. Adjust this outside on the lining, allowing a slight bag all the way around. Shirr the fullness at the top to fit the lining at yoke line. Position yoke and join to front and back. Gather the flounce and join it to the upper portions, leaving a heading at the top. If the shirred tucks illustrated are desired allow for them. They are about 3/4 inch wide. Join the sleeve and adjust in armseye, shirring the fullness several times at the top to fit the armseye. Join cuff. Gather fullness at sleeve bottom to fit cuff and join.

This gown should be made of soft material. The one illustrated is made of chiffon cloth and trimmed with lace. Allover lace is used for the yoke. Bands of the material fagoted together with circles of handwork adorn front at yoke line, as well as sleeves.

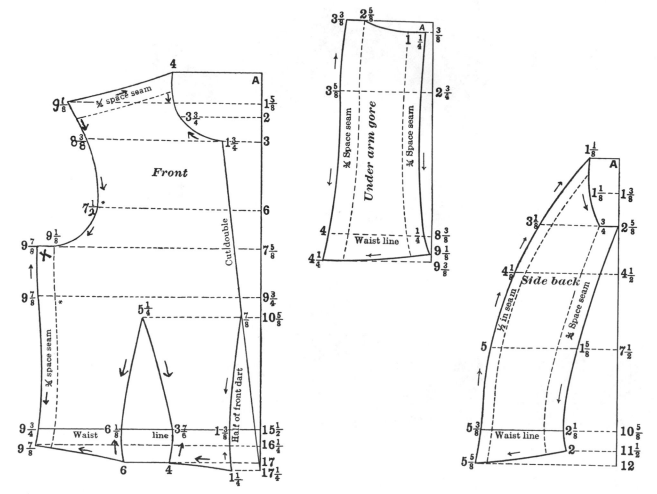

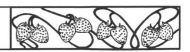

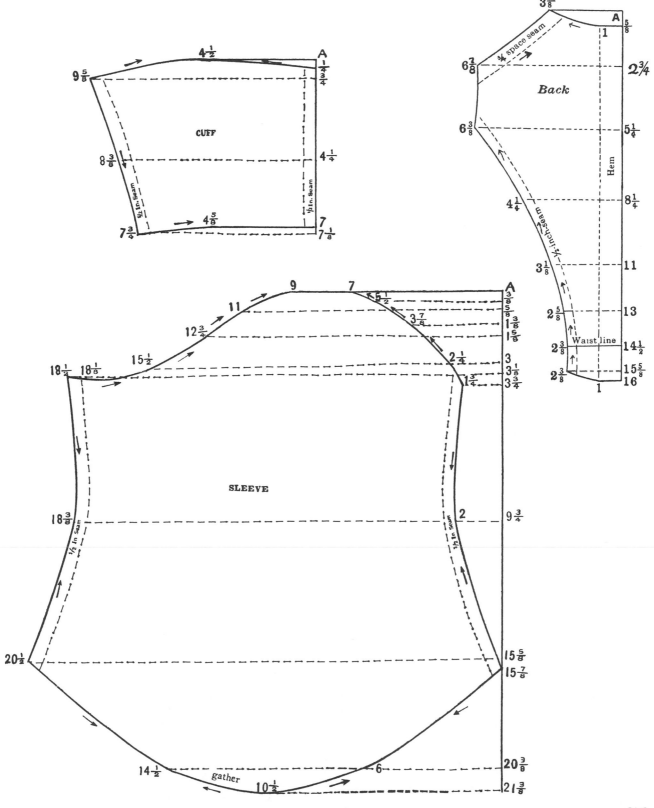

May 1904

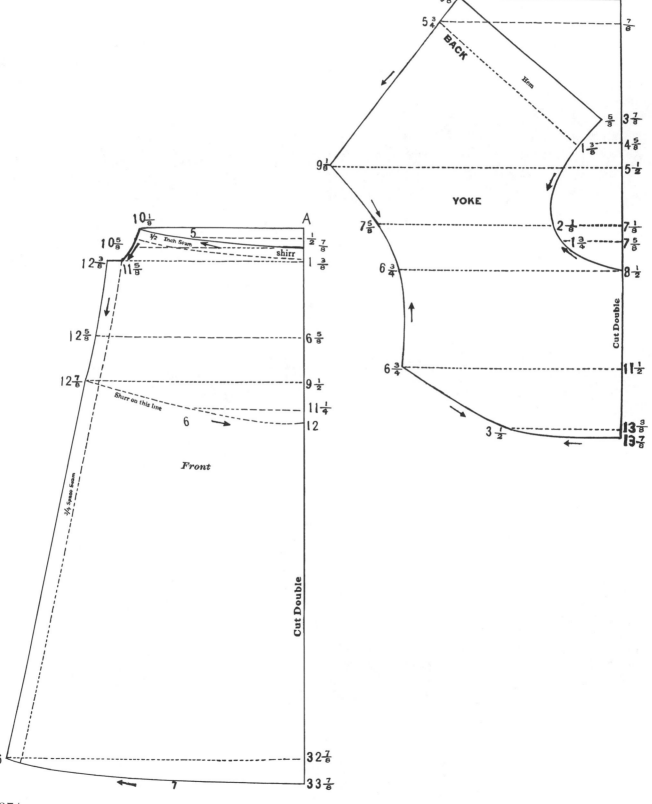

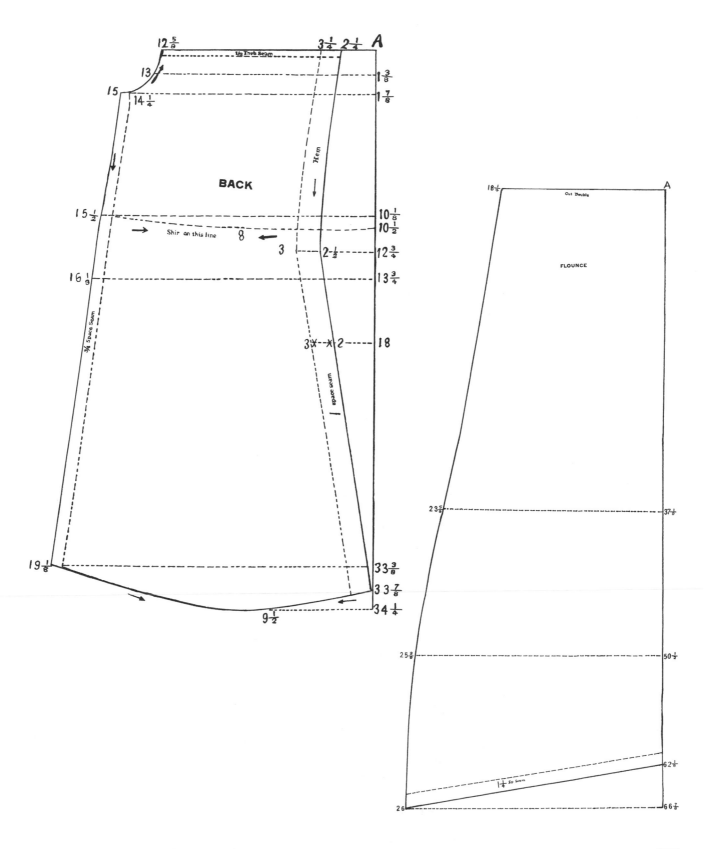

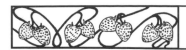 

Ladies' Reception Gown

Use the scale corresponding to the bust measure to draft the waist, which consists of back, front, yoke, collar, sleeve, and cuff. Use the scale corresponding to the waist measure to draft the four skirt portions. Regulate all lengths by the tape measure.

Tuck all goods before cutting. Join front to back at underarm seam. Gather the fullness at front and back to fit the yoke and join. The yoke is finished with a ruffle of chiffon in collar effect. Join the sleeve. Adjust in armseye, placing point of yoke at shoulder with the corresponding point of sleeve.

Shirr the fullness on each side to fit the yoke between the Xs. Adjust the remaining portion of the sleeve in the usual way. Position cuff and gather fullness at the bottom of the sleeve to fit it. Bind neck and adjust collar in the usual way.

Join skirt seams according to the Xs. Finish at top and bottom in the usual way.

This gown is made of chiffon and adorned with small ruffles. Shirred tucks adorn the waist and sleeves. A lace yoke in collar effect completes the costume.

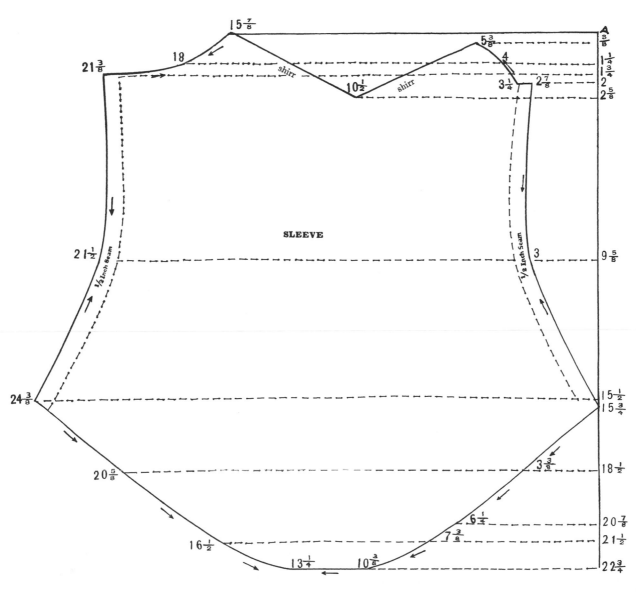

377

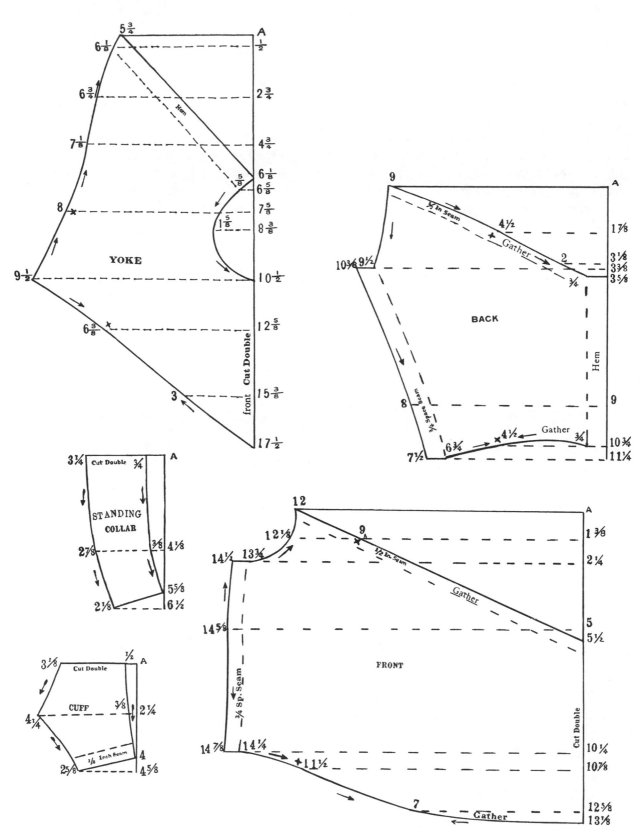

YOKE

STANDING COLLAR

Cut Double

CUFF

BACK

FRONT

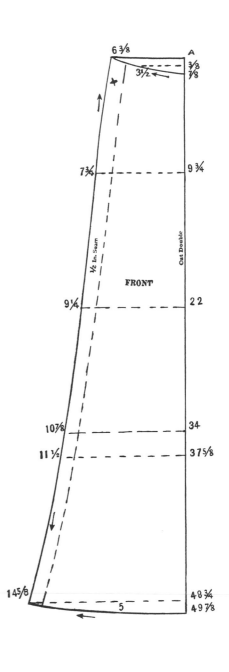

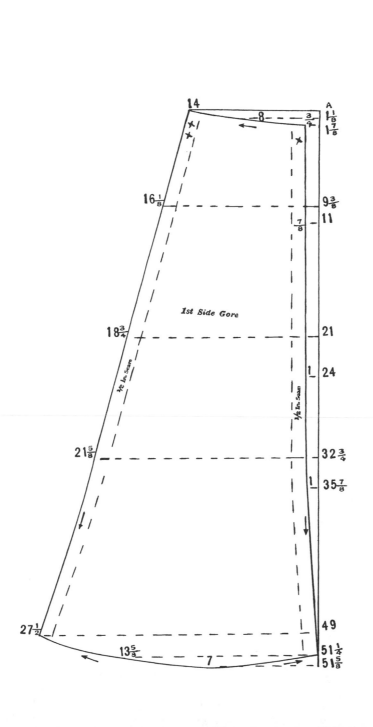

379

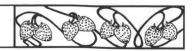
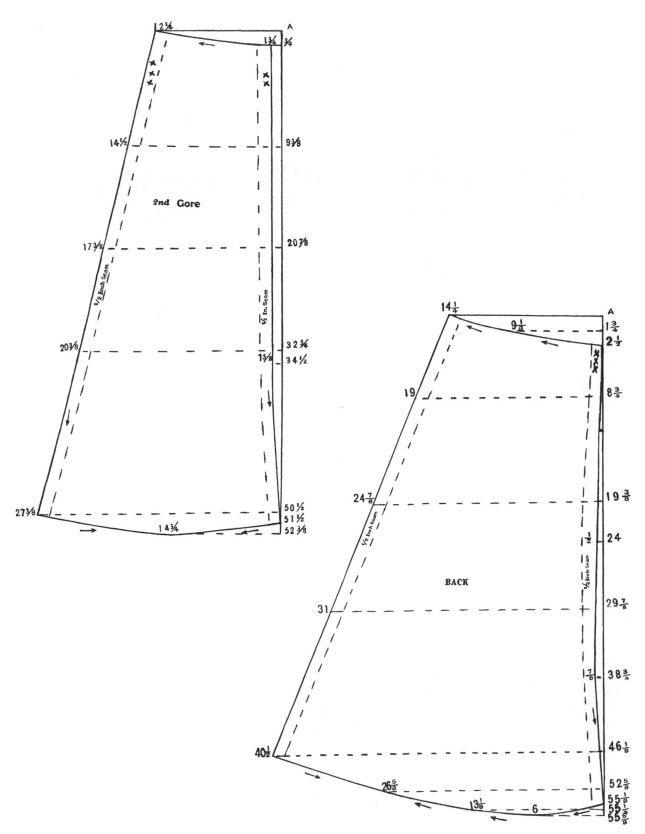

Shirtwaist

Use the scale corresponding to the bust measure to draft this waist, which consists of back, front, back and front pleat, collar, and sleeve. Regulate all lengths by the tape measure.

Join front to back at shoulder and underarm seams. Join front pleat to back pleat at shoulder seam. Place center of back pleat to center of waist back and extend over shoulder down fronts, as illustrated. Place a straight piece, of any desired material, in pleat effect down front. Gather fullness of back and front to fit the waistline and hold in position with a tape. Slash the sleeve a short distance from bottom at back on the line indicated. Join the sleeve and gather only a portion of the fullness at the bottom into the cuff, leaving the remainder open, as illustrated. Face the open portions and fasten them together with buttons. Adjust sleeve in armseye, gathering fullness at top to fit armseye. Bind neck and adjust collar in the usual way.

A waist made of contrasting materials develops very prettily in this style.

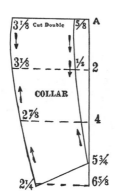

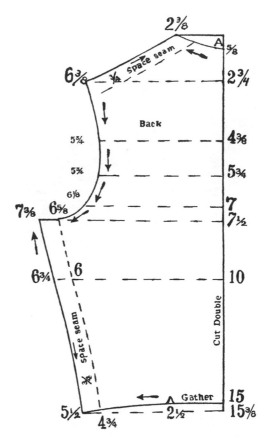

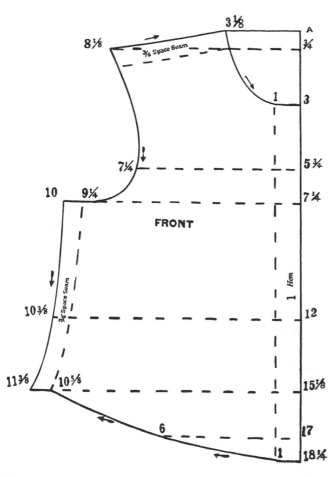

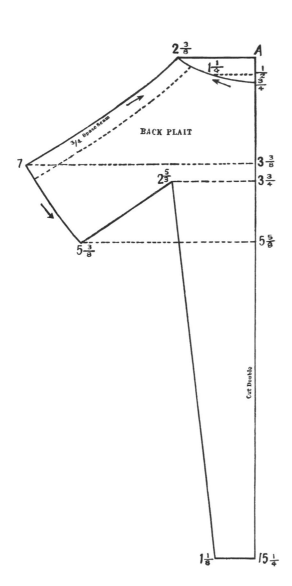

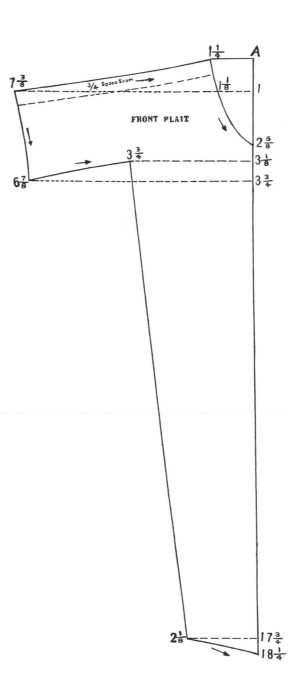

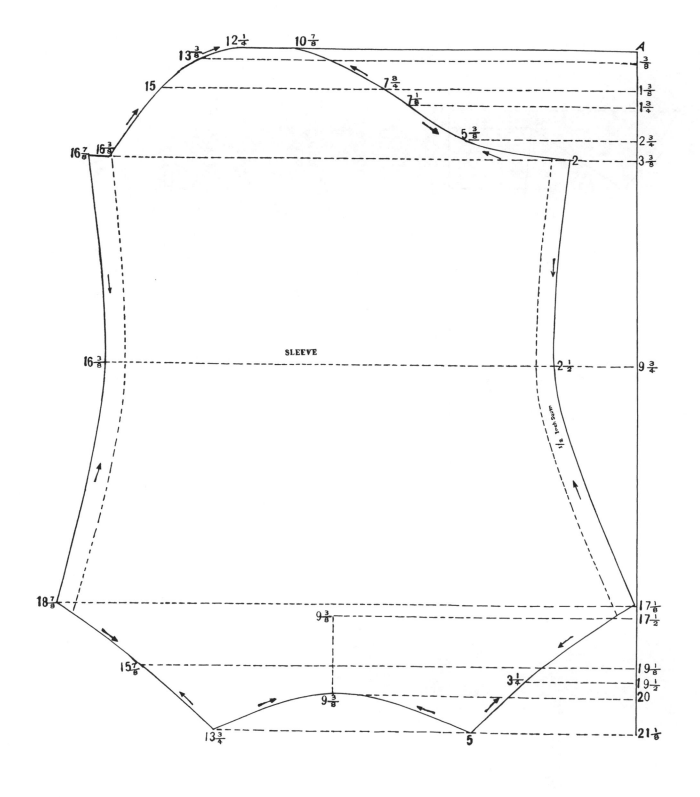

 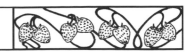

Shirtwaist

Use the scale corresponding to the bust measure to draft this waist, which consists of back, front, yoke, collar, and sleeve. Regulate all lengths by the tape measure.

Tuck all goods before cutting. The yoke is tucked and trimmed with lace wheels. Cut the yokes as indicated on the draft. Lay the pleat in front and back as indicated. Arrange the remaining fullness in the fronts in small pin tucks terminating a short distance from the yoke line, as illustrated. Join the front to the yoke at yoke line, allowing the right side to overlap the left and fasten at left side. Join the waist at the shoulder and underarm seams. Gather fullness to fit the waistline and hold in position with a tape. Bind neck and adjust collar in the usual way. Join the sleeve and adjust in armseye. Gather any surplus fullness at top to fit armseye and at bottom to fit cuff.

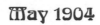
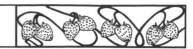

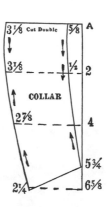

COLLAR

3⅛ Cut Double ⅝ A
3⅛ ½ 2
2⅞ 4
2¼ 5¾
6⅝

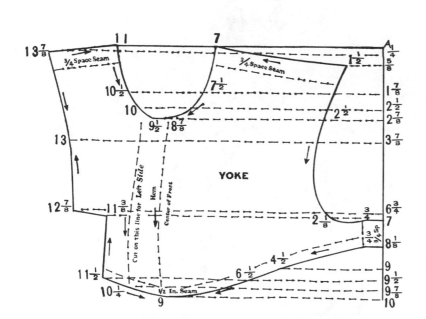

YOKE

13⅞ 11 7 A¼ ⅝
¾ Space Seam ¾ Space Seam ½
10½ 1½ 1⅞
10 7½ 2½ 2⅝ 2⅞
9½ 8⅞ 3⅞
13
Cut on this line for Left Side
Hem Center of Front
12⅞ 11⅜ 6¾ 7
2⅛ ¾ ¾ Sp
¾ 8⅛
11½ 4½ 9 9½ 9⅞
6½ 10
10¼ ½ In. Seam
9

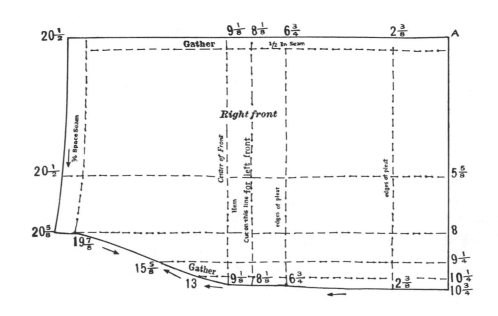

20½ 9⅛ 8⅛ 6¾ 2⅜ A
Gather ½ In. Seam
Right front
¾ Space Seam
Center of Front
Hem
Cut on this line for left front
edges of pleat
edges of pleat
20½ 5⅝
8
20⅝ 9¼
19⅞ 10¼
15⅝ Gather 9⅛ 8⅛ 6¾ 2⅜ 10¾
13

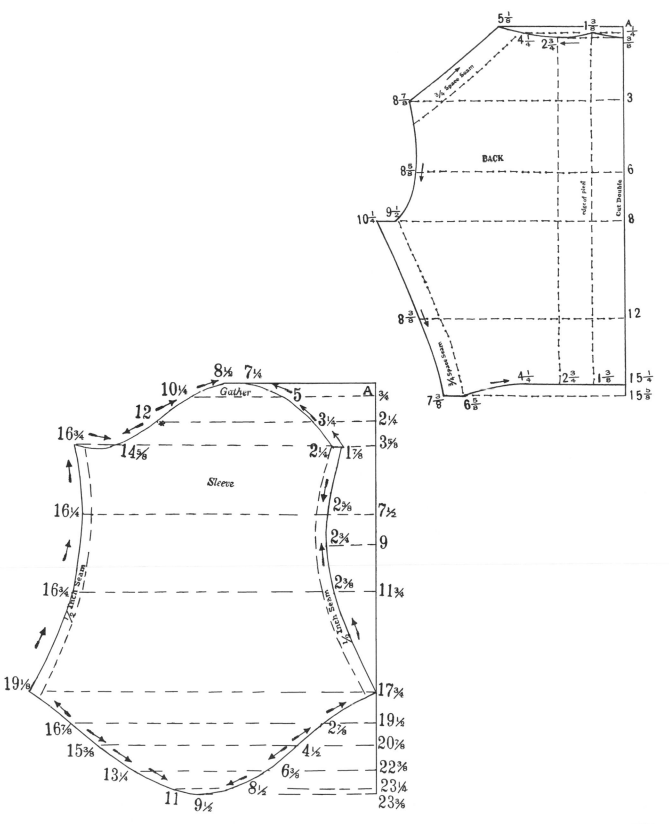

November 1904

The vogue of the full skirt is quite established. Avoid heavy materials in this style; rather express your ideas in soft effects such as crepe, liberty satin, chiffon, silk mull, net, etc. A certain amount of symmetry is noticeable in the use of tuckings, gaugings, shirrings, and smockings, which, as a rule, extend a short distance below the waistline, imparting a certain snugness to the hips.

In tailor-made suits the full and ungored skirt is impracticable. A certain amount of fullness at the feet may be obtained by a numerous arrangement of pleats. Plaids will be very popular for the winter season; the plain circular skirt is particularly adapted for this style of goods.

A great feature is the deep girdle. It is made of taffeta or liberty silk cut on the bias. It is fashioned so deep in front as to extend just below the bust line and terminate in a sharp point. It is crushed over a fitted lining and terminates at the waistline in the back of about 3 inches in depth. Some end in a sash flowing to the foot of the skirt. This adaptation of the girdle removes all possibility of the blouse effect.

The blouse does not pouch as much at the front as formerly, only a slight droop upon the belt being permissible. A general bagginess, however, seems to be the thing in smart gowns, and they are decidedly a loose fit. The bodice is not held tightly in the back, but is permitted to issue from the belt in a careless fashion.

Sleeves have become distinguished by their amplitude, especially at the top where much fullness is gathered into the armseye, but they do not stand up above the shoulder. Many are constructed to only reach the elbow, and when long are joined to a closely fitting cuff. The leg-of-mutton sleeve has again made its appearance with many variations. The shirtwaist sleeve is still held in moderation.

A general roundness of figure is what we now aim to reach. The pointed girdle adds greatly to the bodice in front, while the lengthening of shoulders and fullness of sleeves gives the broadening effect and makes the waistline appear much smaller.

Owing to the largeness of sleeves, capes have been conveniently revived. A very popular cape is the garrick. It may be a triple or quadruple cape just escaping the waist. It is possible to construct it of cloth or silk, and it may match the dress with which it is worn.

The short jacket, the three-quarter length, and the long coat seem alike in vogue. Most jackets are tight fitting in the back with box or half-fitted fronts. In most instances where a belt is utilized, the back is half fitted with a slight fullness at the waistline, which is held in position by the belt. Long coats are varied, some being tight fitting and others having box fronts. Pleats are utilized in many instances.

Fur will be greatly used in combination with one or more varieties, such as mink and squirrel, and chinchilla and moleskin. Many little stoles and neckties of fur are seen, making elegant adjuncts to a toilet.

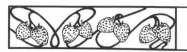 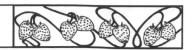
Evening Costume

Use the scale corresponding to the bust measure to draft the waist, which consists of back, front, yoke, collar, standing collar, and sleeve. Use the scale corresponding to the waist measure to draft the three skirt portions. Regulate all lengths by the tape measure.

Gather the fullness in the front to fit the front portion of the yoke. Join the front to the yoke at this point. Gather the fullness in the back to fit the back portion of the yoke, and join it to the yoke at this point. Join the whole at the underarm seam. Gather the fullness at the waistline to fit the waist measurement and hold in position with a tape (unless a lining is used). Place center back of large collar to the center of the waist back, and allow it to fall into position around front as illustrated. Bind neck and adjust standing collar in the usual way. The sleeve is a puff sleeve ending with a triple ruffle at the elbow. Join it and adjust in armseye, gathering fullness at top to fit the armseye. Gather fullness at bottom to fit the elbow, or just above. Hold in position and join ruffles.

Join the skirt portions. Finish at top and bottom in the usual way. Arrange the fullness at the top in deep folds, except the front gore which is left perfectly plain.

This costume will develop very nicely in silk or any soft material. The one illustrated has a large collar of allover lace, edged with ruffles of the material. Embroidery extends down the front panel, and around the bottom, of the skirt. Two clusters of wide tucks, two in each cluster, also adorn the skirt bottom.

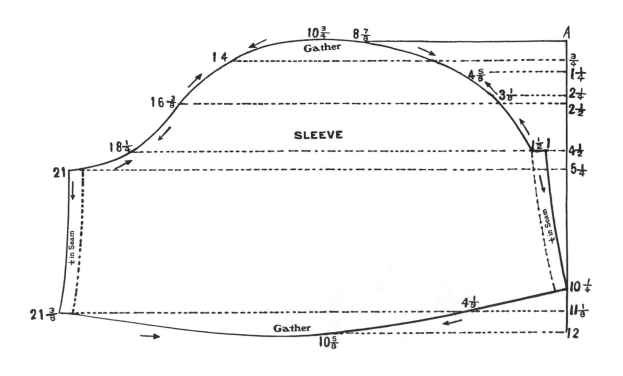

 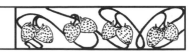

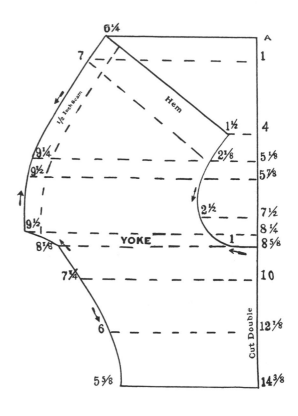

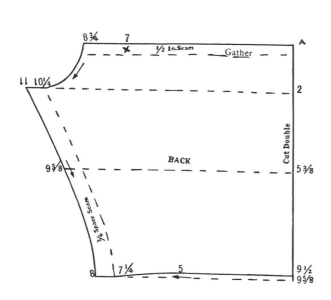

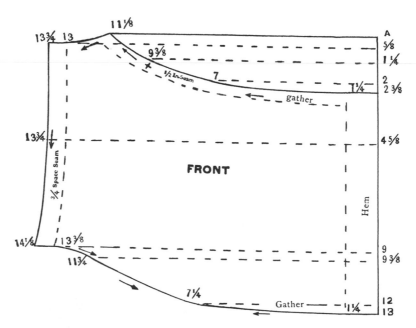

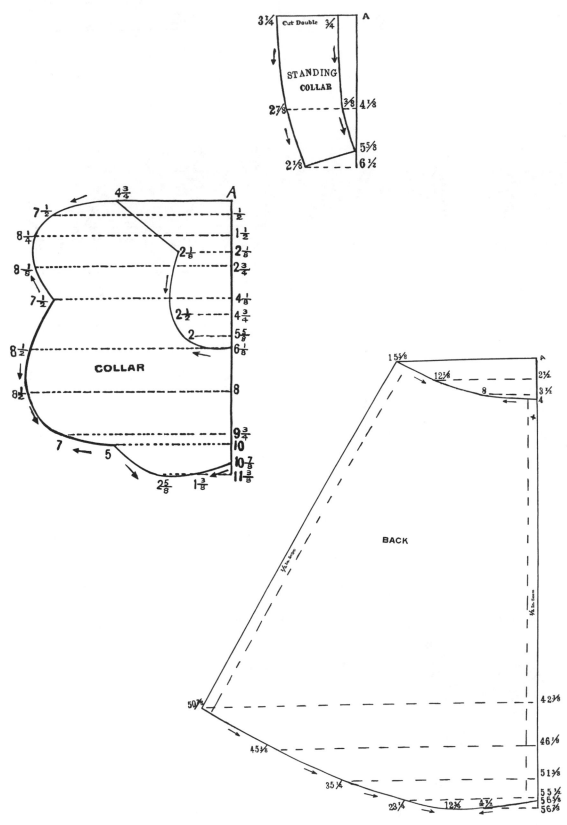

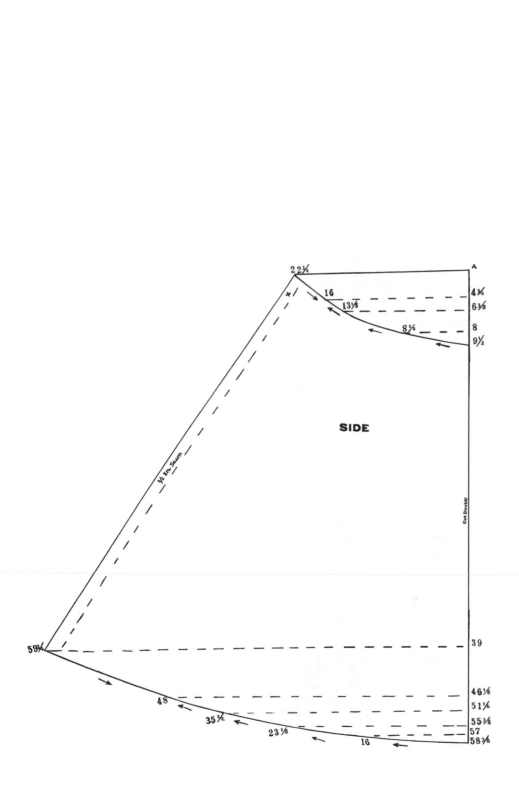

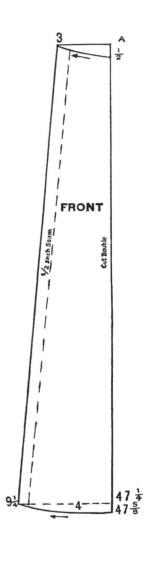

SIDE

FRONT

2 2¼

16

13⅛

8½

4¾

6⅜

8

9½

A

½ In. Seam

Cut Double

59¾

39

48

35½

23⅛

16

46⅛

51¼

55⅜

57

58⅜

3

A

½

FRONT

½ Inch Seam

Cut Double

9¼

4

47 ¼

47 ⅝

Coat

Use the scale corresponding to the bust measure to draft this coat, which consists of back, side front, front, collar, two sleeve portions, and cuff. Regulate all lengths by the tape measure.

Lay the pleat on the pleat line indicated on the front, and overlap this on the side front according to the Xs, the depth of 1 1/4 inches. Stitch back from pleat line 1 inch, forming a pleat of that depth. Lay the pleats in the back, turning the ones in the center toward the center, and the one at the outer edge toward the sleeve. Stitch back from pleat line 1 inch, forming a pleat of that depth. Join the coat at the shoulder and underarm seams. Adjust any fullness in back at waistline, holding it in position with a belt that extends only to the underarm seam.

Place the center of collar to center of back. Join collar to neck around front and down revers as illustrated. Fold the sleeve pleat on the pleat line and overlap this on the other sleeve portion. Stitch back from edge 1 inch, forming a pleat of that depth. Join the sleeve thus formed. Adjust it in armseye, gathering fullness at the top to fit the armseye and at the bottom to fit the cuff.

This coat may be made of any heavy material suitable for winter wear.

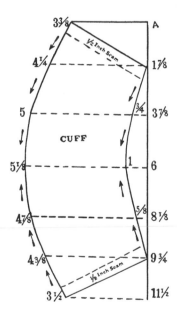

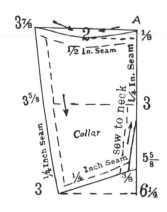

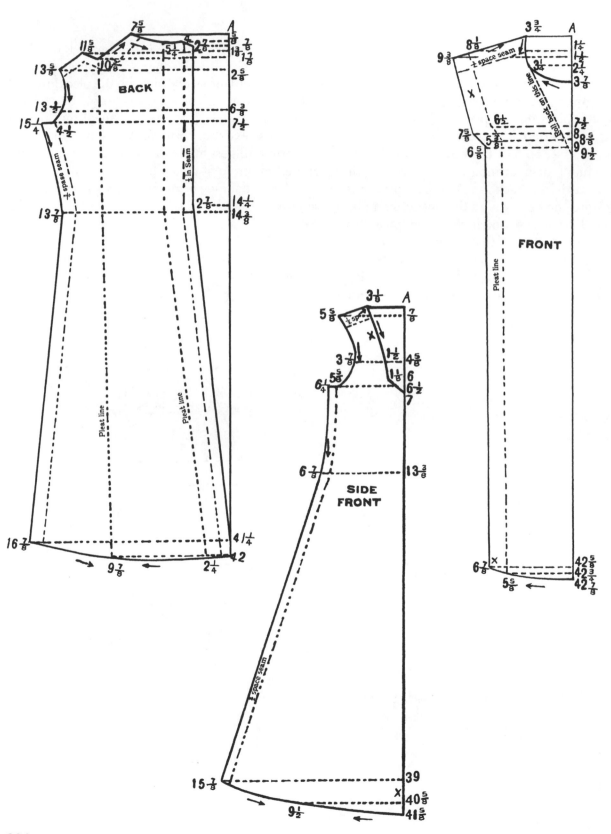

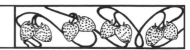
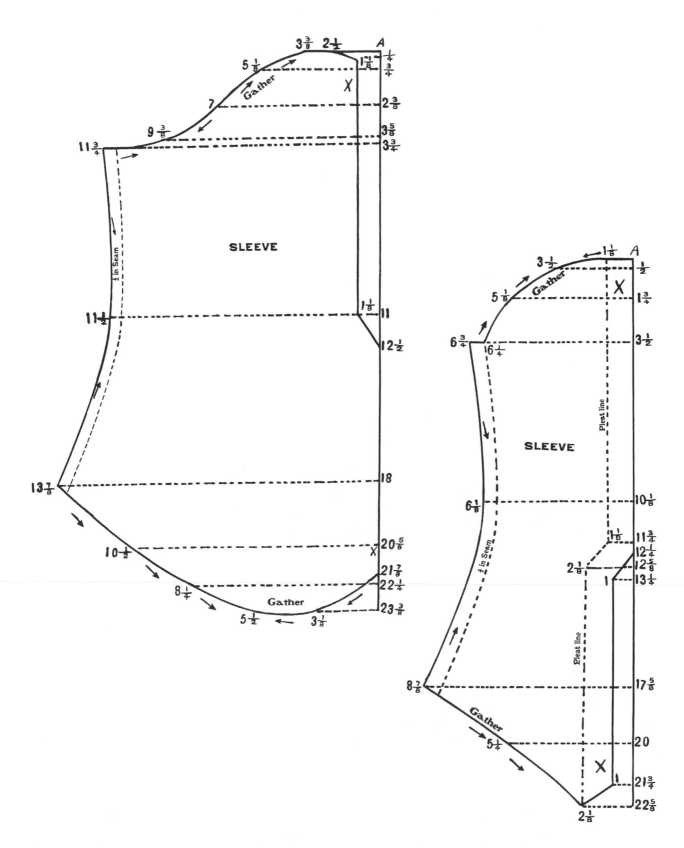

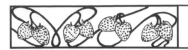

Cape

Use the scale corresponding to the bust measure to draft this cape, which consists of first cape, second cape, and cape. Regulate all lengths by the tape measure. Place the three capes consecutively, with corresponding portions together. Join them at the neck and finish. Turn back the cape proper on the dotted line in rever effect. Make of any desired material.

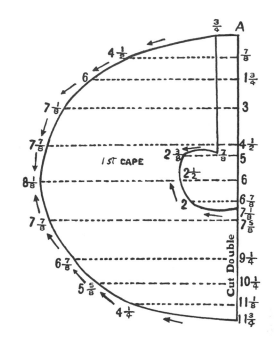

1ST CAPE

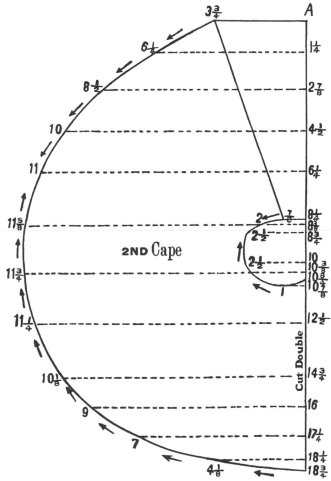

2ND Cape

399

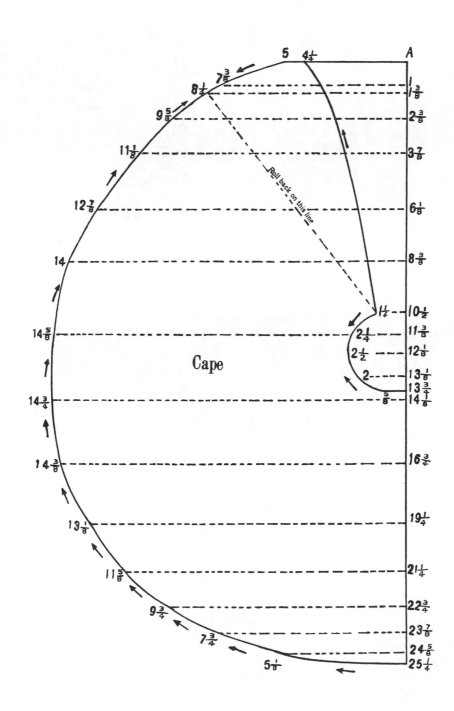

Cape

Roll back on this line

August 1905

The circular skirt, in many varied forms, seems to have come into popular favor. These fit closely about the hip with much fullness at the feet. One of the smartest and newest designs has the modish seam down the front. The draped skirt is also quite a new feature. We still have the moderately full skirt with its many shirrings, pleatings, and tuckings.

Shirtwaist suits have taken on quite a new form in the way of suspender effects. These may be arranged in straps, meeting at the waistline or crossing over. Or they may be arranged in wide berthas or revers of different designs.

Trimmings on skirts are massed about the feet. A very popular style of bodice is the surplice. Broad, square-shouldered effects are aimed at, as shown in the short full sleeves now so popular. Even the outside jacket has short sleeves. Mousquetaire gloves play an important part in the completion of such toilets. Of course many full-length sleeves are seen, especially for house and street wear.

There are dainty yokes, collars, and fichus without number, made of any sheer material such as lace, chiffon, or batiste. They are worn as outside accessories and render an otherwise plain gown a thing of beauty. Many of the newest blouses have a V or small yoke at neck, which may often be filled in with a fancy chemisette of allover lace or mull. These are detachable and may figure in more than one blouse, or one blouse may have more than one chemisette. The linen and piqué cuffs and collars worn on coats and jackets are also very neat accessories. Some are embroidered. Some of the flowered ribbons make beautiful girdles as well as suspender effects.

This has been a season of white. Thin India linens and mulls with a few tucks, lace, and insertion make soft, pretty effects. Embroidered linen in white is also very beautiful. Even for tennis and outdoor games white is exclusively worn, cheviots, serges, and flannels being used for these more simple costumes. A bright tie or belt is the only distinguishing note of color.

The tailor-made suit is still as necessary as the business suit is to men. The English shirt blouse is most suitably worn with it. It is made of cashmere or linen and its very simplicity imparts an air of distinction.

As a rule the more dressy blouses or bodices must match the skirt with which they are worn. They should be worn with a deep girdle of the same material as the gown, or else silk of the same tint. Even the shoes, hose, gloves, and hat should harmonize with the gown. Notwithstanding, we are still blessed with the odd waists more commonly known as shirtwaists. The surplice model is favored. A small V at neck and a small yoke are another feature, while elbow sleeves are promiscuously selected.

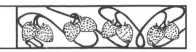

Evening Costume

Use the scale corresponding to the bust measure to draft the waist, which consists of lining back, underarm gore, and front; back; front; yoke; collar; and sleeve. Use the scale corresponding to the waist measure to draft the four skirt portions. Regulate all lengths by the tape measure.

Join the lining back to the side back. Place the outside back on them. Arrange the fullness at top and bottom to fit the lining. Take up the darts in the lining fronts. Place outside fronts on them with corresponding portions together. Gather the fullness to fit the lining. Join the waist at the shoulder and underarm seams. Place center of yoke back to center of waist back and allow it to fall in position around to front. Stitch in place. A straight full front (no draft) fills in the remaining portion of the front. Gather the fullness in front and back to fit the waist-line. Bind neck and adjust collar in the usual way. Join the sleeve and adjust in armseye, gathering fullness at top to fit the armseye. Gather fullness at bottom to fit the forearm. Finish sleeve at bottom with a ruffle.

Join the skirt seams according to the Xs. Arrange fullness at top in small tucks to fit the waist measurement. Arrange five small tucks, 1/4 inch in depth, at each curve of the flounce. Place flounce on bottom of skirt, cutting out skirt to correspond with curves in flounce. Finish at top and bottom in the usual way.

This costume is made of dotted veiling and trimmed with allover lace and velvet bands.

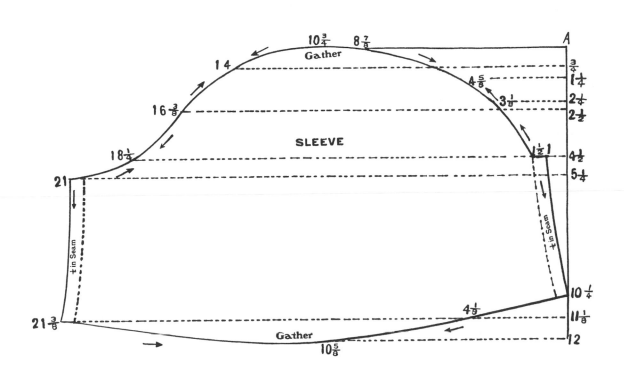

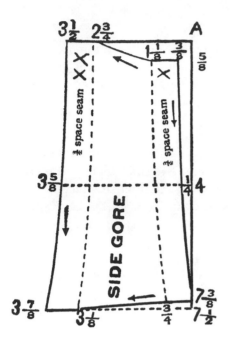

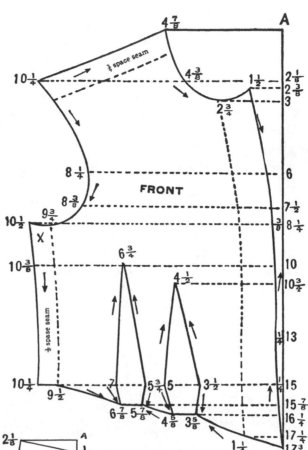

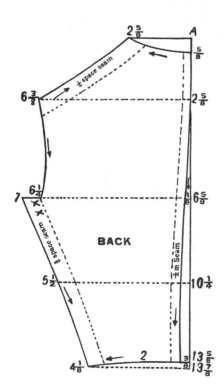

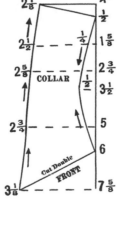

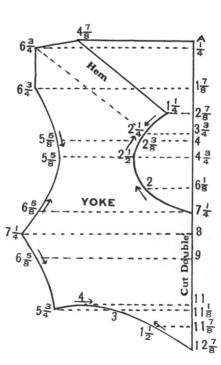

 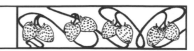

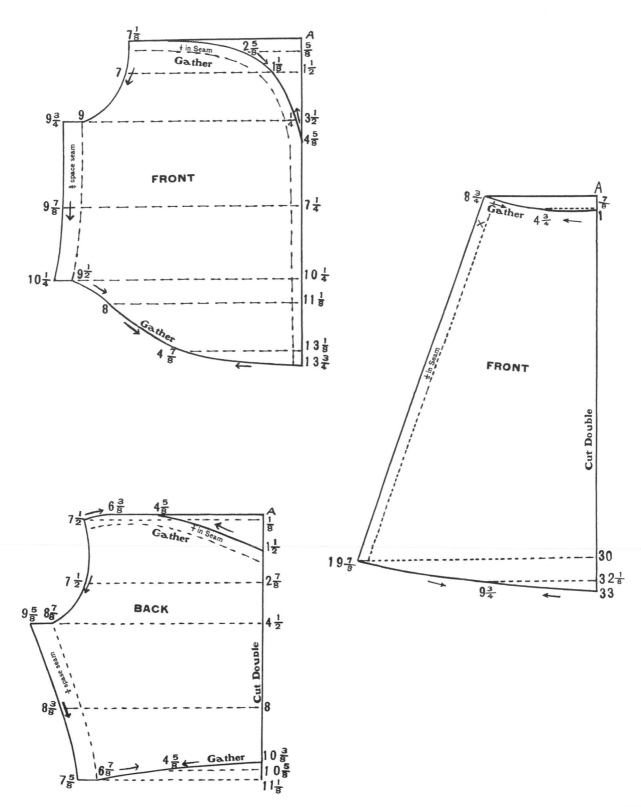

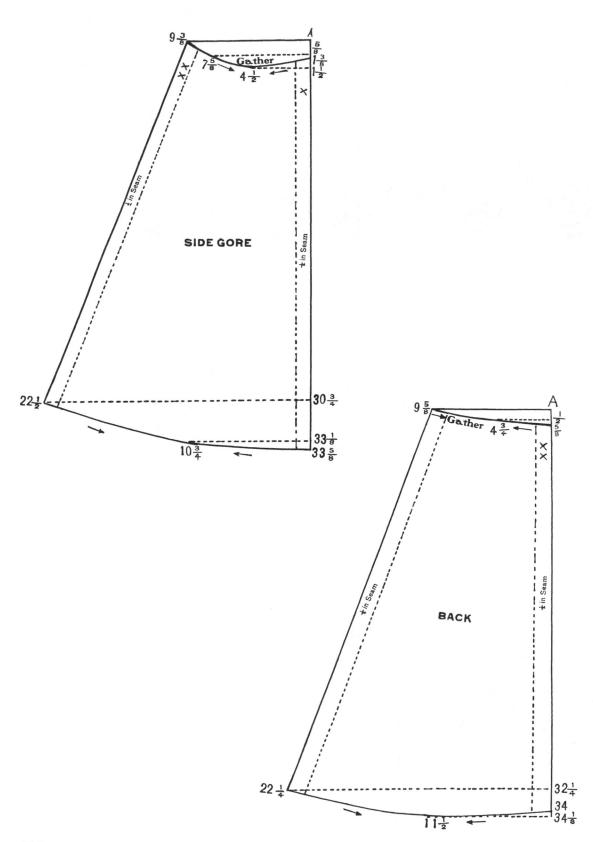

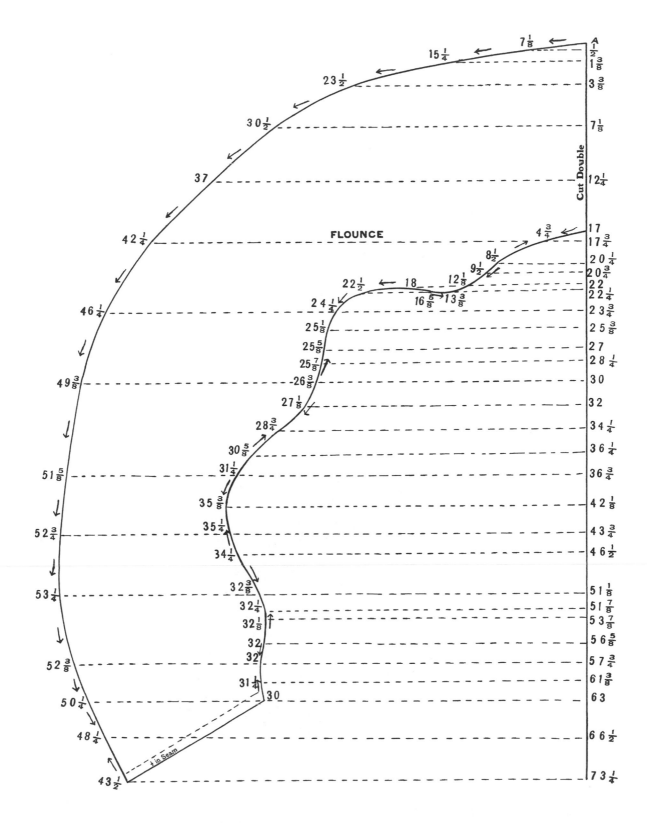

407

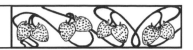
Afternoon Toilet

Use the scale corresponding to the bust measure to draft the waist, which consists of back, front, yoke, collar, and two sleeve portions. Use the scale corresponding to the waist measure to draft the three skirt portions. Regulate all lengths by the tape measure.

Lay the pleat in the front as indicated on the draft. Join front and back to yoke and gather the fullness to fit the yoke. Join the waist at the underarm seam. Gather the fullness at waistline to fit the waist measurement, and hold in position with a tape. Make a small opening in the front yoke, as illustrated, by cutting at the lines on the draft. The small revers for this opening have not been drafted. Cut three-cornered pieces and fit them in place.

Fill in the small yoke at neck, as indicated on the draft, with any contrasting material. Bind neck and adjust collar in the usual way. Join the sleeve and adjust in armseye, gathering fullness at top to fit the armseye. Finish at bottom in the usual way.

Take up the darts in the skirt lining. Join the flounce to it. Join skirt at back. Join the overskirt front and back. Gather the fullness at top to fit the lining or the waist measurement. Finish skirt at top and bottom in the usual way.

This dress is made of embroidered pongee and trimmed with lace.

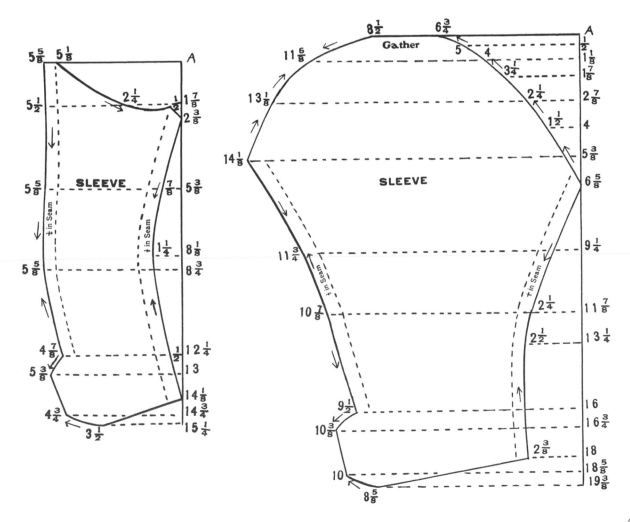

409

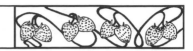

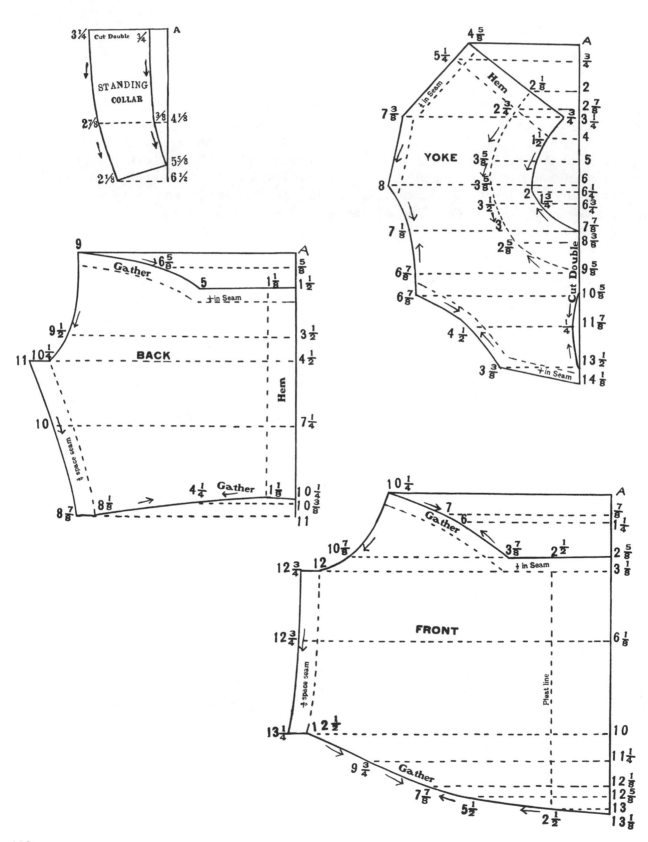

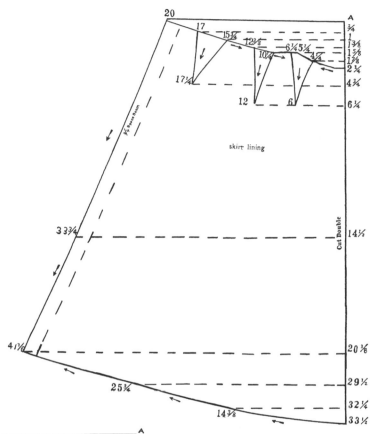

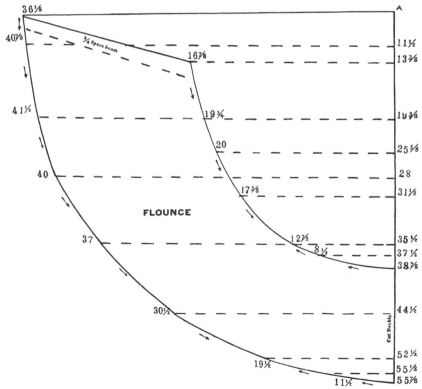

FLOUNCE

411

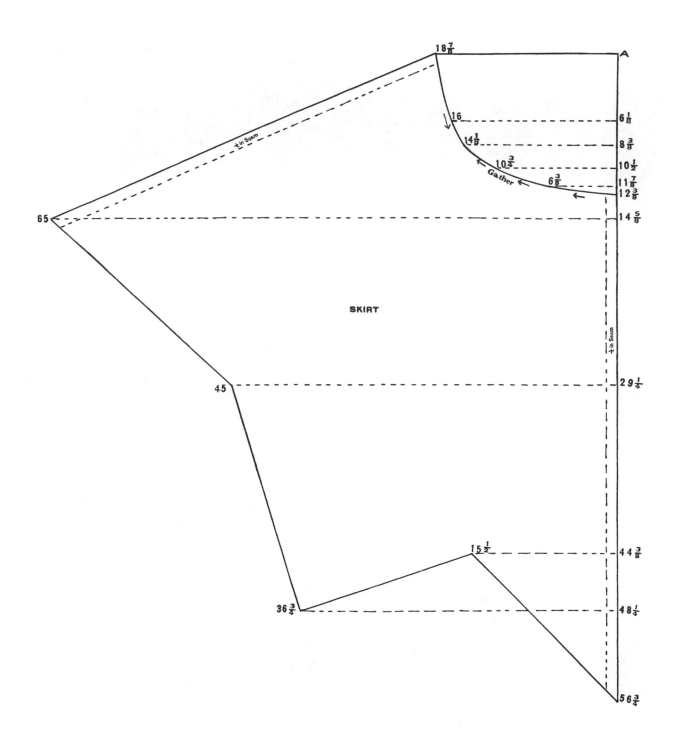

 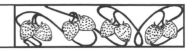

Cravenette

Use the scale corresponding to the bust measure to draft this coat, which consists of back, front, collar, belt, and two sleeve portions. Regulate all lengths by the tape measure.

Join the back portions at the back seam. Arrange the pleat down the center of the back, as indicated on the draft, and stitch in place. Also take up the other box pleats. Stitch the slot seams on the fronts, following the lines on the draft. Join the underarm gore to the front. Join the whole at the remaining seams. Adjust the waistline fullness by placing the belt in position. The collar is drafted in one piece, but should be cut in three sections. Cut on the dotted lines, arrange sections one over the other, and stitch in place. Join triple collar to neck by placing center back of collar to center back of coat and allow collar to fall into position around the neck. Join the sleeve and adjust in armseye, gathering fullness at top to fit the armseye. Finish at bottom in the usual way. Hem coat at bottom. Finish at center front with buttons and buttonholes. A stitched strap (no draft) covers the slot effect partway down the front.

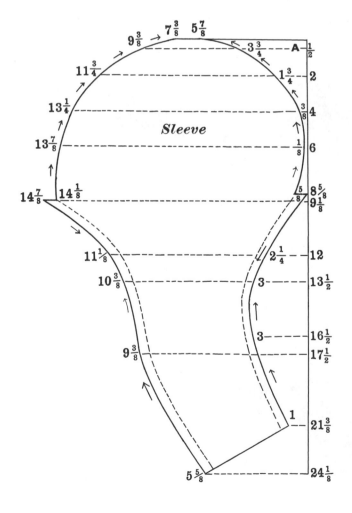

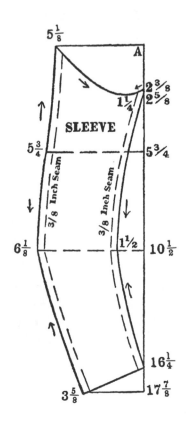

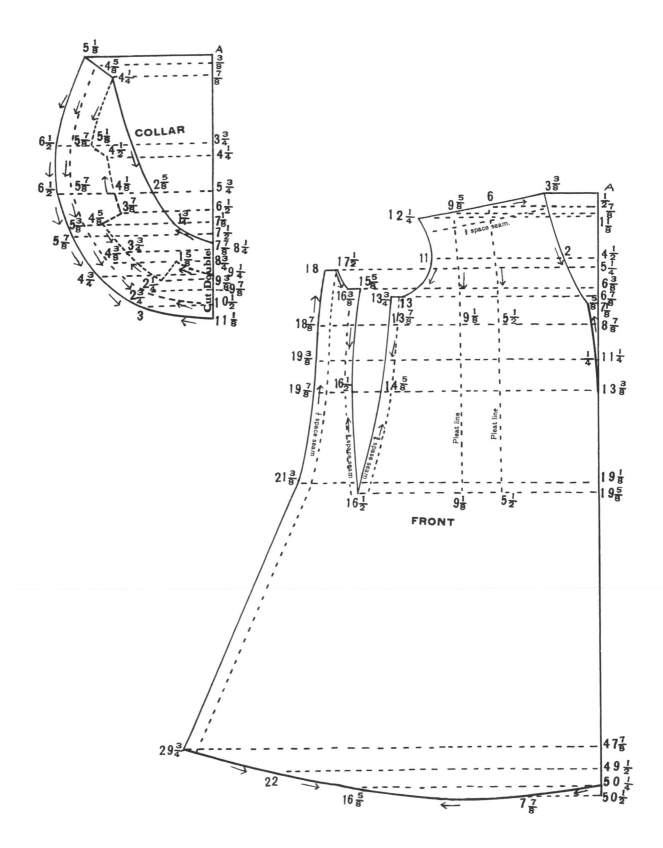

COLLAR

Cut Double

FRONT

¼ space seam.

¾ space seam

¼ space seam

⅛ space seam

Pleat line

Pleat line

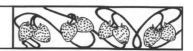

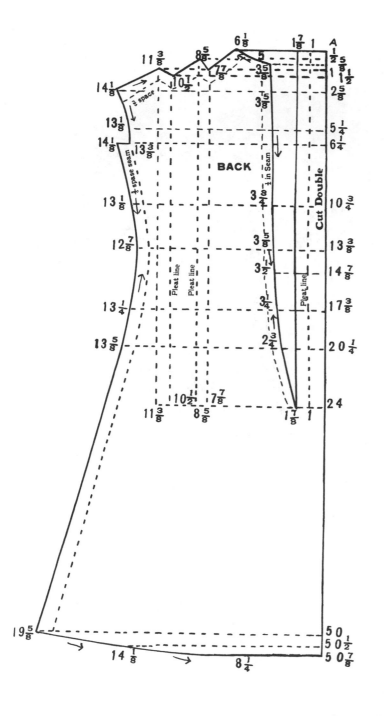

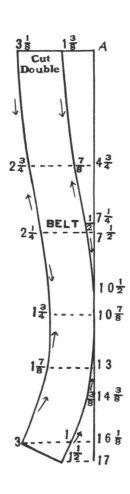

Fancy Shirtwaist

Use the scale corresponding to the bust measure to draft this waist, which consists of back, front, yoke, collar, and sleeve. Regulate all lengths by the tape measure.

Tuck goods before cutting. If desired you may avoid an underarm seam by placing the waist portions together at the underarm and cutting goods in one piece. Fit the fullness in front to the shoulder and neck measurement. Join waist at the shoulder seam. Place center front of yoke to center front of waist and allow yoke to extend around neck to center back. Stitch in position. Fold hem in back. Gather the fullness at waistline to fit the waist measurement. Bind neck and adjust collar in the usual way. Join the sleeve and adjust in armseye, gathering fullness at top to fit the armseye. Gather fullness at bottom to fit the cuff (no draft).

This waist will make up in soft material very nicely. It is trimmed with lace.

 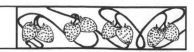

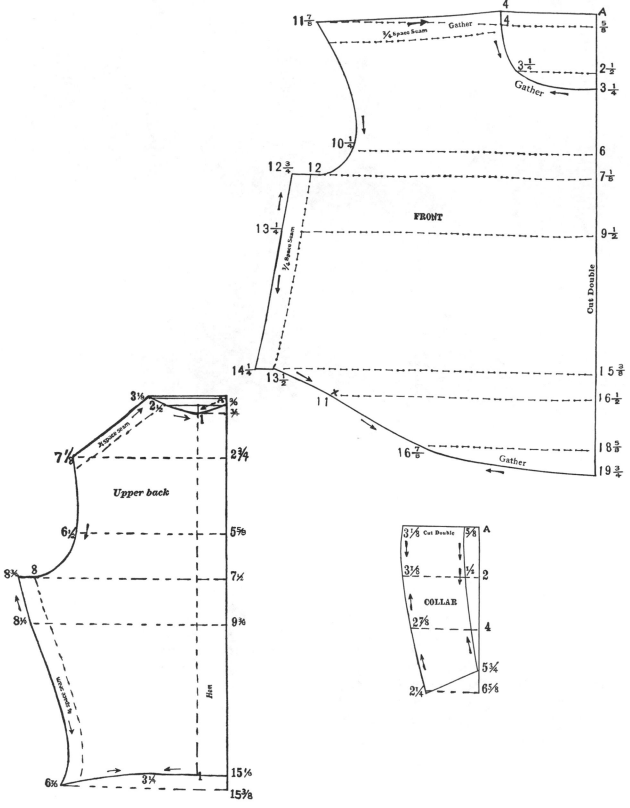

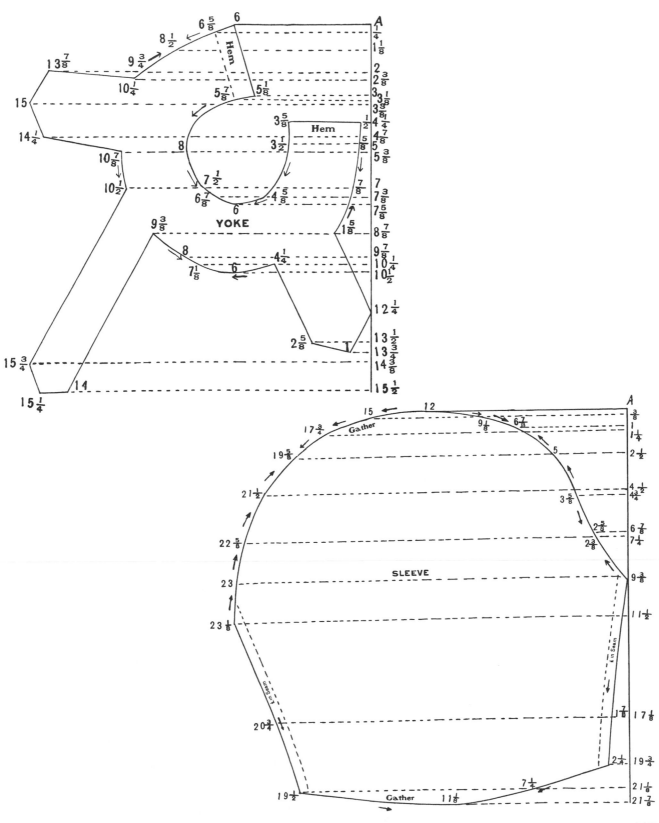

419

Shirtwaist

Use the scale corresponding to the bust measure to draft this waist, which consists of back, front, vest, collar, and sleeve. Regulate all lengths by the tape measure.

Place vest on front underneath right front, allowing it to overlap left front and fasten at left side. Join waist at shoulder and underarm seams. Arrange the fullness in the front at shoulder seam in four small tucks. Gather the fullness at bottom to fit the waist measurement and hold in place with a tape. Bind neck and adjust collar in the usual way. Join the sleeve and adjust in armseye, gathering fullness at top to fit the armseye. Arrange fullness at bottom in small tucks, after which join cuff (no draft).

This waist may be made of any suitable shirtwaist material.

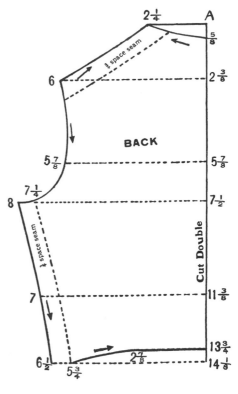

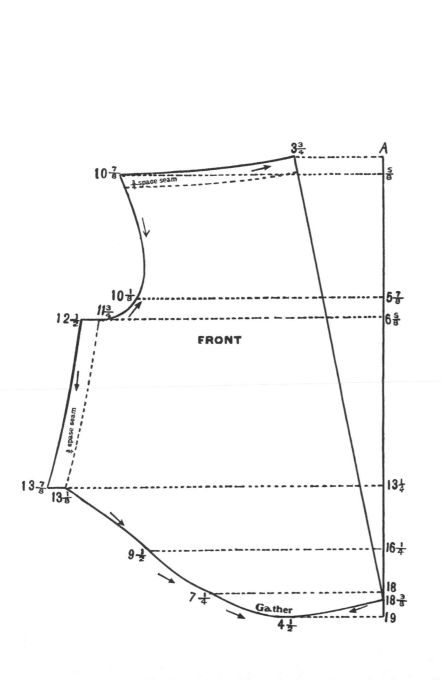

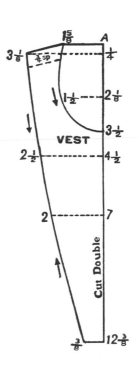

 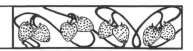
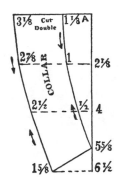

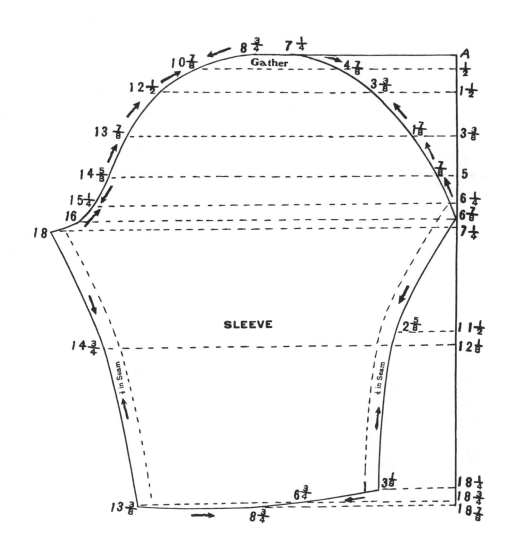

May 1906

A great wave of white is now surging through all high-class establishments, overwhelming every department from parasols and hats to hosiery and shoes.

Morning frocks, strictly tailor made, are shown in piqué, linen, and in serge. They are made in shirt-waist style, on naval lines, and in short coat suits. To wear with them, the new sailor hat is shown, and a simple white linen parasol, embroidered at the edge in the fashionable dimity scallop. White stockings, gloves, and shoes complete the costume.

All the morning frocks shown in the smart shops are on simple lines. Some introduce hedebo and eyelet work; others again are absolutely plain, rows of stitched straps and tiny linen-covered buttons being their sole trimming. The skirts of these suits clear the ground, and the coats end generally at the waistline. Most of the coats are square cut in the new and popular style called the pony coat. Others follow the becoming eton-bolero effect, plain or laid in pleats that open at the bottom. To accompany the coat suit, the tailors recommend a white linen shirtwaist, cut on severe lines and showing a turn-down collar and a handkerchief pocket upon the left breast. But the fact that many of the smartest dressers are ordering soft lingerie blouses to wear with the plain morning frock will make them equally correct. The naval suit is very becoming to slender figures and since it is quite as correct for morning wear as a shirtwaist suit, it lends a pleasing variety to one's wardrobe.

Chambray, duck, piqué, linen, and mercerized cotton, with or without a woven dot or figure, are the correct tub materials for morning gowns. Later in the season, we shall see dainty dimities, plain or printed with tiny figures, worn in the city streets as well as out of town. Lines of valenciennes lace, or snowflake net, are sparingly introduced in them. A narrow girdle of black velvet, dipping slightly toward the front, finishes the pretty frocks.

Morning frocks, quite suitable for informal afternoon wear, show more elaborate trimming, but the same simple lines. Very smart for these frocks is a new material seen in lustrous white and delicate blue, gray, pink, and wisteria tones. Woven half of silk and half of cotton, it is corded like eolienne and shot with tiny rough touches like rajah. A cross between the two, it is light and supple as silk, but shows more body. It is used for dressy costumes for the afternoon as well as for simpler ones, and it serves also as a good background for embroidered bands and medallions used as trimming on gowns of cloth or linen.

Wool morning gowns are of serge, tweed and voile; but heather mixtures, checks, and the popular shadow and clan plaids are in demand for traveling and for actual service. These frocks show flat trimming effects, chiefly straps, buttoned tabs, and borders of silk braid. In response to the fashionable demand for trimming lavished upon trimming, the straps and the lines of silk braids are ornamented with soutache applied in whorls and in running geometric designs, or with disks cut from the gown material and couched into place with fine gold or black silk cord. This style of trimming lends itself to elaborate effects, and permits that hitherto most rare opportunity of securing originality in a tailored gown. These flat trimmings are also seen on the semitailored gowns of voile, silk, or fine cloth meant for visiting and driving.

Princess and bolero effects are still the height of fashion.

A new and smart combination for an afternoon gown shows a box or a cape coat of supple moiré, unlined, worn over a circular skirt of hair-striped silk voile, or of chiffon broadcloth. Charming color effects may thus be brought within reach, such as dove-gray with silver embroidery, worn with a skirt of pearl gray or of white.

Shirred bindings are a new feature this season, decidedly French, and applicable in many ways. The narrower they can be made the more decorative is the effect. I have seen silk braid thus bound on both edges, and then applied in band and scroll pattern with excellent effect. This shirred edge is seen bordering motifs and medallions of lace or embroidery. It finishes flounces, top and bottom. It binds the raw edges of collars, cuffs, and stole ends cut from piece lace, and it is seen on the edges of chiffon frills on gowns and wraps and parasols. It is often softened with a finish of richelieu pleating.

The newest designs in nets and organdies are so tempting that one can scarcely pass them by. The blurred effects of last season are still with us, changed however in their coloring. Instead of a confused melange of flower and leaf tints, the new color scheme is confined to misty tones of a single color. The effect is more delicate, and the gown assumes a more definite hue. The newest of these printed cottons show crossbars of gleaming satin, adding both beauty and body to the airy gowns.

Another new idea in sheer textiles is a combination of silk mesh grenadine stripes and medallions of flowered mull. The effect is very lacy and elegant. New piece goods from St. Gall show small designs wrought in raised cotton embroidery in white or in self-color. These charming materials come in all the delicate tints fashion now prescribes, including the new biscuit tones and pearl grays. Plumetis comes in new and very pretty designs, and at a distance has nearly the same effect as the St. Gall products. In white and in ecru it will be largely used for the simple afternoon gowns required at country resorts during the summer.

In making up these textiles, dainty effects are absolutely essential. Lingerie and the finest of hand embroidery are introduced to as great an extent as one's purse permits. Smart women who are forced to economize on making as well as on material, select silk mull and fine dimity, and insert in it bands and motifs of allover valenciennes, or of net in snowflake or ring-spot design, bordering them with gathered baby ribbon. They find, too, that a little money invested in a dozen or so of embroidered or lace-trimmed pocket handkerchiefs, such as bargain tables frequently offer, goes a long way in providing pretty and original effects in berthas, sleeve frills, and tiny boleros.

For the more elegant gowns, nothing can be better or smarter than the new band trimming that combines in itself all the fashionable lingerie and lace effects. It serves as cuffs upon the full puffed sleeves of elaborate lace or lingerie coats and wraps, and is frequently used to build up boleros and yokes. Alternate medallions of valenciennes lace and pintucked linen batiste are joined in hand effect, by an intricate but most successful combination of irish lace, point de venise, and mull, embroidered in heavy laid work and in broderie anglaise.

There is literally no end to the amount of lingerie work and hand embroidery, as well as combinations of irish and baby laces, on the spring and early summer gowns. Chiffon voile, silk batiste, drap d'eté, and chiffon broadcloth are used for the gowns intended for Easter, and post-Easter festivities and functions.

Transparent coats are shown of irish and baby irish lace and of silk cord passementerie. Few of them are lined other than with knife-pleated net or mousseline.

Parasols of irish lace laid over chiffon, and of firm white linen showing a pretty combination of stiletto work and raised embroidery, are shown. The practical parasol is a thing quite of the vanished past. Its nearest kin is the parasol of ombré taffeta, shading outward from a center so pale as to be almost white, into a middle tone of brown, blue, rose, violet, or gray at the edge.

The most distinctive shape in hats this season is the new sailor with its flat, inch-high crown, and tilted on the left by a bandeau (much lower than in the winter hats). This shape is seen in straw, but as yet mainly in hats of lingerie and of embroidered linen. The crown is a flat piece of hand embroidery, a bit suggestive in shape, and at times in decoration, of a circular doily. The flat brim is hidden under a shaped piece of linen finished with dimity

scallops along the edge, and embroidered in continued eyelet and filled work. Three folds of soft radium silk in different tones of pink are twisted about the low crown, and then tied in long bows and pointed ends that lie against the tilted brim. Two quills, extra long and extra wide, project upward and backward from the bow, and flowers or a chou of tulle cover the hat.

Another shape is of unbleached leghorn. Its crown is like an inverted finger bowl, and a rolling brim of moderate dimensions is dented against it irregularly on the left side. The edge is bound in velvet, and a shaped fold of velvet encircles the crown. A pair of quills curiously fashioned from uncut velvet are thrust into the hat at a becoming angle. Flowers nestle in the indentations of the crown, giving the hat a highly finished look.

Bridesmaids' hats follow picture lines, as usual, and appear to be fashioned of metal gauze, tulle, and plumes. The latter are wide and graceful, rather than long. When worn with colored gowns, only the tips of the plumes are dyed to match the costume, the rest being left pure white. At some approaching weddings the bridesmaids will carry muffs constructed of delicate gauze ribbon and natural flowers.

Wedding gowns continue to be made of rich white satin, though now and again a bride prefers the soft effect of misty chiffon, or the youthful appearance of brussels lace and net. Satin gowns show quantities of point and duchesse lace and frills; in rarer instances they are almost overlaid with the priceless fabrics. Hand embroidery is seen on many rich wedding gowns. The orange blossom is the usual flower motif, and silver, seed pearls, and tiny rhinestones are seen gleaming in it here and there.

 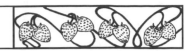

Tea Jacket

Use the scale corresponding to the bust measure to draft this pattern, which consists of back, front, and sleeve. Regulate all lengths by the tape measure.

Join the back to the front at the shoulder and underarm seams. Lay the inverted pleat in back according to the directions on the draft. Finish jacket at top and bottom in the usual way. Join the sleeve and adjust in armseye, gathering any surplus fullness at top to fit the armseye.

This jacket may be made of any soft material. It has lace draped down the front and arranged around the bottom of thc waist and sleeves. A bow of ribbon at the neck completes the jacket.

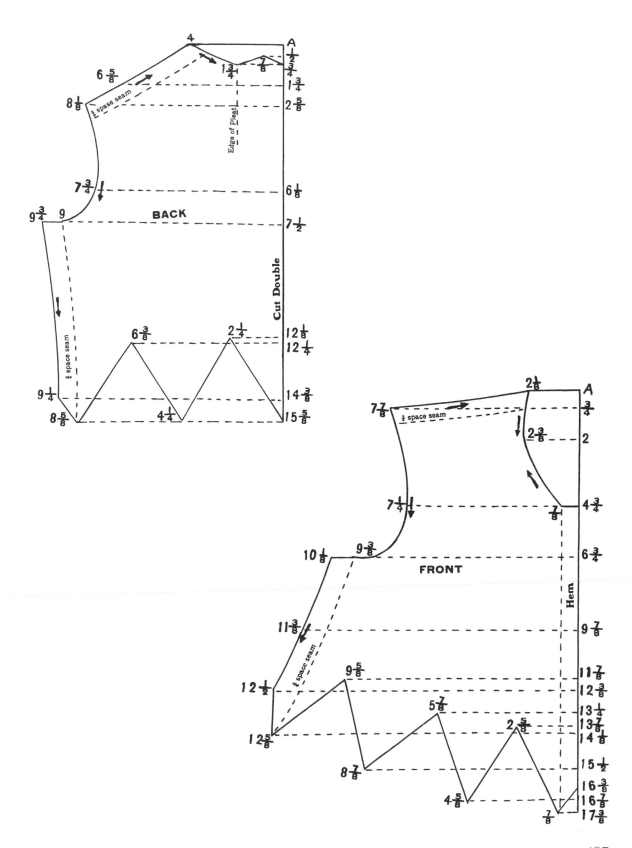

427

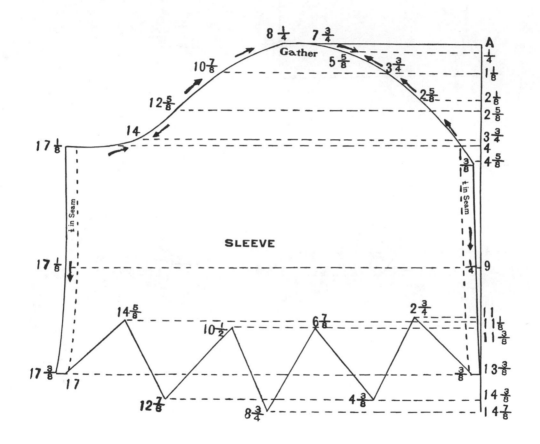

Princess Gown

Use the scale corresponding to the bust measure to draft this pattern, which consists of lining back, side back, underarm gore, and front; waist; yoke; collar; sleeve lining; sleeve; and five skirt portions. Regulate all lengths by the tape measure.

Join the waist lining seams according to the Xs. Fold the hem in the backs and take up the darts in the fronts. Place the yoke on the lining with corresponding portions together. Place the waist on the lining, gathering it at top and bottom. Join it to the yoke at the top. Arrange it at the bottom so that the princess portion of the gown will come just above the place where it is joined to the lining. Bind neck and adjust collar in the usual way. Join the sleeve and place it on the sleeve lining with corresponding portions together. Gather the fullness at top and bottom to fit the lining. Adjust sleeve in armseye and join.

Join the skirt seams according to the Xs. Arrange the fullness in back in an inverted box pleat and leave sufficient space for the placket. Finish at top and bottom in the usual way.

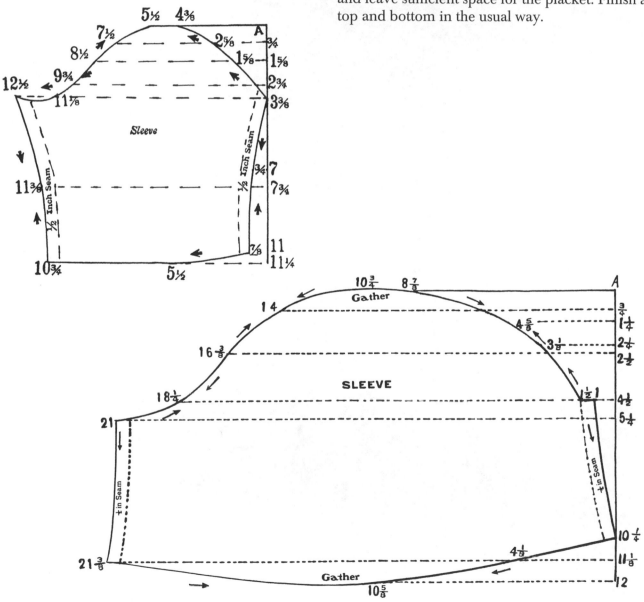

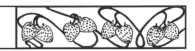
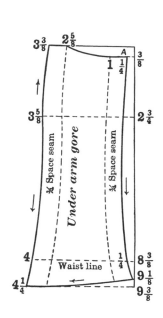

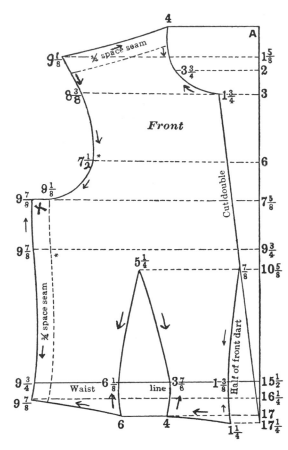

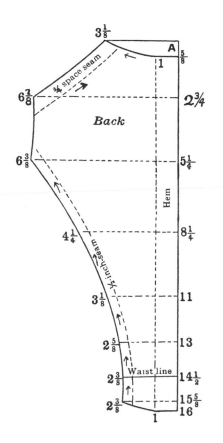

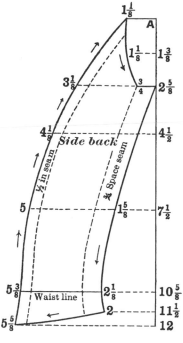

431

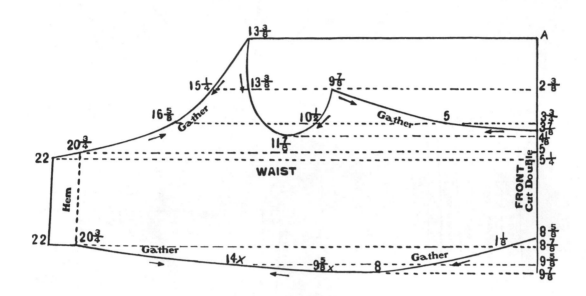

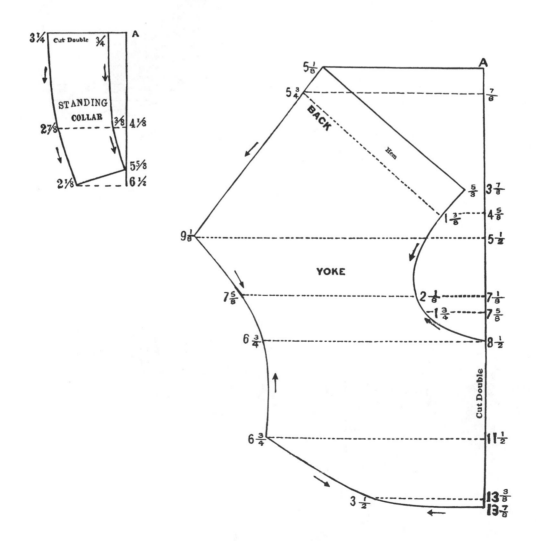

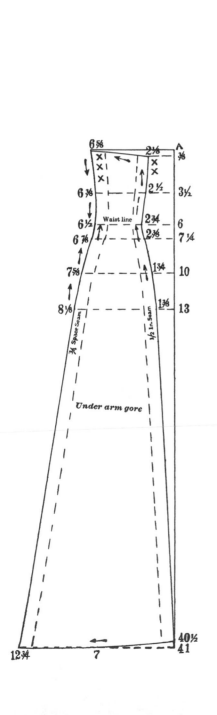

Under arm gore

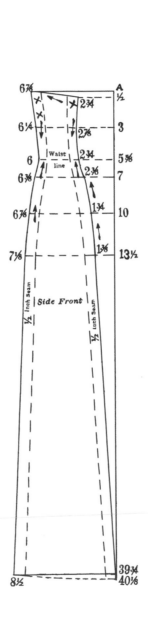

Side Front

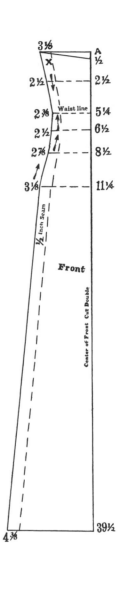

Front

Center of Front Cut Double

433

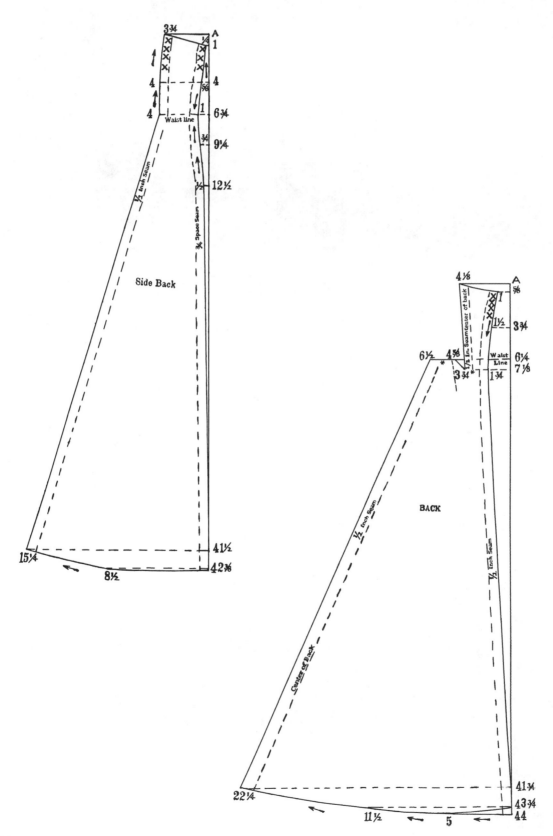

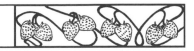

Shirtwaist

Use the scale corresponding to the bust measure to draft this waist, which consists of back, front, vest, collar, sleeve, and cuff. Regulate all lengths by the tape measure.

Join the waist at the shoulder and underarm seams. Shirr the fullness at neck, both back and front, into position. Gather the fullness at bottom to fit the waist measurement and hold in place with a tape. Place vest underneath right front, allowing it to overlap left front and fasten at left side. Gather vest into position. Bind neck and adjust collar in the usual way. Finish waist around neck and vest in any desired way. Join the sleeve. Shirr it at the top to fit the armseye and join in armseye. Cut two cuffs and arrange one above the other as illustrated. Gather the fullness at bottom of sleeve to fit these cuffs.

This waist may be made of any desired shirtwaist material.

435

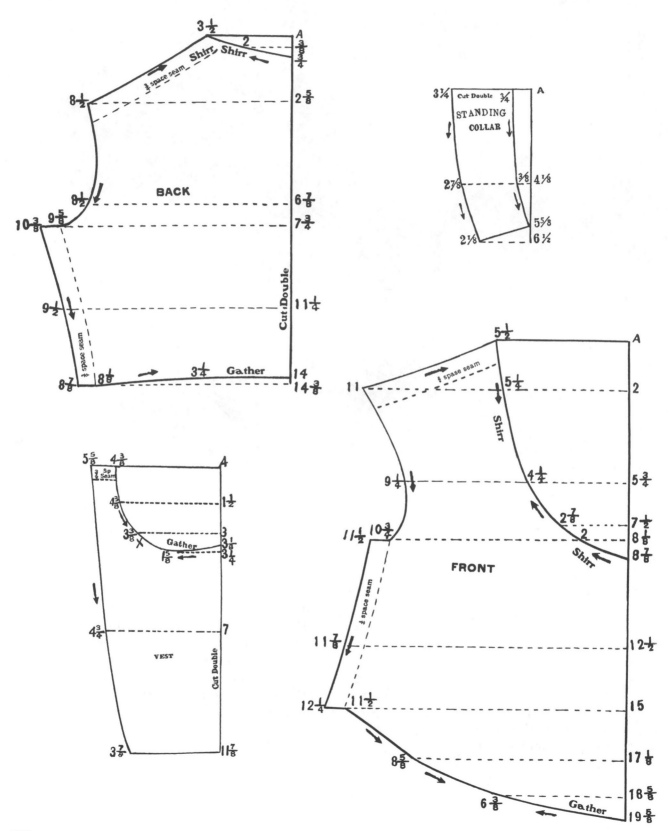

BACK

STANDING COLLAR

Cut Double

FRONT

VEST

Cut Double

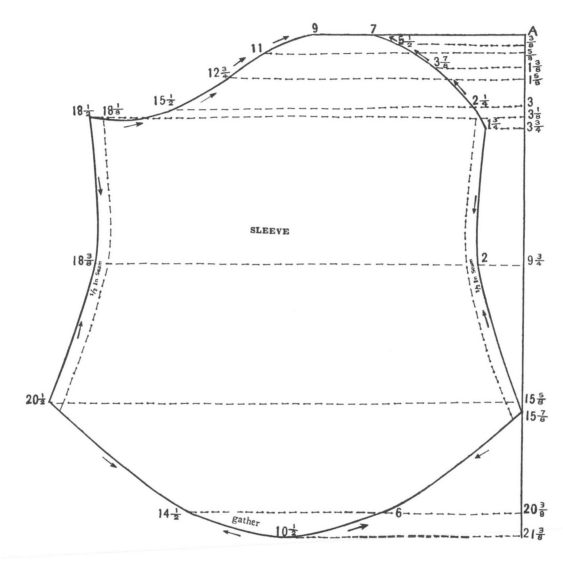

SLEEVE

A

9   7   5½
11
12¾
15½
18½ 18⅛
½ In Seam
18⅜   m   2   9¾
3
3⅛
3¾
3⅞
3⅝
5⅝
3⅝
1⅜
1⅝
2¼
1¾
2
½ In Seam

20½   15⅝
15⅞

14½
gather
10½   6   20⅜
21⅜

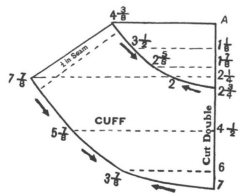

4⅜   A
3½   1⅛
2⅝   1⅞
7⅞   2   2⅜
2¾
½ In Seam
CUFF   Cut Double   4½
5⅞
3⅞   6
7

437

Appendix A
Diamond Cutting System Rulers

To aid you in enlarging the *Voice of Fashion* patterns, I had the Diamond Cutting System rulers reconstructed from a partial set of original rulers, plus information in the magazines. They may be used either for drafting or to determine the size a pattern piece should be projected to.

Instead of inches, the patterns are labeled with whole and fractional units. Unit size varies with the ruler, so the same number of units is used for any size pattern. For example, to draft a bodice with a 34-inch bust, you would choose the size 34 ruler to draw all straight lines. To draft a bodice with a 36-inch bust you'd draw lines with the size 36 ruler, and so on. A tab has been added to each ruler to indicate the inch measurement it is used for, plus the (rounded) metric equivalent.

Only ten units have been provided for each ruler, as on the originals (plus a little extra length to facilitate pasting). These rulers are too short to draw some pattern lines. The book page size prevented me from lengthening them. In fact most rulers had to be broken into halves. However, a ruler long enough to draw any line can be created by photocopying.

First figure out which rulers you need to enlarge the desired pattern (see the introduction and "Using the Diamond Cutting System"). Then find the longest line to be drawn with each ruler. The number of units the line requires is indicated on the end farthest from the baseline. Lengthen the ruler to at least that many units.

The rulers read top to bottom for vertical lines and right to left for horizontal ones, due to the placement of the pattern baselines. If a ruler was not broken into halves, copy it as many times as required. Cut out the copies. Lay the first segment of the ruler vertically on a table with the identifying tab at the top. On the second segment, fold under the tab at the heavy line under the label. Align this line with the line indicating the "10" unit on the first segment, covering the "1" of the "10." Tape or glue in place. Use a pen to rewrite the covered "1," or change it to "2" to indicate 20 units. Paste any additional segments the same way.

If the ruler was broken, make one copy of each half. Paste the 6–10 segment to the 1–5 segment. Copy and paste this ten-unit ruler as described above.

The rulers may then be pasted onto cardboard or inexpensive yardsticks and used for drafting. Or they may be used for measurement only, and lines drawn with a yardstick.

18 in.
46 cm

19 in.
48 cm

20 in.
51 cm

21 in.
53 cm

22 in.
56 cm

22 in.
56 cm

23 in.
58 cm

23 in.
58 cm

24 in.
61 cm

25 in.
63.5 cm

24 in.
61 cm

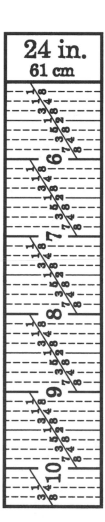

25 in.
63.5 cm

26 in.
66 cm

26 in.
66 cm

27 in.
69 cm

27 in.
69 cm

28 in.
71 cm

28 in.
71 cm

29 in.
74 cm

29 in.
74 cm

30 in.
76 cm

30 in.
76 cm

31 in.
79 cm

31 in.
79 cm

32 in.
81 cm

32 in.
81 cm

33 in.
84 cm

33 in.
84 cm

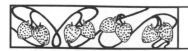 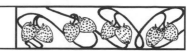 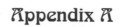
34 in.
86 cm

34 in.
86 cm

35 in.
89 cm

35 in.
89 cm

36 in.
91 cm

36 in.
91 cm

37 in.
94 cm

37 in.
94 cm

  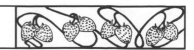

38 in.
96.5 cm

38 in.
96.5 cm

39 in.
99 cm

39 in.
99 cm

 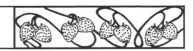
40 in.
102 cm

40 in.
102 cm

41 in.
104 cm

41 in.
104 cm

42 in.
107 cm

42 in.
107 cm

43 in.
109 cm

43 in.
109 cm

44 in.
112 cm

44 in.
112 cm

45 in.
114 cm

45 in.
114 cm

Appendix B
Metric Conversion Table

This table contains the English and metric equivalents of measurements often used in sewing. Numbers running to several decimal places and (most) fractions under 1/16 inch have been rounded for easy use.

English Measurement	Metric Equivalent	Metric Measurement	English Equivalent
1/8 in.	3.2 mm	1 mm	1/32 in.
1/4 in.	6.4 mm	2 mm	1/16 in.
3/8 in.	9.5 mm	3 mm	1/8 in.
1/2 in.	1.3 cm	4 mm	5/32 in.
5/8 in.	1.6 cm	5 mm	7/32 in.
3/4 in.	1.9 cm	6 mm	1/4 in.
7/8 in.	2.2 cm	7 mm	9/32 in.
1 in.	2.5 cm	8 mm	5/16 in.
1 1/4 in.	3.2 cm	9 mm	11/32 in.
1 1/2 in.	3.8 cm	10 mm (1 cm)	13/32 in.
1 3/4 in.	4.4 cm	2 cm	3/4 in.
2 in.	5.1 cm	3 cm	1 3/16 in.
2 1/4 in.	5.7 cm	4 cm	1 9/16 in.
2 1/2 in.	6.4 cm	5 cm	2 in.
2 3/4 in.	7.0 cm	6 cm	2 3/8 in.
3 in.	7.6 cm	7 cm	2 3/4 in.
3 1/4 in.	8.3 cm	8 cm	3 1/8 in.
3 1/2 in.	8.9 cm	9 cm	3 1/2 in.
3 3/4 in.	9.5 cm	10 cm	3 15/16 in.
4 in.	10.2 cm	15 cm	5 7/8 in.
4 1/2 in.	11.4 cm	20 cm	7 7/8 in.
5 in.	12.7 cm	25 cm	9 13/16 in.
5 1/2 in.	14.0 cm	30 cm	11 13/16 in.

 # Metric Conversion Table

English Measurement	Metric Equivalent	Metric Measurement	English Equivalent
6 in.	15.2 cm	35 cm	13 3/4 in.
6 1/2 in.	16.5 cm	40 cm	15 3/4 in.
7 in.	17.8 cm	45 cm	17 11/16 in.
7 1/2 in.	19.1 cm	50 cm	19 11/16 in.
8 in.	20.3 cm	55 cm	21 5/8 in.
8 1/2 in.	21.6 cm	60 cm	23 5/8 in.
9 in. (1/4 yd.)	22.9 cm	65 cm	25 9/16 in.
9 1/2 in.	24.1 cm	70 cm	27 9/16 in.
10 in.	25.4 cm	75 cm	29 1/2 in.
10 1/2 in.	26.7 cm	80 cm	31 1/2 in.
11 in.	27.9 cm	85 cm	33 7/16 in.
11 1/2 in.	29.2 cm	90 cm	35 7/16 in.
12 in. (1 ft.)	30.5 cm	95 cm	37 3/8 in.
1/2 yd. (18 in.)	45.7 cm	100 cm (1 m)	39 3/8 in.
3/4 yd. (27 in.)	68.6 cm	1.25 m	1 yd. 13 3/16 in.
1 yd. (36 in.)	91.4 cm	1.50 m	1 yd. 23 1/16 in.
1 1/4 yd.	1.14 m	1.75 m	1 yd. 32 7/8 in.
1 1/2 yd.	1.37 m	2.00 m	2 yd. 6 3/4 in.
1 3/4 yd.	1.60 m	2.50 m	2 yd. 26 7/16 in.
2 yd.	1.83 m	3.00 m	3 yd. 10 1/8 in.
2 1/2 yd.	2.29 m	3.50 m	3 yd. 29 13/16 in.
3 yd.	2.74 m	4.00 m	4 yd. 13 1/2 in.
3 1/2 yd.	3.20 m	4.50 m	4 yd. 33 3/16 in.
4 yd.	3.66 m	5.00 m	5 yd. 16 7/8 in.
4 1/2 yd.	4.11 m	5.50 m	6 yd. 9/16 in.
5 yd.	4.57 m	6.00 m	6 yd. 20 1/4 in.
5 1/2 yd.	5.03 m	6.50 m	7 yd. 3 7/8 in.
6 yd.	5.49 m	7.00 m	7 yd. 23 9/16 in.
6 1/2 yd.	5.94 m	7.50 m	8 yd. 7 1/4 in.
7 yd.	6.40 m	8.00 m	8 yd. 26 15/16 in.
7 1/2 yd.	6.86 m	8.50 m	9 yd. 10 5/8 in.
8 yd.	7.32 m	9.00 m	9 yd. 30 5/16 in.

Appendix C
Edwardian Dressmaking Terms

This glossary was published in *The Complete Dressmaker,* edited by Clara E. Laughlin, in 1907. The original introduction follows.

Terms and expressions which occur in fashion notes and books are very often unintelligible to many home dressmakers. Therefore, the introduction of them here may be helpful. We get our fashions from the French people, and many of them have never been translated into our own language, but always retain the French names.

Accordion pleating: One pleat laid on another by machinery, steamed and dried so as to retain this position.

Ajour: An open effect produced by joining two parts together by a cross or catch stitch.

Antique: A word used to designate an old-style material or fashion such as has been used in times long past—*moiré antique.*

Appliqué: Laces or embroidery joined to or applied to a material. It may be a piece, or a design of leaves, figures, etc.

Arabesque: A scroll effect or design which may be made with cords, stitchery, or applied pieces outlined.

Armure: A fancy weave of silk which has a small raised pebble design. It is much affected in mourning wear.

Bag seam: A seam stitched on the right side and then on the wrong, hiding the raw edges.

Basque: A tight-fitting waist which extends below the waistline; taken from the costume of the Basque peasants of France.

Batiste: A fine cotton muslin having a good deal of dressing, resembling lawn, batiste being slightly heavier.

Bayadere: A design in dress materials in which the stripes run from selvage to selvage giving a round appearance.

Beige: A soft, fine material made of yarns in the natural color. May be either twilled or plain.

Bengaline: A plain round-corded weave of silk and wool, in which the wool is used as a filling covered by the silk. It is smooth in surface and small in grain. When the cord takes a fancy appearance the fabric is called *crystal.*

Bertha: A ruffle or shaped cape following the line of a low-cut waist around the shoulders. It may be of lace, silk, or velvet.

Beurre: A name given to materials or lace having a yellow color resembling butter.

Bishop sleeve: Named for a sleeve in the robe of a bishop of the Episcopal Church. It is gathered at the top and again at the wrist with a straight cuff.

Blouse: A loose waist usually gathered on a drawstring at the bottom; to blouse a waist is to puff up from the waist, back and front.

Boa: A round neck scarf, either short or long, made of net, chiffon, lace and ribbon, and various soft materials. Fur and feathers are made into boas also.

Bodice: A tight-fitting waist; it is also applied to a high-fitted belt or girdle.

Bolero: A Spanish jacket; a small sleeveless jacket worn over a loose blouse. Many styles have this effect produced on lace or velvet.

Border: Any trimming put on an edge or above it and used as a finish to a garment.

Bouclé: A woolen material whose surface is raised in little tufts at regular intervals or in patterns; a rough material.

Bouffant: Used to express a very full or puffy effect—as *bouffant sleeves.*

Bouillouée: A narrow puffing used for fancy trimming, sometimes corded. It is often made in chiffon or soft satin.

Bourette: A kind of material on which rough threads or knots appear as straight or broken stripes.

Brandenburg: A military ornament of braid and loops with which a jacket is fastened.

Bretelle: A sort of cape which extends from the belt in front over the shoulders to the belt at the back of a waist. It is much wider at the shoulders and slopes at the waist.

Broché: An embroidered effect obtained by weaving; also called brocade.

Cabochons: A jet, glass, steel, or pearl flat bead or nail head, used for dress trimming or millinery.

Challis: An extremely lightweight dress fabric of cotton and wool, woven without twill; soft and free from dressing.

Chameleon: A changeable effect obtained by weaving two or three colors together.

Chiffon: The finest, sheerest silk material manufactured.

Chiffon cloth: A firmer fabric than chiffon.

Chiffon (Liberty): A chiffon cloth with a satin finish.

Chiné: Effects obtained by printing the warp before weaving, making the filling of a plain color.

Choux: A rosette of any soft material which will look like a cabbage.

Circular flounce: A flounce cut to fit the skirt at about the knee, but which flares in a circle at the foot of the skirt.

Collarette: A large collar or cape which fits the shoulders.

Collet: A small cape or large collar.

Covert cloth: Lightweight summer cloths, originally made of natural or undyed wool, resulting in gray, drab, or fawn colors.

Crash: A rough, loose linen material used for toweling and also for dresses. Often spoken of as *Russia crash*.

Crepe de chine: A soft silk fabric which lends itself to graceful folds.

Crepe tissue: A very fine transparent, crimpy material which is worn very much for mourning ruchings and trimmings.

Crepon: A woolen or silk-and-wool material with a crepe or crinkled effect.

Cuirasse: A perfectly plain tight-fitting waist.

Demassé: A fabric ornamented on the surface with a rich design, the running figure woven, but not printed, like damask.

Drap d'eté: An all-wool fabric with a twilled surface, woven as a twill and finished as a broadcloth.

Dresden effects: Warp-printed flowers and figures like those used on Dresden china.

Drop skirt: A lining skirt which is intended for one special dress, and is often hung or attached to the outer skirt.

Duchesse: The finest satin fabrics woven.

Dutch neck: A square or round neck cut only 2 inches below the throat.

Epaulette: A trimming which falls over the shoulders like a small cape.

Etamine: A canvas weave with a wide-open mesh rendering it more or less transparent. Sometimes woven with a silk stripe.

Eton: A short jacket or coat reaching to the waistline, dipping slightly to a point at the center back—after the style of uniform worn at the Eton School, England.

Faconni: Fancy, elaborate.

Fagoting: An embroidery stitch which fills the space between two edges, holding them together. It differs from the catch or herringbone stitch in being worked through the edges, and not flat on them.

Faille Française: A silken material having a soft cord with a cotton filling.

Featherstitching: Very much like bias or cord stitchery used in embroidery and with very good effect in dressmaking.

Fichu: A draped scarf or cape having long ends which fall from a knot at the breast.

Foulard: A soft, thin dress silk woven without twill. Twilled foulard is known as a silk serge.

French gathers: Made of one long stitch on the outside and one underneath, and alternating.

French knot: An embroidery stitch in which from four to eight or nine twists are made on the needle. The needle is pushed back through the same opening to the wrong side while the loops are held on the right side.

Frogs: Ornaments made of braid in a fancy pattern having a loop which fastens on the opposite button or olive. There are always a pair of these ornaments used for each fastening.

Full back: The straight-back widths of a skirt gathered in two rows at the top.

Galloon or passementerie: Trimming made of beads, spangles, or silk, into bands and fancy designs.

Gauffié: An effect seen in silk when the material is pressed into shapes or patterns.

Gauntlet: A cuff shaped like a gauntlet or riding glove, similar to the spreading cuffs seen on costumes of past centuries.

Gigot: A sleeve with a large puff at the top and fitting close to the lower arm like a leg-of-mutton sleeve.

Girdle: A belt of shaped cincture for the waistline.

Glacé: A shiny surface, applied to gloves and silk materials.

Granite: A raised pebbly effect in silk or woolen goods like armure.

Grenadine: An openwork diaphanous silk, wool, or cotton.

Grosgrain: A silk fabric with a cord or ribbed effect.

Guimpe: A yoke or waist usually made of white materials and worn with low-cut dresses—worn very much by children.

Habutai: A plain woven silk made in Japan on hand looms. It is smooth and even in texture.

Harlequin: Made of three or more separate colors.

Huckaback: A dicelike pattern, very heavy, used for toweling.

Iridescent: Changeable, having a rainbow effect.

Jabot: A trimming, usually of lace or chiffon, gathered full and allowed to fall in cascades or shells.

Jaconet: A fine muslin heavier than cambric, free from starch or dressing, but glazed by calendering.

Jacquard: Applied to materials made on jacquard looms, which automatically select the threads and make the designs, formerly produced by hand looms only.

Jardinière: Of many colors, resembling a garden of flowers.

Jupon: A short petticoat applied to double or triple skirts. The upper skirt is the jupon.

Khaki: A Japanese silk plain woven and less fine in weave than habutai.

Lancé: Shot effects, small dots—also called *petit pois*.

Liberty satin: A soft shiny satin.

Louis XVI; Regence; Directoire; Empire; Colonial: Certain styles peculiar to special periods in different countries.

Louisine: A soft, thin silk fabric.

Maline: A very fine gauzelike texture.

Matelassé: Woolen or silk cloth which has a raised pattern on the surface as if quilted or padded.

Medici: A collar for cloaks and dresses, very high and stiffened, rolling outward at the top.

Melangé: Mixtures of color applied in weaving; also mixtures of cotton warp and wool weft.

Melton: A stout smooth cloth used for men's clothing and women's coats. The nap is sheared close to the surface and is finished without pressing or glossing.

Mercerize: A chemical process of rendering cotton threads lustrous. The thread is shortened and hardened, producing a silky effect.

Merino: A soft woolen material.

Merveilleux: A satin fabric woven in a sort of twill pattern.

Mirror velvet: A smooth, shiny effect produced by ironing velvet with the nap.

Mitaine: A form of sleeve in which the lower part below the elbow resembles a mitten.

Moiré: A watered effect like spreading waves over a silk, cotton, or woolen material.

Motif: A portion of a design—as a leaf from a spray of flowers.

Mousseline de soie: A transparent, very thin material used for gowns or veiling satins or silks.

Nacié: A mother-of-pearl effect.

Natté: Like a basket weave.

Natural color: The grayish flax color–known as *undyed*.

Oriental; Persian; Cashmere: Names applied to a series of colors and patterns found in cashmere shawls.

Ottoman: A name applied to silk or woolen material with a large rep or cord.

Oxford: Originally a wool fabric in dark gray and white mixtures (90 percent of the former and 10 percent of the latter). Of late, heavy cotton and linen fabrics have been known by this name.

Pailette: Spangles of gelatin.

Panel: A piece of material placed either in the front or sides of a skirt, usually outlined by rows of trimming giving the appearance of an inlay.

Passementerie: Heavy embroideries or edgings and galloons, especially those made of rich gimps, braids, beads, silks, and tinsel.

Pastel shades: Very light tints, somewhat opaque in character.

Peau de cygne: One of the popular weaves of soft, highly finished silk; closely resembling peau de soie.

Peau de soie: A tough satin fabric.

Percale: A kind of cambric closely and firmly woven with more dressing than ordinary, and may be either printed or plain.

Picot: A small loop used as an ornamental edging on ribbons and laces.

Piping: A bias fold or cord put on the edge of a band or garment as a finish.

Placket: The opening left in a skirt to allow the garment to be put on and off the person; an opening in a shirtwaist sleeve.

Plastron: A full or draped vest for a waist.

Pleat: A trimming made by folding the material over on itself.

    Box pleat: A fold turned toward either side.

    Double box pleats: Box pleats having two folds.

    Kilt pleats: Large single folds turned one way.

    Knife pleats: Narrow folds turned to one side.

    Triple box pleats: Box pleats having three folds.

Plissé: Pleated.

Plumetis: A fine, sheer fabric in which a design is produced by means of loose tufts or spots.

Pointillé: Dotted with small spots or polka dots.

Polonaise: A waist and overskirt combined in one garment. It is taken from the Polish national costume.

Pompadour: Mixed colorings in light shades, such as were worn in the time of Louis XV and Mme. de Pompadour.

Pongee: A thin, soft silk fabric, woven from the natural uncolored raw silk.

Postilion: An extension of the back pieces of a basque or extra tabs set onto a basque at the back.

Pres de soie: A fine, cotton lining used for underskirts.

Princess: A style of dress in which the waist and skirt are made in continuous breadths from neck to feet.

Quilling: A narrow-pleated effect; a *rose quilling* is a very full triple box pleating stitched through the center, having the effect of a row of full-blown roses.

Redingote: An outside garment cut princess style, showing a skirt front beneath.

Rep: A style of weaving in which the surface has a crosswise appearance as a distinction from cords, which extend lengthwise in the fabrics.

Revers: Pointed or square pieces usually turned back or reversed on the front of a waist or coat.

Ruche: A trimming of lace, silk, crepe, or chiffon, gathered or stitched in the middle.

Shantung: A heavy grade of pongee silk in which the natural color of the material is preserved.

457

Shirr: Two or more rows of gathers having a space between.

Sicilienne: A mohair of heavy weight, either plain or with a fancy pattern.

Smocking: Accordion pleating caught together alternately in rows, making an elastic fabric.

Soutache: Narrow worsted mohair or silk braid used in dress trimmings.

Stock collar: A full or plain collar in imitation of the stocks of 50 years ago.

Suede: Undressed kid; a skin from which the outer part has been rubbed off or skinned.

Surah: A soft silk woven in nearly invisible cords or twills.

Taffeta: A smooth weave of silk.

Tussah: A coarse silk produced by silkworms which are fed on oak leaves.

Tuxor: A soft, rich satin or silk cloth.

Vandyke: Pointed effects seen in laces, trimmings, etc.

Venetian: An all-wool material of a broadcloth construction, except that the face is twilled.

Vest: A flat center front trimming for a waist, also a separate garment.

Vigomeux: A worsted material which is printed in several colors, giving a melangé effect.

Voile or veiling: A wool or silk-and-wool fabric similar to the old-fashioned nun's veiling. Some voiles are extremely thin and transparent; these are called *chiffon voile.*

Watteau pleat: A box pleat down the center of the back of a princess gown which is laid from the neck to the waistline and then hangs freely to the bottom of the skirt.

Zibeline: A shiny, woolen material having long hairs.

Appendix D
Further Reading

Cabrera, Roberto and Patricia Flaherty Myers. *Classic Tailoring Techniques: A Construction Guide for Women's Wear.* New York: Fairchild Publications, 1984.

Information on molding and shaping garments, which can be adapted to period styles.

Elite Styles Co. *Elite Fashions Catalog, 1904.* Mineola: Dover Publications, 1996.

Reproduces the majority of fashion drawings from the May 1904 Elite Styles pattern catalog.

Grimble, Frances. *After a Fashion: How to Reproduce, Restore, and Wear Vintage Styles.* San Francisco: Lavolta Press, 1993.

Covers medieval through Art Deco styles for women and men. Guides readers through each stage of a reproduction project and advises them on all aspects of collecting vintage clothes.

Grimble, Frances, ed. *The Edwardian Modiste: 85 Authentic Patterns with Instructions, Fashion Plates, and Period Sewing Techniques.* San Francisco: Lavolta Press, 1997.

Women's patterns for 1905 through 1909, selected from *The American Garment Cutter Instruction and Diagram Book* and *The American Modiste.* Includes chapters of a 1907 dressmaking manual and rulers for the American System of Cutting.

Harris, Kristina, ed. *59 Authentic Turn-of-the-Century Fashion Patterns.* New York: Dover Publications, 1994.

Women's, children's, and some men's patterns from 1890s issues of *The Voice of Fashion.* The enlargement instructions are incorrect; they assume the pattern measurements are inches.

Kidwell, Claudia. *Cutting a Fashionable Fit: Dressmaker's Drafting Systems in the United States.* Washington: Smithsonian Institution Press, 1979.

A history and analysis of 19th-century patent drafting systems.

Kliot, Jules and Kaethe Kliot, eds. *Garment Patterns 1889 with Instructions.* Berkeley: Lacis Publications, 1996.

Everyday garments for men, women, and children, reprinted from *The National Garment Cutter Book of Diagrams* and *The National Garment Cutter Instruction Book.* These patterns probably require the same rulers as *The Voice of Fashion.*

La Barre, Kathleen M. and Kay D. La Barre. *Reference Book of Women's Vintage Clothing 1900–1919.* Portland: La Barre Books, 1990.

Illustrations from fashion magazines pasted up alphabetically by category—bags, belts, bathing suits, etc. and details such as skirt lengths and trims—and by year within each category. Alongside runs text that probably summarizes the original descriptions.

Shaeffer, Claire B. *Couture Sewing Techniques.* Newtown: Taunton Press, 1993.

Construction as practiced in couture workrooms, where Edwardian techniques are still used.

Index

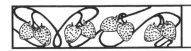 

The Edwardian Modiste
85 Authentic Patterns with Instructions, Fashion Plates, and Period Sewing Techniques

Edited and with Additional Material by Frances Grimble

Women's styles from 1905 through 1909
8 1/2" x 11" quality paperback, 430 pages
85 patterns, 91 fashion plates, 21 sewing illustrations

The Edwardian Modiste contains patterns and fashion plates for all major women's styles and most garments from 1905 through 1909. These years saw a transition from the turn-of-the-century S-curve silhouette to the straighter line of the 1910s. The patterns are selected from *The American Garment Cutter Instruction and Diagram Book* and 12 issues of the quarterly magazine *The American Modiste*.

The 85 patterns include:
- ◆ 29 day, afternoon, and evening dresses
- ◆ 18 suits (some with additional blouses)
- ◆ 10 blouses and waists
- ◆ 8 outer coats, motor coats, raincoats, and evening wraps
- ◆ 15 items of lingerie and foundation linings
- ◆ 2 home robes
- ◆ 3 sports outfits

This 430-page book also includes:
- ◆ Drafting rulers for the American System of Cutting used with the original publications
- ◆ Complete instructions for pattern enlargement by drafting and by projection
- ◆ Fashion columns describing styles, fabrics, trims, colors, and construction

And:
- ◆ Substantial illustrated sections from a 1907 manual, *The Complete Dressmaker,* which give detailed directions for dressmaking and ladies' tailoring

The Edwardian Modiste can be purchased for $42 in bookstores or ordered from Lavolta Press at 20 Meadowbrook Drive, San Francisco, CA 94132. If mail ordered, shipping is $4; California purchasers must add sales tax. Prices subject to change without notice.